INDIA

Author:
Antonio Monroy

Photographs:
Antonio Martinelli and
Roberto Meazza

Layout:
Bob Noorda

ORBIS·LONDON
INDIA BOOK DISTRIBUTORS

... the earth when I look at it
Makes me aware
Of the hubbub of a huge concourse
Of ordinary people
Led along many paths and in various groups
By man's common urges,
From age to age, through life and death.
They go on pulling at oars,
Guiding the rudder,
Sowing seeds in the fields,
Cutting ripe paddy.
The work –
In cities and in fields.
Imperial canopies collapse,
Battle-drums stop,
Victory-pillars, like idiots, forget what their own words mean;
Battle-crazed eyes and blood-smeared weapons
Live on only in children's stories,
Their menace veiled.
But people work –
Here and in other regions,
Bengal, Bihar, Gujurat –
Filling the passage of their lives with a rumbling and thundering
Woven by day and by night –
The sonorous rhythm
Of Life's liturgy in all its pain and elation,
Gloom and light.
Over the ruins of hundreds of empires
The people work.

Rabindranath Tagore (1861-1941)

Extract from the poem *Recovery 10*
translated by William Radice

© 1985 by Touring Club Italiano

First published in Great Britain by Orbis Publishing Limited, London 1985.

All rights reserved. No part of this publication may be reproduced, stored in a retrieval system, or transmitted, in any form or by any means, electronic, mechanical, photocopying, recording or otherwise, without the prior permission of the publishers. Such permission, if granted, is subject to a fee depending on the nature of the use.

Editor:
Maria Raffaella Fiory Ceccopieri

Edition Editor:
Rossella Bigi

Secretary:
Luisa Molteni

Production:
Giovanni Schiona

Foreign rights:
Annamaria Mannucci

The map used was specially created for this book by the Cartographic Department of the T.C.I.

Publishing consultant and coordinator of the international editions:
Nebojša Bato Tomašević

English translation by:
Babel Translations, London

The lines on page 3 are reproduced from Rabindranath Tagore's *Selected Poems*, translated by William Radice and published in Penguin Modern Classics, 1985: translation (c) William Radice, reproduced by permission of Penguin Books.

Printed in Italy by:
Arti Grafiche Amilcare Pizzi S.p.A.
Cinisello Balsamo (Milan)
Binding:
Legatoria Editoriale G. Olivotto (Vicenza)
Typesetting:
Centro Grafico Linate,
S. Donato Milanese (Milan)
Colour Separations:
Fotolito Farini, Milan

Contents

India: Unity and Variety   13
History is the History of Myths. A Day in the life of Brahma.... / The Indian Village. "Permanence" of the Castes. / Geography and History. / The Monsoon Cycle. / Unity in the mark of caste and religious tolerance. / The European Race for India; the British East India Company. / The Mutiny. The Victorian Empire. / Congress, Gandhi, and the Stages on the Road to Independence. / The New Nation: New Myths and New Rites.

Myths, Religions, Cults   57
The Significance of Religion in India. / Brahmanism and Hinduism. Vishnu, Shiva, Devi-Shakti. / A Thousand Years of Buddhism. The Religion of Mahavira. / The Presence of Islam. / Pilgrimages and Great Religious Assemblies. Holy Cities and Major Sanctuaries.

Art and Architecture   129
The Indian Concept of Art. / Sanctuaries and Monasteries cut into Mountainsides. / The Evolution of the Hindu Temple. / Indo-Islamic Architecture. The Schools of Painting. / Dance, Music, and Literature in the Regional Traditions.

Society and Caste   169
A Uniquely Indian System: Caste. / The Indian Village. / Family, Marriage, and Communal Life in Villages. Festivities, Cults, and Magico-religious Practices. / The India of the Tribes.

The New Urban Condition   233
The City in Indian History. / The Great Cities Today. / Modern Architecture. The Indian Cinema Industry.

Chronology.	285
Glossary.	286
Photographic Credits.	287
Acknowledgements.	287

'Nothing in India is identifiable, the mere asking of a question causes it to disappear or to merge into something else'.

E.M. Forster *A Passage to India*

India: Variety and Unity

The idea of India, as a projection of an ideal geography of the universe, has ancient origins. It dates back to a mythical past and is the fruit of a uniquely Hindu cosmological vision: India is the *Bharatvarsha*, the homeland of Bharat, the favoured place of the lands which form the legendary continent of Jambudvipa at whose centre was the 'axis of the world', the mountain of gold called Meru. Bharat is also the name of the ancient Aryan peoples who inhabited the northern region. Because of the extent of its territory and above all because it was thought of as the land of the ancient fathers, Bharat became the name of India itself; it is now the second name which the new republic, seeking to associate itself with its own origins, adopted at independence.

Myth therefore is at the root of the idea of India, which, although it is ever present in the culture and spirit of India, seems in many ways to be far removed from India's historical development and the objective reality of events. This vast portion of southern Asia has been inhabited by an infinite variety of peoples since remote antiquity — a rich and complex mosaix of diverse races, ethnic groups, and societies. Many of these peoples came from far off and settled in various parts of the subcontinent; others developed in totally isolated areas, whilst others were in close contact or even integrated with nearby groups, so forming new cultures and ways of life. The rigid caste laws kept the numerous castes separate and prevented them from intermingling their blood. Even today the Indian population is a multi-coloured mosaic of the past, which in its entirety displays an organic design, although its innumerable strands still preserve their own individuality. The most obvious proof of this is provided by the survival of a thousand different languages and dialects, some of which display considerable linguistic and literary independence. The material cultures display considerable differences between one community and another, ranging from unbelievably primitive conditions, as in some of the tribes of central India, to highly civilized and refined societies displayed by groups living in the great cultural and economic centres of the country.

Although India may be regarded as one nation, it is so in a unique and unusual way. It seems to contradict the modern theory of the constituent principles which determine the existence of a nation. The unity of India, in fact, if it ever existed in the past, was certainly not political but essentially religious.

History is the History of Myths

The inheritance of Indian civilization and culture is based on a particular concept of time and history with a specific metaphysical and religious vision. The ancient history of India is the history of myths which have come down to us through a noble oral tradition and which, prior to the introduction of writing, held the memory of immense periods of civilization and consciousness. Sacred history long remained the only history passed on, and oral transmission the only means held valid and sacred by the brahmins for the perpetuation of the memories, above all the 'knowledge' of the *Vedas*, created by poets and sages who were ignorant of writing. Myth and history are indivisible and when the great inheritance of ancient civilization was written down in Sanskrit, the epics, the myths, and the memories of the poets continued to pass on the memory of deeds and events together with stories, legends, and myths. These scriptures have the character and development of biblical tales; in their religious authority, and through the fact that they are the

On the preceeding pages:
1. On the road between Patna and Nalanda in Bihar, travelling from village to village with the local bus.
2. Tamil fishermen off the coast of the Bay of Bengal.
3. At dawn, a multitude of the faithful pilgrims take part in the procession of the god Alagar, brother of the goddess Minakshi, patron of the city of Madurai in Tamil Nadu. According to mythology, the god was coming to the wedding of his sister to the god Shiva. Tradition has it that, because of frequent stops amongst the devotees, Alagar did not reach the ceremony in time and, annoyed and offended that the wedding had gone ahead without him, he returned home precipitously, without entering the city and without leaving his wedding presents.

Vamana Murta, one of the incarnations of the god Vishnu.

sole sources of recorded history, they assume the status of the 'revealed' truth, religiously lived and commemorated by the Indian people of every age.

The finite view of history which seems to shape the history of Christian Europe is foreign to Indian thought. Time is not linear but cyclical; the rhythm of centuries is replaced by the 'great year', which may last for millennia, with a curve of growth and decay, burning out in a universal conflagration only to begin anew ad infinitum. 'This is clearly a religious time, as is the Christian eternity, but it differs from eternity as transmigration differs from resurrection. A cosmic cycle runs to more than four million years; a day of Brahma, four billion and a cycle of Brahma more than three hundred billion; whatever the number, Hinduism has a multiple for it...' (Malraux). Beyond history on a human scale, the historical cycles were overlaid by cosmic cycles, which, although they did not repeat themselves unaltered, were subject to the law of the 'eternal return'. The sickness which marks a particular period — such as ours, known as *Kaliyuga* — is explained by the fact that a decadent phase is in force, influenced by an era of renewal and growth. In order to escape from time and the perennial repetition of the cycles, speculative and religious thought points the way to liberation or annihilation in '*moksha*' or '*nirvana*'.

The Importance of the Village

'If India seems to make fun of history, this is because it has never known a development such as we have from the times of Tacitus and Caesar and which we call history. The dynasties and the succession of kingdoms, the enlargement of the "national territory", were all regarded as anecdotal and of very little importance'. The concept of Indian history rests on the certainty of the perennial nature of the caste system. National history is overlaid by the history of individual caste communities, the *jati*, bound together by a prized inheritance of memories of the genealogists or poets, whose task it was to repeat endlessly the wanderings of mythical ancestors, so reviving the eternal models of the tradition. Rather than the history of the kingdoms and dynasties — and just to list them would fill this chapter — it is the village, the natural base of the jati, which is the true India, the source of a possible history, indeed of hundreds of thousands of histories. 'In truth all these princes, even the greatest, are as if they had never existed... Even when they were alive, the Hindu village did not bother itself very much about them; how subsequently could they people its memory?' (Deleury).

Geography and History

We know that geographical and climatic characteristics are decisive factors in the history of any country, but nowhere else in the world is this effect so clear and obvious as in India. The Indian subcontinent may be divided into three main zones. In the north is the mountainous belt of the Himalayas, whose peaks mark the traditional limits of India. Although the impassable Himalayan barrier has blocked the descent of invaders from the north — the Mongol hordes, for example, which overran other parts of Asia — to the west, along the Afghan border, there was an opening, the Khyber Pass, down which waves of invaders flowed over the centuries, from the Aryans to the army of Alexander the Great, from the Huns to the Scythians of Kushan and the armies of Islam. The second zone is formed by the immense Ganges plain, the traditional target of invading conquerors; washed, as it is, by the Indus, Ganges, and Brahmaputra rivers and running from the interior of present-day Pakistan to the borders of East Bengal

(now the Bangladesh frontier). This vast lowland is the celebrated *Aryavarta*, the sacred 'home of the Aryans', recorded in the codex of Manu and sung of in the epics, and the scene of great battles between the indigenous peoples and the invaders. The third zone is bounded by the Vindhya mountains of central India which, together with the Narmada river, form a natural barrier between the Ganges plain and the Deccan or *Dakshinapatha*, meaning 'region of the right, or south'. Although not particularly high, the Vindhya did form an effective barrier to the expansion of the peoples of the north, allowing the peoples of the southern region to maintain their own culture relatively intact. The various peoples of the north gradually flowed into the great triangular *cul de sac* of the peninsula, coming into contact with the mysterious Dravidian peoples and their magico-religious cults, their crowds of gods, and their fertility symbols.
The other natural and more extensive border is the ocean which surrounds the peninsula. The long coastline is almost always low and uniform, with few natural bays. Although so exposed to the sea India has never willingly turned to it, developing neither a seafaring culture nor a maritime empire. The only period of seaward expansion in India's history came in the eleventh century, when the Tamils of the southern Chola dynasty built a maritime empire that extended as far as Malacca, Java, and Sumatra, creating a vast area of dominion in South East Asia where their cultural influence has led to the concept of *India Magna*. It was, however, an isolated episode and lasted just a century. For thousands of years the coasts of India remained inviolate, touched only by peaceful navigators and merchants, whose objectives were limited to commercial exchanges along the trade routes which linked the coasts of Africa and India. Around the first century AD there was intense trade between Rome and India. Rome sent manufactured goods and merchandise to the great Indian trading centres of the southern coast in exchange for silk and spices, cottons and precious stones. The Arabs also engaged in trade with the kingdoms of the south and numerous merchants settled peacefully along the coasts. However, it was from the sea that the last and most final conquest of India began. Beginning in 1498 the forerunners of the great European mercantile empires began to touch on its coasts — first the Portuguese, then the Dutch and the French, and finally the British.

The Monsoon Cycle

The Indian region lies largely within the torrid and tropical zone — the Tropic of Cancer runs across its centre — and, apart from its high mountains, it is one of the hottest countries in the world. The climate of India is characterized by a long dry season, broken by the periodic event of the monsoon, which affects the whole of southern Asia. To understand India one must know the monsoon. Travellers of all ages have observed the importance of this tremendous phenomenon and the crucial role it has played in the survival of this sun-drenched land. Marco Polo, the first and most famous of a long line, wrote in his celebrated *Travels*; 'It grows so hot, that one cannot conceive it' and that without the cooling effect of the summer rains 'the heat would be such that no one would survive'. When one remembers that the majority of the Indian population live in the vast areas of the countryside one can see how the seasonal rhythm of the monsoon is vital to the life and economy of the country. The *kharif*, the monsoon harvest, has been and still is the corner-stone of Indian food production and the failure of this harvest because of the lack of rain or, sometimes, because of too much rain, can cause famine. The annual cycle of the monsoon and the apparent movement of the sun has led to the notion of a precise time-table, a notion that has existed since antiquity, of the cycle of life which governs everything in nature. It is not surprising that popular culture, religion, and mythology, as well as music, the arts, and literature all celebrate the monsoon, not only as the source of life but as the most fascinating face of nature.

Unity, Caste, and Religious Tolerance

A series of factors - not always clearly definable — link with an unbroken thread the innumerable generations of men who have settled on Indian soil. This continuity is the key to a view of India and its history. Whatever the popular beliefs identified with the inheritance of myths or the metaphysical idea of death and eternity, the product of a peculiar concept of time and history, or the particular natural and climatic conditions of India which have so marked the customs and the ways of life, it is certain that these factors and many others are the constant and invariable companions of the composite Indian people in the millennia of history upon which they have left their mark. The capacity for assimilation of Indian civilization, which has been subject to invasions and occupation by foreign peoples to a greater extent than any other country, is a well-known phenomenon, but the result is that all these incoming peoples have become integrated into Indian culture, without, however, completely losing their own distinctive characters. India maintains its unity in its multiplicity of cultures and religions and one of the essential factors in this process is undoubtedly its peculiar social organization. The formation and permanent establishment of the castes dates back to the settlement of the Aryans in the regions of northern India. The caste system, with its subdivision into distinct groups placed in a rigid hierarchy, was and is still the unifying element in the structure of the entire Indian social order. Justified by the doctrinal principles of the brahmins and protected by religious sanctions, it has been interwoven since Vedic times with the deeds and events of Indian history, influencing the behaviour, customs, and cultural traditions of the population right up to the present time. Even such foreign rulers as the Moguls and the British had to come to terms with a caste-based society, taking its strength and capacity for resistance into account in their government of public affairs and often acquiescing to its inflexible rules for fear of dangerous reaction.

A naga, *or divine snake, from a bas relief on the roof of cave I at Badami (by S. Lefmann, 1900).*

Moments of universal peace amongst the various peoples are rare in Indian history but when they have occurred they have almost always been the result of a policy of tolerance by the sovereign power towards the religious cults and practices of the people. Such an attitude also implicitly entails tolerance and respect for the caste system and its religio-ritual aspects. Historically, such a policy was adopted by two rulers who lived at different periods and belonged to totally different cultures. These were the Emperor Ashoka Maurya of third century BC and the Mogul Emperor Akbar, who lived in the sixteenth century AD. It was under Ashoka Maurya that almost the whole Indian subcontinent was first unified politically. After the conquest of Kalinga ended in victory for his dynasty and in the unification of the Indian kingdoms under a single empire, Ashoka, faced by 100,000 dead, was, according to the chroniclers of the time, profoundly troubled and in the end decided to transform his life, embracing Buddhism and its symbols of peace and non-violence. He himself preached the teachings of the Buddha, sent missionaries to every corner of India, and raised Buddhism to the status of a state religion, although without compulsion. Yet it was at this very time that the devotional cults and pilgrimages to numerous sacred Hindu sites became established in Hinduism.

The history of the first millenium AD is marked by numerous attempts at territorial unification by various dynasties, which grew from small kingdoms by a process of expansion and annexation of large parts of India. Hindu sovereigns of

From an engraving by W. Daniell, 1834.

great moral and political stature as well as patrons of the arts emerged. These included all the rulers of the Gupta dynasty, creators of one of the most exuberant periods in literature and the arts; of these the fourth-century Chandragupta Vilkramaditya is outstanding. The sixth century saw the short but important reign of Harsha, who managed to extend his dominion over almost the whole of the Ganges plain. In the south two local dynasties, first the Pallava and then the Chola, managed to unite under their rule a large part of the Deccan. Despite the unification of fairly large parts of India none of these dynasties was able to realize the ambitious project of uniting the whole of India in a single religious and political entity as Ashoka Maurya had managed. It would fall to a foreign race, the Moguls, to achieve the objective of national unity, which finally came about in the sixteenth century, under the third Mogul Emperor, Akbar the Great. Under Akbar the imperial sway extended over almost two thirds of India, but at the same time, at the wish of the sovereign, there was general religious peace. Akbar was the greatest of the Muslim rulers and his reign lasted almost half a century. He is remembered first of all as a pacifier, a ruler who displayed profound religious tolerance, He was the heir of the Persian concept of royalty; the emperor, the source of all justice, was also the protector of the religions of the people. Although a Muslim in his culture and faith, Akbar experienced a personal religious tension which drove him to deepen his knowledge of other doctrines and above all to settle the conflicts and establish peace between Muslims and Hindus. After having suffered centuries of religious persecution the Hindu communities finally felt themselves protected and as a result they gave their loyalty to the empire, so consolidating its political unity. The successors of Akbar departed from the political and religious policy of the great sovereign until the last of the Moguls, Aurangzeb, administered the *coup de grace* to the empire by his fanatical observance of Muslim orthodoxy. However, the Mogul period laid the foundations for what India was to become over the following centuries. The idea of national unity, despite the ever-present and profound differences of culture and religion, was from then on viewed by all Indians as a concrete and achievable objective.

The Europeans in India

With the arrival of the Europeans in India its history took an entirely new and, in certain ways, dramatic turn, which resulted in a profound transformation of the Indian people. Initially, the Western presence in India was spasmodic and secondary, motivated only by commercial interests, but subsequently — and mainly under the British — it changed into actual territorial conquest as the British built the largest colonial empire of the modern world — an empire whose jewel was India.

'Since remote antiquity the aspirations and desires of all nations have been directed towards obtaining access to the inestimable treasures which this land of marvels produces... The way in which the West managed to seize these riches is a fact of worldwide historical importance, closely bound to the destiny of nations' (Hegel). To Westerners, India has always appeared a strange, mysterious, and incredibly rich land. Although this is partly true, much of it was the product of

A map of the Mogul Empire (by J. Fraser, 1742).

pure fanatasy and lack of real, first-hand knowledge. Information was based on the vague and picturesque accounts of travellers and merchants who had visited India in earlier centuries. However, India remained the land of spices, silk, and a tremendous wealth of materials and products which became essential to the requirements and economy of the Europeans.

In 1498, some years before the accession to the throne of the first Mogul emperor, the Portuguese led by Vasco da Gama arrived by sea and founded prosperous colonies along the southern coasts. Right from the outset the Portuguese presence was marked by a controlled process of conquest, confined to the west coast overlooking the sea, the interior being totally ignored. The Portuguese supplanted the Muslim merchants and gained absolute domination of the trade routes through the eastern seas, maintaining a monopoly over spices throughout Europe for about a century. This quickly stimulated the interest of mercantile companies in various other European countries and these, over a period of time, founded the first trading posts along the coasts of India. After about a century and half it was the British East India Company which gradually established itself in India and then came to dominate the other mercantile enterprises. On the death of the Mogul Emperor Aurangzeb, at the beginning of the eighteenth century, the Muslim empire began a slow but irreversible process of economic and territorial disintegration and there was a resurgence of the Hindu forces and kingdoms which had been subjugated for centuries. Some of these, the Marathas, formed themselves into a single, powerful confederacy led by Shivaji, a petty regional prince. The offensive against the Muslim army resulted in the conquest by the Marathas of the whole of central and northern India. The new empire was governed by the Peshwa Brahmins of Pune.

By the first half of the eighteenth century — when the country was divided into distinct areas of influence — the only trading companies still active in India were the French and the British. These were soon in conflict, both economic and military. In 1757, with the victory at Plassey over the Muslim ruler of Bengal, the British East India Company became master of a vast zone of India and one of the great potentates of India in its own right. In 1773 the British government passed the Regulation Act which restricted the freedom of action of the company and unified all the conquered territories. At this juncture the British conquest of India was not yet absolute but profiting from internal conflict within the Maratha confederation, the only power which could hinder British expansionism. The British succeeded, partly by force and partly by a series of alliances, in annexing virtually all the territory of the declining Muslim empire. In 1805 British forces raised the Union Jack over the fort at Delhi and assumed in the name of the British Crown the sovereignty, by now only symbolic, of the Great Mogul.

The first phase of colonization, in which all the European trading companies took part, began with a colossal, though patchy, plundering of the resources and products of the country; but the second phase, which began with territorial expansion and political control by the British, saw the conquest of the Indian economy through the systematic acquisition of the means of production. Protected by preferential customs tariffs, emergent British capitalism made numerous massive capital investments in the various productive centres of the Indian economy — in manufacturing and craft-based industries — and succeeded first in overcoming and then in destroying the flourishing local industries. Raw materials were exported from the colony and then manufactured goods were reimported at competitive prices, resulting, for example, in the total collapse of the existing Indian cotton industry. The situation in the countryside, where the techniques of production had remained unaltered for thousands of years, was no different. Its progressive impoverishment was due to many causes but the principal one was the introduction of private ownership of land. This led to the creation of a powerful class of landowners — and to the conversion of the land back to the single crops (cotton, jute, tea, coffee, opium) intended for export and for the exclusive benefit of colonial interests. The slightest natural disaster led to terrible famines which decimated the malnourished population. It is calculated that, despite the attempts of the British administration to improve matters by introducing reforms, more than 100 million people starved to death in the nineteenth century. In 1857, a century after the fateful battle of Plassey had opened the way for British mastery of the subcontinent, an event occurred which was of great significance in the history of modern India.

The Victorian Empire

Kipling's 'Black Year' began with the mutiny of certain sepoy units, (Indian soldiers in the service of East India Company) which spread to large parts of the civilian population. One of the reasons for this explosion was the deep-rooted disquiet aroused by the policy of annexation pursued by the British company which sought, on various arbitrary pretexts, to extend its sway over native principalities. This was coupled with widespread unease among the population created by social and economic disintegration and a feeling of revolt and protest over the systematic corruption of the religious and cultural values of the Indian tradition by a foreign culture. The whole of northern India went up in flames and after taking Delhi the rebels proclaimed the restoration of the Mogul empire. Bloody repression followed and the British, exploiting the rivalry which existed between the Indian rulers, managed to quell the uprising. The Mutiny gave the British government the opportunity to dissolve the East India Company and to formally annex India to the Crown, officially taking over the government of its overseas possession. The Mutiny — a more important event that it might seem — profoundly disturbed Anglo-Indian relations, which were never the same again. Above all it upset the entire colonial policy. In 1876 the Prime Minister, Disraeli, introduced a Bill proclaiming Queen Victoria the Empress of India, which was ruled by her direct representative, the Viceroy. This act was both a culmination of British policy and the beginning of the final phase of colonialism. For more than seventy years the imperial government ruled through an immense bureaucratic and centralized apparatus, which administered India with increasingly British laws. Beneath this there was an array of Indian princes and chiefs — more than 650 Hindu and Muslim rulers enjoyed considerable autonomy in their own states — all of whom were subject and owed loyalty to the British Crown.

Although the Mutiny was not a true 'war of independence' — as historians of certain political persuasions see it — it did excite a nationalist feeling amongst Indians and a consciousness of their national identity. The British, for their part, abandoned the reformist policy which had been begun prior to the Mutiny. The conditions of the mass of Indian people could not be raised nor the compromised local industries rescued. All that remained was to impose a system of government based on out-and-out control and the containment of the internal situation — which included the use of military force — and to concentrate every effort into converting the colonial system to serve the interests of the empire. The government concerned itself with consolidating its administration and improving the infrastructure, by building roads and railways, but taking no interest at all in the miserable conditions in the countryside.

The policy of cultural domination, begun early in the nineteenth century, continued with the spread of the English language and the teaching of western sciences. The Indian Civil Service was established with a view to producing a narrow class of chosen Indians, bureaucrats and officials, who would be faithful

A sipahi *or sepoy, one of the native soldiers employed by the British East India Company (by Ferramo, early nineteenth century).*

subjects of the imperial crown. Universities and military schools were founded with the intention that they should provide the minor officials and officers. However, when this mass of Indian students came into contact with the new, liberal ideas being debated in Europe, which stressed nationalist values, liberty, and self-government for the people, it provided the stimulus for the development of a new concept of the nation and also a source of criticism of the largely autocratic excercise of power by the British. The local press expanded enormously and the first political associations began to be formed, associations which channelled the involvement of the educated classes towards a political objective and a single consciousness. Thus Indians began to reclaim for themselves an increasing share in the government of their own country.

The Road to Independence

The remote origins of the idea of Indian unity were never political in nature and throughout the nineteenth century, in the meeting with western civilization, the reforms and changes were mainly of a religious and spiritual character. It was with the foundation in 1885 of the Indian National Congress that the idea of possible political unity took shape. Initially regarded by the British as largely innocuous, the Congress gradually became the focus of the various groups and associations working for a national cause. Then, with the foundation of the Muslim League, Indian nationalism gradually assumed the status of an organized and conscious pan-Indian movement.
In its early years Congress was moderate and confined itself to discussions, but with the great Maratha leader Lokamanya Gangadhara Tilak the policy of the

An eighteenth-century 'Company drawing'.

nationalists became more radical and the unrest spread to the Hindu masses. The famine at the end of the last century and the high-handed division of the province of Bengal led to extensive outbreaks of terrorism in this region. Congress, backed by public opinion, launched *swaraj*, the campaign for the self-government and independence of India. The British response was based on an attempt to exploit the usual Hindu-Muslim rivalries, which consequently became more marked and foreshadowed what was to happen between the two groups. The Indian contribution of men and resources to the British during the First World War should have resulted in a more liberal reform of the colonial administration, but instead a harsh policy of repression was put into effect.

It was at this point that the figure of Mohandas Karanchand Gandhi, later known as the *Mahatma*, 'great spirit', emerged. In 1921, at the helm of Congress, he launched the non-collaboration movement which mobilized the rural and urban masses in continuous unrest. The approach inspired by Gandhi was totally new. It was based on non-violent resistance, civil disobedience, the boycotting of British goods, and the non-payment of taxes. All this caused enormous difficulties for the colonial government and forced it to introduce more liberal reform. The political action of the Mahatama, which was inspired by the religious rule of *ahimsa* (non-violence) in a grandiose philosophical vision of uniting the social, cultural, and religious spheres, was a potent detonator which awakened a new spirit of unity amongst all the social groups and castes. For the first time, the mass of poor and under-privileged were involved, including the untouchables. The latter were championed by Gandhi, who castigated the perverse laws of untouchability. The socio-ethical Gandhian theory was opposed to the western idea of progress, putting forward instead a gradual alternative reform of the economy. It required a strict containment of industrial and technological development in order to preserve the ancient framework of production, both agricultural and craft-based, from excessive strains.

*'Mr Gandhi, the man of the moment',
from* Indian Business, *1921.*

In 1928 the political leadership of the movement passed to a more radical generation, with Jawaharlal Nehru and Subhash Chandra Bose. At the same time, under its undisputed head, Muhammad Ali Jinnah, the Muslim League was reorganized and anti-Hindu feeling grew amongst its members, with the League calling for the creation of a purely Islamic state, Pakistan. The First World War gave the nationalist movement considerable impetus but the Second World War made it irresistible, creating an irreversible situation which would lead to the end of India's colonial status. Beset by war, the British government asked the representatives of the Congress to co-operate in fighting the Axis. Congress would not agree unless Britain gave a solemn promise to grant independence once the war was over. The British refused and the nationalists decided to embark on a series of disturbances under the slogan 'Quit India!'. The reaction was harsh and over 100,000 militants ended up in prison, along with the historical leaders of the movement. However, the War had provided the Muslim nationalist movement, now the favoured ally of the British, with the chance to obtain the partition of the peninsula into two separate states, one Muslim, the other Hindu. Events took over and the British could no longer control the situation. They decided to demobilize and leave India. On 15 August 1947 power was officially transferred and India became an independent nation. It was the end of foreign domination but the beginning of a blood bath. The antagonism between the Muslims and Hindus reached fever pitch and, with the departure of the British, who had provided a balancing factor between the two groups, the result was an appalling tragedy. An exodus involving 15 million people, Hindus living in Pakistan and Muslims living in India, began and seized by panic they clashed, resulting in a massacre which left hundreds of thousands of people dead. Another victim of this carnage was the Mahatma, who was assassinated on 30 January 1948.

The New Nation

India has achieved *swaraj*, independence and self-government, although the price it has paid in freeing itself from foreign domination has been high: massacres and the division of its territory into two distinct parts. In this century, the ancient ideal of a unity founded on religious peace has become the political unity of its two separate parts. The two national entities, India and Pakistan, now run along their independent paths towards increasingly divergent goals.

India, in which a large Muslim minority, indeed the second largest cultural and religious minority, still lives, is continuing along the lines formulated at its origins, from the archetypal idea of India of the Bharats, through the few moments of religious peace and political unification imposed by the Mogul Empire to the last two centuries under the British Raj. However, the new national unity, inspired by a concept which belongs at root to the culture of the West, has, paradoxically, flourished and matured in India, precisely because of the struggle and the opposition to that same culture. This one nation, artificial and perhaps fragile and uncertain, has displayed to date a great capacity for resilience and tenacity. The social, caste, religious, and linguistic diversity of India and the tremendous variety of its social fabric have long been moulded by this nationalist ideology and by the national commitment of its political and intellectual class. In January 1950 the nation officially adopted a republican constitution, which was to make it the 'largest democracy in the world', and confirmed its institutional integrity.

However, in 1953 the Nehru government was forced by popular opinion to subdivide the peninsula into a number of states (a federation of twenty-two states and several federal territories) based on linguistic groups — a move which confirmed the reality of a marked and subsequently stronger trend towards politico-cultural regionalization and the potential growth of various internal nationalist movements, with the consequent risk of threatening the present unity of the nation.

On the economic and development front, reforms aimed at accelerating the industrialization of the country were promoted in the nineteen-fifties, in total contrast to the aspirations of Mahatma Gandhi. Under the leadership of Nehru, who opted for a socialist and semi self-sufficient model, industries were nationalized and a series of five-year plans were laid down. Although India is still mainly agricultural, the agricultural sector was in fact neglected, leading to a productive and social imbalance in the various regions, aggravated by the failure of the agrarian reforms and the redistribution of land.

In the early nineteen-sixties the subcontinent faced a new, external danger that threatened its territorial integrity. In the north the Chinese army crossed the border and seized various areas of Indian territory. The incident was unilaterally provoked by the Chinese, who got the better of a number of clashes before they decided to withdraw to an almost acceptable frontier. However, the incident did lead to an Indian military build-up and to a policy of strength — yet another contradiction of Gandhian theory — a policy that was confirmed some time later by the explosion of India's first atomic bomb in 1970. In the meantime, relations between India and Pakistan became increasingly tense as a result of border incidents and the issue of East Pakistan, culminating in a series of bitter border clashes in 1965, 1971, and 1972. The military victories of India led to the creation of a new sovereign state, Bangladesh.

The protagonist and indeed almost the symbol of this phase in the nation's history was Pandit Nehru's daughter, Indira Gandhi, the Prime Minister for five terms. During this period India was to show the world its growth as a young nation, although one already capable of deploying formidable military force and of wiping out the image of a poor Third World nation, aspiring to the role of a major

4. This great stupa, the traditional form of Buddhist reliquary, stands near the village of Tikse, 13,125 ft up in Ladakh. The village is mainly inhabited by monks and a short distance away flows the river Indus, with the mountain range of Zanskhar in the background. The stupa is surrounded by high-altitude crops, mainly barley, which is one of the region's basic foodstuffs. The monks, as well as the peasants, cultivate the fields.
On the following pages:
5. The sky clears for a moment during an October dawn over the Kanchenjunga massif (28,200 ft), which dominates Darjeeling, the 'City of Lightning'. For more than a century this was one of the most beautiful and typical of the British hill stations and today Darjeeling still has an Anglo-Indian appearance, with bungalows, parks, a zoo, and places for recreation.

economic and industrial power in Asia. In some ways the country is on the verge, if not of achieving, at least of coming near to this objective. Even though there have been painful imbalances and enormous difficulties, the overall economy of the country displays a sustained and vigorous growth. Nevertheless, in recent years clear signs have emerged of opposition challenging the old ideals of unity. India is becoming increasingly divided into regions and this seriously impinges on the idea of national unity — an idea cultivated since the first years of the independence struggle and which provided the motivation for the efforts devoted to the creation of a free and united nation. The conflict between Hindu and Muslim, the often perverse game of coalition of opposing groups in the workings of a parliamentary democracy, the bloody disputes between ethnic and social groups, the attempts at secession by extremist fringes which aim at the separation of major parts of India (the Punjab, Assam) can obscure a path which has been followed for better or for worse, even if only partly. At present it does not seem that there are alternative routes or directions to pursue. The strength of the controversial government of Indira Gandhi has been in firmly containing the centrifugal tendencies and in re-establishing the central national ideal, although the rebuilding of the country after the continual rifts absorbs all its political energy, diverting it from other vital sectors. India is living today — full of hope and vitality — through one of the most critical moments in its modern history, a phase that is crucial for the years to come.

6. High paths running along the Zanskhar river in Ladakh, with people gathering wood for the severe winter of the region. The climate is dry and it rains only occasionally during the year.

7. The Lamaist monastery of Rizong Gompa, which can only be reached on foot. Ladakh is also known as 'Little Tibet', because, besides its altitude, it shares the social, cultural, and religious characteristics of Tibet. The capital of Ladakh is Leh, an ancient caravan and monastery city.

8. A whole family at work in the valley of Leh. The peasants often work to the accompaniment of songs and when resting they drink chang, an alcoholic beverage.

7

8

9. Morning calm on Lake Wular, Kashmir's largest lake.
10. Lake Chilka, in Orissa.

11. The boats of fishermen on the banks of the Ganges, near Varanasi.
12. Half submerged by the river in flood, some stone votive symbols and statuettes at Hardwar. The city of Hardwar occupies one of the holiest sites on the river and is a pilgrimage and devotional centre.

12

On the following pages:
13. The Narmada river.
14. Dusk in the great plain of Kutch, a frontier zone on the Pakistan border. A hunter ventures into the desert in search of game.

15. The splendid fortified city of Jaisalmer rises up in the middle of the Thar desert, Rajasthan. It is an ancient caravan city and was the capital of the 'lunar' Jaisal Rajput dynasty. Some tribes of nomads are employed in building the roads.

16. Between Jaipur and Amber in Rajasthan, a small lake covered with aquatic plants and, in the middle, the summer pavilion of Jai Mahal, built in the eighteenth century by Jai Singh, the ruler of Jaipur. The lake was once the home of crocodiles.

17. White cows gathered in the shade of a banyan tree. This special Gujarati breed is regarded as one of India's finest. Despite various changes, the peasant population remains largely opposed to the butchery and eating of beef. The ancient tradition of the cow's sacredness has deep roots in religion and in the philosophy of ahimsa *(non-violence); but it also persists for functional reasons. The cattle form the centre around which the entire economy of single family subsistence farming revolves.*
18. Monsoon landscape from the hill of Palitana, on whose summit there stands an ancient Jain holy city, with some 900 temples, sanctuaries, and shelters for pilgrims.

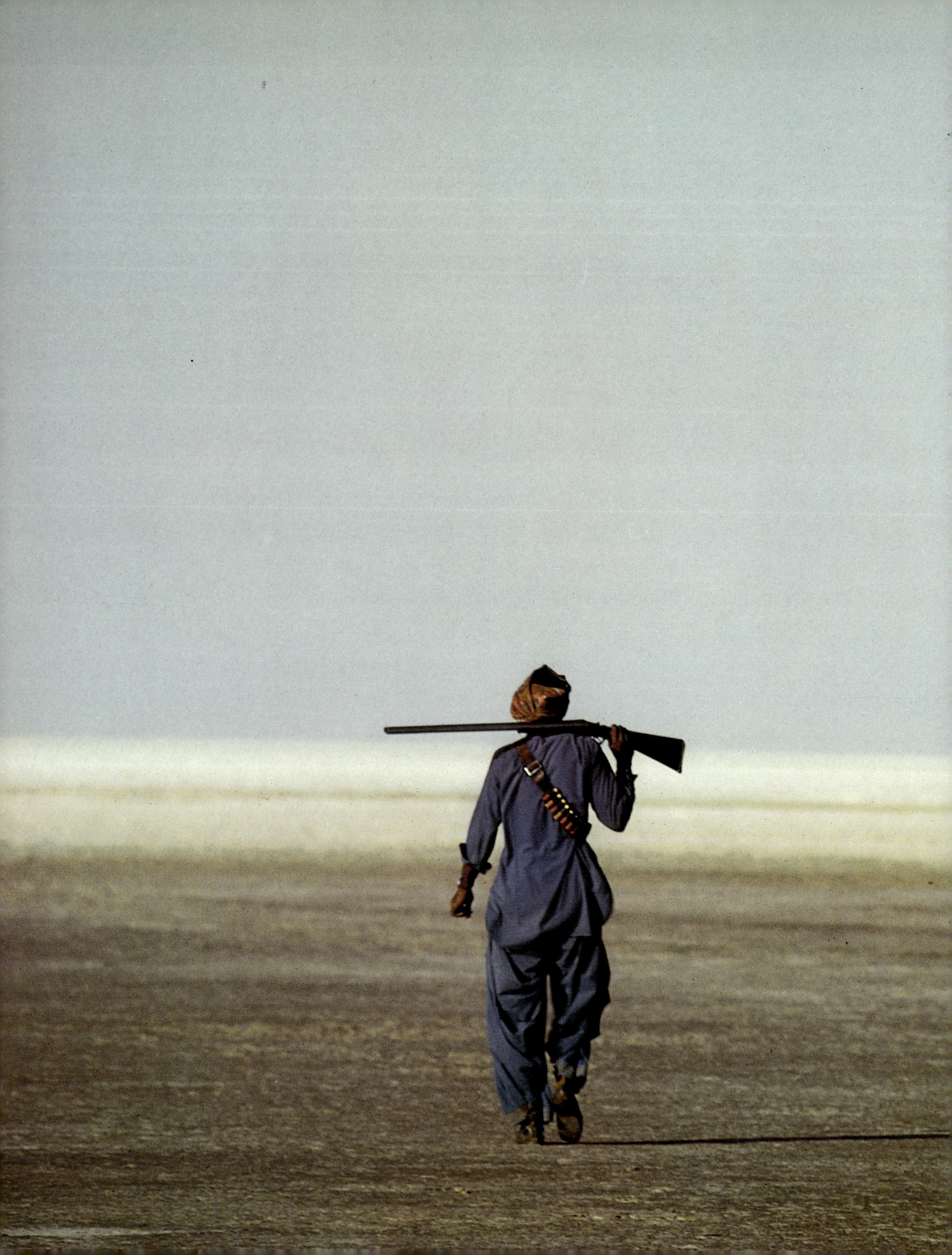

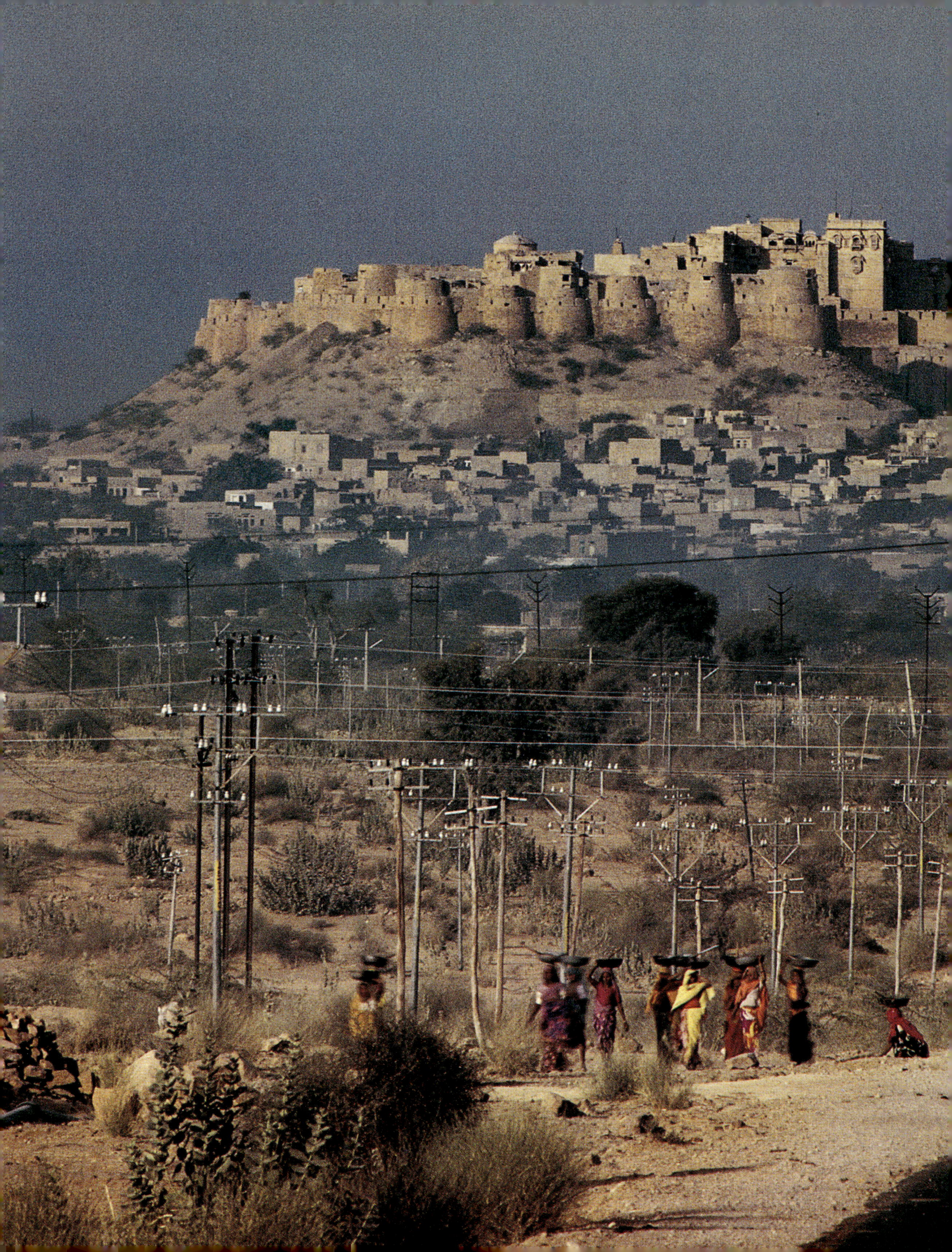

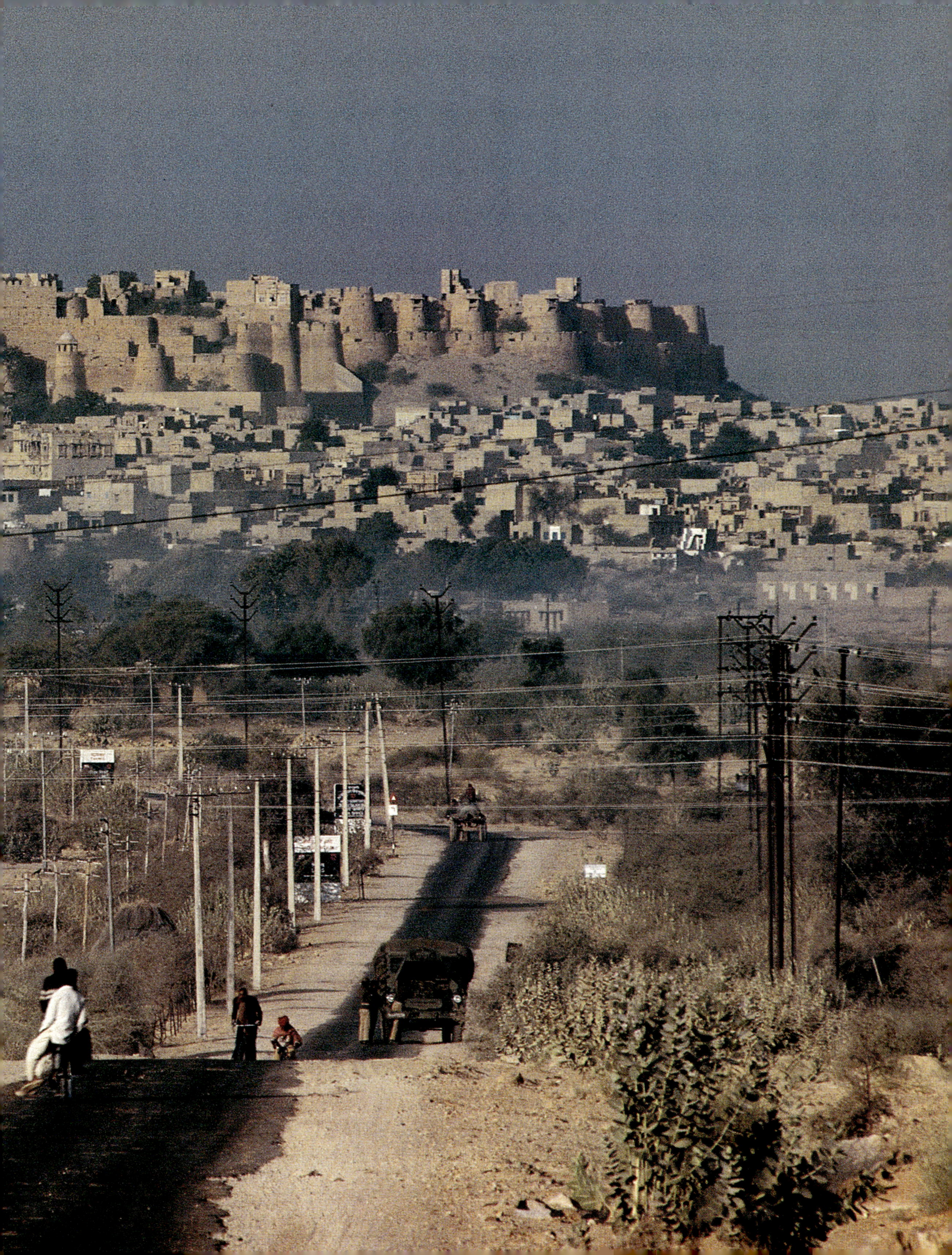

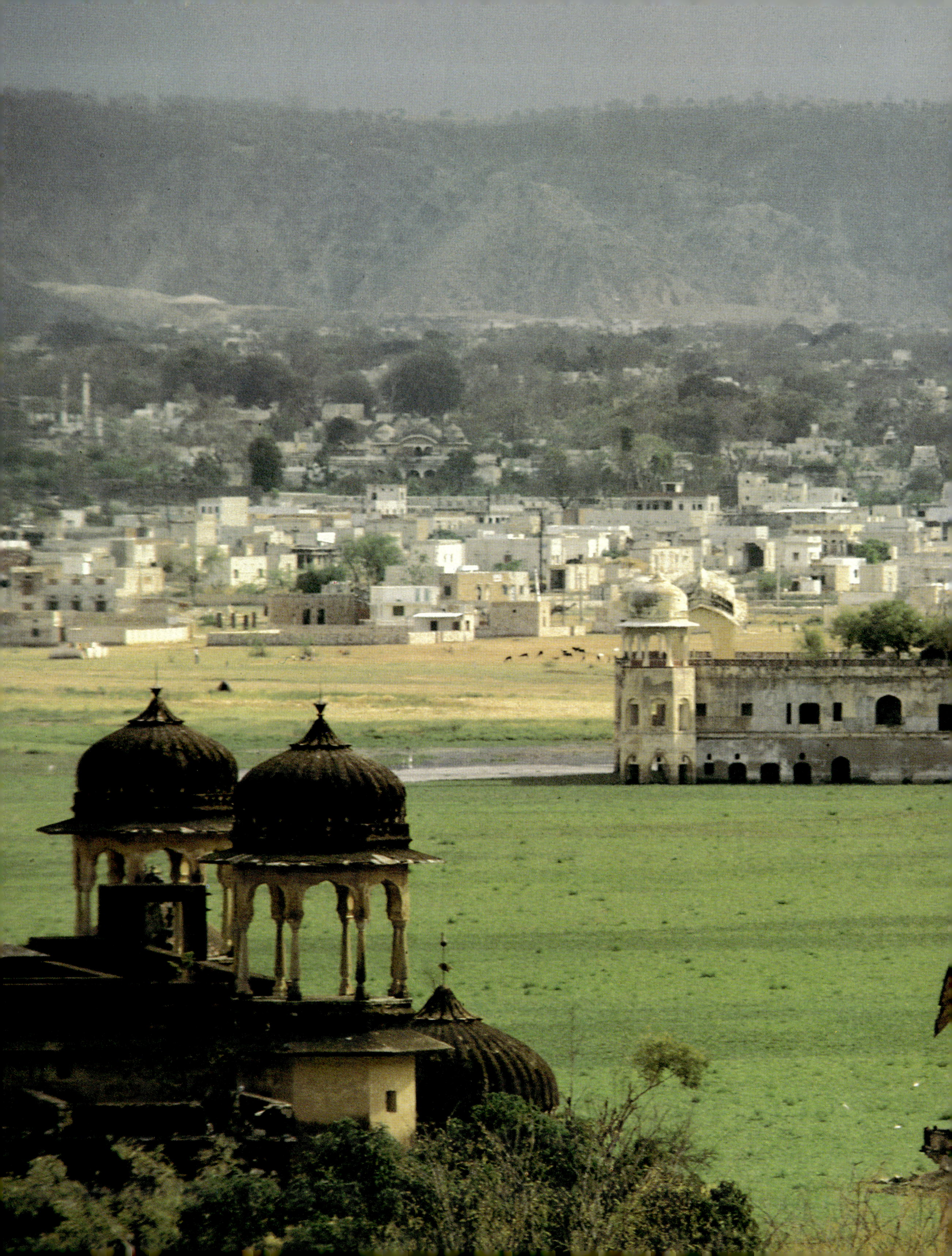

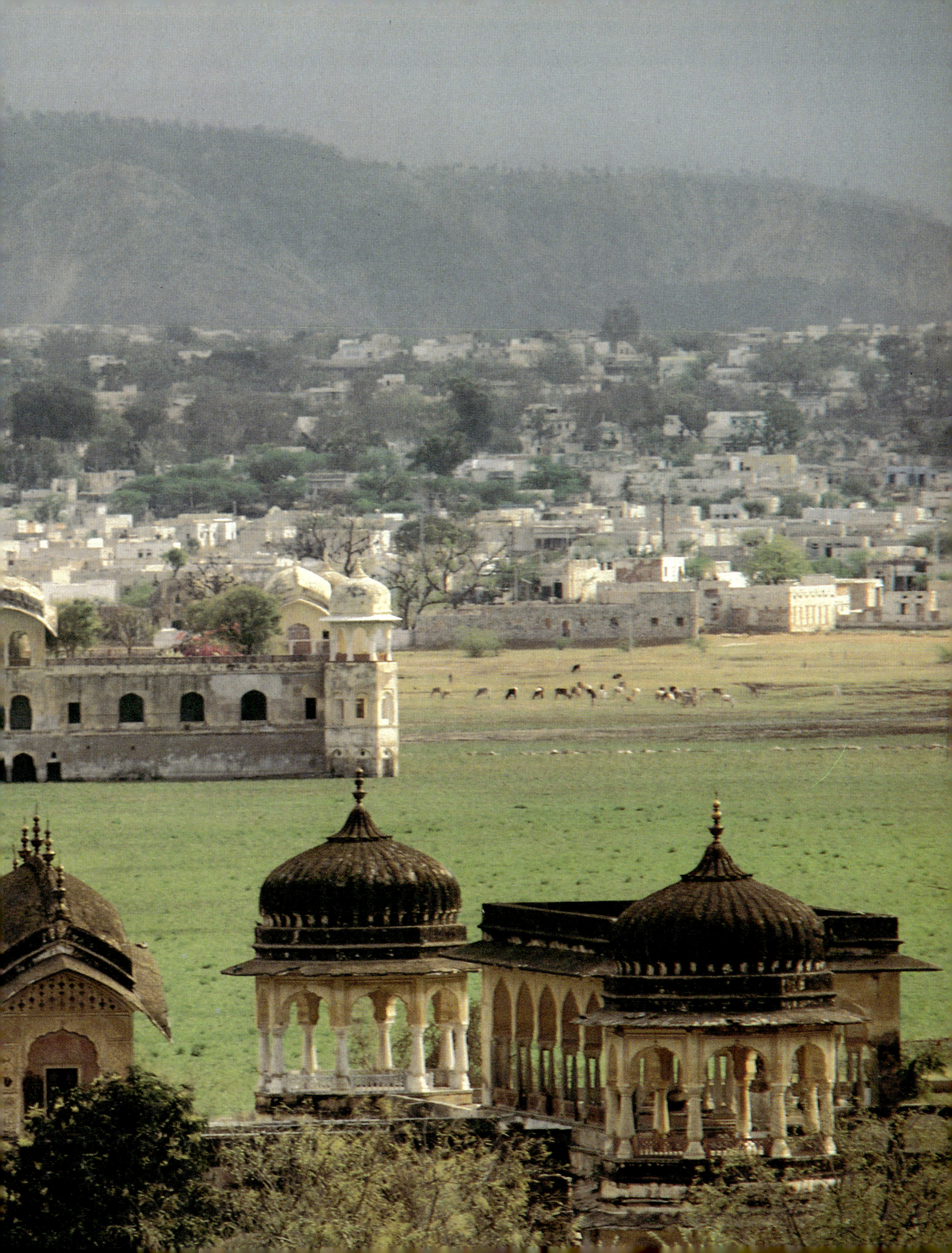

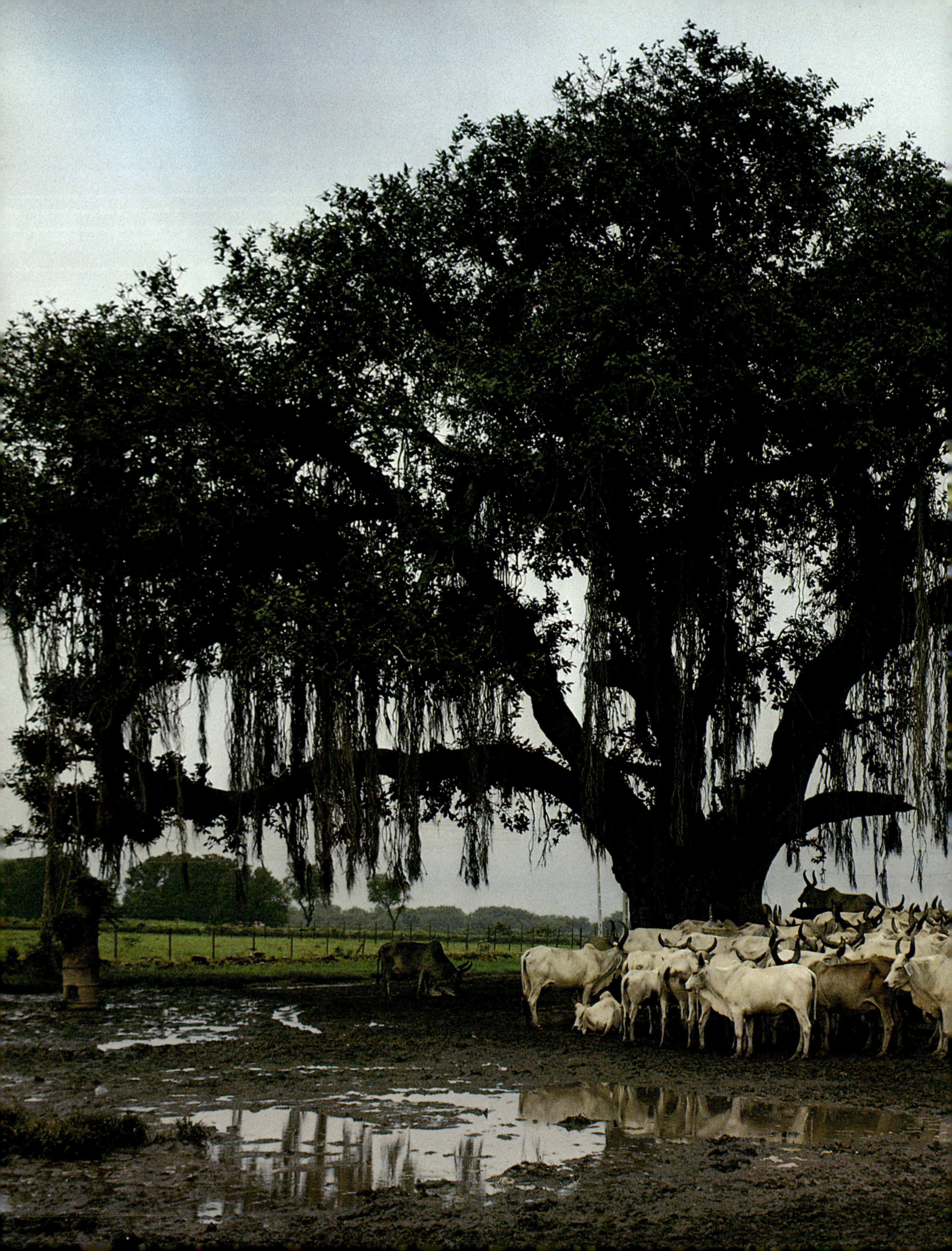

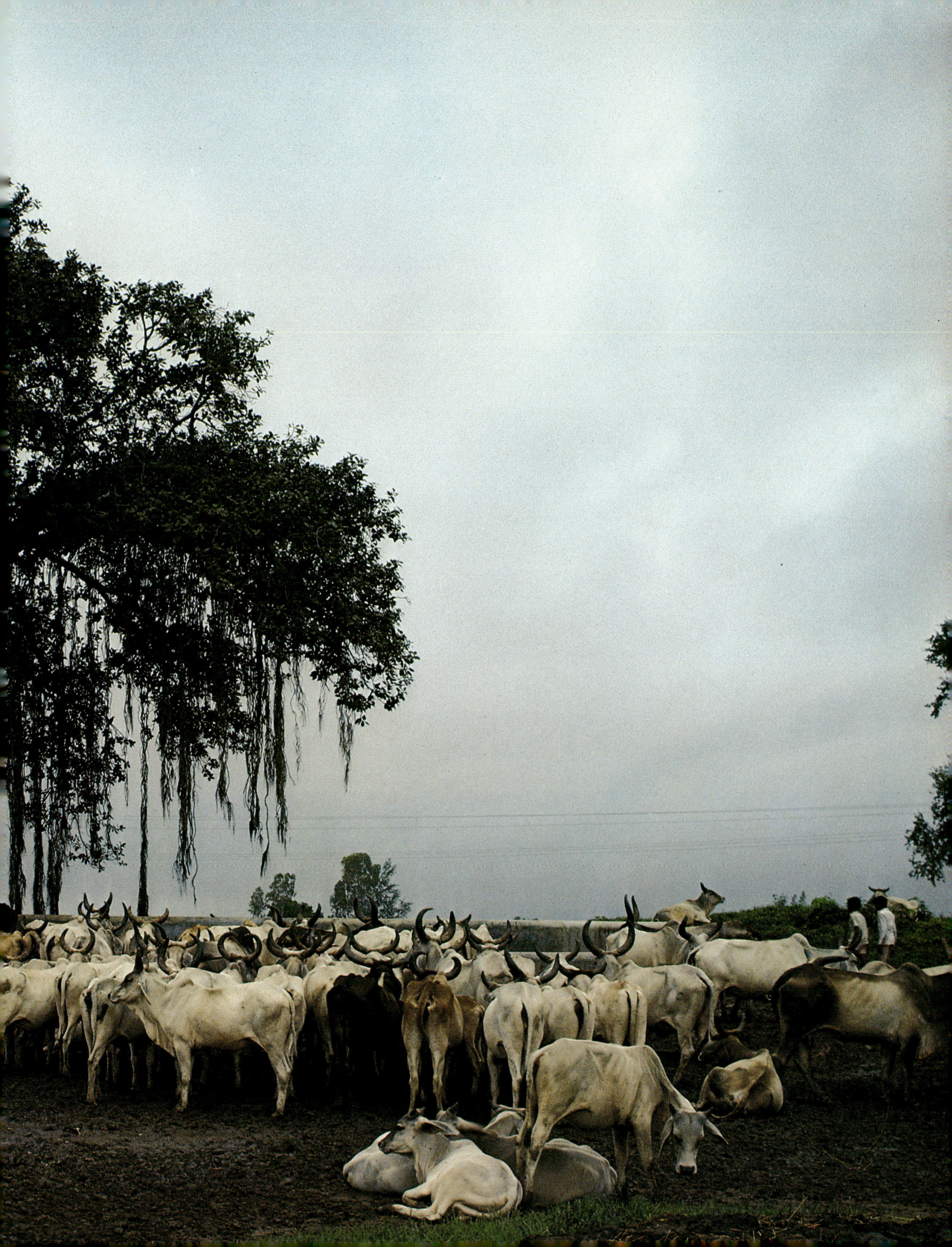

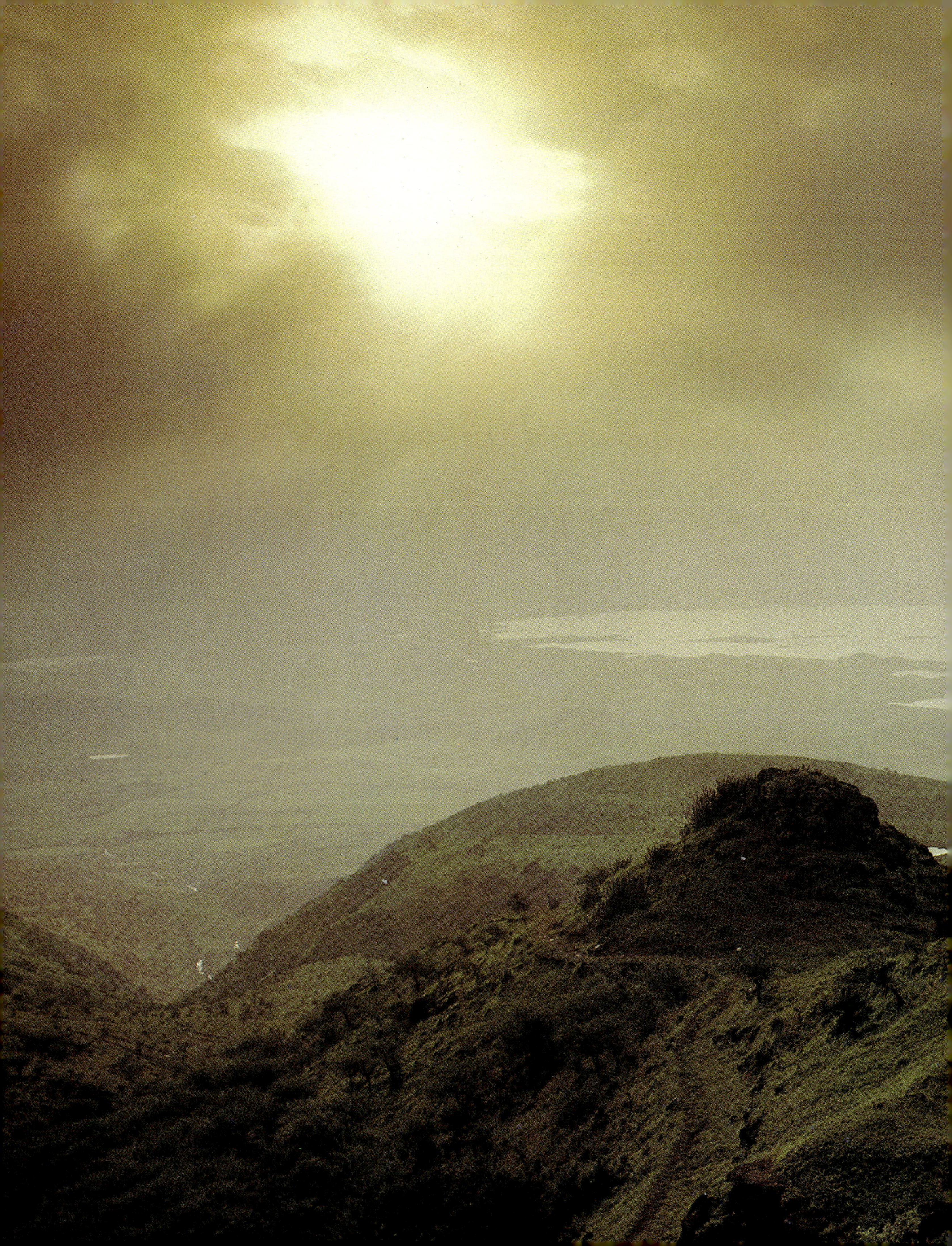

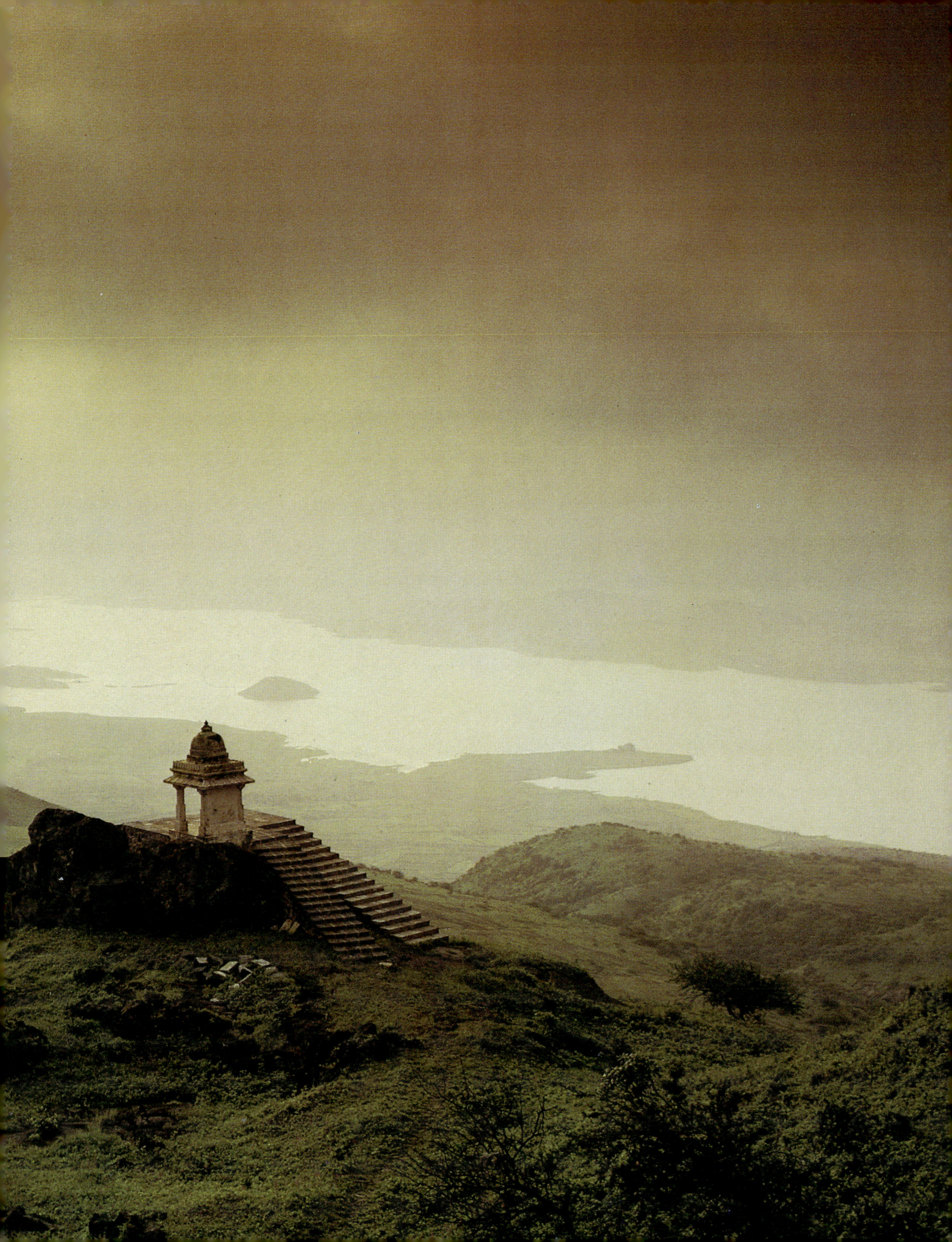

19. The arid countryside around Daulatabad, an ancient Islamic fortress in Maharashtra.

20. The ruins of Hampi, the ancient capital of the Hindu empire of Vijayanagar, in the state of northern Karnataka. The 'City of the Victory' covers an area of 12.75 square miles and is surrounded by seven concentric rings of fortified cyclopean walls, within which lie the ruins of palaces, temples, and fortifications. The ruins and erratic rocks with their pinkish coloration which are scattered everywhere create a strange, picturesque, almost enchanted landscape.

21. A mandapa, or stone pavilion, on the banks of the lake at Hampi. It is also a dobhi ghat, *a place used for the washing of clothes.*

On the following pages:
22. A majestic camel, whose coat has been clipped in decorative patterns, at the camel market in the village of Nagaur, between Jodhpur and Bikaner, in the middle of the desert of Rajasthan.

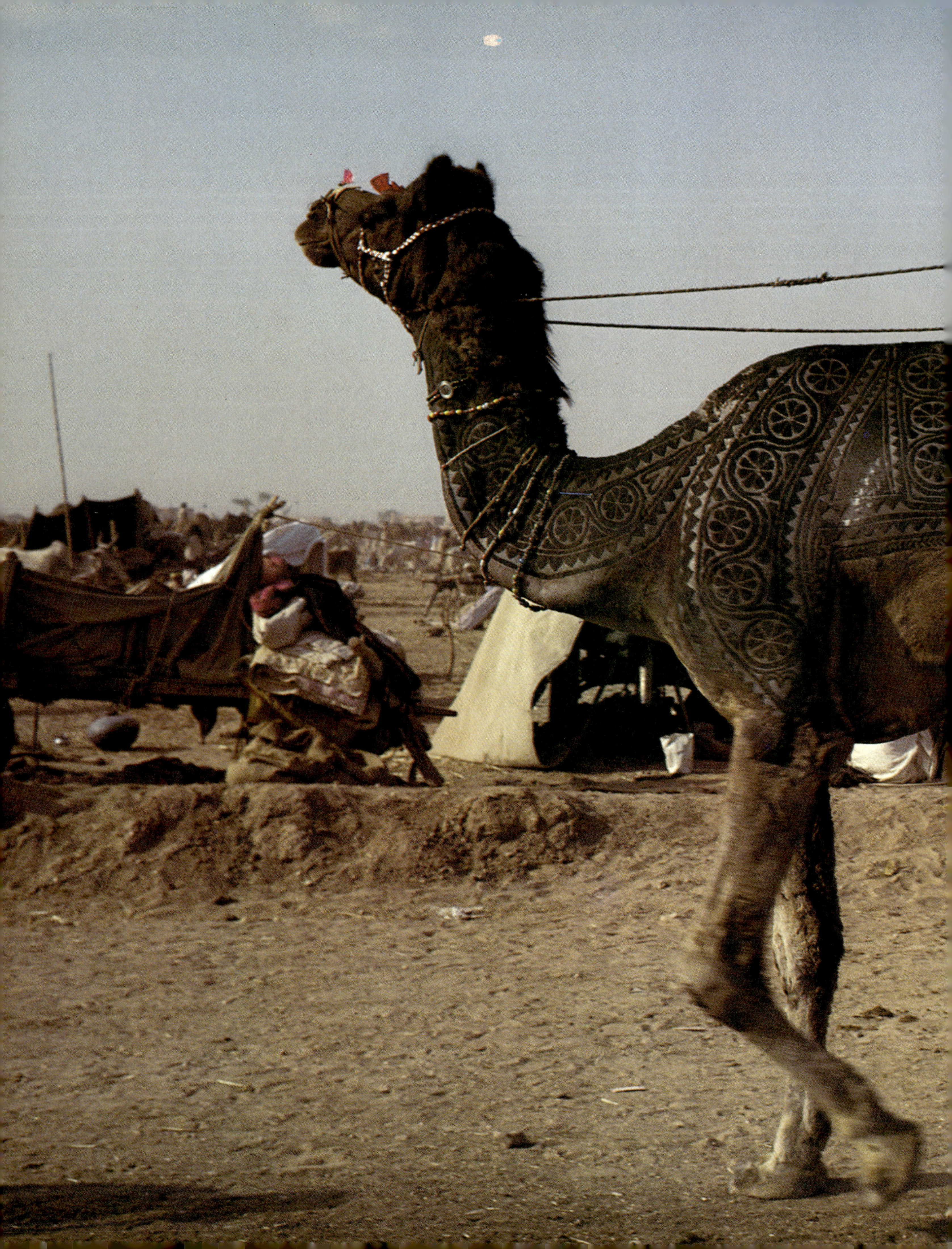

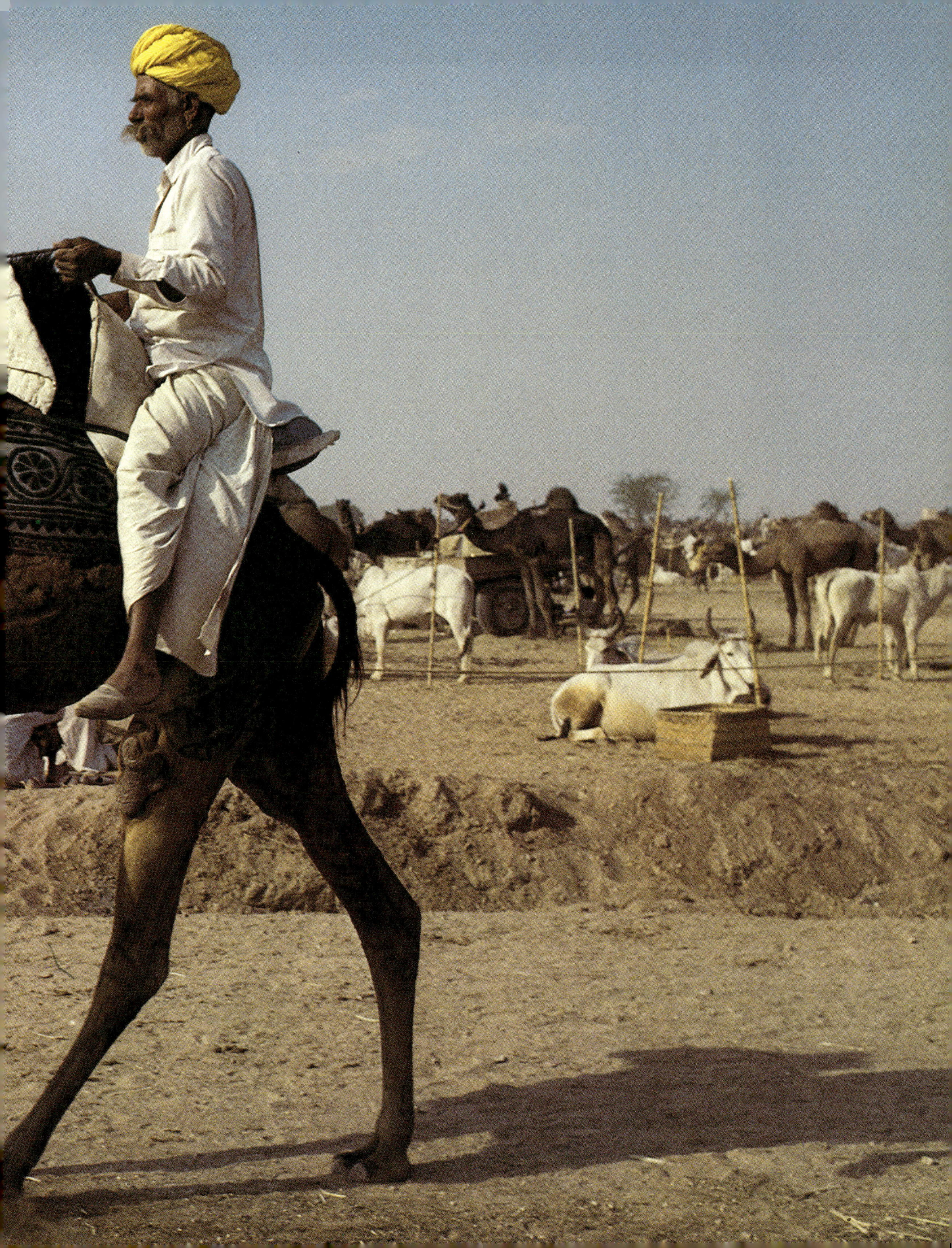

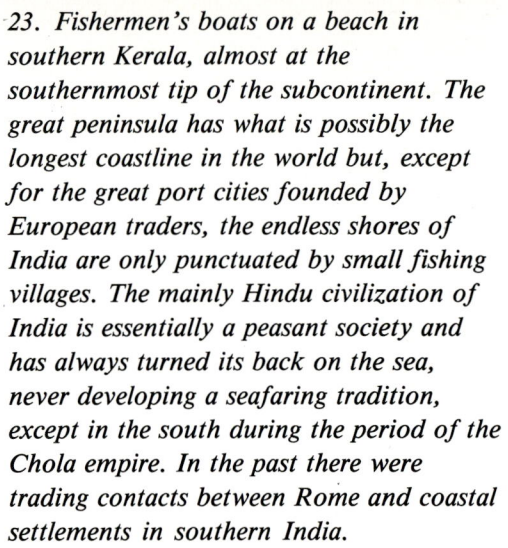

23. Fishermen's boats on a beach in southern Kerala, almost at the southernmost tip of the subcontinent. The great peninsula has what is possibly the longest coastline in the world but, except for the great port cities founded by European traders, the endless shores of India are only punctuated by small fishing villages. The mainly Hindu civilization of India is essentially a peasant society and has always turned its back on the sea, never developing a seafaring tradition, except in the south during the period of the Chola empire. In the past there were trading contacts between Rome and coastal settlements in southern India.

*24. Fishermen and catamarans on the beach of Mahabalipuram, a few miles south of Madras. The catamarans (*kattumaram *or 'tied trunks' in Tamil) are to be found in their thousands along the coasts. These primitive, ancient boats consist of between three and seven shaped trunks bound together by ropes. They move with the waves and are virtually unsinkable.*

25. Boats plying the backwater canals and lagoons behind the coastline which form a vast comunications and transport network in Kerala. Because of the humid, tropical climate, the vegetation, especially in the palm forests, is luxuriant. The Kerala coast is one of the parts of India that is most exposed to the monsoon and there are heavy rains every year. Kerala's economy is mainly based on plantations of spices, pepper, cardamom, peanuts, coffee, tea, coconuts, areca, and rubber.

26. The great serpent boat during the festival of Thiruonam (Holy Onam), in a lagoon near Alleppey. The festival, which takes place in the months of August and September at the end of the summer monsoon, commemorates the return home of the legendary King Mahabali, a beloved sovereign from a distant, happy, and prosperous epoch. The festival lasts ten days and includes processions, dances, and songs; but the most spectacular moment is the race of the serpent boats, or Chundan Vallum.

27. High monsoon in Kerala. The Indian climate is marked by a long dry season broken by the great phenomenon of the monsoon, which lasts for about three months. Ninety percent of the Indian irrigational system depends upon monsoon rains, which are often unpredictable and variable – a variability which governs the fate of vast areas of India.

28

28. A typical scene during the monsoon season along the Kerala railway. The entire culture, both classical and popular religion, mythology, arts, music, and literature of India bear the stamp of the monsoon, which has always been regarded as the source of life in a basically agricultural country, where the chances of survival depend upon the amount of water which descends from the skies. Often the rains are too heavy, the crops rot, and floods devastate the countryside. At other times, when they are not heavy enough, there is no water to store for other harvests. If the monsoon is late the peasants of various parts of India perform rites in honour of the divinities asking for the blessing of abundant rains for the fields. A popular song of the south goes 'if the rain does not fall, the world is lost. / Even virtue is lost, if the rain does not fall...'.
29. Waiting for a train in the rain.

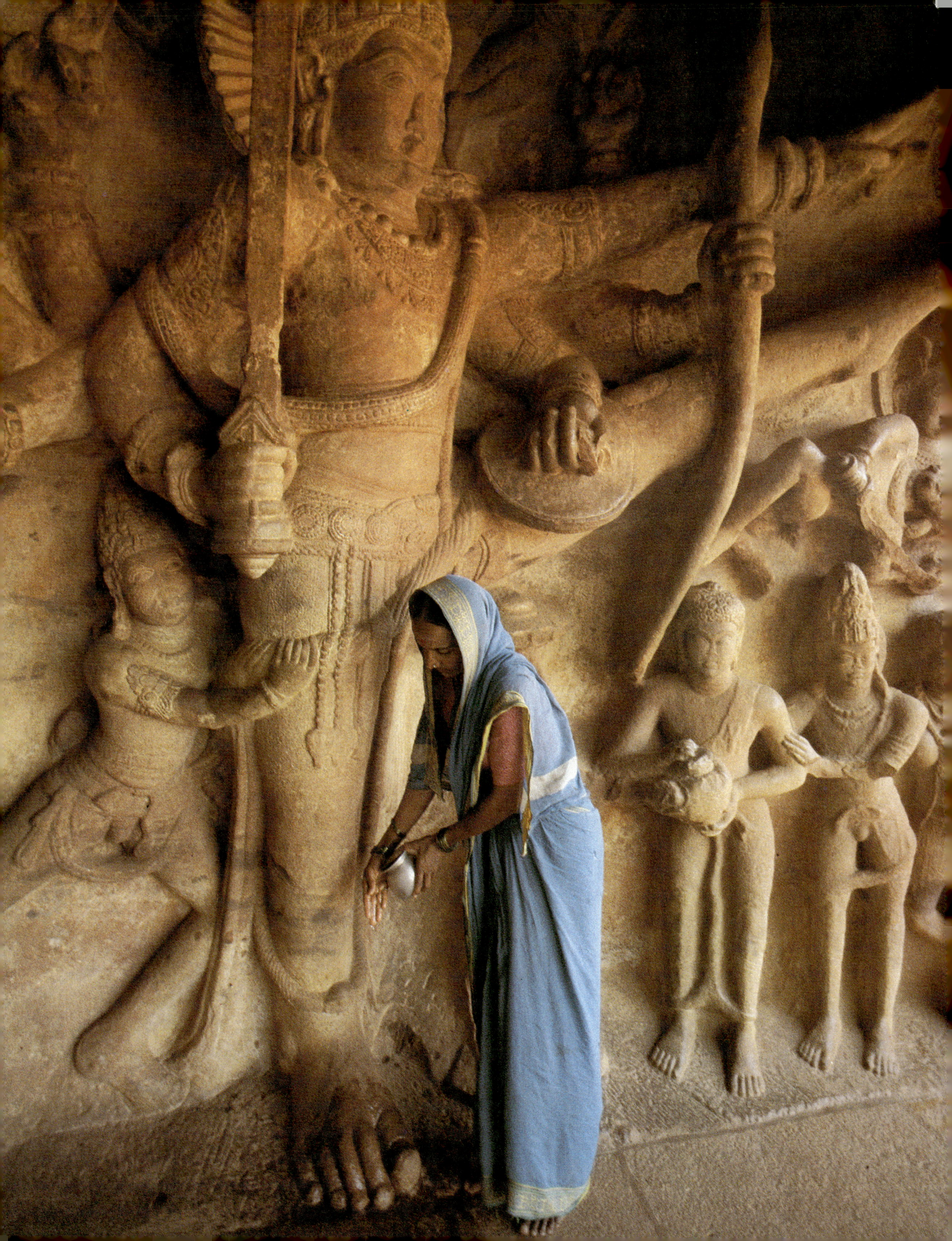

A true Hindu will call himself a Hindu with great reluctance. Instead he will say: I am called Hindu by those who wish to distinguish me from themselves. It was the Muslims who first called me Hindu, meaning by that I was not Muslim. The Christians too call us Hindus, in order to separate us from them'.
                                                            Raimundo Panikkar

Myths, Religions, Cults

The term Hindu does not exist in the ancient Sanskrit scriptures and has no equivalent in the Indian languages. It is Persian in origin and relatively recent in date, having been adopted by the Europeans, for whom Hinduism signified the ancient religion shared by virtually all the peoples of the subcontinent. Hinduism is the dominant religion and 80 percent of the population belong to it and are known as Hindus. There is then a large minority of Muslims making up eleven percent. The remainder, excluding the aboriginal communities, is composed of a variety of creeds and sects, including Sikhs, Christians, Jains, Parsis, and a number of Buddhists.

Unlike the conventionally defined monotheistic religions such as Judaism, Christianity, and Islam, Hinduism does not proffer itself as a revealed religion — at least not in the intense Western sense; nor does it lay down dogmas or a collective interpretation of the concept of god which is intended to overrule the purely individual one. A Hindu is born as such and may be a good Hindu even if he does not declare his faith in a single god or in a multitude of gods or even if he is a complete atheist. No founder of Hinduism is known, nor are there any prophetic messengers of an immutable truth and nor is a messiah expected; furthermore there is no official teaching which imposes an orthodox reading of its doctrinal scriptures. It is therefore not a religion in the strict sense or at least not a religion organized as such. Hinduism is first of all a complete system of life and a particular social order and it is difficult to think of its spread without the adoption of the characteristic form of Indian life. It is impossible to separate the subdivision of Indian society into castes from the Hindu religion, because the caste system is inextricably linked to the doctrinal framework of Hinduism — hence it is also a philosophy of life and a mode of philosophical and religious thought.

The almost total absence of proselytism in Hinduism suggests that it is not what one might term a militant religion. This does not mean that it lacks unity — the primary tendency of every religious creed. The unusual feature of Hinduism is its unified nature which combines the most diverse and contradictory doctrinal concepts, religious tendencies, and cults. What distinguishes it further is its extreme tolerance of other religions, in that it regards all spiritual roads as good, so long as the faith is lived genuinely and to the full. It is said that Hinduism does not have a true concept of sin, nor does it affirm a rigorous ethical code or commandments without whose observance it is impossible to attain salvation. Although it is true that it has ethical and moral laws, respect for these does not necessarily offer the chance of salvation, because the fate of every individual being (*svadharma*) is unique, and transcends any laws or commandments laid down by a collective religion.

It is difficult in a brief survey to illustrate properly the profound doctrinal complexity of what we call Hinduism but there are some fundamental concepts which can give an idea of its special features. These concepts have remained unaltered over the centuries and form the common basis not only of the Hindu schools and sects but of all the religious movements born in India, even heterodox doctrines such as Buddhism and Jainism. *Dharma*, the first of these concepts, has a double meaning. The first is that of the law whose purpose is to maintain the harmony of the social order, the result of which has been the formation of the

30. A woman pours water over the foot of a large statue of Vishnu Vamana, inside cave II at Badami, in upper Karnataka. This is an act of veneration, or puja, *dedicated to the divinity of whom she is a devotee. Popular acts, rites, and objects of devotion can be seen everywhere in India; in the countryside, a tree, a stone, a hollow in the rock may all become spots invested with holiness. As a result, small altars are built and the rites of homage to the divinity who presides over the site are performed daily. In the cities, too, in the houses and even in offices, there are images or altars dedicated to divinities or saints, to whom fresh garlands of flowers and incense are offered every day.*

Dharma-shastra, the codes of conduct which govern the relations between men, their rights and civil and religious duties and, above, all, the rules concerning the ritual purity of the castes. In this respect therefore it is an ethic, a moral law which, although religious in origin, bears a human and temporal imprint. The other meaning of Dharma is purely metaphysical, Dharma being conceived as the 'law which governs the universal order, the permanent support of the universe', from which all proceeds and on which all depends, including the moral laws of men and even the transcendent world of the gods. Dharma *is* the truth, unrevealed, in short 'the religion', not as a series of doctrines and religious concepts which are to be believed in but as the process and action to be 'realized' Man must realize the Dharma and because it is mysterious and ineffable he must perservere, to the limits of his abilities, with becoming part of the cosmic order. In the Dharmic conception there is another essential premise, the doctrine of the transmigration of the soul, known as *samsara*. Time, seen as a wheel which turns unendingly on itself, carries beings in an eternal transmigration from existence to existence. However, it is *karma*, (literally 'action', the law of causality), which acts as the motor of infinite rebirth. Every act implies a retribution which reverberates through subsequent lives, just as every earthly event is the product of the accumulated actions of past lives. Hindus thought that, however, desirable and gratifying an existence might be, the result was always a painful and unavoidable path ending in death and total dissolution. Despite the fact that it was possible to rise in the karmic scale to reach higher levels in subsequent lives, the return to existence confirmed at each recurrence the state of servitude to the laws of karma. It is at this point that Hinduism, pervaded by man's tormenting desire to free himself, elaborated the doctrine of salvation in the hope of putting an end to the tyranny of karma. Indian soteriology — called the doctrine of *moksha* (liberation) first formulated at the time of the ancient *Upanishads* — lays down, in line with the variety of human inclinations, a plurality of lives or spiritual courses. These may be classified in brief as follows: the life of action or *karmamarg*, the normal life which provides for the observance of religious duties and the application of the acts prescribed by the scriptures but which in its highest form signifies the perfect realization of the karma in a progression towards liberation or god; the life of knowledge or *jnanamarg*, reserved for chosen minds, which use knowledge as a means of choice between the real and unreal and which only succeed in realizing themselves in the absolute comprehension of god; the life of concentration or *yogamarg*, which favours the ascetic life, inspired by ecstatic doctrines and contemplation, such as yoga. Yoga literally means 'yoking' — perfect discipline and control of the psycho-physical impulses to dominate the forces which chain man and hinder him from transcending his earthly condition. Although the final aim is moksha, the knowledge of god and the most direct way of attaining it lies in Yoga. 'Aimed at mastering the senses and the mind, so that the mirror of the soul, unpolluted by temporal preoccupations, can perfectly reflect that god which "hides in the hearth" (Zaehner). The final course is the life of devotion or *bhaktimarg*: the approach to god through love and absolute devotion, the mystical relationship in which the gift of grace and the loving and compassionate gaze of god is contemplated.

Strictly speaking, the cult of the gods, the rites, the pilgrimages, and all the devotional acts are only the first steps which prepare the soul for the necessary purity on the long path leading to the absolute, atemporal personality of the *brahman*, the ultimate absence of the universe. The principal *marg* or way which Hinduism seems to have chosen over its long process of evolution is *bhakti*, which is summarized as 'the supreme good to which one must aspire is the perennial contemplation of god'. According to this concept, the soul in an absolute mystic ecstasy tends to overcome the state of duality which separates it from god and its great natural aspiration, to being reabsorbed back into the eternal, undifferentiated brahman (for Buddhists this is Nirvana). The yogi who reaches the total state of unity is said to be touched by brahman, in absolute communion with the ultimate entity of the universe. The *Bhagavad Gita*, one of the most important of Hindu scriptures, declares that it is the state of 'absolute oneness'. Modern Hinduism, which has largely lost its Vedic and Brahmanic connotations, sees the emergence of new trends and new mystics. Amongst the religious masses there is an almost spontaneous trend towards the life of bhakti, the mystic and trusting adoration of a single god and it is significant that the *Bhagavad Gita* has become the gospel of all Hindu believers. It comprises a collection of legends, myths, cosmogonies, and the doctrinal foundations of all Hinduism and is in essence the major scripture of bakhti-yoga. As Ananda K. Coomaraswami, a great Indian scholar, has stated, 'it is studied in every part of India, recited daily from memory by millions of Hindus of every sect and cult, and may be regarded as the fire which feeds all Indian spirituality'.

Brahmanism and Hinduism: Vishnu, Shiva, Devi-Shakti

The most ancient body of Brahmanical doctrine consists of the *Vedas* or 'sacred wisdom', the body of the mythical beliefs and philosophical and theological conceptions of the Aryan tribes which invaded northern India in a series of waves between 2000 and 1000 BC. These are four collections or *sambita* of hymns and magico-sacrificial formulas which were once passed on orally. The *Rig Veda*, the oldest and most important, introduces the principal divinities and the Vedic myths, whereas the *Sama, Yajur,* and *Atharva Vedas* are liturgical compilations for rites and sacrifices. The later *Brahmana*, prose treatises which deal more thoroughly with the procedures for the celebration of sacrifices, also belong to the Vedic literature. In the *Vedas* ritual and sacrifice are of absolute importance and this exalts the importance of the priestly caste which officiated at the sacrifices. The priest was held 'higher than the gods' because he possessed a perfect ritualistic apparatus and collection of magic formulas, through which — as the *Atharva Veda* says — 'he supports the heaven and the earth'. The power of Vedic sacrifice is such that it became the fundamental law, not only of individual destiny, but of the universal order. For this reason the brahmins or priests, the 'invokers' of the gods, enjoyed particular prestige which established the absolute superiority of their caste over other groups.

The Aryans, first in the Punjab and then in other parts of northern India, introduced new ways and customs and, most important of all, Sanskrit, which was to become the sacred language throughout India. Originally, theirs was a nomadic and pastoral economy, with a rigidly patriarchal system of authority in the family and the tribe. In their descent into India they confronted the older, more highly evolved civilization of the Indus. The Aryans overwhelmed it, absorbing certain aspects of its culture, and continued in their migration towards the upper valley of the Ganges where they settled and began to farm. It was inevitable that in their contacts with the people of the Indian plains, the aborigines and the Dravidians, the Aryans would absorb many of their religious customs and concepts. The Vedic pantheon of Agni, Indra, Varuna, and Mitra, vague divinities with no corresponding definite image, was supplemented by a multitude of Dravidian gods and idols connected with the cult of fertility. Although not universally accepted, it has been cogently argued that it was at this period that the caste system arose and that its function was initially to preserve the racial purity of the Aryans from pollution by the blood of the subjugated peoples and secondly to protect the privileges of the priestly class. The caste system was imposed by the brahmins with

Hari-Hara, a composite figure combining Shiva and Vishnu (by D.D. Kosambi).

Murugan (Subrahmany, Karttikeya), a highly popular divinity among the southern Tamil, from a modern religious picture.

rigid hereditary criteria for status and social functions, preserved by religious laws and sanctions. The caste hierarchy is already well defined in a hymn in the *Rig Veda*, where it is divided into four canonical *varna* (the Sanskrit term for caste): priests (*Brahman*), rulers and warriors (*Kshatriya*), merchants or craftsmen (*Vaishya*), cultivators or servants (*Shudra*).

The *Vedas* and the subsequent *Upanishads* completed the cycle of scriptures known as the *shruti*, which means 'revelation', the doctrinal basis of the brahmanical religion. The *Upanishads* represents the most highly evolved brahmanical thought, which arrives at the formulation of a fundamental metaphysical concept: the *atman-brahma* (soul-god) relationship. The doctrine of transmigration (*samsara*) appears for the first time, together with two complementary concepts; *karma*, action, and *moksha*, the possibility of salvation. The sages of the *Upanishad* schools based their reflection on the primacy of *atman*, the inner man: 'the brahma will no longer be the god of the cosmic sacrifice', as in the first Vedism, 'but that of the spiritual search' (Zaehner).

The first commentaries on the *Vedas* appeared in the seventh and sixth centuries BC. These introduced the next phase in the literature which includes the *Dharma-Shastra*, scientific and legal treatises which codify the various spheres of human activity on the basis of a new interpretation of the Vedic principles. It is at this moment that Brahmanism is regarded as becoming Hinduism, in which the speculative thought tended to integrate popular spirituality with the systematic elaboration of the philosophy. At the same time as the evolution of the six *darshan*, defined as the orthodox philosophical systems of Hindu culture, the cult of images developed amongst the mass of believers together with the building of temples (in the Vedic period neither images nor temples existed), the celebration of popular religious festivities, and the pilgrimages to holy places (*tirtha*). Popular religious feeling profoundly inspired the creators of epic poems and mythological tales. These fantastic works of legend, myth and profound moral teaching clearly indicate Hinduism's development towards a popular, monotheistic religion. This trend was to be confirmed by the appearance of philosopher saints, who founded the new schools of spirituality: Shankara in the eighth century AD, Ramanuja in the twelfth century and Madhva in the thirteenth century. In the final phase of the establishment of Hinduism, from the sixth to the fifteenth century BC, three major religious streams formed: Vaishnavite, Shaivite, and Shaktite, the cults of the gods Vishnu, Shiva, and Shakti. They were inspired by the sacred epics, the *Ramayana*, the *Mahabharata*, the *Purana* and the Tantric books, which then became the highest doctrinal authority of Hinduism until the modern period. Vishnu, who occupies a secondary position in the *Veda* and is identified as the divine being who presides over the energy of the sun, is acknowledged by his faithful as the single Supreme Reality, the 'Lord of the Universe'. However, it is in the doctrine of the *avatar* (incarnations or divine descents) in particular that Vishnu assumes a position of the first rank, in a series of different and specific incarnations. God descends to the earth from time to time to save the world and set it back on the right course. This is how Krishna, the most authentic incarnation of Vishnu, addresses Arjuna, and therefore men, in an episode of the 'Song of the Lord', at the heart of the *Mahabharata*: 'for the protection of the good and the destruction of the evil, to re-establish the order, I return in successive epochs' (*Bhagavad Gita*, IV, 8).

There are ten classic avatars which are of great importance in the sacred iconography and which led to the formation of autonomous sects and cults. They mark the various periods in the history of humanity, beginning with prehistoric myths (Matsya, Kurma, Varaha, Narasimha) up to incarnations in human form (some of which are identified with historical personages), Vamana, Parashurama, and Rama (this last being the incarnation of the hero-king, the protagonist of the epic poem the *Ramayana*); Krishna, the eighth avatar, has become the most popular modern divinity — not simply an incarnation but the most complete manifestation of Vishnu. Krishna is the object of extraordinary adoration amongst Hindus, the supreme lord of the bhakti cults, a devotional religious form akin to the Western notion of 'grace'. He is the divine protagonist of the *Bhagavad Gita*, the most important and popular sacred text of modern India. This is a religious and doctrinal treatise but also a splendid literary work. Buddha is regarded, although not by all Vaishnavite sects, as the ninth incarnation of Vishnu. Finally there is Kalki, the tenth and last avatar, who is yet to descend and who will appear at the end of our era (*Kaliyuga* or 'age of iron') in the shape of a hero bearing a sword and riding a white horse, in order to restore the dharma, the law of justice and purity.

In his specific manifestation Vishnu is Nara Narayan, the Lord of the Primordial Waters, who rests on the serpent Adishesa (who represents eternity), stretched out on the surface of the Ocean. Beside him is his wife Sri or Lakashmi, goddess of prosperity and the mediator between Vishnu and man. In Vishnu the helpful and merciful aspect of god is emphasized and the relationship of the faithful with the

Hanuman the monkey god and Ravana the demon god talking together in the shade of a mango tree (from a modern illustration from southern India).

Shiva Nataraja, in a drawing based on a bronze by Tiruvelangadu (eleventh century AD, Madras Museum, from The Dance of Shiva *by A.K. Coomaraswamy).*

divinity is one of loving and trusting abandonment. In Vaishnavism, and particularly in the avatars of Krishna, *bhakti,* the devotional attitude towards god, takes on a central position and the conviction is affirmed that redemption is possible for all, even the lowest castes, because the god himself, as is confirmed by the doctrine of the avatars, displays concern and compassion for man. Vaishnavism has followed two paths, the Pancharatra and the Bhagavata; the former is based on the ritualistic and magical texts and, like certain Shaivite traditions, has advanced the concept of *shakti,* which takes place with the intervention of Lakshmi, the wife of Vishnu. The Bhagavata places the emphasis on the devotional aspect, bhakti, which has inspired poets and mystics in particular. The most representative of these were the Alvar, mystical poets who lived in Tamil areas in the eighth century AD. Their poetry was founded on absolute devotion to Krishna, continually insisting upon the universal availability of divine grace to all creatures.

Shiva, to whom the other major religious tradition is dedicated, has a cult which is spread throughout the peninsula. There are thousands of temples dedicated to him. In pre-Vedic times the god was Rudra, a terrifying divinity who presided over the natural elements and brought storms. He was given a propitiatory epithet, Shiva, meaning benevolent, propitious and in the second century BC the personality of Rudra-Shiva underwent a profound change, rapidly assuming the personality of an absolute divinity. For his followers, who form a powerful current in the history of Hinduism, Shiva is the Supreme Being, to whom are attributed the powers of the evolution, preservation, and dissolution of the world. Shiva dances in a circle of fire as he squashes the world in the form of a demon, but his frenetic rhythm re-creates a new world. In this manifestation, which is splendidly represented in the Dravidian statuary and in the Chola bronzes, he is called Nataraja ('King of the Dance').

In the creation manifestation the *lingam,* a phallic emblem (generally a cylindrical stone of varied size), symbolizes the generative principle, which has assumed prime importance in the Shaivite cult. Represented with the *yoni,* the symbol of the female genitalia, Shiva combines in himself the two primordial elements of nature, the male and the female. The cult of the lingam is extremely ancient and probably represents the prehistoric fertility cults practised by the aborigines of the subcontinent. However, the fertility aspect which is attributed to Shiva dates from the Puranic period and the Tantric texts and the epics. The faithful believe that the emblem has powerful magical and miraculous powers. The act of venerating the linga-yoni, besides guaranteeing the gift of fertility, brings a state of grace which cancels out all sins.

Shiva is Mahayogi, the great ascetic, master of the sadhu and the yogi, eternally immobile in meditation (the opposite of Nataraja, who is eternally in motion). The third eye in the centre of his forehead has destructive powers. His numerous arms hold the trident, the tambourine, and the axe. Many of his faithful adorn themselves in this way and imitate him in long and terrible self-mortifications. In many images Shiva rides the bull Nandi, which is sometimes understood as the symbol itself of the divinity. The permanent residence of Shiva and his consort Parvati is Mount Kailash in the Himalayas. The divine family also includes two sons: Skanda (Karttikeya, Subrahmanya, or the Tamil name of Murugan), a six-headed martial divinity and patron of the brahmin priests; and Ganesh or Ganapati, the elephant-headed god, one of the most popular divinities in India. If Vaishnavism exhibits a profound doctrinal complexity, the same is also true of Shiva, although the apparently contradictory nature of his figure, his ability to synthesize antithetic natures, and above all the ascetic and esoteric stamp of his sects have made him inaccessible to the masses, who are more spontaneously attracted to the devotional cult of a mild and protective god. His followers include devotees of asceticism and the monastic life, who are grouped in numerous sects and congregations: Pashupata, the Natha-Yoghin of the north; the Shaivites of Kashmir; and, in the south, the Shaiva-Siddhanta, the Virashaiva or Lingayat. The divinity has been at the centre of a *bhakti* cult, a form of devotion more widespread amongst Vaishnavites, of mystic Tamil poets who lived between the sixth and eighth century AD and whose faith was summarized in the message that salvation was only possible through self-abandonment to Shiva, the one true god. In Shiva of the 'thousand names' and the thousand manifestations there is one which represents one of the subtlest and most pregnant concepts in Hinduism. Shiva Ardhanarishwara, a composite figure of the god and his wife, the perfect union of the fundamental principles of existence. Iconographically half the body appears male and the other half female. It is the symbol of the divine duality, the synthesis of the opposing parts, the male god with his *shakti*, the "female energy", with which he becomes "active" and "potent". However, the goddess too, who is known by the generic name of Devi, is adored under an infinite variety of names and manifestations: Parvayi, Uma, Ambika, but also Durga, the

The battle between Rama and Hanuman and the army of monkeys on one side and on the other Ravana, with his ten heads and twenty arms, leading the army of Rakshacha demons (from a nineteenth-century illustration).

warrior goddess, and finally Kali, the Black, the Great Mother, who drives the natural cycle of life and who through death allows the regeneration of life itself in the world. Throughout India *pitha*, centres of sacrifice, are dedicated to the great goddess, with the presence of devout shakta, who principally venerate the female manifestation of the god. Other schools return to the principle of the shakti and religious and philosophical works of an initiation cult, concerning the ritual and even the practices of sexual mysticism. In the doctrines of the *Tantra*, literally 'thread', not only all the Shaivite sects but also Buddhists and some Vaishnavites and Jainists come together.

The primitive Brahmanic pantheon, mixed with Vedic divinities, was replaced in the period which we term the Indian Middle Ages by a triad of religious traditions and schools, each of which developed along monotheistic lines and which formed the main strands in the final theological order of Hinduism and have continued up to the present day.

The concept of *trimurti*, the synthesis of Brahma, Vishnu, and Shiva — as described in the accounts of European travellers — never truly existed and neither did its cult. What the travellers may have described is one of the many attempts at Hindu syncretism or, according to some historians, an attempt by a Brahmanic sect to prevent the total eclipse of the god Brahma. Brahma never enjoyed the importance of the other two divinities and his cult disappeared after the Gupta period (roughly AD 320-540). However, Brahma, who was defined as the 'creator' in the *Vedas*, has survived in the concept of *brahma*, the ultimate synthesis of the monotheistic vision of the religion. Images of Brahma are uncommon and there is only one temple, at Pushkar, now dedicated to him. The wife of Brahma is Sarasvati, the goddess of the arts and music.

A Thousand Years of Buddhism

In the course of its evolution Brahmanism became interwoven and clashed with various confessional movements and trends of various kinds and of varying degrees of importance. Some were heretical or schismatic offshoots of Brahmanism itself, others came from cultures or places that lay outside India. Many of the religious communities which have descended from the heterodox movements are alive and widespread and retain a distinct position even today. others, which arose at certain points in the long history of India, have subsequently disappeared.

Buddhism, which has deeply influenced certain Hindu doctrinal concepts, is a significant example. From the appearance of the Buddha in the sixth century BC to the onset of the decline of the movement he founded, Buddhism spread throughout India, attaining the status of a national religion under Ashoka in the third century BC. This period, on which Buddhism left a deep impression, lasted at least a thousand years. With the Brahmanical renaissance of the sixth and seventh century AD Buddhism retreated into small communities of monks, or to the Himalayas or to Sri Lanka. It finally disappeared from India at about the turn of the millennium — the religion of the Sublime left the great peninsula for distant countries.

The illustrious son of India, the 'Light of Asia', the Buddha, born at Kapilavastu in 558 BC of a noble family of the warrior caste, belonged to the Sakya race. He was given the name of Siddhartha Gautama (the latter being his family name).

Over the centuries legends and fantastic tales were added to the historical figure of the Prince Siddhartha. The known facts are few, but we do know that at the age of twenty-nine he abandoned his parent's house and his family, that at thirty-five he obtained Illumination (acquiring the title of the Buddha), and that he died at the age of eighty. For forty-five years the Buddha led a wandering life through the various parts of India, preferring isolated places surrounded by nature. He preached everywhere, converting by the strength of his word and his example. Numerous miracles are also attributed to him. 'No biography was written until centuries after his death. His true identity — that of the awakened one (*Buddha*) — was proclaimed publicly and accepted by his disciples, his life was transfigured and he took on the specific mythological dimension of Great Saviours. As a result the Buddha came to be the founder of a religion but Buddhism is the only religion whose founder did not declare himself the prophet or messenger of a god and indeed he rejected the idea of god' (Eliade).

In Buddhist thought the connection between life and sorrow is of prime importance. This gives rise to the 'Four Noble Truths' (expounded in the first sermon at Benares): first, life is sorrow; second, sorrow is born from desire (because all is transitory, 'impermanent'); third, liberation from sorrow consists of the abolition of desires; the fourth shows the way to extinguish sorrow. This is also known as the 'Middle Path', and is expanded in eight rules of moral conduct ('The Eight Part Way'), whose observance is the road which leads to *nirvana*.

Avalokiteshwar, the Buddha of Compassion.

In its fundamental principles Buddhist doctrine expresses a form of life that is only feasible for monks, because renunciation was of overwhelming importance in the doctrine and even though the Buddha himself preached the 'middle way', a temperate asceticism, it was thought desirable that a certain number of people should embark on a course whose end is spiritual illumination. In its doctrine there are profound affinities with the *Upanishads*, the scriptures which represent the most highly evolved philosophical essence of Brahmanism, as well as traces of the Samkhya, one of the six orthodox Hindu philosophical systems and of the theistic Yoga, whose principles and techniques became a point of reference in Buddhist morals. The Buddha, in fact, does not represent a true antithesis of Brahmanism and his behaviour in this respect is significant. He says nothing on the nature of the soul, he does not deny the existence of gods, nor does he say anything against the caste system, even though the Buddhist community abolished all caste discrimination. What was important to him was to declare that all things were transitory (caste, race, forms, and even the world of the gods expressed by man), because everything is destined to disappear. It is essential that there are men desirous only of ascending, of chosing the life of renunciation and asceticism. The Buddha maintains a solemn silence on the Ultimate Reality and does not seek to give his teaching a systematic structure, but takes great care in defining the dominion of cause and effect. Existence is dominated by the law of *samsara*, the perpetual cycle of existences, to which man is bound by *karma*, the chain of actions whose fruits reverberate through subsequent lives. The only way of breaking the infinite cycle is, for the Illuminate, the destruction of passion and the elimination of ignorance through the doctrine which demonstrates the 'impermanence of all things'. To the concept of karma, which is similar to the Brahmanical one, Buddhism adds intention as a criterion of judgement. Karma can only be generated if an intentional will exists.

Upon the death of the Buddha his disciples held numerous councils and it was these which led to the sectarian divisions and heresies which afflicted the religious community. The most important of these include Hinayana Buddhism or Theravada (The Lesser Vehicle) and Mahayana Buddhism (The Great Vehicle). Therava is the school of wisdom founded by Sariputra, one of the best of the Buddha's disciples. It is based on three orthodox principles: the Buddha as master; dharma as doctrine; *samgha* (the monastic community) as the way of life. Descended from early Buddhism, it has no place for divinity or the soul, and it believes in the impermanence of things and the instability of phenomena. The sorrow of the world is generated by life and by reincarnation, from which release can be obtained by reaching nirvana. It abolished temples, ceremonies, and rituals and only allowed the veneration of relics and statues, as well as pilgrimages to places made sacred by the presence of the Buddha.

The other major tradition is called Mahayana (The Great Vehicle), which stems from transcendental metaphysics with a theistic development. The figure of the Buddha is transfigured and every word of the Master assumes an esoteric sense, divine in nature, and in essence the Buddha is adored as a divinity. The fundamental virtues of Mahayana are compassion, charity, and altruism. The ideal example is the *bodhisattva*, the being destined for illumination and nirvana, which he renounces to help other creatures reach the same condition. It is the ideal of universal compassion (*karuna*) through self-sacrifice.

Lamaism is a manifestation of Mahayana Buddhism (also known as Vayrana Buddhism) which developed in the seventh century AD in Tibet and Ladakh, or Little Tibet, within the borders of India. It is based on elaborate ritualism, religious cults, and rigidly hierarchical communities of monks, which reflected the structure of the whole of Tibetan society. The invasion of Tibet by Communist China in 1959 caused enormous changes in Tibetan life, whose consequences,

Iconometric diagram for use in drawing the Buddha.

particularly in the religious sphere, still can not be ascertained.

The reasons for Buddhism's disappearance from India are not clear. It appears that it may have been due to the tendency for Buddhist communities to become centres for the exercise of power over culture and the cities, unleashing interminable rivalries between opposed groups; in the religious field, the renaissance of Hinduism offered the mass of faithful a cult with a supreme divinity which was more accessible than the values of asceticism and the monastic life.

During the supremacy of Buddhism, which over long periods also enjoyed political autocracy, Hinduism silently continued on its course. In the subsequent development of the great Hindu theistic traditions, the figure of the Buddha was in a certain sense absorbed in Vaishnavism, becoming for his followers, although not for all, an incarnation of Vishnu. Hindus say that the Buddha descended from heaven not to bring a new order but to restore the ancient order.

The twentieth century has seen a return of Buddhism to India, but it is a movement that is totally foreign to the historical development of Buddhism. What has occurred this century is the phenomenon of self-conversion to Buddhism — not only as a religion but also for its egalitarian principles — of hundreds of thousands of untouchables of the Mahar community in Maharashtra. The founder of this neo-Buddhist movement was Bhimaro Ramji Ambedkar (1893-1956), a member of the Congress during the long struggle for independence and also a member of the Mahar caste. He chose the religious life as a way of showing the Indian untouchables a way of eradicating caste discrimination and escaping from the lowly position in which Brahmanical society had kept them for millennia. Ambedkar began openly to criticize Hinduism and lay the grounds for the schism in the nineteen-thirties. In 1956, following the famous formula of renunciation ('... I renounce the gods of Hinduism, Brahma, Vishnu, Rama, Krishna, and I adhere to Buddhism'), 30,000 Ambedkar and Mahars converted to the religion of the Buddha. Today the Buddhist untouchables number some four million, two thirds of whom live in Maharashtra, the home of Ambedkar.

The Religion of Mahavira

Jainism (from *jina*, the 'victorious') is one of the most ancient Indian religious movements and it is still of great doctrinal importance, with more than two million followers divided into two sects. These, historically, have differed more in the social rules inherent in monastic discipline than over doctrinal matters. The *Digambara* (literally 'clad in space') were radical and ascetic, even at one time demanding total nudity. The *Svetambara* ('clad in white') were of a less rigid orthodoxy and as their name suggests only wore white garments. The Svetambara Sthanakavasi were an offshoot of the latter who did not venerate icons and did not have temples.

Right from the time of its foundation Jainism assumed the character of an order of itinerant monks, known for the rigour of their ascetic practices and by their tradition of pilgrimage to places sacred to Jainism, scattered all over India. Later they also added a lay branch of followers, which now predominates, who usually belong to the merchant classes.

Jainism denies the existence of an absolute divinity and does not believe in a creator as the Prime Cause, because the universe did not have a beginning and will not have an end. The Jain venerate the *Jina*, people who, having triunphed over passions, have achieved *moksha* ('liberation') through devotional acts and asceticism and have freed themselves from the perpetual cycle of rebirth. It is a pillar of doctrine that Jainism shares with Buddhism and to a degree with

Hinduism. Twenty-four saints or *Tirthankara* ('creators of passage') are venerated. These legendary figures appeared on the earth to show man the path to liberation. History records the actual existence of the last two, Parshavanatha (2700 years ago) and Vardhamana, known as Mahavira (Great Hero), who lived about 200 years later, at about the same time as the Buddha. Mahavira, the twenty-fourth and last tirthankara, is regarded as the historical founder of Jainism.

In the doctrine of Mahavira there is a marked anti-Brahmanic tendency. His heretical position is based on the denial of a supreme god, the refusal to recognize the infallibility of the assertions of the *Vedas*, the rejection of caste, and the view that sacrifice is useless. Nevertheless, Mahavira does not deny the existence of gods, to whom he attributed a certain holiness, although they too are condemned to extinction. Men must escape from the tyranny of karma since it enslaves them to the cycle of reincarnations. Liberation is achieved when any contact with matter ceases, a separation which may be achieved by rigorous ascetic practices, including chastity and lack of property (*aparigraha*), affirmation of the truth (*satyagraha*), and 'not causing of harm to anyone' (*ahimsa*). In theory, only the monastic life allows one to aspire to salvation; for the Digambara, even being a woman removes the possibility of achieving salvation, other than by being reborn as a man in the lives to come.

Although Jainism refuses to believe in an absolute god, it does admit the existence of the soul (*jiva*); indeed, everything that exists in the world possesses a soul or vital spirit, not just humans but animals, plants, and, to varying degrees, even inorganic matter. Respect for life, *ahimsa* (non-violence, although in doctrine its significance is the non-interference in someone else's karma), is therefore the most important commandment, which forms the core of Jainism. This rule has been popularized in modern times because Mahatma Gandhi, although a Hindu, adopted it as a spiritual guide and as a practical policy in the struggle for Indian independence. The doctrine of ahimsa has never been of such absolute importance to Hindus as it has to Jainists, but it has often been associated with the inviolability of the cow and with vegetarianism.

It is the followers of Mahavira who display the most thorough and absolute faithfulness to the concept of ahimsa, even when the consequences are extreme. The most orthodox monks have adopted rigid practices, such as covering their mouths with a net so as not to kill insects that might fly in and walking about with a broom to sweep ants and other insects out of their path before they are crushed. They are strictly vegetarian and some of them only eat plants whose fruit can be collected without destroying the plant itself. They abstain from drinking unfiltered water and they eat before dusk so as to avoid accidentally eating any nocturnal insect attracted by the lights. The concentration of Jainists in commerce, finance, and banking (they are known for their attitude to usury and also their donations toward the construction of their temples) or in certain crafts — generally goldsmiths — stems from their being unable to farm because work in the fields involves the destruction of living beings. Fasting and an austere life are regarded as essential for purification; the most sublime example, which was attained by Parshvanatha and Mahavira but is regarded as an impossible one for the majority of men to follow, is slow suicide by fasting.

The Emperor Akbar (from India *by Dubois de Jancigny and S. Raymond, 1846).*

The Presence of Islam

A little over a century after the death of the Prophet Muhammad in AD 632, the first Muslim traders and missionaries reached the borders of northern India. However, it was not until the eleventh century that the first massive penetration of India by Islam began. The armies of Mahmud of Ghazni and Muhammad Ghori crossed the Khyber Pass and conquered the Punjab and the neighbouring provinces. In the thirteenth century the first Turco-Afghan Sultanate was established in Delhi. The profound Islamicization of India came with the Mogul Emperors, beginning in 1526 with Babar, the first of the imperial dynasty which was to govern the whole country for almost two centuries. The Moguls, who originated in Central Asia and were the descendants of Genghis Khan and Timur (Tamerlane), gave India not only political unity but also a distinct culture, subsequently termed Indo-Islamic by historians, which entailed the profound transformation of administrative and military institutions, the creation of new capital cities, and widespread planning of the territory. The Mogul emperors were great builders of cities, fostering original architectural styles, as well as arts and crafts, music and literature. The death of the Emperor Aurangzeb at the beginning of the eighteenth century, when the empire was at its greatest geographical extent, marked the onset of the decline of Mogul sovereignty and the simultaneous resurgence of the Hindu forces and rulers. The coming of Islam to the subcontinent led to the most large-scale and violent clash between different civilizations and cultures that it had seen. It penetrated to the heart of Brahmanical civilization and spread throughout the peninsula. For Indians, Islam was something new and absolutely irreconcilable — in religious terms, there could not be a more marked divergence than between Islam and Hinduism. Although true integration was impossible, the two communities did over the centuries establish a bearable co-existence; the influence of the two communities on each other and the exchanges between them enriched them both but neither was capable of corrupting the other, nor could they fuse. Islam in India did succeed in imposing an almost absolute political supremacy but it was never able to complete its conquest in the religious sphere.

In the early centuries of the Muslim presence, the Hindu world suffered severely through the religious fanaticism and iconoclastic violence of the Muslims. Countless sacred centres and Hindu sanctuaries were destroyed, the stones of the temples and other sites being used in the building of Islamic mosques or palaces. Apart from the Rajputs in the northwest, who were the only Hindus courageously to oppose the invaders, the peoples of India at the time were politically divided and militarily defenceless. In short, they were in no position to oppose the Islamic fury. The predatory expeditions and the destruction of the Brahmanical temples were followed by harsh religious discrimination and fiscal oppression, one example being the *jiziya*, a special tax imposed by the Mogul emperors on all Hindus. Today many of India's Muslims are descendants of the first converts to Islam, who belonged to Hindu communities which occupied the Punjab in the first few centuries of the present millennium. Despite the Muslim proclivity for forced proselytism, the Mogul period did not see mass conversions of the Hindus. Many converted spontaneously, particularly groups outside the high Brahmanical castes and those who would subsequently be termed 'untouchables'. Conversion to Islam was a means of escaping the discriminatory rules imposed by the Hindu caste system.

There are some eighty million Muslims in India today, making up eleven percent of the population. The greatest concentrations are in states such as Uttar Pradesh, Bihar, West Bengal, and Kashmir. In 1930, prior to the bloody partition of the subcontinent and the creation of the two Pakistans, Muslims formed almost a third of the population. Though a minority, they were a considerable political force in the struggle for independence, which was to a large extent the cause of the division of India and the formation of an exclusively Muslim nation.

Islamic doctrine praises a society without castes, and is founded on the principle of confessional brotherhood. Its doctrine abolishes all differences based on birth or race, but secular contact with Hindu society, with its caste system, has influenced the Muslims of India. There are two basic subdivisions (not castes), the Sunni and the Shiite Muslims; who follow different schools of Koranic law and theology. In particular they differ in their interpretation of the right of succession from Muhammad. However, because Islam is a revealed religion the doctrinal differences are minimal. It is not therefore a true split and intermarriage is not unusual. The Muslims of India are therefore a multi-racial society of varied descent ranging from Arabs to groups from Central Asia, such as the Pathans and the Afghans, as well as the converted Hindus.

Within the two main traditions there are some seventy minor sects, though there is no hierarchy and they tend to intermingle. Some communities have retained the caste system as it was prior to conversion and some professional groups are also hereditary sects, such as the Dawoodi Bohra, merchants who live in Mahrashtra and Gujarat, the Sulaimi Bohra, the Memon who originated from the Kutch and Sind and are concentrated around Bombay, and the Ismaili Khoja, whose spiritual head is the Aga Khan, a direct descendant of Ali. The Moplah in Kerala form a large minority in southern India and they retain Tamil customs and traditions, although they have belonged to Islam since the first Arab merchant settlements along the Malabar coast in the seventh century.

Almost all Indian Muslims observe — often in a more orthodox fashion than in other Muslim countries — the principle rules of Islam, including the offering, the Muslim calendar based on the Hejira, the ritual prayers, the pilgrimage to Mecca, the traditional festivals (Ramadan, which in India is called Ramzan). Islam does not provide for a specific clergy for the rituals. The congregations, which occur in almost all Indian cities, are guided by an *imam* (leader) or *mullah* or *maulvi* (theologian), who attend to the mosque and to the religious activities of the community. They still officiate over the more traditional ceremonies, such as circumcision and the funeral rites which precede burial. Marriage is not a sacrament but a civil contract governed by a specific Muslim code, which permits polygamy. Muslim women, despite legal changes, are still today restricted by the rigid rules of female segregation (*purdah*). The religious festivals of the Muslim calendar are celebrated with great solemnity and devotion throughout India. The death of Hussein, the son of Ali and Fatima who was killed in the battle of Kerbala in AD 680, is celebrated in the month of Moharran or the month of grief. It was originally a Shiite festival but today it is celebrated by all believers. Having lived together for centuries, the Hindu and Muslim communities have spent years in relative peace and tranquillity, punctuated by moments of great tension and conflict. Relations today are fairly peaceful apart from intermittent, scattered clashes. The Muslims who remained in India after the creation of Pakistan have often had to face the increasing 'Hindu nationalism' of certain extremist groups. Some Muslim customs, such as the butchering of cows, are not willingly accepted by the Hindu communities and in the cities they often become the spark for serious incidents, although they are in fact merely pretexts which conceal economic and political conflicts. The Islamicization of the lower Hindu castes, a process which began in the Mogul period, continues today, with the collective conversion of whole groups of *harijans* (untouchables) such as recently occurred in Tamil Nadu. These changes of faith deeply concern the Hindu leaders and the implicit change in electoral loyalty of the newly converted groups also concerns the politicians.

Certain aspects of the religious tradition have displayed a rapprochement, which has led to an intense and reciprocal exchange. In the sixteenth century the interest which the Emperor Akbar, the most enlightened of the Moguls, displayed in the Brahmanical religion and his tolerance towards its followers was a source of great hope to the Hindus. The Emperor did not favour orthodox Islam and wished to found a new faith which would include the doctrines shared by the various religions, including Hinduism. The *tawhid ilahi* or *din ilahi* (divine unity or divine faith), as the new creed was called, attracted few followers and did not survive the sovereign's death. The Muslim *sufi* tradition, which was very similar to the Hindu bhakti cults, had a marked influence on Brahmanical religious thought. Sufism, an esoteric movement which arose within the largest movement in Islam and which was composed of ascetic monks who lived in confraternities, was inspired by a mystical and tolerant form of religion, unlike the rigid formalism and the supremacy of the law of Islam. Through Sufism, whose principles also influenced several Mogul emperors, Indian Muslims partly absorbed the religious permissiveness of the Hindu religion. The veneration of Muslim saints and the establishment of a pilgrimage tradition to Sufi tombs are clearly Hindu in origin. In northern India the cult of the *piroshaikh* (saints venerated by Hindus and Muslims alike) is still popular.

Large crowds of Muslim pilgrims (both Sunni and Shiite) continue to gather at Ajmer, the site of the tomb of a venerated saint, Khwaja Moinuddin Chisthi, the twelfth-century founder of a Sufi community. They sing religious hyms and hold meetings of poets, including Hindu ones, at which poems specially composed in honour of the saint are recited.

In the Mylapore quarter of Madras, inside the Kapalishwara temple dedicated to the cult of Shiva and his wife Parvati, an unusual and touching event has taken place for the last 200 years on the tenth day of the Muslim month of Moharran. A crowd of Muslims from all parts of the city approach the ritual basin of the temple and, offering prayers in homage to Hindu deities, immerse the *panja* (symbols wich traditionally represent the family of the prophet) in the water.

Religious Renewal in Modern Hinduism

Although Islam was never able fully to establish itself in the religious life of India, it did force Hindu culture to examine itself and to react. Profound changes were discussed at length in the period between the establishment of the Mogul Emperors in the sixteenth century and the rise of a new foreign power on Indian soil in the eighteenth century. Some religious reforms amongst the Hindus in the last century were largely caused by the influence of Christianity and by Western philosphical and social ideas. Exposed to the influence first of Islam and then of Christianity, the architects of the reforms were great religious thinkers and figures from a variety of Hindu traditions, almost all from the north, even though their movements were widespread and continue to cause reverberations down to the present day. Indian spirituality began a process of renewal in the middle of the Muslim period, with the speculative commentators (Vallabha, Chaitanya) and the highly popular mystics (Ramananda, Tulsida, Tukaran, Mirabai, Kabir). Kabir (1440-1518), a disciple of Ramananda, the celebrated Hindu master, was the proponent of a new religious concept which indicated a mystic personal path in conjunction with a universal god. He preached against the idolatry of the Hindus and the excessive ritualism of the brahmin priests, as well as Muslim dogmatism. He predicted the birth of a great community of believers, united and not constantly torn by antagonisms between religious groups.

Under the influence of Kabir, Nanak Dev (1469-1538), later called Guru Nanak, founded the Sikh community (from the Sanskrit *shishya* and the Pali *sikka*, disciple). The movement was based from the beginning on the canons of non-violence and the mystic conceptions of the Vaishnavite bhakti, which entailed absolute devotion to a single god. Guru Nanak, like his master Kabir, was also inspired by the Muslim mystical movement of the Sufi. The figure of the *guru* (master) is of fundamental importance in the Sikh religion and nine gurus

The Jesuit Roberto de Nobili, shown here in the garb of a sannyasi *or holy man, lived in India as a missionary in the first half of the seventeenth century. He was one of the Europeans most open to the value of Indian culture.*

followed Nanak in the leadership of the brotherhood. After their death these were venerated as chosen spirits, the intermediaries between man and god. Because of the persecutions the sect suffered under the Mogul Emperors, the tenth and last guru, Gobind Singh, turned it into an out-and-out army, known as the *Khalsa*, 'the purity', with distinctive customs and characteristics, including the use of the name *Singh*, 'lion'. The tradition of sanctified gurus ended with Gobind Singh but the Sikhs continued to venerate the sacred book, the *Granth Sahib*, a collection of mystical hymns and prayers from various sources. The Sikh religion rejected Hindu ritualism and idolatry, and the division of society into castes, although there are clan divisions very like castes. There are now some twelve million Sikhs, the great majority of whom live in the Punjab, which in modern India is now a rich and prosperous state. The Sikh community is regarded as one of the most active and hard-working in the country, being dedicated to farming, trade, and various technical professions. Its martial tradition has resulted in a massive Sikh presence in the Indian army. Religious choices, but above all the troubled history of the community, have made the Sikhs a warlike and militant sect who to a great extent seem to feel themselves part of a 'nation' distinct from the rest of the country. In recent years this trend has been accentuated to the point where the extremists in the brotherhood (particularly the Nihang, called the armed fist of the Khalsa) are calling for political independence for the Punjab, in order to form an independent nation governed exclusively by Sikhs (Khalistan).

Although important in the religious history of India, Christianity has made little headway. Unlike the situation in other countries colonized by European nations, there are relatively few Christians in India and at present the churches only account for 2.5 percent of the population (eight million Catholics, six million in various Protestant churches, and two Syrian Orthodox groups, almost entirely confined to Kerala).

Christianity in India has a complex history and a variety of traditions. The eastern church is certainly the oldest, dating back to the traditional arrival of the church in India with the arrival of the Apostle Thomas in India in AD 52. A more extensive process of Christianization began in the sixteenth century with the arrival on the coast of Malabar of missionaries in the wake of the Portuguese conquerors. The missionaries were mostly Franciscans and Dominicans and they founded a number of local churches and missions in southern India. Subsequently, the local churches experienced a series of schisms, due to the policy of the church of Rome and because of conflicts over the choice of liturgy. Today, two distinct churches exist, although both are within Christian Catholicism; the Mathoma Church and the Malankara Syrian Orthodox Church.

It has now been historically established — and accepted — that the 'evangelization' mission proceeded hand in hand with colonial expansion, often reflecting the interests of the colonizers. As with Islam, the bulk of the converts to Christianity belonged to the low and untouchable castes. In other instances the Cross was imposed by force and at one point, in Goa, even the Inquisition was in force. The decline of the Catholic church in India paralleled that of Portuguese power, although the Catholics continued with their proselytism, modifying their missionary policy with time. Today, their activity in the field of education, which is offered to both Christians and the members of other religions, is regarded as important. A local clergy has taken over the hierarchy and the liturgy has undergone a process of 'Indianization', taking on a character that is closer to Indian customs and traditions.

The last to reach India were the Protestant churches. Their arrival coincided with the decline of the Catholic churches and the rise to economic and territorial dominance of the British East India Company. The first mission began in India and then subsequently the various denominations became active throughout the

A Shivaite holy man who is practising extreme ascetism offers a floral tribute to the lingam, *the phallic symbol of the god Shiva (from an illustration in the seventeenth-century* History of the Moguls *by Nicolo Manucci).*

subcontinent. The exact form of their involvement depended upon their various doctrinal approaches and organizational capacities. Many missions, almost all of them British, acted separately before coming together in the National Christian Council, although they retained their own denomination and independence. Like the Catholic missions, the Protestant ones intensified their efforts in schools and social assistance, with the result that today thousands of schools, aid institutions, hospices, and orphanages are run by them. The presence of Christianity in India over such a long period and the intense social activity of the churches considerably disturbed the religious thought of certain Hindu groups and from the beginning of the last century onwards there were attempts to reform the Hindu religious institutions and certain customs. It was the ethical and social character of Christianity which struck the elite of Indian intellectuals and thinkers more than its theological and doctrinal concepts, above all in conbination with the empirical and pragmatic spirit of Anglo-Saxon culture.

One of the best-known movements of renewals was the Brahmo Samaj, a theistic religious group which opposed the use of images and preached a collective cult and the importance of various reforms in Indian society. It was founded in the last century in Calcutta by a Bengalese brahmin, Rammohan Roy, He was profoundly struck by the practical and ethical character of Christianity and he believed that in the future it could become the basis for a universal religion. The decline of the Brahmo Samaj was largely due to its excessively critical attitude towards the fundamental values of Hinduism and by the fact that it favoured a religion from outside India and associated with the culture of foreign rulers.

Another movement, the Arya Samaj, was completely different in character. Its founder, Swami Dayanand Saraswati, set himself the aim of regenerating Hindu society through the rediscovery of the Vedic tradition, and restoring the sacrifical beliefs and rites of the original Vedism; in short a return to the origins of the religion, shedding the spurious elements and the accretions of the centuries. Opposed to idolatry and the scriptures dating from after the first *Vedas*, Arya Samaj became a kind of pure, militant Hinduism and is still widespread today. Together with similar movements it constitutes the basis for a return to a Hindu theocracy, an 'integralism' born of nationalism and in a sense opposed to the tolerant and open spirit of the Hindu tradition.

There were countless new trends and reformist movements in the period prior to independence and they resulted in marked changes in the religious and social behaviour of the Indians, or at least of some of them. In other parts of the country the ancient religious traditions of historical Hinduism have remained intact up to the present day. Whilst modern reforms and initiatives are in full flood, archaic cults and ancient magico-religious beliefs and practices continue to survive unaltered in certain areas. Yet again the Hindu religious world displays its capacity for adaptation, its innate tolerance and capacity for co-existence despite the diversity of spiritual trends.

During the years of struggle against colonial domination, Hindu religion again appeared against an environment that was usually foreign to its tradition. It was Mahatma Gandhi, the father of modern India, who was to develop — through a greater awareness of Hindu religious values, examined in comparison with the message of Christianity and other religions — a way of life inspired by a new religious vision, in which involvement in the world and a deep religious consciousness were not different faces of a single reality. The inspired reader of the *Bhagavad Gita* would be the 'saint' and 'politician', a fusion of a single synthesis and religious practice. There is a quotation from the Mahatma which, more than any other message, clarifies this concept: 'It is stated that religion and politics belong to two different spheres of life. But I would like to say, without a moment's hesitation and in full simplicity, that those who say it do not know hat religion is'. It was in the light of this remark by Mahatma Gandhi that two of his best disciples, Vinobha Bhave and Jayaprakash Narayan, inspired by the ideals and the methods of the Master, founded the Sarvodaya Samaj movement in modern times. It is a fundamentally religious movement, but also politically active in every aspect of human existence.

Pilgrimages, Holy Cities, and Sanctuaries

No other people in the world display so marked a taste for pilgrimages as the Indians do. It is an unusual religious phenomenon which manifests itself in unbroken movements of great masses of pilgrims during religious festivals towards the holy cities or gathering places for the great religious assemblies. These sites, which are scattered throughout the subcontinent, parallel the distribution of religious occurrences which punctuate the history of India.

It is not just the Hindus; Muslims too ply the traditional routes across the length and breadth of the subcontinent, making pilgrimages to a Sufi saint or a sanctuary where one of the regular Muslim festivals is celebrated. Ajmer is sacred to the Shiite Muslims, just as Dwarka is to the Krishnaite Hindus. The Jain, a small group of austere and disciplined monks, anoint the stone colossus of Bahubali, an image of one of their saints, every twelve or fourteen years. The last Jain gathering, Maha Mastakabhisheka, was held at Sravana Belgola, in the region of Karnataka, in 1982. About a million believers, or about half the membership of the sect, attended. Every sect or brotherhood of the various religions in India has its holy centres and its times for pilgrimage, but the real originator of the tradition of pilgrimages and great religious gatherings was the Hindu people, and they are still its mainstay. It is not in the domestic cults or in the liturgies in the millions of rural temples or cult sites of the various caste congregations that the majestic spectable of the Indian religious spirit is displayed, but in these ecumenical manifestations of Hinduism. It is the religious duty of an observant Hindu to celebrate dozens of rites and events in the course of his life, but he acquires merit by undertaking a devotional journey (*yatra*) to one of the holy centres of Hinduism or to participate in the great, mass religious assemblies (Kumbh Mela, Magh Mela, Mahamakha, Eclipses) at least once in his life. Often it is in fulfilment of a vow, sometimes the observance of a rule of his caste (*dharma-varna*); the motives for a pilgrimage may be more mundane; to ensure the birth of sons, to gain wealth, or to obtain a better harvest. In general it is regarded as a religious deed, encouraged by all the doctrinal schools, and one which allows the pilgrim to attain an absolute state of purification, obtaining remission for all his sins. In terms of salvation, such devotional acts constitute an effective support on the spiritual path to the realization of *dharma*, 'the cosmic law', and will ease the ascent of the individual soul towards the ultimate goal of the Hindu faith: liberation from the perpetual cycle of rebirth. A pilgrimage, for example, to the holy city of Varanasi undertaken at a particular moment in one's existence can, in a similar fashion to the plenary indulgences granted in Holy Years to Christians who had travelled to Rome, secure the believer on the road to salvation.

The cult of the *tirtha* (Sanskrit meaning the 'place of the sacred glance'), sites which the magico-religious world of the Indians regards as sanctified by miraculous events or by the belief in the presence or revelation of a divinity, has grown up since antiquity in post-Vedic India. Many tirtha are recorded in the holy scriptures, in the epic poems or in the ancient mythological compilations, such as the *Mahabharata*, the *Ramayana*, and the *Purana*. These are veritable handbooks for pilgrimages to sites dedicated to specific divinities (Shiva, Vishnu, Devi-

Shakti). The Puranic tradition even advances a hierarchy of the tirtha. In other instances, these places are believed to have been the residence of sages or seers (*rishi*), sanctified by the veneration of the people. The Buddha helped establish a tradition of visiting tirtha. Before he died he instructed his disciples to make pilgrimages to the sites sanctified by his presence.

Such sanctified sites led to the building of temples and even cities. Whole mountains became sacred, just as the banks of rivers are packed with an interminable series of tirtha. According to the *Mataya Purana*, one of the most ancient mythological accounts, there were over six hundred million tirtha along the river Narmanda from its source to its mouth. For the Indian religious spirit, so focused on the sacred sphere (a pervasive holiness which proliferates without ceasing), the tirtha have a magical, almost sacramental efficacy. Viewed in this way, India is a dense map of 'luminous' centres, 'charged with energy', from which grace is obtained, grace being 'power' or 'cosmic energy' (*shakti*) for Hindus. Millions of faithful pilgrims unceasingly move from one tirtha to another, driven on by a profound religious thirst and by the desire for purification and salvation.

These manifestations have what might be termed a 'pan-Indian' character, being found in all parts of India and common to all the peoples who inhabit this region of southern Asia. The proliferation of sites has covered the land with a communications network between the major regions, which has given India a trans-cultural and trans-religious unity since antiquity. Many of the modern roads and motorways which traverse India follow ancient pilgrimage routes, passing from one holy city to another or from an ancient sanctuary to the site of a fervent cult. These roads serve the same purpose today, although almost all modern pilgrims prefer the cars, buses, and trains of the twentieth century, rather than walking, as they would have done in the past. The railway network — built up under the British and one of the most extensive in the world — is perhaps the means of transport most used by the mass of devotees. During the great festivals, hundreds upon hundreds of trains are used to carry literally millions of pilgrims. Varanasi, also known as Benares and Kashi, has always been the holiest of sites for the Hindus. Dedicated to Shiva, the city is open to all the creeds and traditions of Hinduism. Above all, it is here that the conditions exist for the attainment of supreme liberation, because those who die at Varanasi — as is confirmed by all the religious literature — do so in the certainty of liberation from the infinite cycle of rebirth. The belief is widespread that Shiva himself, Mahadeva, the tutelary divinity of the city and the cremation sites, whispers the sacred formula, the *mantra* of final departure, in the ear of the dying. Hundreds of pilgrims flock to Varanasi by road and rail from all parts of India; indeed many even walk there, covering great distances in doing so. Frequently, pilgrims come to see the sacred centre of Hinduism at least once during their life; others, thinking themselves to be close to death, make a final effort to realize the dream of their existence — to spend their last moments on the bank of the river and to receive a draught of its water.

The city is built on the left bank of the Ganges, between two of its tributaries, the Varuna and the Asi; hence the name Varanasi. It has steps down to the river (*ghat*) stretching for almost two miles and these are crowded from dawn do dusk by the devout, by pilgrims, *yogi* and *panda*, ascetics and officiating priests, intent on rituals, purificatory ablutions, and cremations on funeral pyres. In the past the city was a famous centre of culture and schools of the Indian sciences. Great masters and saints (Ramananda, Chaitanya, Kabir, Tulsida), religious men who fully shared the sanctity of the site and in their turn conferred greater holiness on the city. Varanasi owes its sanctity mainly to the Ganges, the Mother Ganga, thought of by Indians as the river of life, which descends from heaven and whose

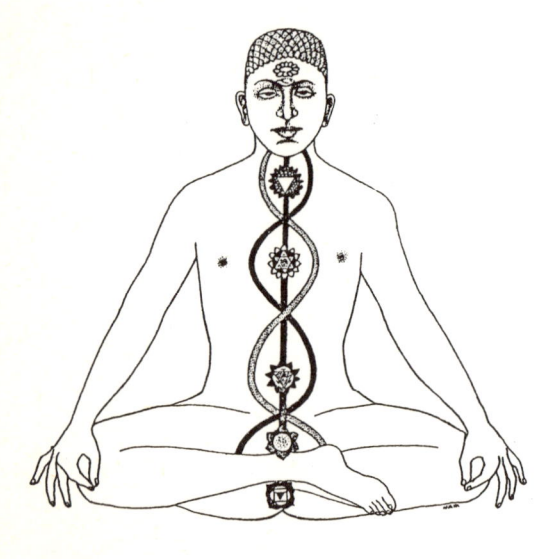

Muladhara chakra, from the kundalini *of* Tantric yoga *(from* Incredible India *by P. Thomas, 1966.*

waters dissolve sins and wash away impurities.
The most influential and, in religious terms, worthwhile pilgrimage for Hindus is that along the Ganges, climbing to its source on the slopes of the Himalaya. However, it is the *pradakshina* (ritual circumambulation) of the river — from source to mouth and back on foot — which profoundly marks the religious life of a devout Hindu. It may last between four and six years and involve difficulty and discomfort; nevertheless thousands of the faithful undertake it in order to acquire the highest merit in terms of salvation. The pradakshina is undertaken along other Indian rivers and, occasionally, one can find holy men and pilgrims on the river Narmada performing the supreme religious rite, which recalls the journeys to the Holy Land undertaken by pilgrims in medieval Europe.

All the sacred sites of India are distinguished by the presence of water, and rivers, which according to mythology are personified by female divinities, are the favoured seats of the sacred. The sources and more extensive estuaries of rivers are regarded as meritorious places of pilgrimage. Water, as the means of purification, symbolizes rebirth. Every water course and every brook is sacred and wherever one looks it is quite normal to see ritual pools and tanks within temple precincts, both in the country and in cities, and extensive steps along the banks of rivers for purificatory ablutions. However, despite the sacredness of rivers, not all stretches along their length are equally holy. As is typical of Indian culture, a hierarchic scale exists in this sphere too. At its peak, without any question, is the stretch of the Ganges in front of Varanasi. Immediately beneath is Hardawar, at the point where the great river, after its precipitous and bounding descent from the peaks of the Himalayas, debouches on to the historic Ganges plain. However, for many Hindus it is Prayag, the city of Allahabad, which is the *tirtharaja*, the 'king of tirtha', the most important of holy places. It becomes so each year on the occasion of the Magh Mela, a religious gathering which takes place in January. It becomes even more so every twelve years at the precise moment of a particular planetary conjunction when the largest religious festival in the world, the Ardh Kumbh Mela, takes place, with an immense crowd of up to seven or eight million pilgrims from every part of India in attendance. At Prayag everyone, in successive waves, bathes in the holy Sangam, the confluence of the rivers Ganga, Tamuna, and the legendary Saraswati (the third river which according to popular belief flows underground into the others during the Kumbh Mela). The astral conjunction which sanctifies the waters of the three confluent rivers as they merge into a single fluvial divinity, the *Trivani* or Triple Plait, occurs at the moment when the Sun enters Ares and Jupiter enters Aquarius.

The genesis of the Kumbh Mela of Prayag, like all Indian religious festivals, is lost in the distant past. There are, however, some historical sources which record a Kumbh Mela in the eighth century BC and the city of Prayag is mentioned in the *Mahabharata*. The Chinese pilgrim Hsuan Tsang, during the reign of Harsha in AD 643, tells of a Kumbh Mela which lasted seventy-five days and involved two-and-a-half million of the faithful. Hindu testimonies in the thirteenth and fourteenth centuries and Muslim ones in the sixteenth, accounts full of wonder given by European travellers some two or three centuries later, and even contemporary descriptions, make it quite clear how little things have changed over the centuries at these gatherings. In mythology, the Kumbh Mela — which in addition to Prayag, is also held at other sites, such as Hardwar, Ujjain, and Nasik, at three-yearly intervals to complete the twelve-year cycle — dates back to an account in the *Purana* which tells of a conflict between three gods and three demons for the possession of the *amrit*, the drink of immortality, contained in a vase, the *kumbh*. In the course of the titanic struggle some drops of the nectar fell on the sites of what were to become the four holy cities where the mythical event is commemorated. Beside the memory of the myth, there are many other

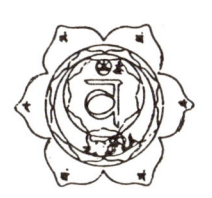

The seven chakra of the human body according to Tantric philosophy (from The Tantric Way *by A. Mookerjee and M. Khanna, 1977).*

motives for events of such size. Initially an annual occurrence, the Magh Mela's original purpose was to obtain the favour of a good harvest from the gods. Typical of a peasant society, the mass gatherings were gigantic fertility rites, held at a moment that coincided with a seasonal event of fundamental importance to the farming economy: the *Uttarayan* or passage of the sun into the northern hemisphere.

For the faithful there is the divine promise, enhanced by myth, of pardon for all faults and the attainment of *moksha*, a special grace which releases the individual from the sentence of over eight million rebirths (as a certain form of popular Hinduism reckons the cycles of *samsara*). The sacramental virtue of the waters at that moment is such that for believers instant death would be highly desirable in their quest for salvation. In fact, in the past, there was a long-standing tradition of ritual suicide, particularly at Prayag, by fanatical believers, who hurled themselves into the waters beneath a large banyan tree on the bank of the river. The profound value of the Kumbh Mela is particularly apparent in the sense of 'mystical' cohesion and 'social' unity expressed on these occasions of Indian religious culture. According to Shankaracharya (eighth century AD), the greatest thinker and reformer of Brahmanism and the first to organize the Mela on a systematic basis, the periodic gigantic embrace in the tirtha between the members of the monastic orders, sannyasi and guru, with the Hindu people, became a symbol of the unity of Hinduism and a means of transmitting the spiritual and ascetic values to the great mass of the faithful. Shankara firmly exhorted his monks to take part in the Kumbh Mela and to lead the people. In fact, the presence of monks and hermits, who even descend from the Himalayas or travel from the temple cities of the south, reflects a precise spiritual duty: that of imparting by example in particular a mystical and solemn lesson in religion to the ordinary men of the earth. In such circumstances, caste and racial divisions, the diversity of cults and traditions, count for nothing.

Today the Kumbh Mela is highly organized. The Indian government and army are mobilized to co-ordinate the immense influx of people converging on a relatively small spot. In the Kumbh Mela at Prayag in 1954 a dispute arose between pilgrims and sadhu over the right to bathe in the river first at the most astrologically propitious moment. The resulting fracas led to the death of over a thousand people. From that time onwards a gigantic temporary city has been erected for each Mela. As well as housing millions of pilgrims and providing *cordons sanitaires* to prevent the spread of epidemics, it is built in such a way as to curb and direct the swirling river of pilgrims.

The climax of the Kumbh Mela is a procession of the sadh led by the Nagi Sadh, a strange sect of naked hermits covered in ashes and bearing the conspicuous markings of their sect on their foreheads. Many of the faithful, particularly the women, throw themselves to the ground at spots touched by the feet of these ascetics. They are followed by the venerable sannyasi of the monastic orders, divided by congregation and by sect, and all wearing ochre garments. Finally, they are followed by the hordes of pilgrims and devotees. It is an immense concentration of humanity, a sea of heads and bodies which sways backwards and forwards as it slowly but inexorably moves towards the river; a mass from which rises the clamour of bells, cymbals, drums, the deep murmur of the chanting of the mantra, the singing of hymns, and the shouting of invocations. '... armies of pilgrims and ascetics, the uproar of the crowd rumbles like a clap of thunder. This alone is enough to make the Ganga the most important of the tirtha, the holy places, in which the age-old holiness has almost solidified into a mysterious and imperishable relationship' (Tucci).

The protagonists of the great sacred gatherings of Hinduism are the *sadhy, sannyasi, yogi, muni, tapaswi, awami, sant, baba, shramana, dandi*, anchorites,

The crowd at a religious gathering at the holy bathing place in the southern temple city of Kumbakonam in Tamil Nadu.

ascetics, hermits, itinerant monks, mendicant devotees — ancient figures still present in the centres of pilgrimage, the temples, the sanctuaries, and sometimes amongst the crowds of the great cities. India abounds in individuals leading a solitary life who have renounced worldly goods. A rough calculation suggests that there are some 80,000 religious institutions (*matha, ashram, akhara, sthana*), temple congregations, orders of monks, caste sects belonging to the two main traditions of Hinduism (Vaishnavite and Shaivite). The total number of holy men is even larger — some 8,000,000. Some of these live permanently in the monasteries scattered throughout India, whilst others live their mystic experience in the most total isolation. The latter have often taken vows of total chastity (*brahmacharya*) and their hermitages consist of caverns dug into the rock, or in the midst of forests, far from towns. The variety of the ways of life and the activities of the sannyasi is vast. They may run schools or hospitals for the poor, work on collective farms, or confine themselves to teaching Vedic mantras or yogic asana. Historically, the monastic period began with the Jain and the Buddhists and then continued with the Brahmanical orders founded by Shankara, Ramanuja, and Madhva. Many monks move from one sacred site to another, from a temple to a monastery, usually staying only a few days at each place, living by begging and often finding hospitality in the shelters for the pilgrims of the temples and of the convents and performing their daily ablutions in the open in water course or rivers. The more demanding orders include, in the Shaivite tradition, the Naga-Sadhy, whose life is governed by rules calling for extreme asceticism. They are generally thought of as wild and somewhat violent in their behaviour; indeed in the past Indian rulers used them as warriors in their struggles against invading armies. They live in remote monasteries called *akhara*, which were once gymnasia and schools of the martial arts. During the religious festivals many sadhu are found along the purificatory steps of holy cities, their bodies and hair covered in ash, where they perform extreme, ascetic exercises, burying themselves in the ground or lying on beds of nails for long periods of time. It is not uncommon to meet a sadhu wearing sandles bristling with nails or another who has taken a vow not to lie down for years, always remaining standing. Today

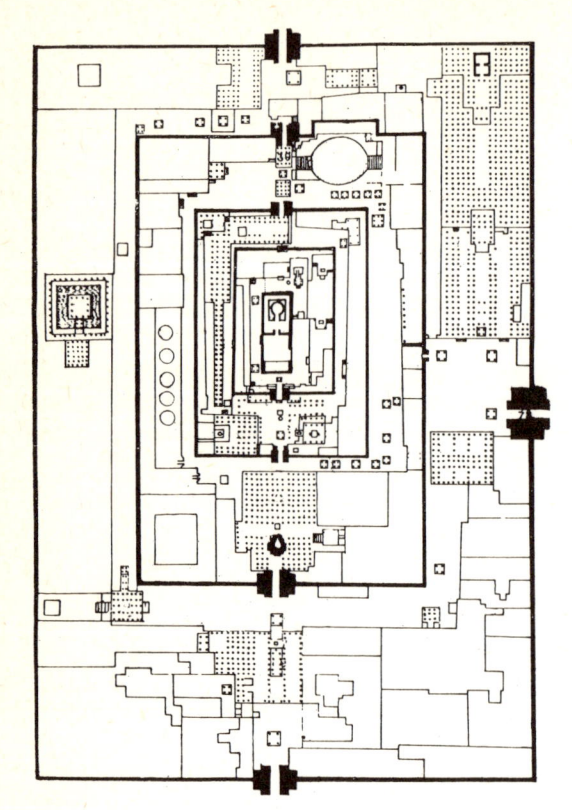

Ground plan of the inner courtyards of the great temple at Srirangam in southern India.

there is a gradual decline in the institutions of the sadhu, whilst the number of false sadhu has increased; nevertheless asceticism still enjoys considerable respect and veneration in Hindu society. It is traditionally believed — as many of the ancient myths say — that the ascetic, by virtue of his extreme penitence, may be able to acquire a spiritual power equal to or even greater than that of the great gods. According to the most deep-rooted Hindu concept, the asceticism of man is a virtue which can confer 'power' against the gods and even foreshadows their overthrow. The yogi practising extreme asceticism (*tapas*) is like Shiva Mahayogi, the divine model of the ascetics, Shiva himself, autonomous and free from the energies, both positive and negative, which the gods usually unleash on man. Although Varanasi and Prayag are the focal centres of pilgrimage, there are countless other sanctuaries scattered throughout India. Some are out-and-out 'cathedral cities', in which the life of the city is almost entirely dedicated to the devotional activity of the temple. There are temples and cities dedicated to Krishna, such as the city of Dwarka, where the god, in legend, reigns as sovereign; or Mathura, the birthplace of Krishna.

On the coast of the Bay of Bengal, 310 miles south of Calcutta, is the celebrated pilgrimage centre of Puri, with its imposing temple of Sri Jagannath, the 'Lord of the Universe', dedicated to Vishnu-Krishna, a particular incarnation. The construction of the present temple, a complex which comprises over thirty buildings, was begun in the thirteenth century, but the cult of the divinity, a combination of Brahmanical and tribal cultures, is more than 2000 years old. The temple of Jagannath, just like a great medieval cathedral, dominates the whole city and all the roads converge on it. More than 6000 people are employed in the service of the temple, including both priests and servants, who are divided into a hierarchy of classes. The cult entails complex daily ceremonies in homage to the idols placed at the centre of the temple, and periodic religious festivals involving pilgrims from all parts of India. The most solemn moment at Puri coincides with the festival of Rath Yatra, celebrated at the beginning of summer. Carts in the form of the temple of Sri Jagannath and those of the two associated divinities are led in solemn procession before hundreds of thousands of people. A crowd draws the carts along a lengthy route through the city from the great temple to a smaller one. It is commonly believed that those who touch the carts gain grace in their quest for salvation. At the end of the festival the enormous wagons, which are built anew each year, are broken into pieces to be distributed to the faithful as relics. Like the other great religious centres of India, Puri, though a small city, has a large number of sanctuaries and temples. The most important of these is one of the four Indian monastic centres founded by the philosopher saint Shankara. It is led by the venerated Jagadguru, 'Teacher of the World', one of the most influential religious figures in India.

Further south, almost level with Madras, is perhaps the largest and most prestigious religious centre of modern India, Tirupati, which even rivals the older city of Varanasi. It is the earthly residence of Balaji, as the divinity of Tirupati, whom the believers regard as the most glorious and auspicious *avatar* (incarnation) of the god Vishnu. Tirupati deserves a more careful examination, because it is an example of the success of pilgrimages in the age of mass communications and consumerism, to which the institutional religion has adapted.

It is thought that the great Dravidian temple was founded in the first century AD and that its growth has been the work of generations of pilgrims, rich and poor, and above all the powerful dynasties of the south who ruled the region one after the other, from the Pallava and Chola to the Vijayanagar sovereigns. The form of adoration and the temple rituals which are still in practice today were introduced by the brahmin saint Ramanuja in the thirteenth century. Legend has it that Ramanuja climbed to the temple of Tirupati, which stands on the summit of a hill, on his knees, because he felt it sacrilegious to approach it on foot. Today, it would be improper to do so by car or bus and so the devout, even if old or ill, slowly walk up to it or, if they are more fortunate, are carried up in a palanquin. Every day, amidst songs, hymns and invocations to Krishna, a long procession of pilgrims snakes along the road which climbs to the sanctuary.

Tirupati is a complex of temples, sanctuaries, civil buildings, entrance towers, porticoes — indeed almost a complete city. The great chapel, with the precious statue of Sri Venkatheshwara (Balaji) is always open for the *darshan*, the vision of the divinity. Thousands of the devout form queues which stretch for miles as they wait six or seven hours to catch a momentary glimpse of the idol. This is the essential rite, the act of devotion which justifies the entire pilgrimage for everybody. In the various sanctuaries of the temple, which are dedicated to other Hindu divinities, the *archaka* (priests) or the *potu mirasidar* (hereditary priestly caste) officiate over ceremonies or rituals in order to procure special grace and indulgences. It is very expensive to attend these functions, which are beyond the reach of the great mass of devotees, but a contribution is asked even for the simple darshan. Those who have nothing must wait for at least fifteen or twenty hours in a queue before reaching the presence of the divinity.

Like some oriental Lourdes, Tirupati is the richest temple in India. It is estimated that some seven or eight million people attend each year and in addition to the ordinary admission dues and the special ones for rituals, there is an immense mass of voluntary offerings, which today are mainly in money. The religious centre is extremely popular with the infinite array of Hindu *bhakta* sects and it reflects the changes in and recharging of modern Hinduism and of the mass cult, as it has come into being in India over the last thirty years. Recently there have been numerous diatribes in the press about the commercialization of religious centres and popular opinion in the great cities views the temple of Tirupati as 'the greatest religious supermarket in the world'. In addition, there are court cases against those responsible for the temples for administrative malpractice and against the *panda*, priests officiating at ceremonies, for general corruption.

Another aspect that is worth mentioning is the fact that some of the most ardent devotees of Sri Venkateshwara are regional and also national political figures, as well as famous film actors. In recent decades, Tirupati has become an important electoral springboard and as a result the temple is visited, especially during elections, by political figures and candidates who want to gain the favour both of the divinity and of the mass of his devotees at Tirupati.

Although the north is regarded as the most important area for pilgrimages, the south does boast a large number of holy cities. These include the extraordinary Dravidian temple-cities, so called because they were founded and planned to incorporate all the religious structures as well as all the utilitarian requirements of a town. Almost all of them are situated in the great region of Tamil Nadu, which is called the 'land of temples'.

At Madurai, the ancient and famous centre of Tamil culture, there is one of the greatest temple complexes in India, whose most immediate and unforgettable image is that of its tall towers climbing heavenwards, covered with a mass of painted gods and figures from the sacred epics. The cult of the temple incorporates several traditions and above all it celebrates the meeting of the indigenous Dravidian culture and the Aryan culture moving down from the north. The marriage of the prehistoric goddess Minakshi, 'the fish-eyed goddess', to the Brahmanical god Shiva, in this incarnation known as Sundareshwara, the 'Lord of Beauty', commemorates a key moment in the religious unity of Hinduism and is celebrated each year at the end of April.

However, the most outstanding of the temple-cities is Srirangam, unique in India and possibly the world, which even today provides an extraordinary example of communal and urban life associated with religion. The outer perimeter measures over half a mile by 800 yards with seven concentric walls which determine the entire plan of the city. They form a series of walkways laid out to meet the demands of ritual, while in between them there are temples, sanctuaries, porticoes for the shelter of pilgrims, spaces, small squares, ritual pools, dwellings for the clergy, schools, shops, and a bazaar. At the gateways in the walls there are twenty-one entrance towers, prism-like in their form and with superimposed plans which are covered with figures from the *Purana* and the ancient epics, the *Ramayana* and the *Mahabharata*. This enormous complex takes its plan and its architecture from the *Mansara*, which lays down rigid rules for the building of temples dedicated to the great divinities and precise canons for the rituals.

The temple of Srirangam is dedicated to Vishnu, in his manifestation as Sri Ranganathaswami, the 'Lord of the Universe'. The god, immersed in the cosmic sleep, is represented reclining on the great serpent Adisesha, at the centre of the Primordial Ocean. Virtually all the great temple-cities of southern India are dedicated to the two great divinities of Shiva and Vishnu.

The temple-city occupies a special place in the history of Indian architecture and in the past constituted a largely independent power within the state, amassing great wealth in the form of lands and villages. It was a major power centre and a place used for commercial transactions, as well as serving as a market for the region. The Islamic and Maratha invasions, the European colonization, first by the French and then by the British, and finally the transformations of contemporary India have broken down its independence; however, the role of the temple-city as a holy place and object of pilgrimage has remained virtually intact. Much of the economy of present-day Srirangam is based on the periodic religious festivals, with the influx of masses of pilgrims from the surrounding regions. In this respect, the radius of the sanctuary's influence is vast, stretching for dozens of miles and, to a lesser extent, throughout India. During the religious festivals, one of the most important of which, the Vaikunta Ekadasi, lasts for between eleven and twenty-one days, processions pass along the walkways of the section reserved for the cult and statues of the divinity are carried ritually on shoulders or on processional carts from one part of the sanctuary to another.

Srirangam appears to be built on the concept of the devotional route and pilgrimage. The plan of the temple, based on the *mandala* (symbolic diagram), represents symbolically the world, a mountain, a pyramid, or an upturned ziggurat, whose centre is reached through intermediate terraces. According to the mystical rules of medieval Hinduism, the devotee proceeds from wall to wall towards the central sanctuary in the expectation of the contemplation of god (darshan), and in doing so gradually sheds, in a sort of purification, the illusory human manifestations, finally reaching the narrow and dark cell which houses the essence of divinity, 'centre and mystical peak of all architecture' (Naudou).

'In the architecture of Hinduism the processional path determines the planning of the Holy of Holies' (Volwahsen). There is a dynamic, an implicit process in the architecture of Srirangam; it is a movement towards a central point, a 'gravitational pole', which governs all the surrounding world. The path along the walls describes a spiral around the *garbha-griha* (cell of the divinity), similar to the *pradakshina* (circumambulation) of the pilgrim before undertaking the liturigical act of the darshan, which crowns the whole movement of the itinerant. The structure of the temple symbolizes and confirms — in solid stone — the concept of a religion founded on pilgrimage, in which the ultimate goal is preceded by a series of passages and thresholds which have to be overcome — like the never-ending movement which governs the life of man — in order to prepare for the final meeting with the divine.

31. Family photograph with the image of Saint Ramdev, the founder of the Santpath order, in the background. The temple of Ramdeora at Pokharam, in the middle of the Thar desert in Rajasthan, is dedicated to the saint. Women come to the temple to ask for the blessing of a son.
On the following pages:
32. Pilgrims and sadhu who have walked from Gangotri, a holy place on the upper Ganges, refresh themselves in the shelter for pilgrims situated on the banks of the river Bagirathi, a tributary of the Ganges in the region of Tehrigarhwal in Uttar Pradesh, some 13,125 ft up. There is a heavy flow of pilgrims and the devout along the course of the Ganges, travelling up to its source and visiting various holy places in order to purify themselves and acquire merit.

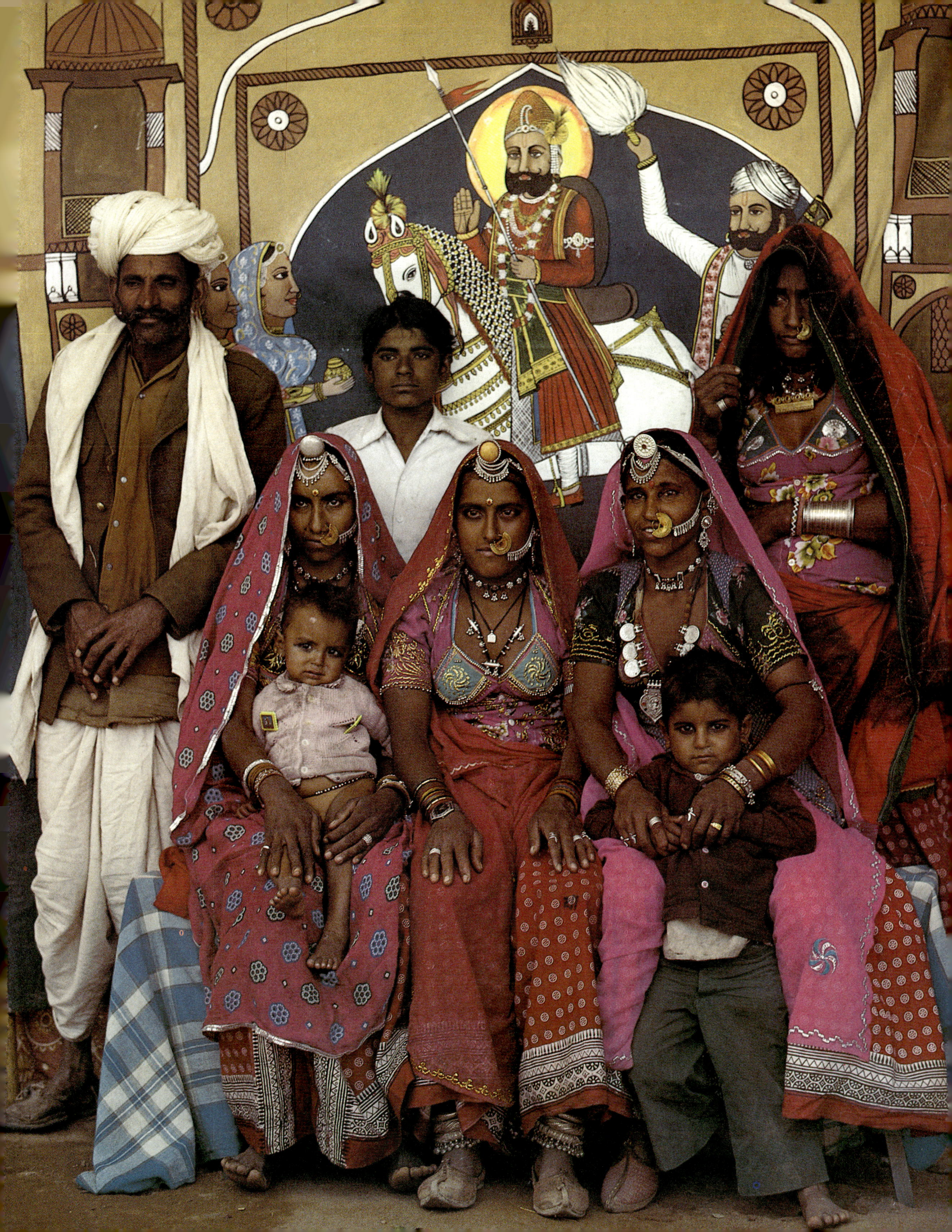

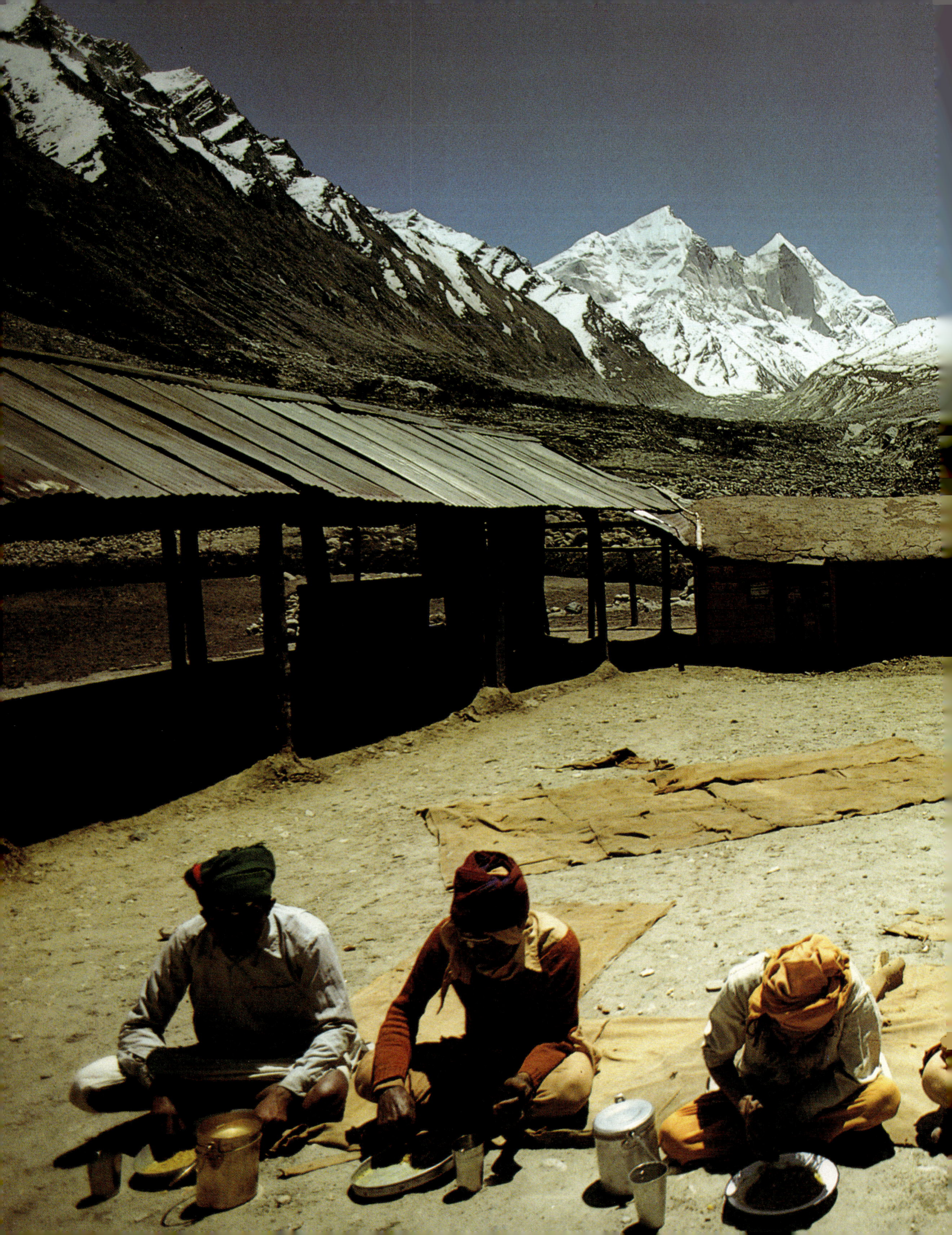

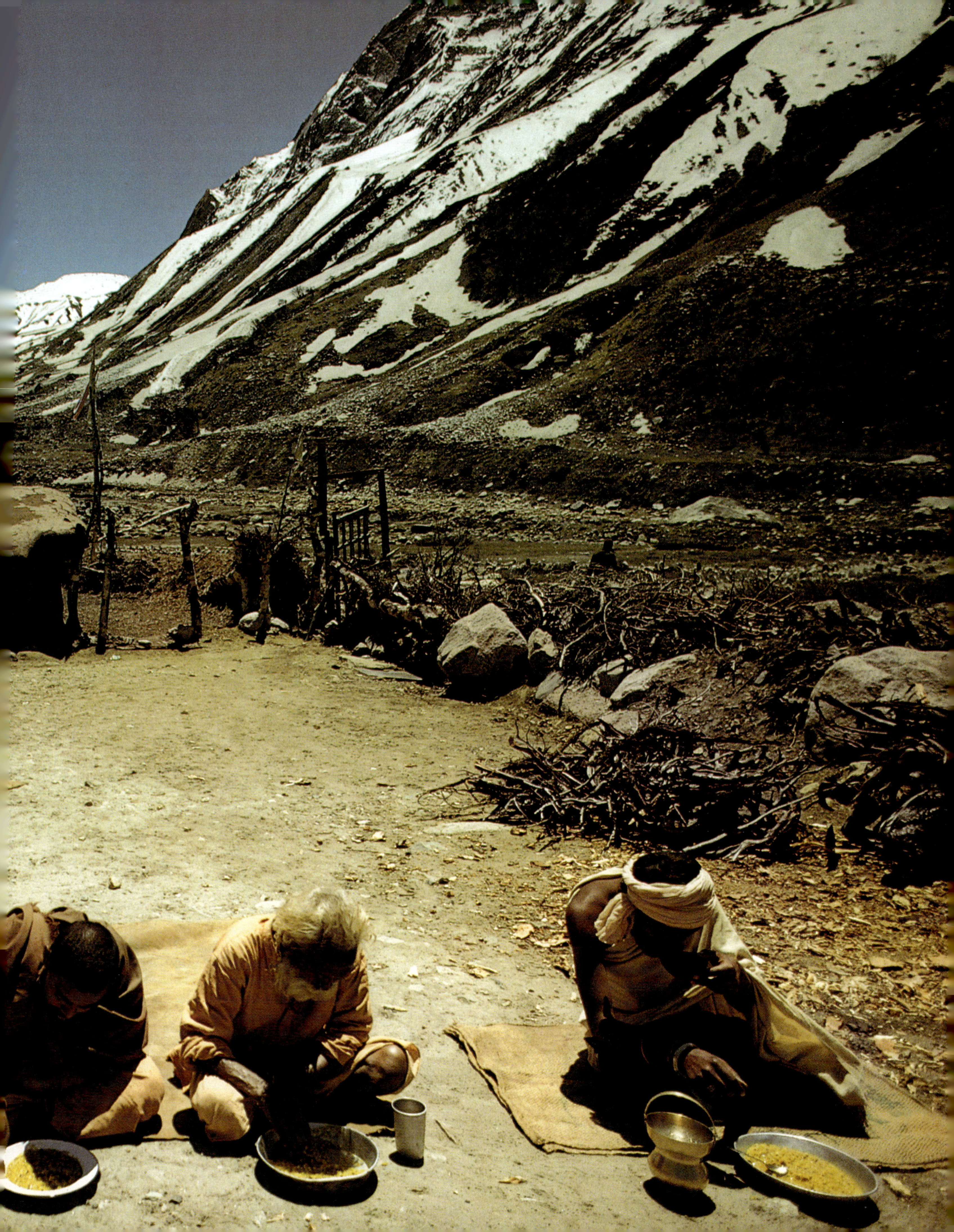

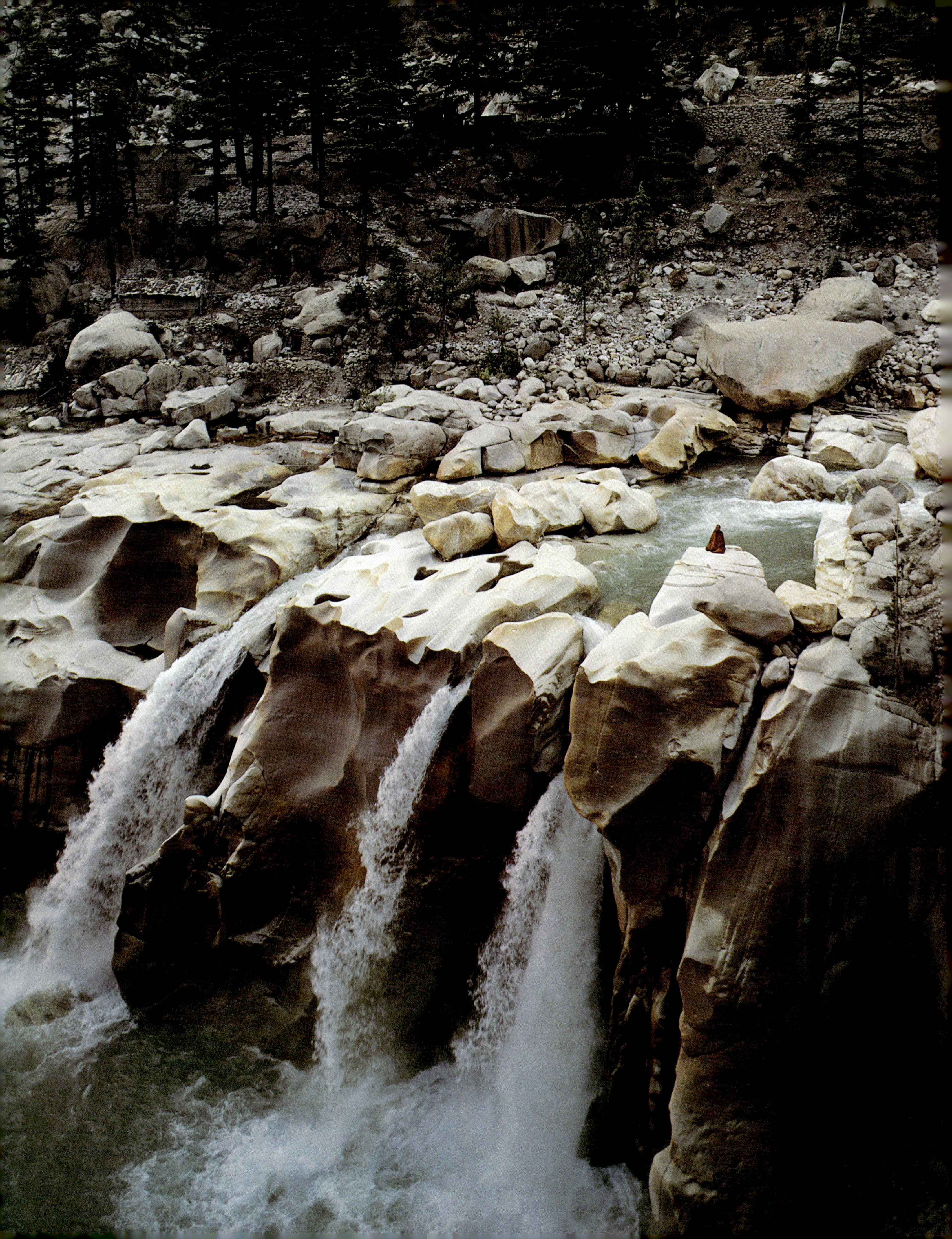

34

33. Waterfall on the river Bagirathi near Gangotri on the upper Ganges. It is an ancient place of hermitage and meditation frequented by pilgrims and sadhu. Ascending the course of the Ganges, the pilgrim passes through Rishikesh, the city of the sadhu, and reaches the confluence of the source streams of the Ganges at Devaprayag. There he performs the traditional rituals in the river and continues towards Bagirathi, then through Tehri, resting at Uttarakashi, the Benares or Kashi of the north, before proceeding to Gangotri and immersing himself in the freezing waters. The next objectives are the sanctuaries of Kedarnath and Badrinath, famous tirtha *(holy places) on the pilgrimage to the sacred sources of the Ganges.*
34. Young actor in the sacred performances, borne in the arms of a devotee, at the site of the celebrations of the annual festival of the Magh Mela at Prayag, also known as the city of Allahabad.
On the following pages:
35. A scene from the portrayal of an episode inspired by the sacred Hindu epics, at the Magh Mela at Prayag. The great religious gatherings, where the devout pilgrims, monks, sannyasi, and sadhu converge, are in essence great fertility rites and occasions of religious and mystical cohesion for Hindus.

85

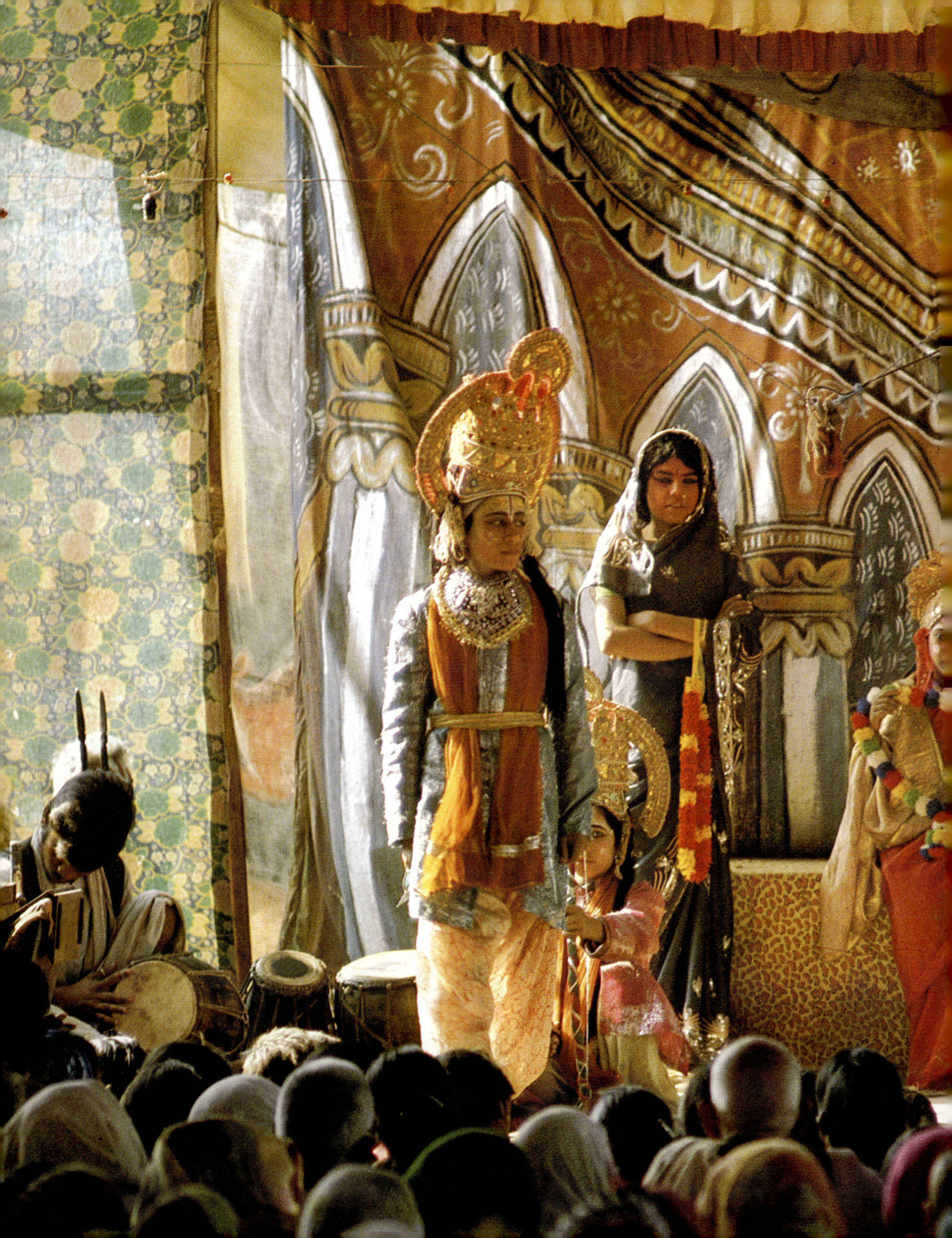

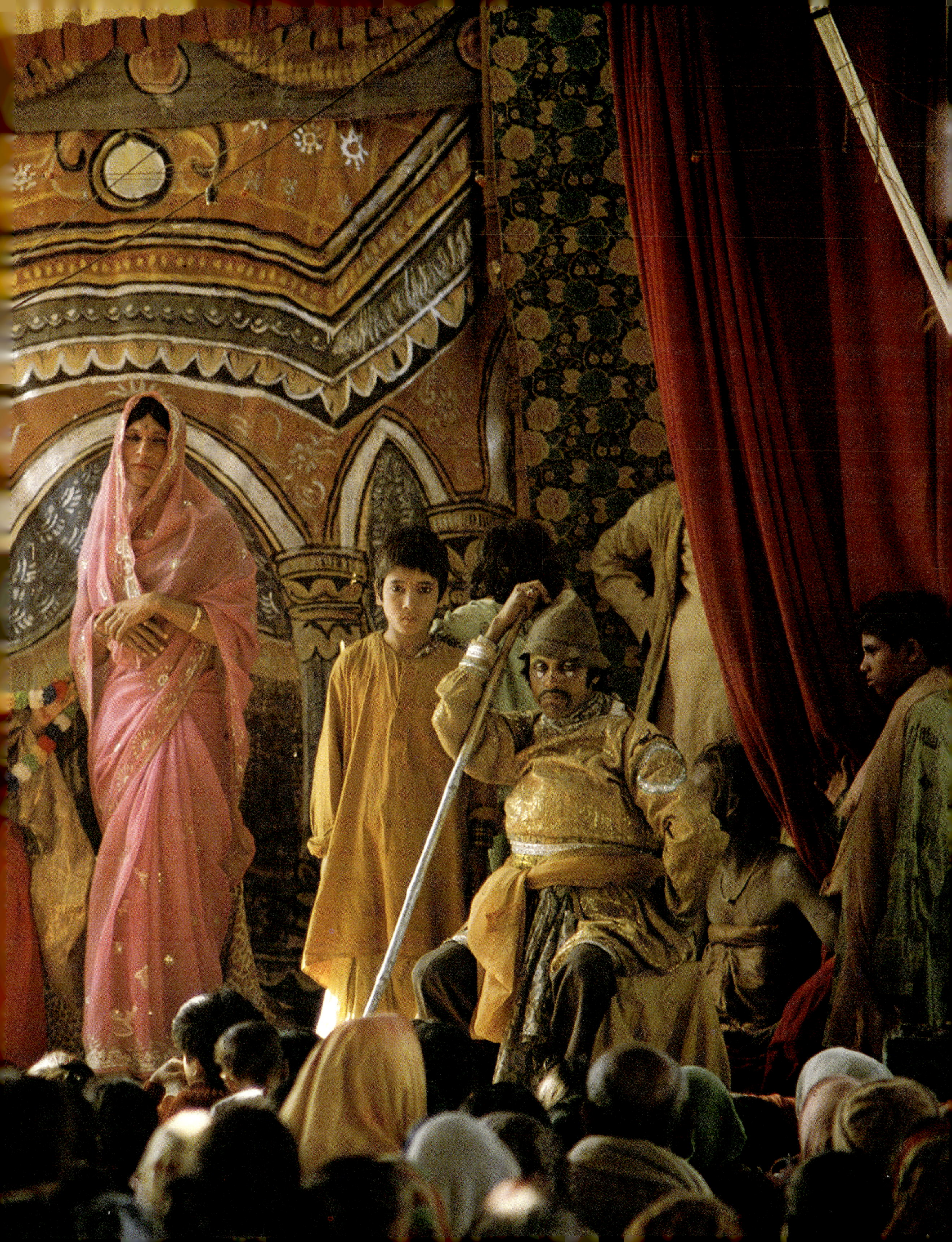

36. In the calm expanse of the Ganges a man is intent on his purificatory ablutions. He is the Maharaja of Jamnagar, Jamsaheb, and he is celebrating the pittrushraddha, *a funeral ceremony which is held in honour of one's ancestors. The various phases of the ceremony, which lasts an entire day, involve the shaving of hair, the votive offering of food and, finally, immersion in the sacred river.*
In India funerary rituals are very important and highly complex, and they are held for quite some time after the death of a relative. The bodies of the deceased are generally cremated, although they are buried on certain occasions.

After the cremation, the ashes are scattered over a river or the sea. Between the tenth and thirty-first day the rite of shraddha *is often celebrated. This is in honour of the deceased relative and its purpose is to show that death does not break the bonds between the past and the present, between the living and the dead. In the case of the death of the head of a family or an important figure in a village, a ritual meal, known as the* nukta, *is organized, to which the relatives and acquaintances are invited. The remains of the meal are offered to the deer, which are tradionally believed to be in touch with the spirit of the dead.*
37. A moment of intense concentration.

38

38. In the shadow of the great stupa of Bodh Gaya, devout Hindus are busy kneading prashad, *the votive offering to the dead in the* shraddha *funerary ritual,* which Hindus must celebrate at least once during their life. At Gaya and Bodhgaya, the rite may be performed privately, but usually it is celebrated collectively, particularly by the poor, in order to reduce the costs of the officiating priests and the ceremonies. Visits and puja to various sanctuaries in the area are undertaken. Bodhgaya is most famous as the place where the Buddha received illumination.
39. A portico on the banks of the lake of Bodhgaya, where the pilgrims purify themselves by bathing.

On the following pages:
40. A wall painting which depicts Shiva and another one of Hari-Hara, a composite figure of Shiva and Vishnu.
41. The Manikarnika Ghat, the holiest and most famous cremation site in Varanasi, seen from above.

ए महा पालिका वाराणसी के
सौजन्य से
दि. 28-5-82

MANI RAM....
MAY 82

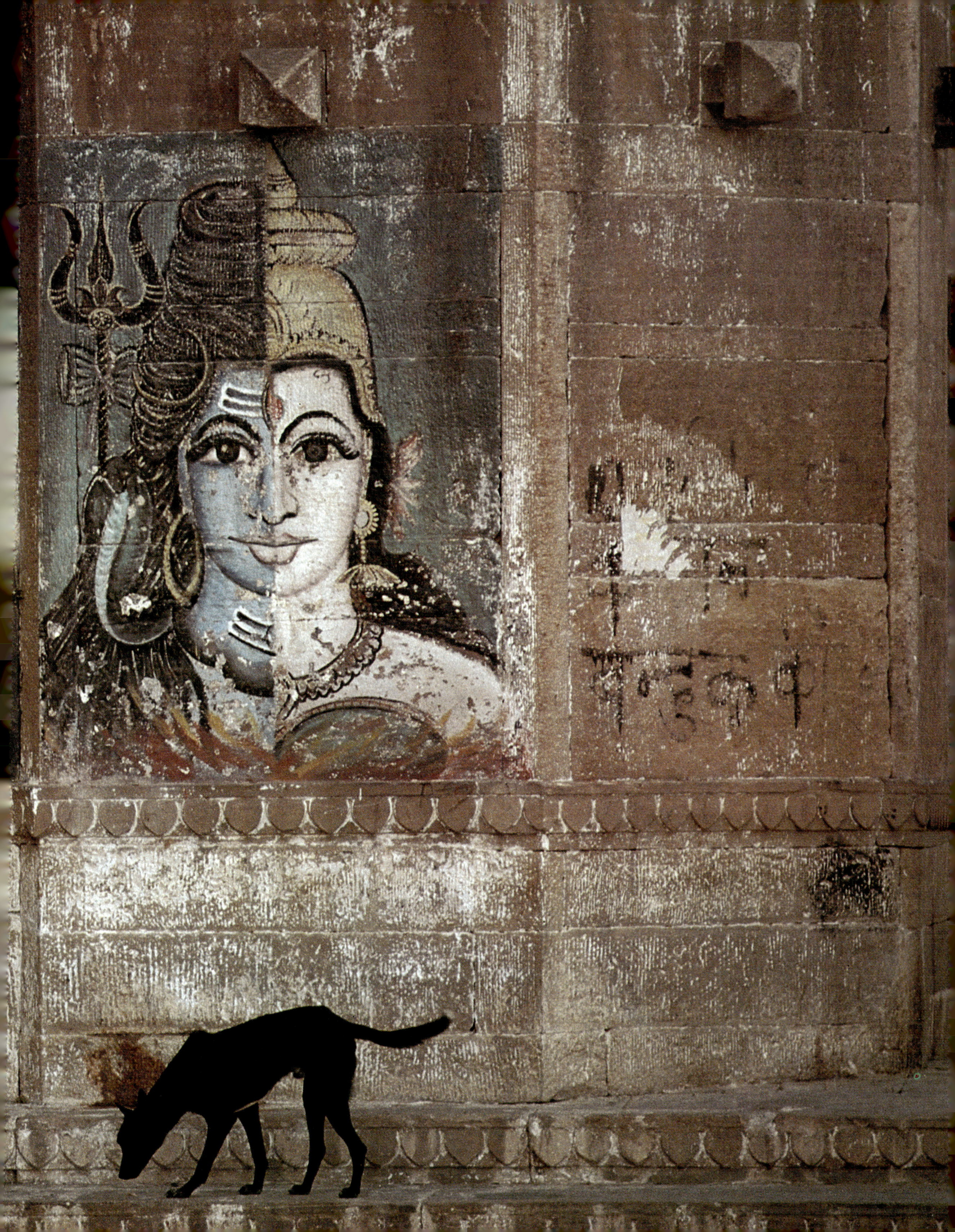

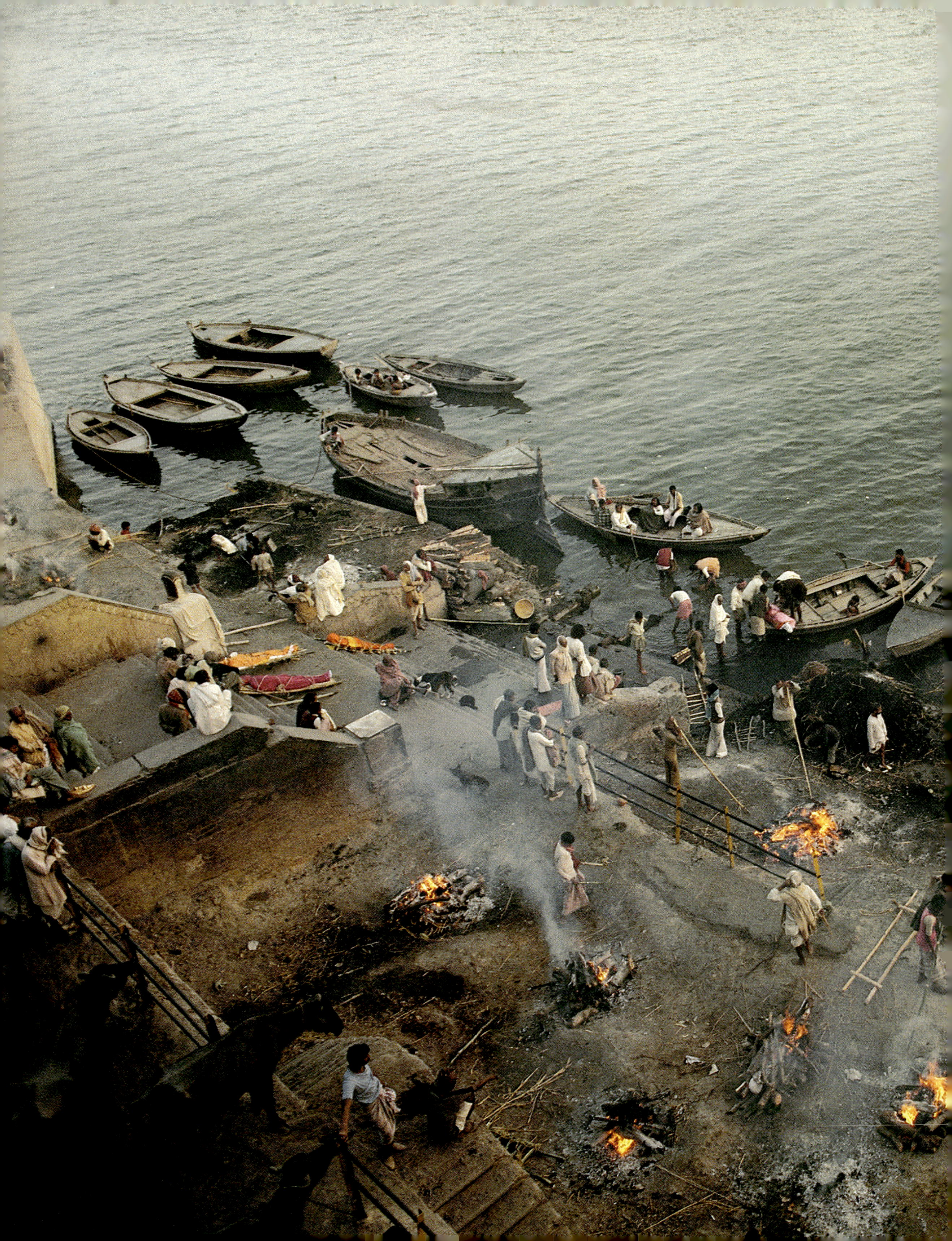

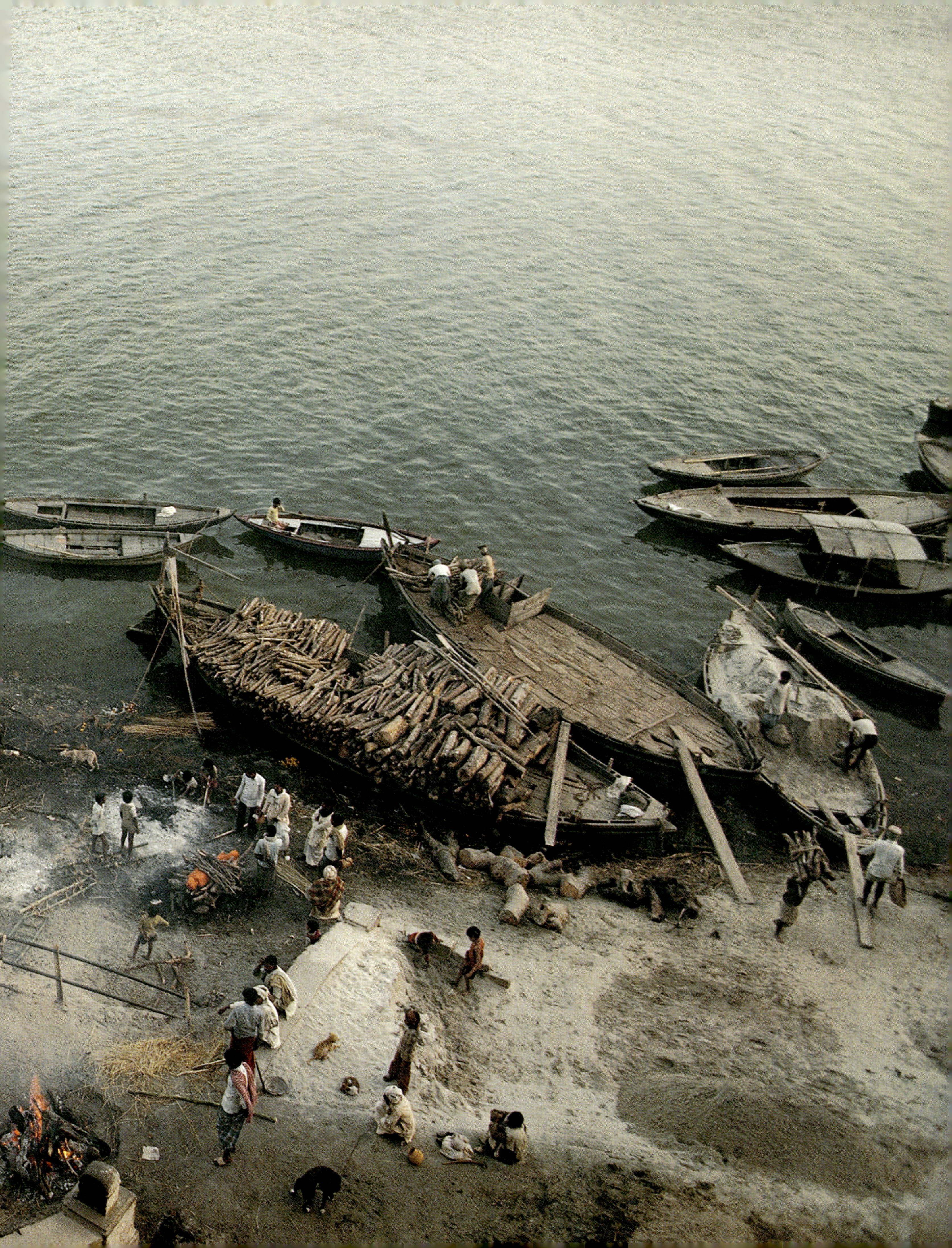

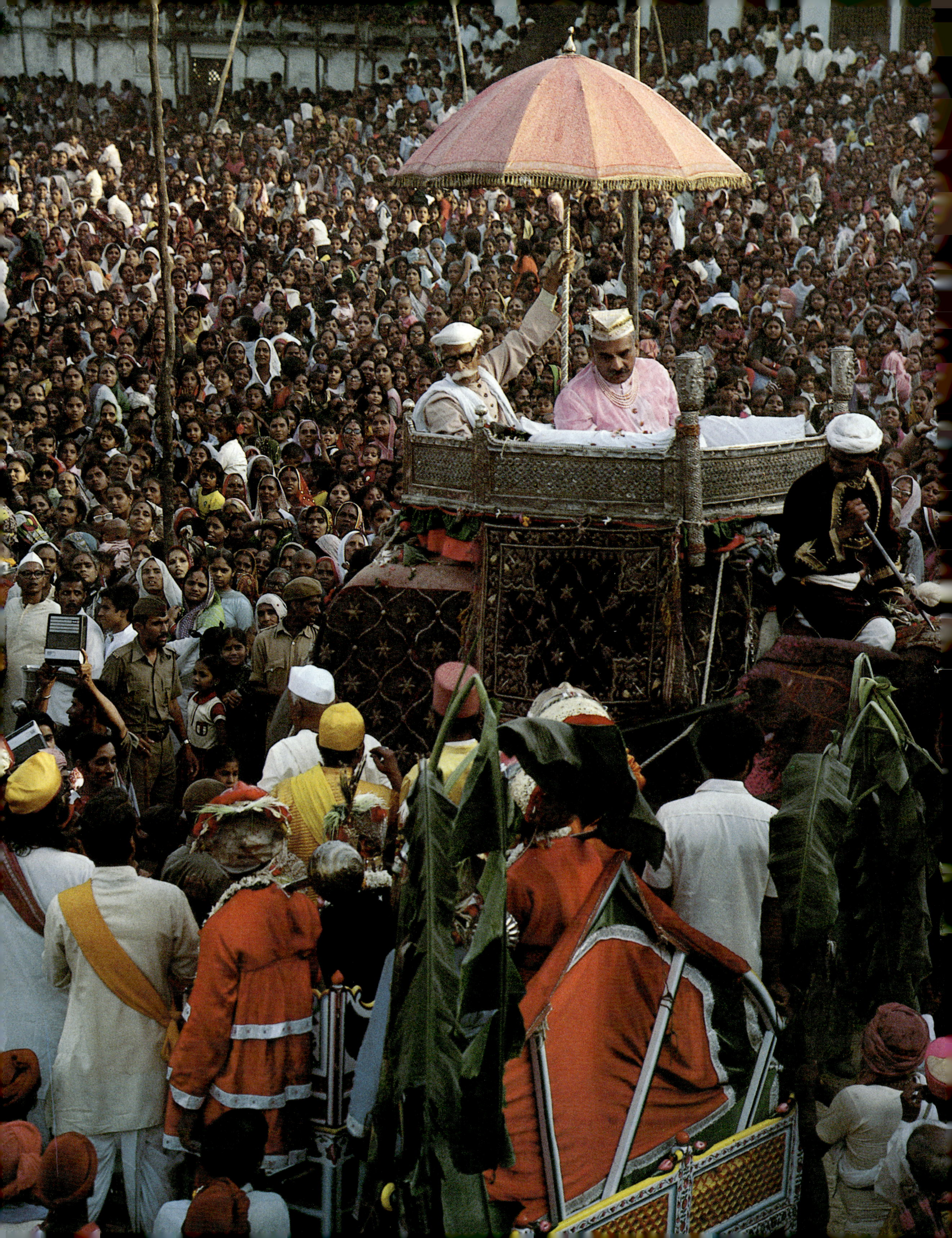

42. *A great procession on the occasion of the festival of Ramlila, in honour of the god-king Rama; on the elephant and underneath the royal umbrella is the Maharaja of Varanasi, regarded as the direct descendant of Rama himself.*
43. *The traditional umbrellas of the* panda *or officiating priests along the steps of the Ganges at Varanasi. Besides ablutions, cremations, and funeral ceremonies, innumerable rites are performed on the steps by large numbers of priests who read sacred texts and horoscopes to the thousands of faithful pilgrims who come to the river every day. In the midst of these crowds at Varanasi one can often come across sadhu, ascetics, or sannyasi remaining motionless in meditation.*

44. Sacred plays with child actors in the celebrations of the Ramlila at Varanasi. Although it is celebrated throughout India, this festival is particularly popular at Varanasi, where it lasts a whole month and every evening there is a performance of an episode from the Ramayana, the great poem whose protagonist is the god Rama.
45. At Bagdogra in western Bengal a craftsman poses in front of his work, a papier-mâché statue which is richly decorated and painted and which represents Durga, the warrior goddess. It has been made for the celebrations in honour of the goddess.

45

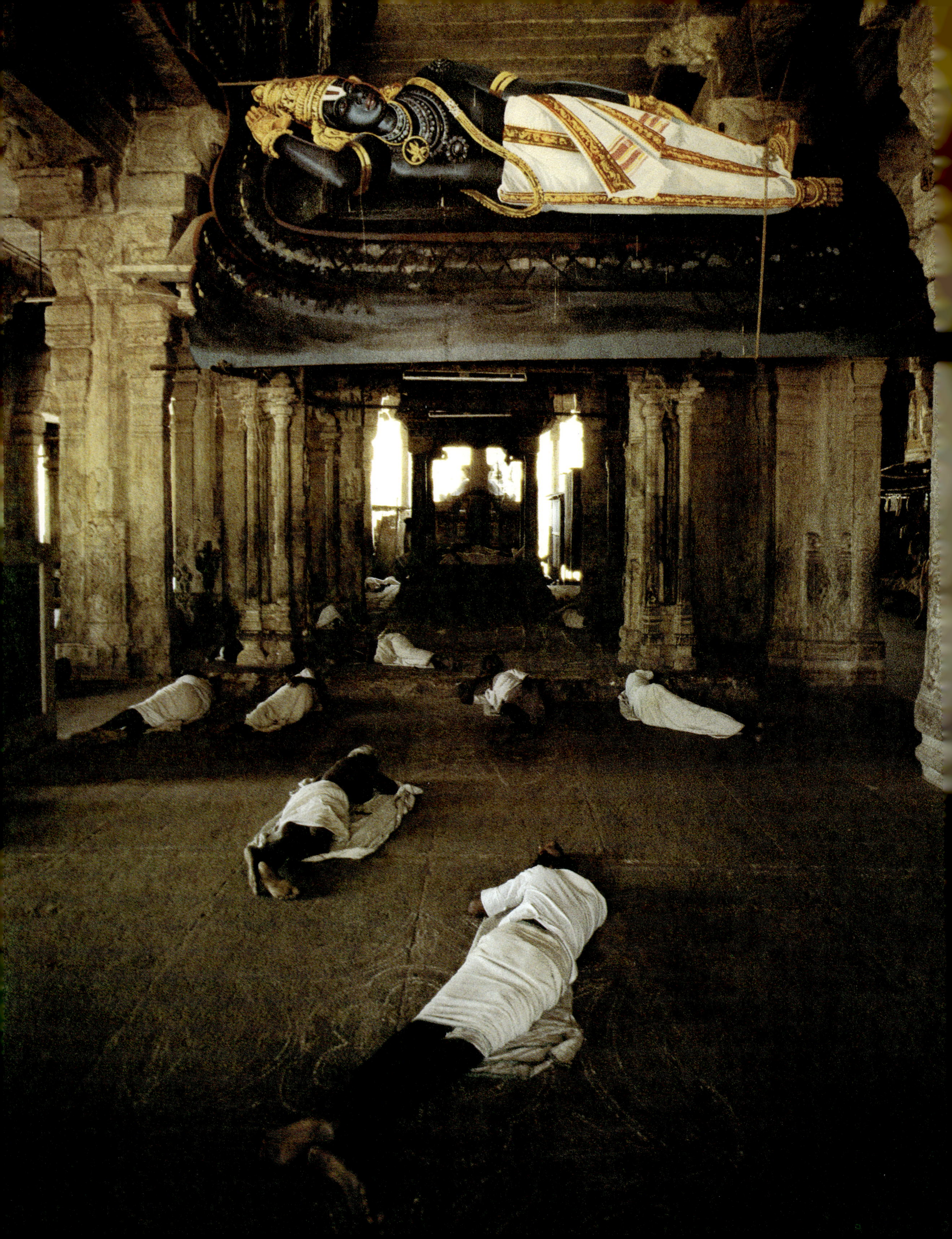

47

46. Beneath the effigy of Vishnu, in the incarnation of Sri Ranganathaswami, the 'Lord of the Universe', deep in a cosmic sleep and reclining on the serpent Adisesha, some servants of the temple of Srirangam take their afternoon sleep in the shade of a portico. Srirangam, in the deep south, is possibly the greatest of the Indian temples; indeed it is a temple city because, as well as the religious buildings, the temple area also contains the dwellings of the Brahmins, schools, shops, stores, and the other features of a true town. It has played a major role in the religious history of southern India, being, both now and in the past, one of the most active centres of the Vaishnavite tradition and for long the home of the great philospher Ramanuja, the founder of the bhakti school, in which the devotional aspect of religion and cult assume prime importance. Major festivals take place in the course of the year and it is one of the most important places of pilgrimage in the south.

47. A devotee of the temple of Srirangam with Vaishnavite markings painted on his forehead.

48. A long gallery with a line of sixty-three statues representing the Noyan-marlal, the so-called guides of Shiva, in the temple of Vellore.
49. A long row of linga-yoni *in the porticoes along the outer perimeter of the temple of Brihadeshwara, at Thanjavur in Tamil Nadu. These are usually votive offerings made by families or communities and dedicated to Shiva. The temple of Thanjavur is one of the most beautiful and best preserved of India's temples. The central tower, the* vimana, *in the tradition of Dravidian architecture is pyramidal in form and rises thirteen storeys to a monolithic stone crown weighing about eighty tons.*
50. Foreshortened view inside the temple of Srirangam.

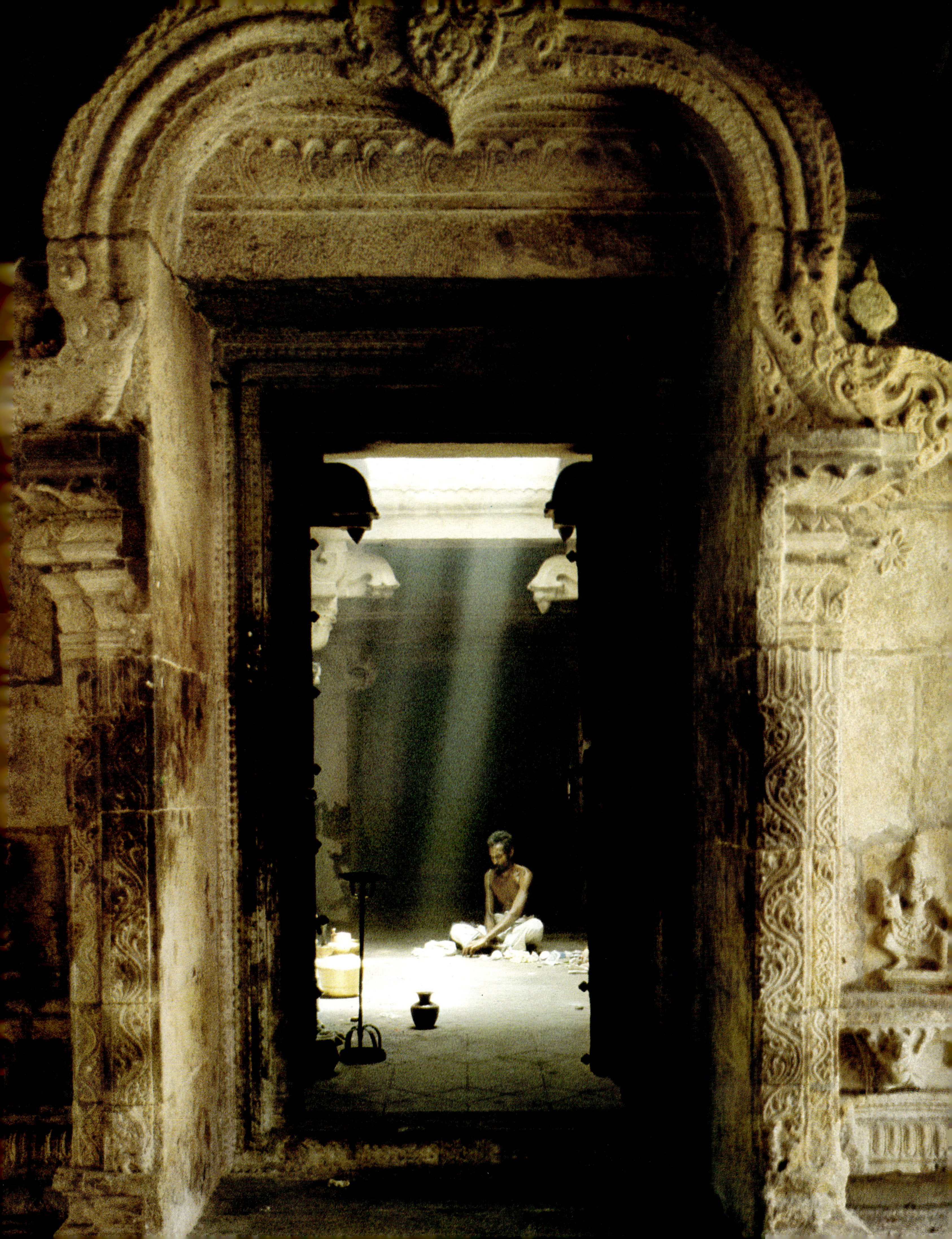

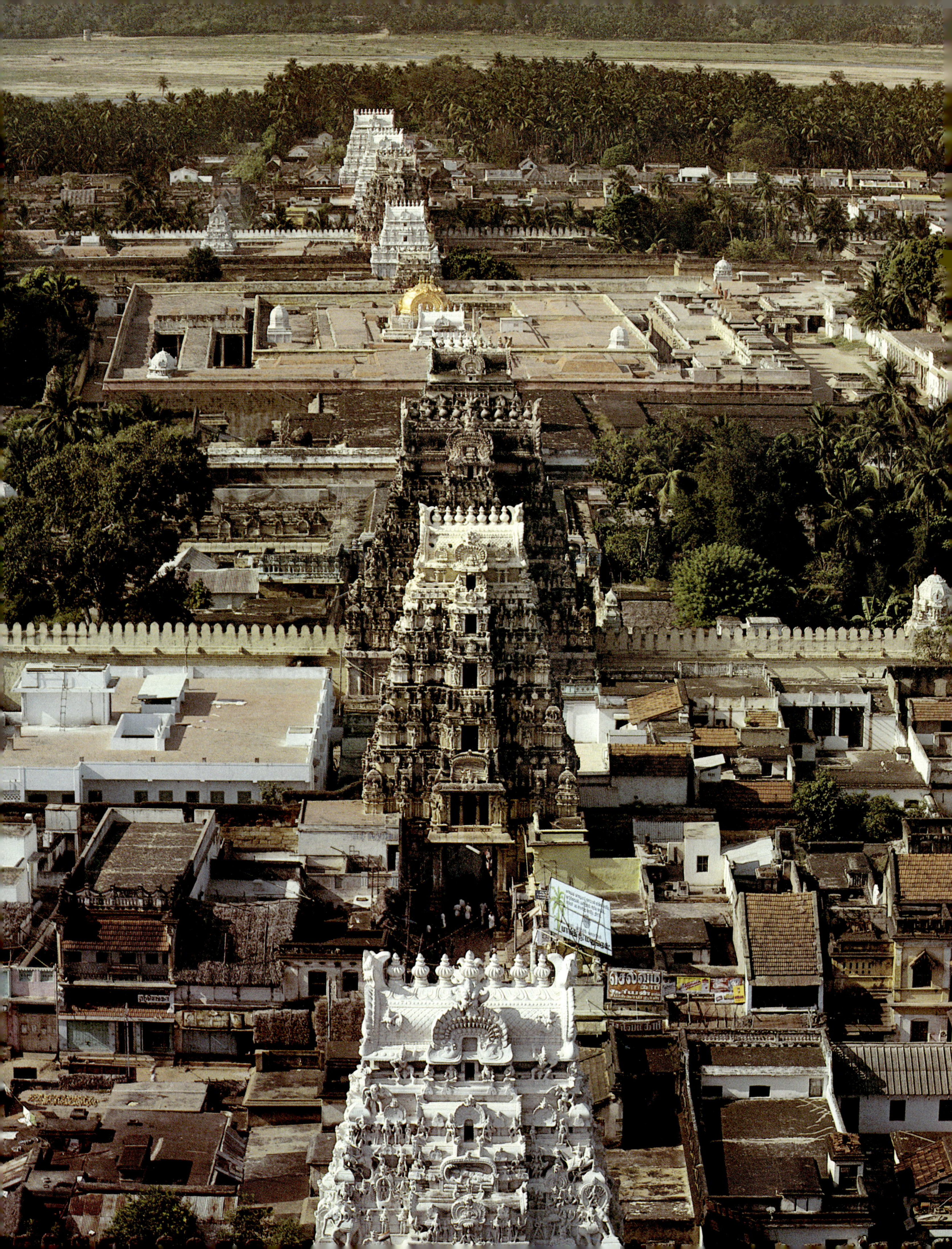

52

51. *A view along the central axis of the temple city of Srirangam showing the series of* gopura, *entrance towers, standing at the intersection of the axis with the seven sets of walls that comprise the temple. There are a total of twenty-one towers at Srirangam, although they were built at different times and some are still unfinished. In the foreground there is a recently built tower. The pyramidal towers which rise several storeys are almost all decorated with statues which represent the Brahminical divinities and episodes from the great sacred poems, the* Ramayana *and the* Mahabharata.

52. *Shesagiri-Mandapa at Srirangam with its pillars of rearing horses.*

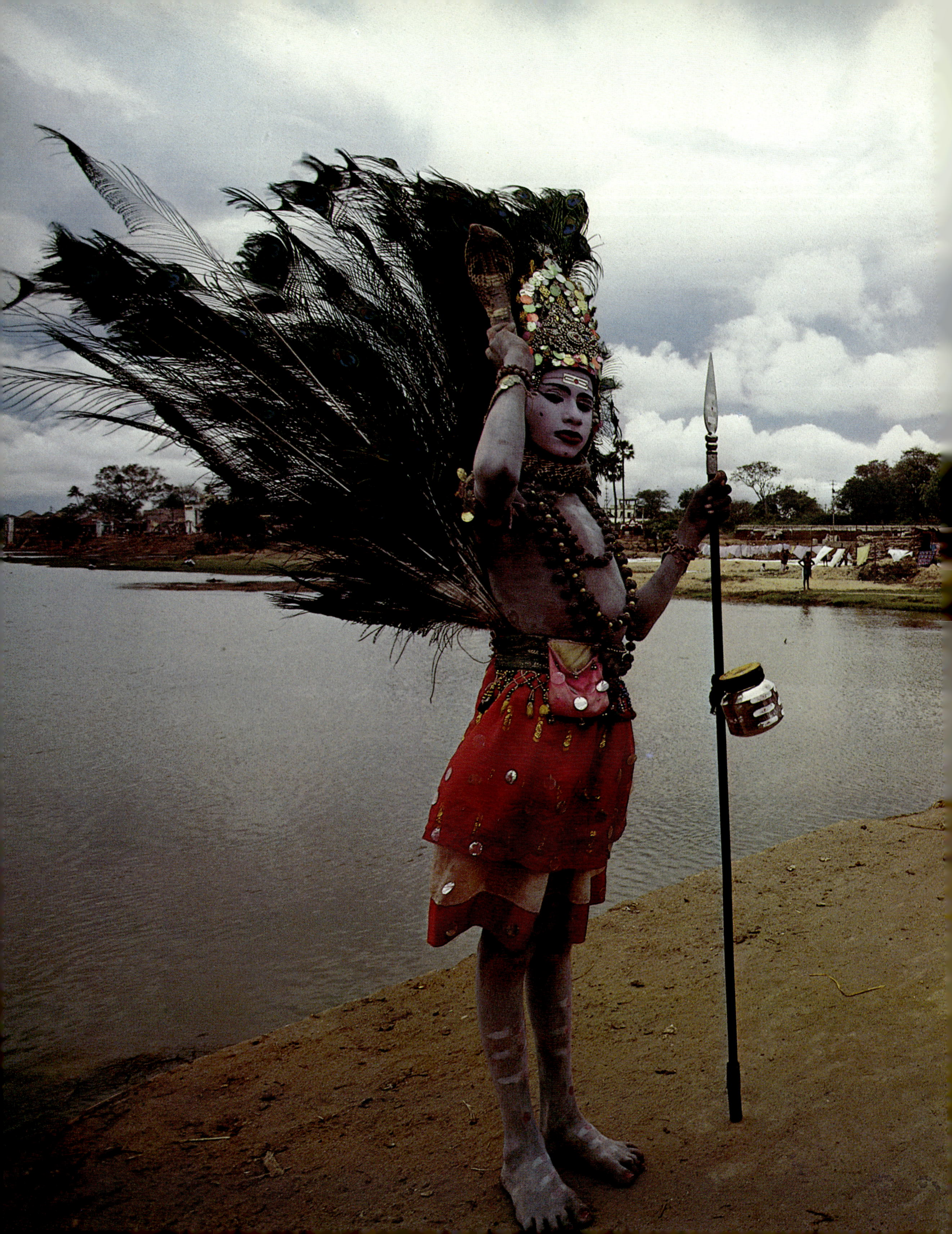

53. At Madurai, during the festival in honour of the goddess Minakshi, a youth plays the highly popular god Subrahmanya, who is known as Murugan, the 'boy god', in the Tamil world. The son of the god Shiva, he is regarded as the patron of the brahmin priests and is borne by a peacock. In the past, besides the usual offerings of flowers, orgiastic dances were performed in his honour. He is never venerated by women, possibly because of his ambiguous origin – according to myth he was not born to the wife of Shiva, Parvati, but from the head of his father. The boy has a cobra wrapped around his neck.

54. Stone statue of the bull Nandi, the divine vehicle of Shiva, in a temple at Pattadakal, in upper Karnataka.

55. *Life inside the great temple of Minakshi, the 'Fish-eyed Goddess'. This sanctuary is another temple city and the various activities that take place within it are not limited to the cult, but include a market, craftsmen's workshops, schools, and even political meetings. The temple has halls and porticoes in order to receive the pilgrims who come from all parts of India for the great religious festivals, the most important of which is the annual celebration of the divine marriage of the goddess to the god Shiva. There are processions even in the streets adjacent to the temples, with gigantic ceremonial carts,* rath, *which carry the idols from one sanctuary to another, across the city.*

56. *Children dressed as* deva *(divinities), on a processional cart for the festival of Minakshi, Madurai.*

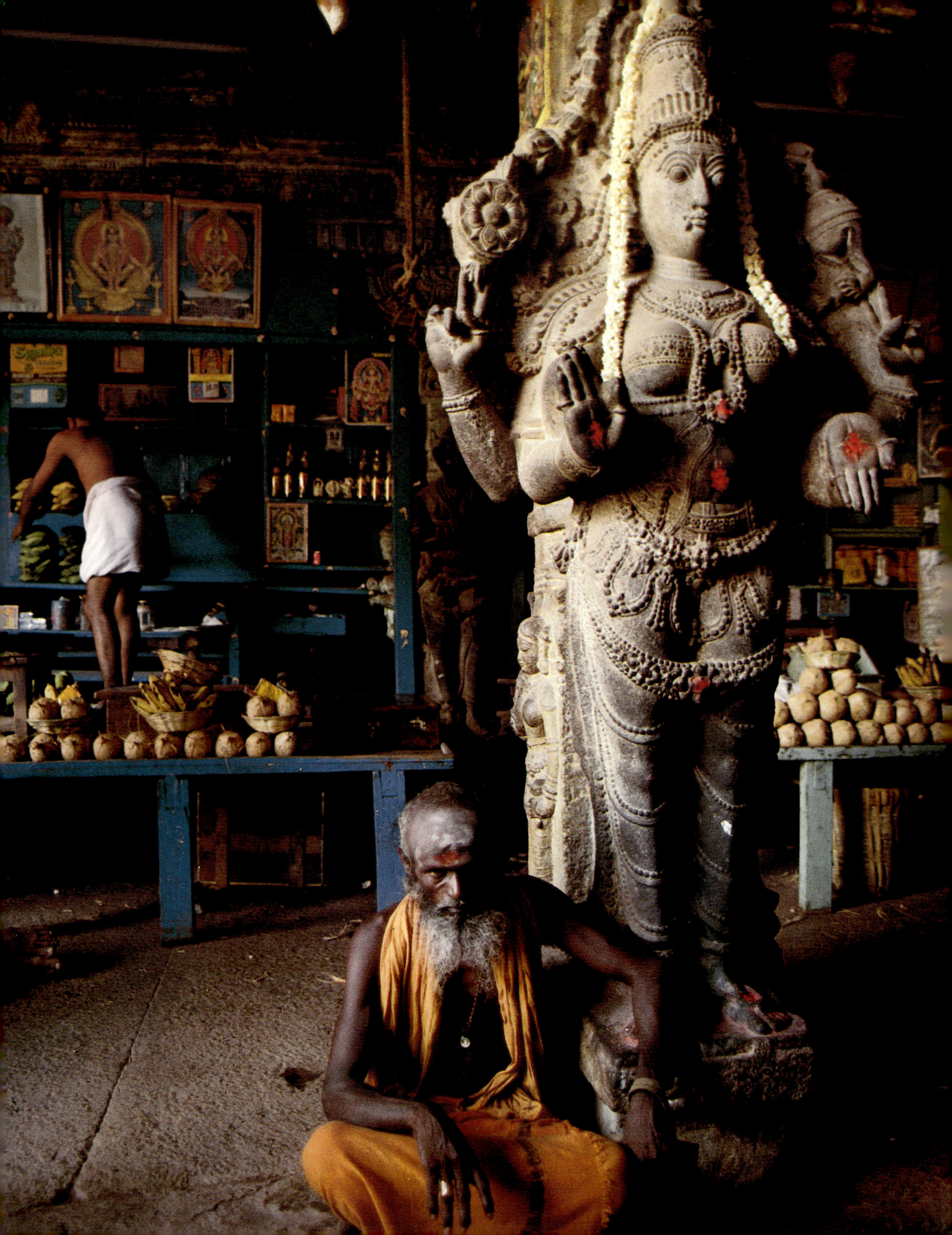

57. Madurai, inside the temple of the goddess Minakshi.
58. Rath Yatra, procession with carts on the occasion of the ceremonial marriage of the tutelary divinities of Madurai.

On the following pages:
59. Gathering of Naga-sadhu for Mahashivaratri, the 'night of Shiva', a religious festival dedicated to Shiva Mahadeva which is held in February, during which ritual bathing takes place at midnight in the sacred pool of the temple. These sadhu represent a way of life that is still widespread in India. Despite the fact that the country is changing fast there are still millions of ascetics, hermits, and itinerant monks. The Naga-sadhu live in isolated monasteries and observe certain rules of extreme asceticism and special practices of chastity. They generally belong to Shaivite sects in which great attention is paid to sexual energy.
60. A sadhu.

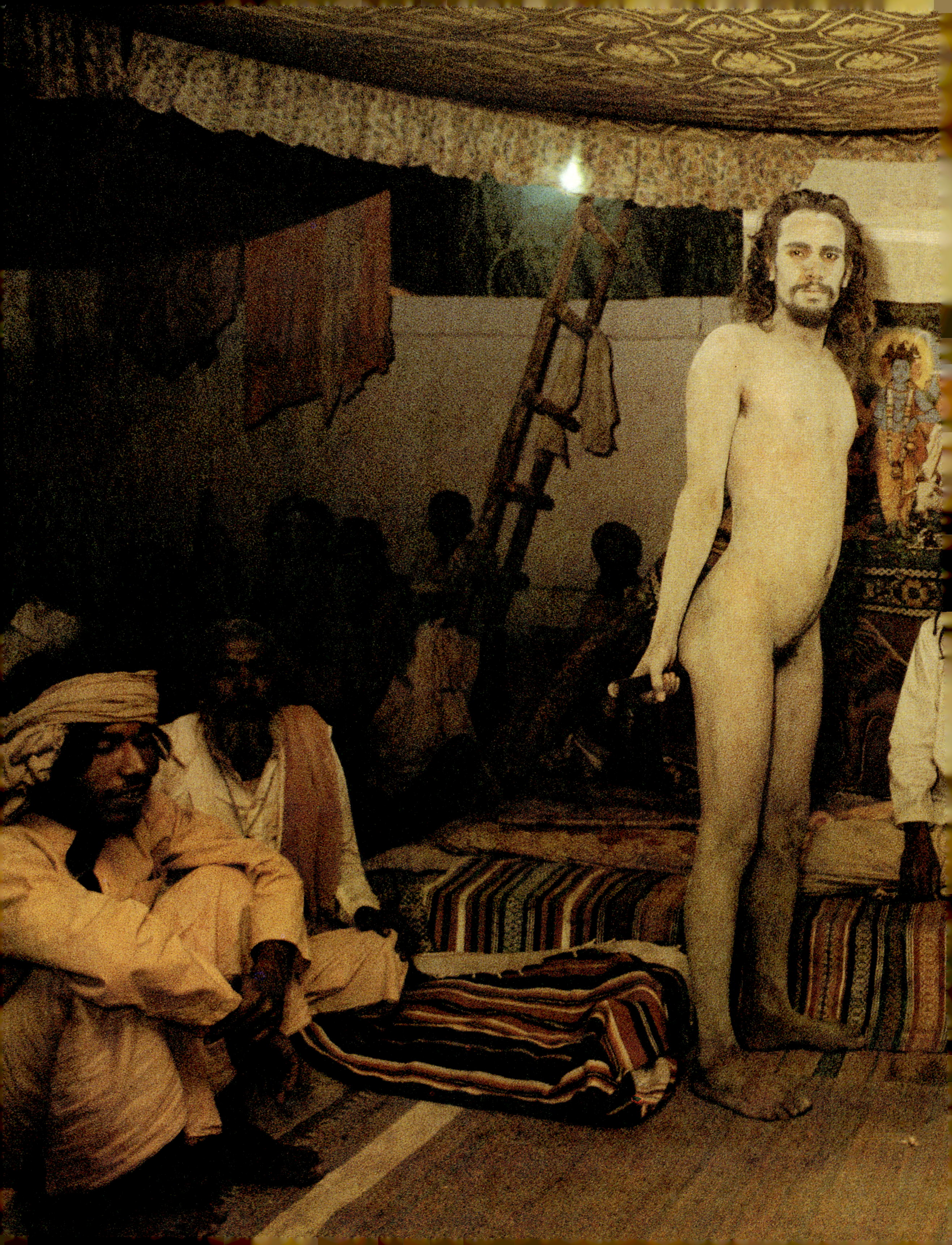

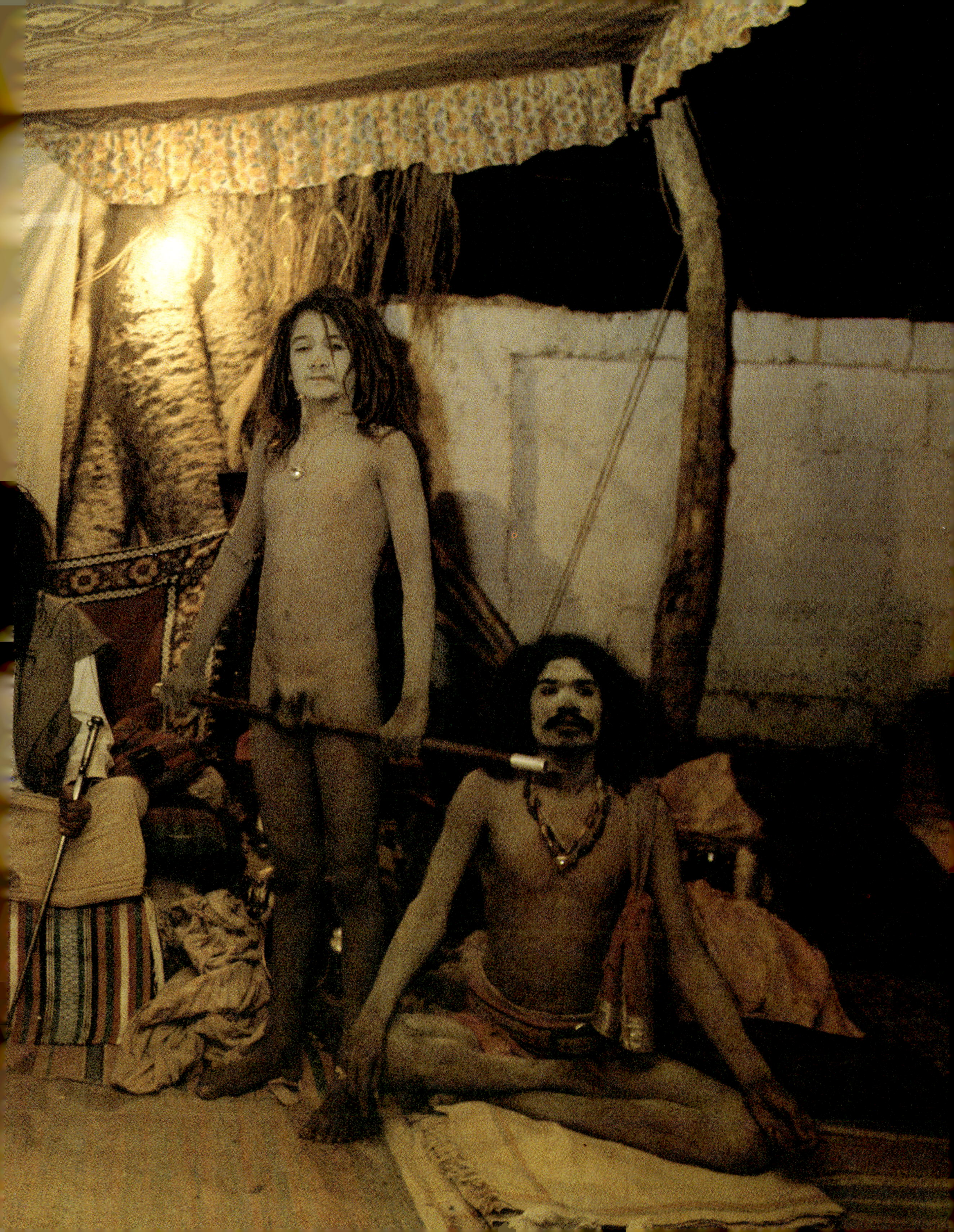

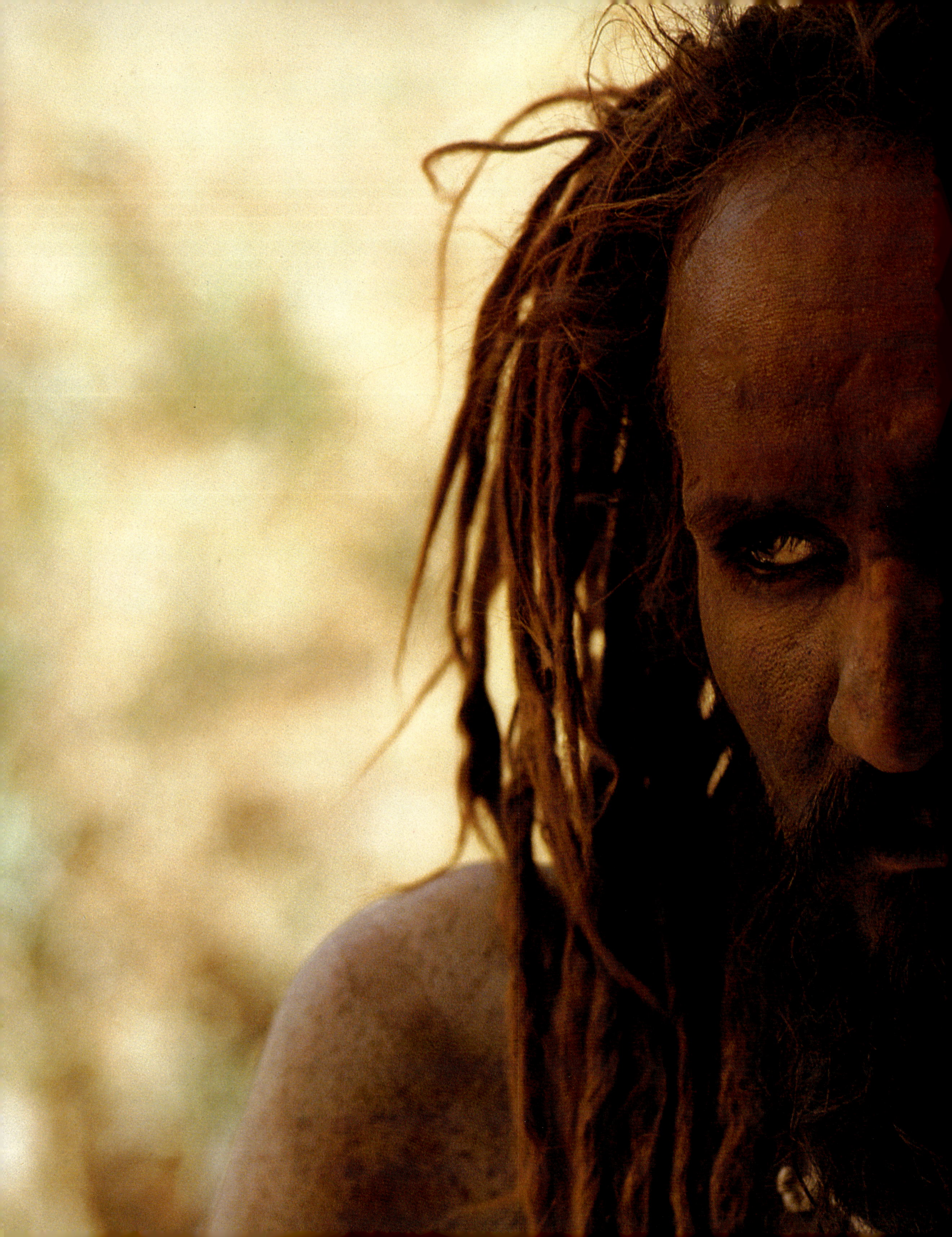

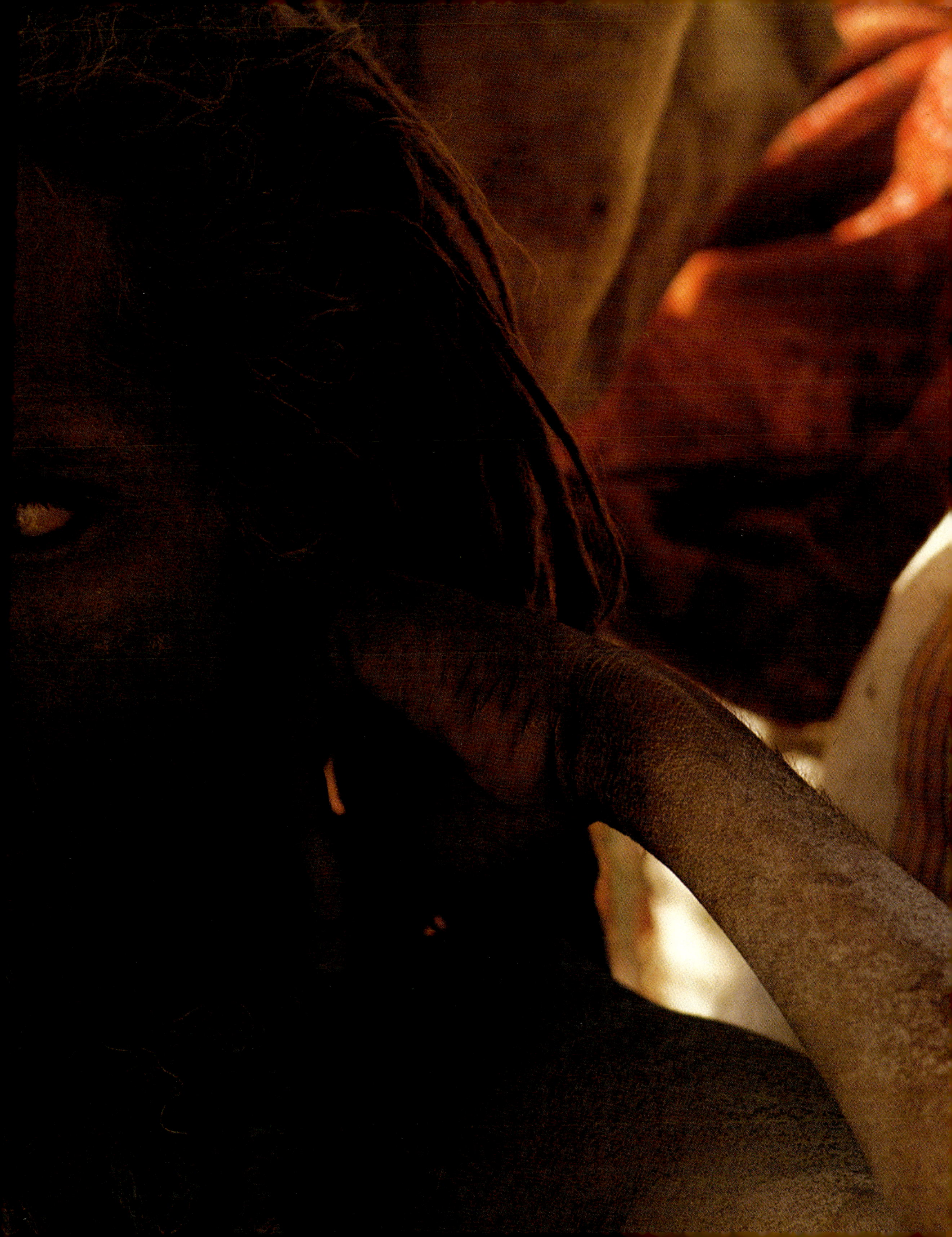

61. *The highly decorated interior of one of the Jain temples of Palitana. The sacred hill of Satrunjyara is one of the most extraordinary sacred citadels in India and it is the most important Jainist one, with more than 900 sanctuaries, both large and small, crowded on the hill. Together with Mt Abu in Rajasthan and Sravana Belgola in the south, it is one of the great centres of Jain pilgrimage.*

62. The porticoed hall of one of the Dilwara temples, situated on the extensive plateau of Mt Abu in the Arawalli mountains in Rajasthan. Built of white marble, the interior is a masterpiece of sculpture and architectural decoration. Columns, ceilings, porticoes, and cells display a highly elaborate, carved working of the marble and figures based on geometrical mandala with superimposed planes and concentric rings in the form of a star. In each cell there is a polished stone idol representing a tirthankara or Jain saint.

On the following pages:
63. At the foot of the colossal statue (about 62 ft high), of the venerated Jain hermit saint Gomateshwara, whose puranic and popular name is Bahubali. The colossus stands at the summit of a large hill of greyish granite, surrounded by various buildings of composite style. The saint is naked, in the posture known as kayotsargi, which shows the impassiveness and serenity of the penitent and ascetic, qualities which Jainists value highly.

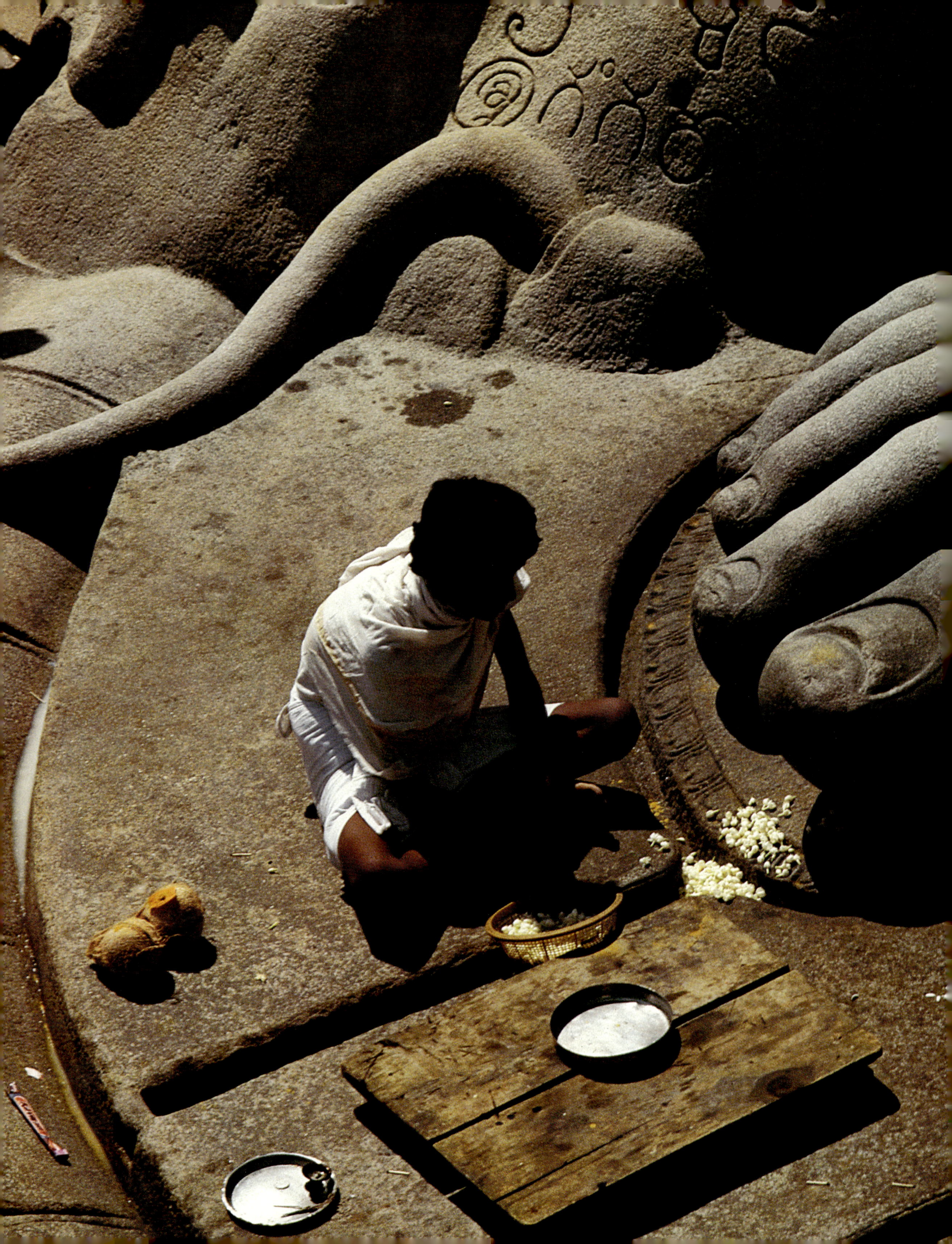

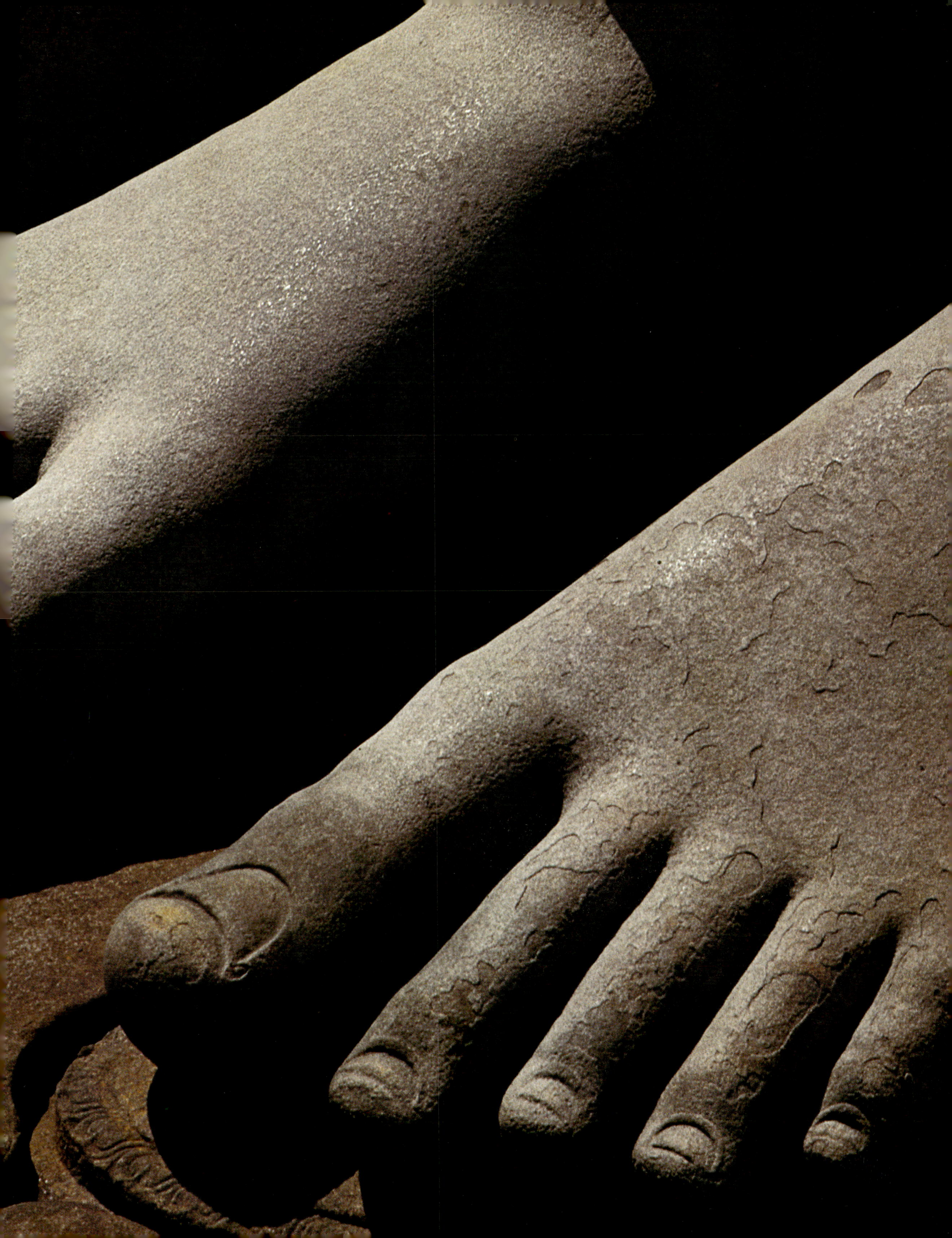

64. An Iberian baroque Christ inside the ancient Carmelite church of St Thomas. The church, which is on the former Portuguese island of Diu, has now been deconsecrated and is part of a hospital. In the sixteenth century the island was one of the main strongholds, together with Daman Chaul, Bassein and the capital Goa, of the Portuguese possessions in India and the main trading centre for the whole area of Portuguese influence; consequently it was also one of the centres of Christianity. The Christians of Diu, unlike Goa, where conversion was even imposed on high-caste Hindus, are descended from communities of low-caste Hindus and untouchables.

65

65. Sculpture on the outer wall of a house in Jamnagar, a city in Gujarat.

On the following pages:
66. The evening prayer of Muslims in the Taj Masjid, a mosque in Bhopal.

121

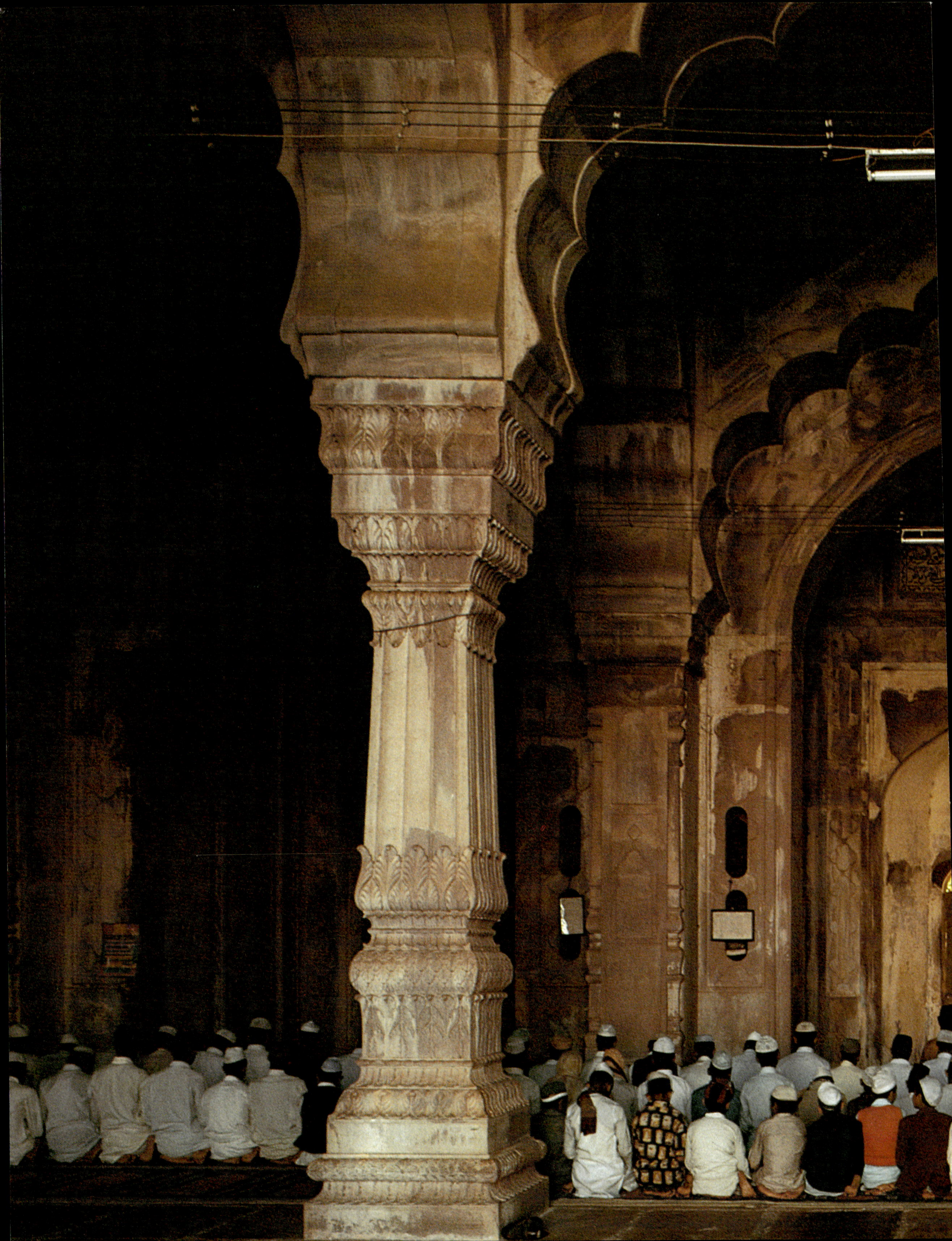

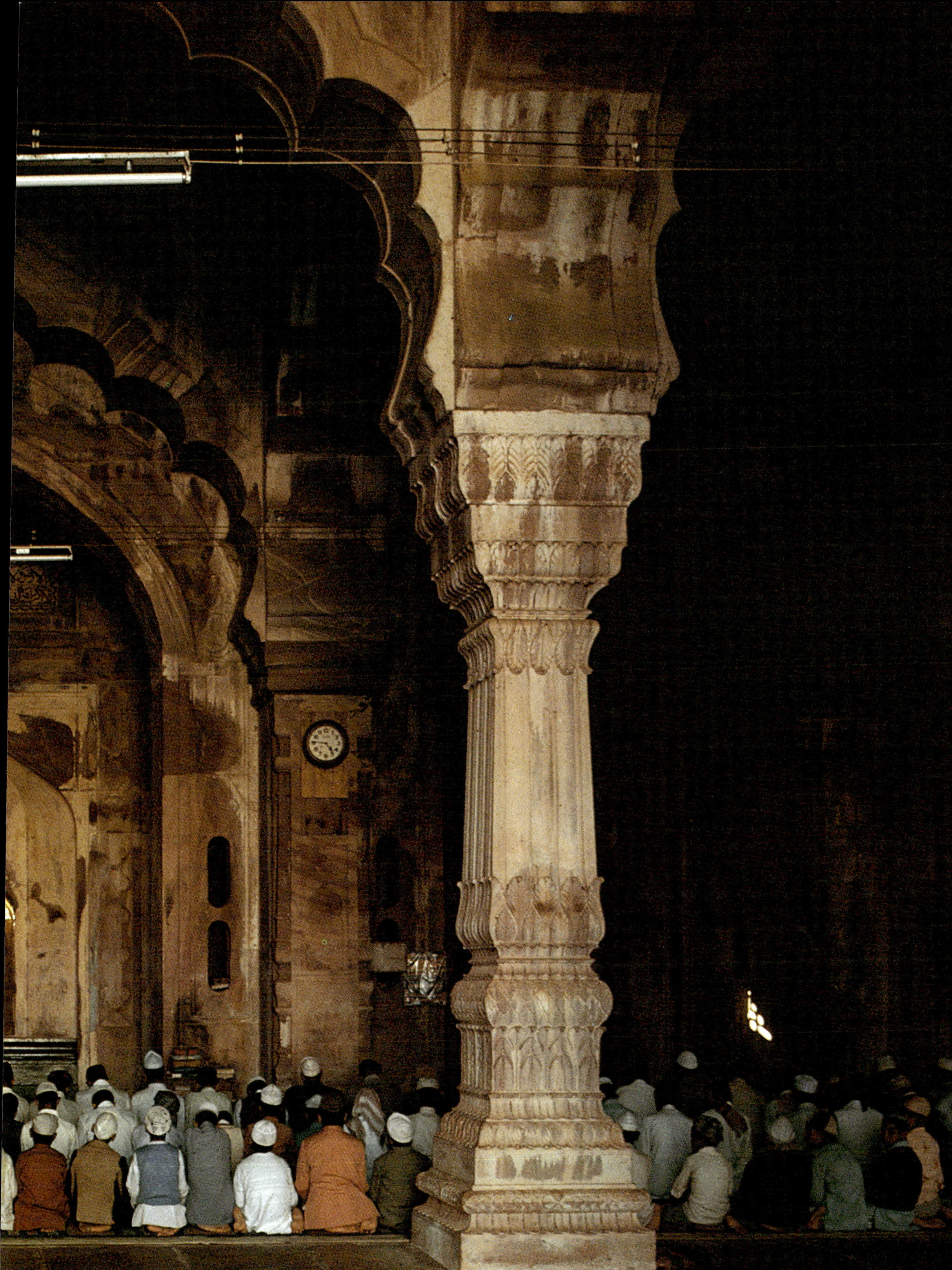

67, 68. The 'Golden Temple' at Amritsar, the holy centre of the Sikhs; some of the Khalsa, the militant, warrior group of the sect.

On the following pages:

69. A great gathering on the occasion of the visit of the Dalai Lama to Manali, in the region of Himachal Pradesh. The waiting lamas and monks throw light muslin scarves into the air, as votive offerings to celebrate the arrival of His Holiness.

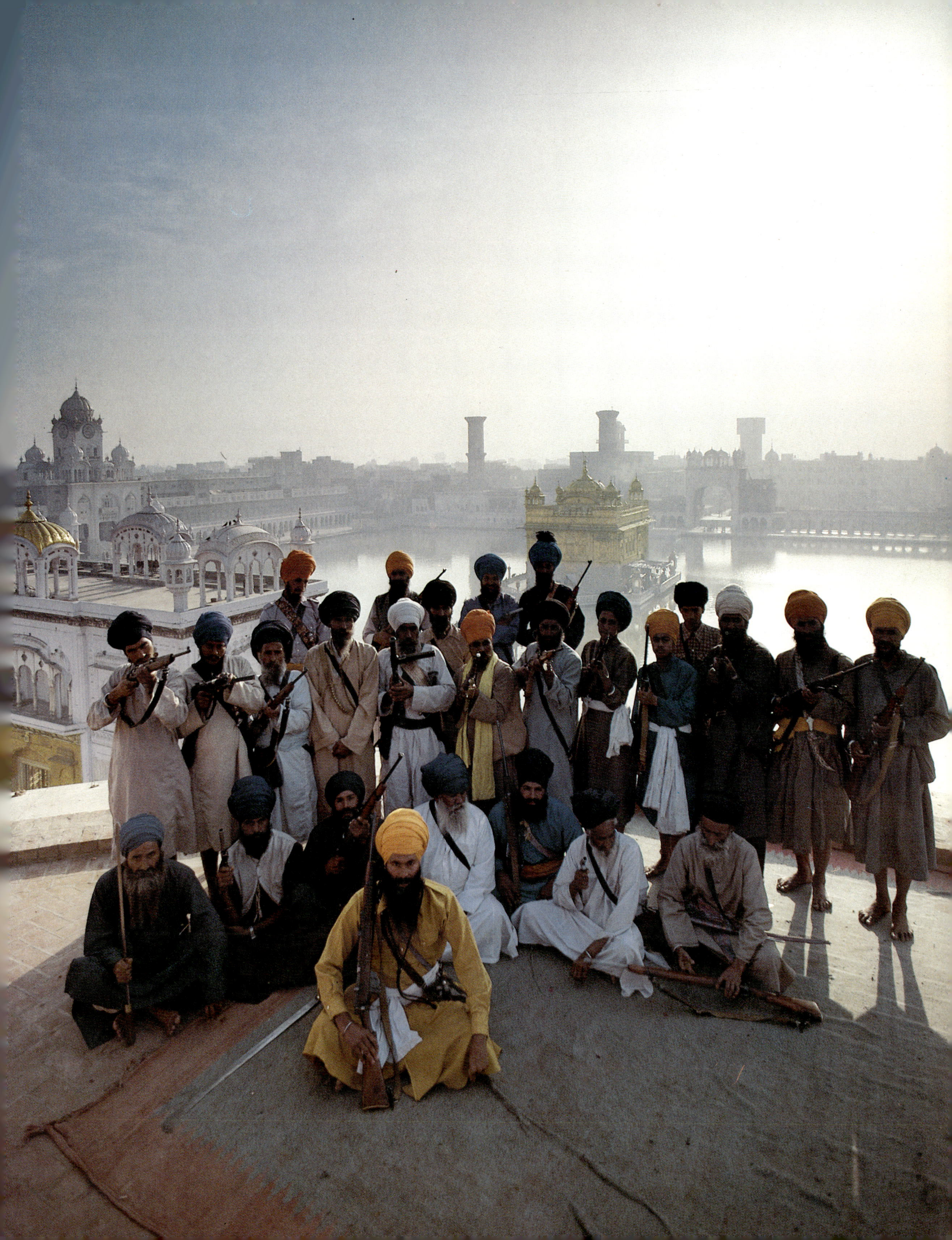

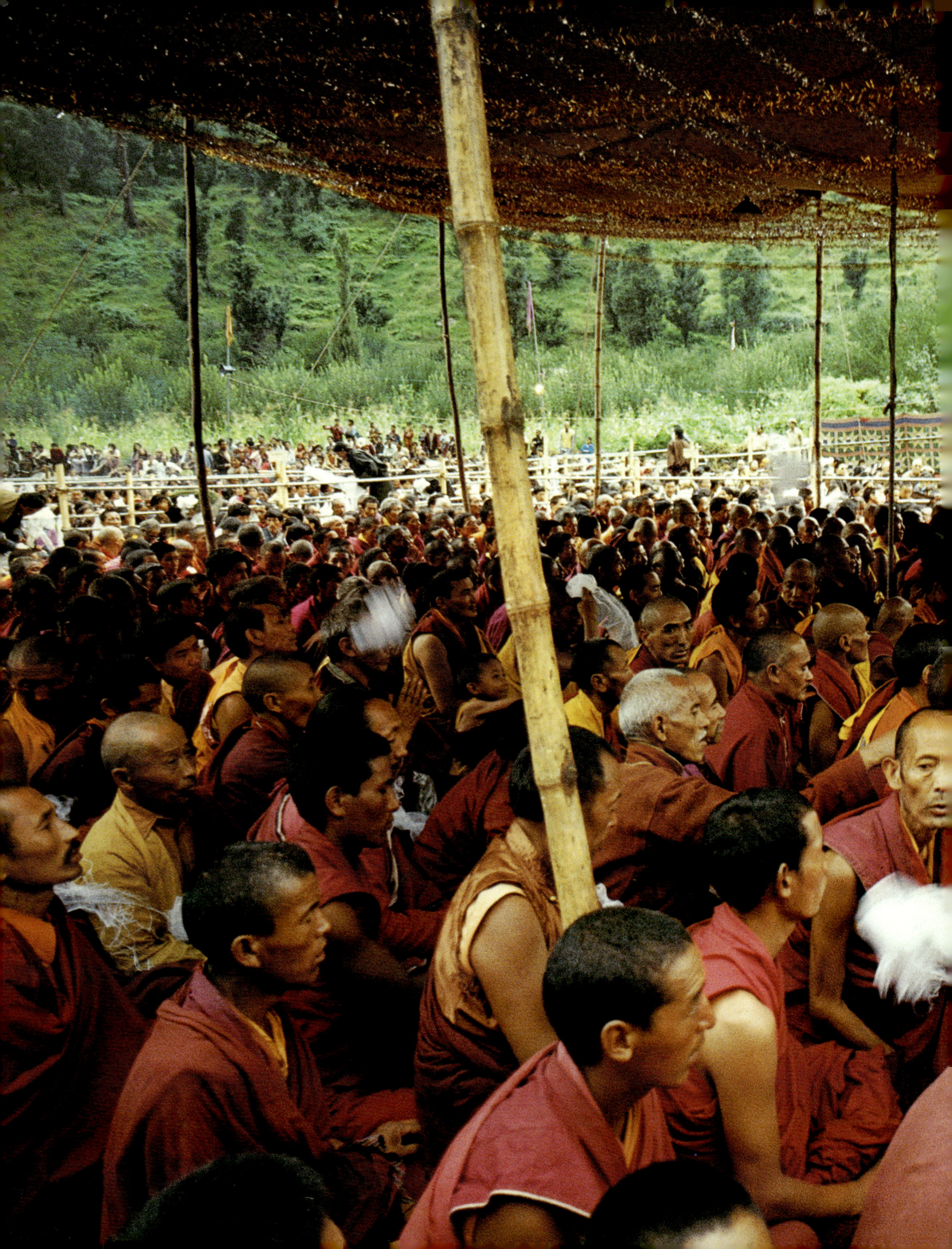

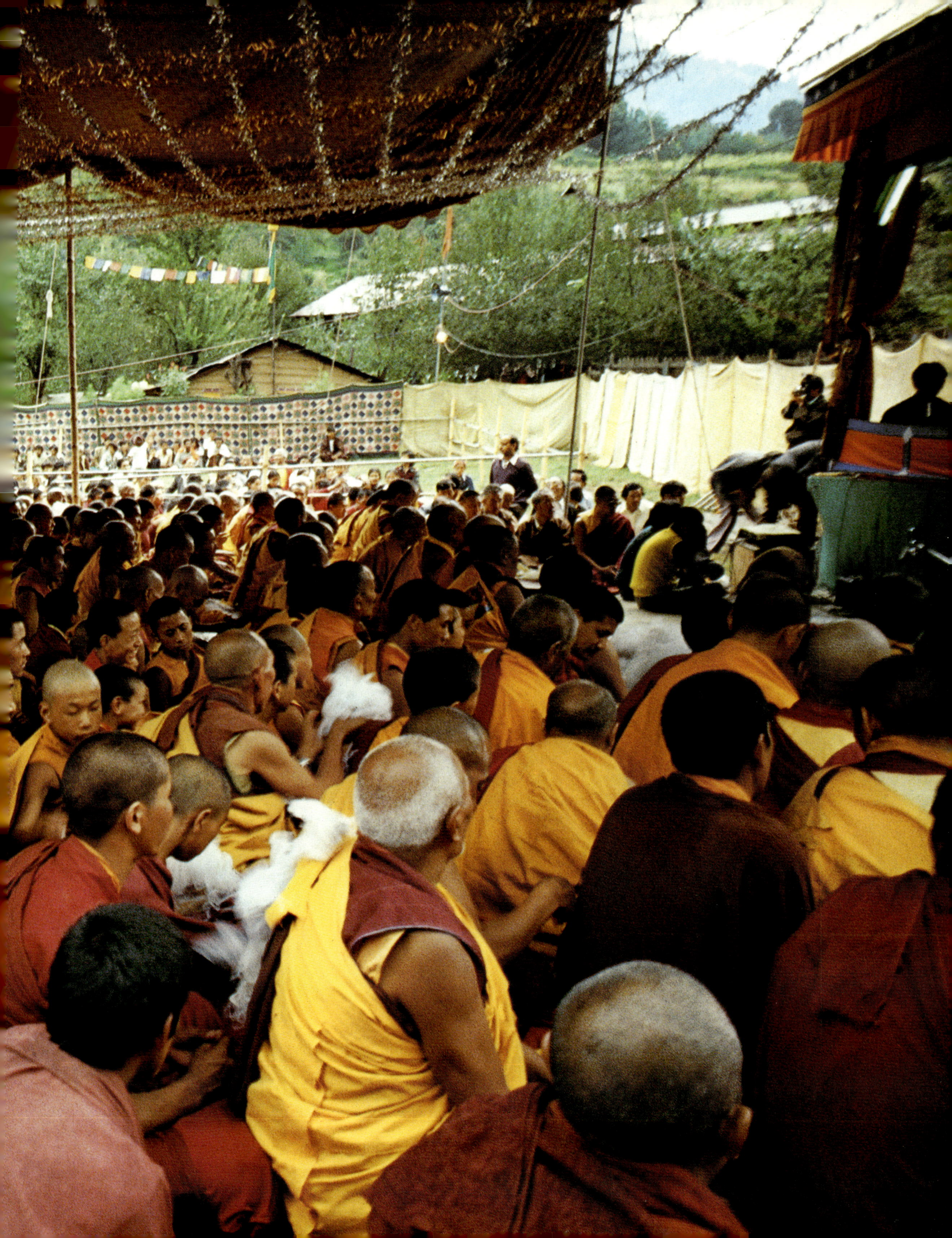

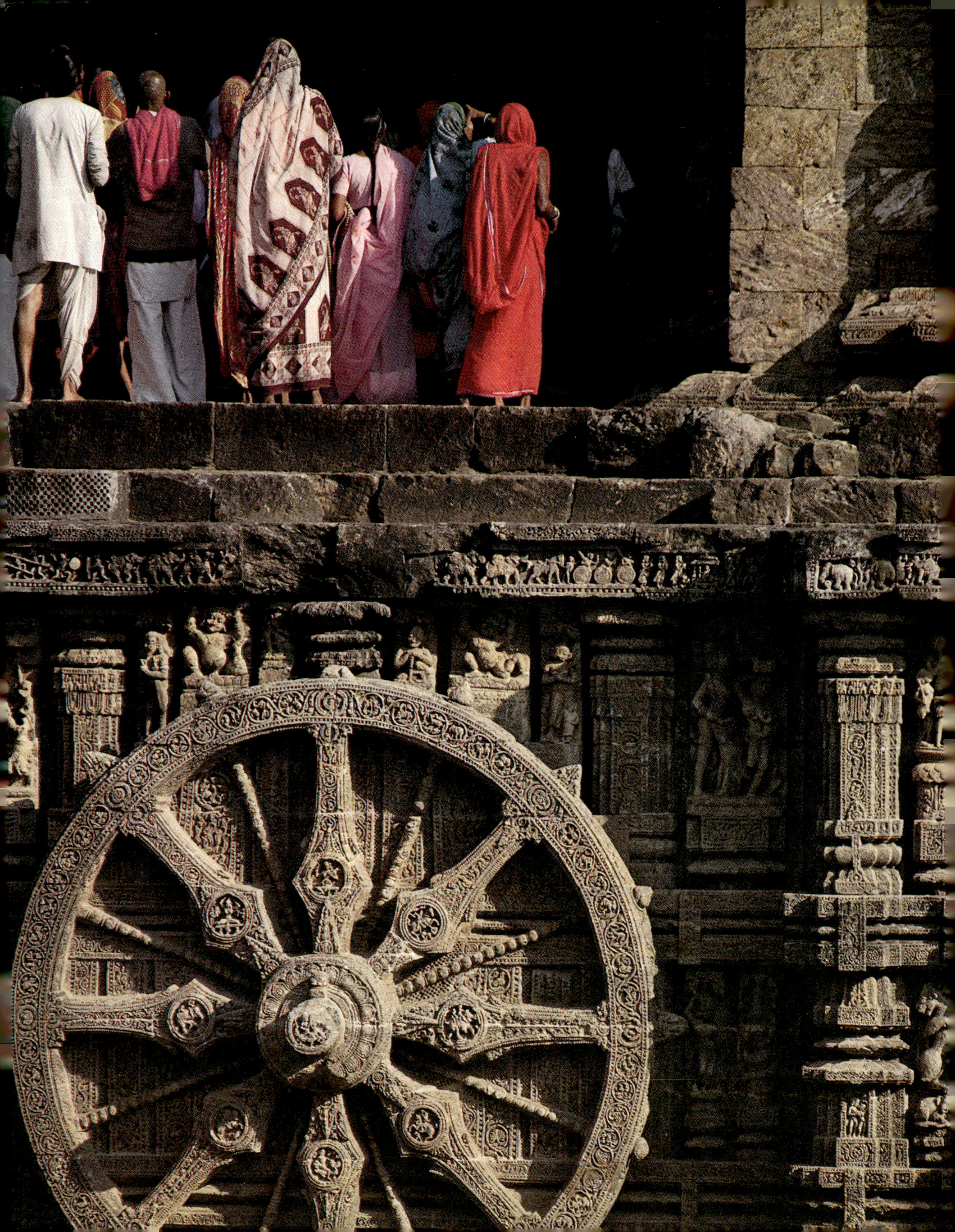

Art and Architecture

To enjoy the sensuous immediacy of Indian art there is no need, however, to study abstruse theories, for this is an art which also expresses a vigorous, extroverted, physical imagination. Even works which embody more subtle metaphysical concepts are accompanied by charming details from ordinary life, born, it would seem, from sheer exuberance and fun. No art is more direct in its approach, more immediate in its appeal, than the minor, small-scale, and intimate work which embellishes the tops, sides, bases, lintels, pillars, doors, and arches of Indian monuments. It is sensuous, vigorous, impetuous, humorous, innocent, bawdy, lyrical, tender; above all it celebrates a state of physical well-being and abundance. Though usually rural in theme, it is not peasant art. Traditions of great refinement penetrated the world of the artisan and craftsman, to be fertilized anew by ebullient folklore, legend, and cult-imagery'.

Richard Lannoy

The cult of images in India is not ancient. Leaving aside the proto-Indian Harappa civilization, whose iconography is rather uncertain, and starting with the Vedic period, there are no images of gods or even temples. It is not until about the fourth century BC, at about the time of the formation of the great monotheistic spiritual schools and the transition from Brahmanism to Hinduism, that images of the fantastic world of the divinities begin to establish themselves. Simultaneously, temples began to be built and the popular cults and pilgrimages to holy places and sanctuaries took root. Above all, there was a growing need for images and idols to replace the abstract doctrinal concepts and the sacrificial ceremonies. The Indian art known to us spans some twenty-one centuries and, despite the vastness of the country and the presence of distinct and often widely separated and isolated regional cultures, India has maintained a conceptual unity and a certain homogeneity in its artistic forms.

It is not arbitrary to say that Indian art is essentially religious, because even in its secular and profane aspects it never completely excludes a sacred component. The works with a religious function — as can be seen from the great body of art which has come down to us — were created to serve a purpose; they are images that provide a means or a support for meditation, with which, by particular processes of concentration, an inner vision is obtained, a reflection of the divine world, represented by the image itself. In Hinduism, the statues of the gods are not objects of adoration, as is commonly believed, but cult symbols, acting as *puja* (homage to, or contact with, the divinity), the essential rite in the daily observances of the Hindu. In order adequately to serve this purpose the creation of the divine images was subject to a series of proportional rules laid down in the ancient treatises of art and craftsmanship, the *shilpa-shastra*. If the rules were observed and the statue of the divinity was 'correct' — that is, it conformed to the sacred canons — the function of the idol was fully respected; it was beneficial and favourable for those who had modelled it and a source of spiritual and mystical life for those who contemplated it.

The artist-craftsman, the *shilpin*, worked on an idol as if it were a liturgical act, preparing himself with meditation and yogic concentration and subsequently, as a second phase, developing a mental image in accordance with the treatises. At the moment in which the right image appeared to his inner vision, he could proceed with the actual execution using the accepted techniques. The treatises do not contain models for copying but rather schemes, such as mandalic diagrams, which stimulated an elaborate mental image from which the artist would proceed directly to creation. The technical process and the psychological method was in fact very similar to the techiniques of concentration in Yoga.

Indian art has never had 'beauty' as a primary aim, although it does not exclude

70. *One of the great stone wheels of the temple of Konarak in Orissa. The gigantic temple was built in the thirteenth century by the Ganga dynasty in the form of a chariot of the sun, with twenty-four richly carved stone wheels and enormous stone horses. The sanctuary, which is now only an archaeological monument, was dedicated to the god who personifies the sun, Surya, a Vedic divinity who was subsequently assimilated by Brahminical culture in the figure of the god Vishnu. Konarak is a masterpiece of Indian art and its sides are carved with innumerable reliefs of mythical beasts, lions, or sea serpents and, above, all, female figures and couples,* mithuna, *in erotic poses.*

it; instead it aims at 'feeling', which is termed *rasa* ('taste' or 'fragrance'), a state of mind excited by various combinations of signs which compose the image or object created. The ultimate, fundamentally religious, aim is to create a dynamic state of consciousness, an 'emotional' resonance, rather than something of purely aesthetic value. All this has freed Indian art from the problems of naturalistic representation, particularly of the human figure, which is the major concern of the Classical and Renaissance art of Europe. Consequently there is a total indifference to the principles of a natural view, the concern for which led to the invention of perspective in Europe.

Although bound by formal liturgical canons, Indian artistic expression enjoyed considerable inventive freedom in conveying its message and this has resulted in an unrestrained proliferation of images in the effort to represent the world of the divinities. The range of rasa is in harmony with the infinite potential of human emotion and the rich universe of the depiction of the heavenly myths; the possibility of communicating contrasting, even antithetic, motifs with the same formal intensity; the gentle with the terrifying, the mystic with sensual and absolute stillness with a frenzy of movement, as for example in the perfect symmetry of a Buddha of the Gupta period and the exuberent anatomical oddities of a Brahmanic deity from the same time, with its numerous heads and arms. Indian artists have been able to confer great force and plastic harmony in their blending of human and animal forms or in their images of figures with dozens of arms, which to a Hindu symbolizes divine power.

At all times and in every regional school Indian visual and plastic arts have created whole cycles of wall paintings and high reliefs, which decorate the great cliff-face complexes or the outer walls of the medieval cathedrals, attaining their highest expression in certain recurrent motifs; in the female figure, for example, in the rhythm of the curves, in the grace of the postures, and in the emphasis on the symbols of feminity. In the representation of movement, often the product of a cult of the portrayals of Indian dance, the shilpin have succeeded in suggesting the rhythm and dynamic balance of the human figure in one of the most pregnant and formally difficult themes, the dancing divinity, such as the image of Shiva Nataraja, immortalized by the splendid Chola bronzes of the twelfth century. In all forms of Indian art, including architecture, it is the *mandala*, the symbolic diagram, which governs the arrangement of lines and spatial fields. In Indian art the mandala, which means 'circle', is the graphical and geometric projection of the centre of the cosmos and its parts. For Tantric sects the mandala is an essential instrument of ritual and support for meditation. Tantrism, which has a tendency towards ritual and liturgical abstraction, has created an immense array of images, symbols, formal syntheses of its cosmology, magico-alchemical experiments, and initiatory rites.

What has survived of the Indian architecture of the past consists mainly of temples and associated buildings. In general, less importance was attached to architecture, which in Sanskrit is *vastu* or 'to enclose', than to the other arts, such as dance or the sculpture of sacred images. However, architects needed to have a thorough knowledge of arts and of the sacred scriptures, of mathematics, and of geography and history. Only in the building of temples did the art of construction become of prime importance. The Indian architect, known as a *sthapati*, was invested with priestly dignity and as well as co-ordinating all the building work he had to preside over the astrological and geometrical operations and the delicate business of deciding the site and the orientation of the building. The construction of a sacred building was seen as a ritual act and sites that were considered 'powerful', the *thirtha*, were chosen for temples. Just as in the creation of a sacred image, the canons of the treatises on architecture, the *Vastu-shastra*, including the famous *Manasara*, had to be respected in the building of a temple.

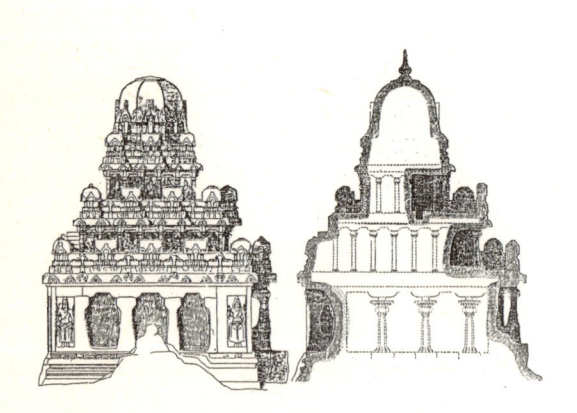

Side elevation and section of the huge Dharmaraja temple at Mahabalipuram in Tamil Nadu (by J. Fergusson, 1876).

The rules principally concerned the plan of the temple and a specific symbolic diagram was used in architecture, the *vastu-mandala*, which gave guidance for the division of space and the forms of elevations. The symbolic diagram, which is a means for identifying the ideal 'centre' of the universe, of which it is a reflection, fixed the central axis of the temple. In addition, the building had to be orientated along the cardinal points, because everything had to be in harmony with universal order. The temple 'is a reconstructed sacred place, that is a "centre", into which the ideal centre of the universe is magically transferred' (Tucci). Just as the statue of a god or the representation of a divine myth must be 'analogous' to the world of the celestial spheres, so the temple becomes an 'analogy' of the whole universe, a cosmogony fixed in stone and space.

In Indian religious thought the building of the temple signified the commemoration of the primordial act of sacrifice which gave rise to the world. This is why it involved the *vastu-purusha-mandala*, the diagram through which the sacred building and its essential parts are identified with the Cosmic Man, the Purusha, the first sacrificial victim, whose body according to the Brahmana was dismembered to form the universe. At the same time the temple is also the axial mountain, the pyramid which goes back to the sacred mountain — Mount Meru — whose peak is the mystical centre of the universe. The entire building is constructed as a path towards the centre in a sort of walkway around the central sanctuary which contains the image of the divinity. Thus the temple is not just the home of the divinity and a gathering place for the faithful, but also the means of the realization of the soul which, by means of a route with identifying marks and a progressive approach, relates the earthly sphere to the celestial one.

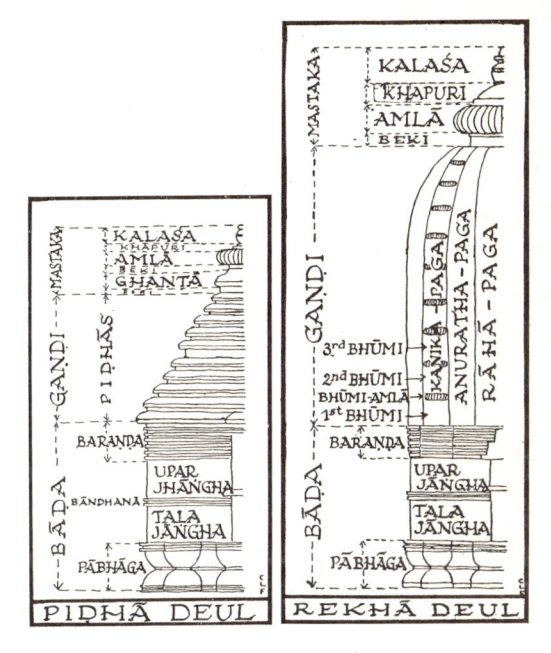

The names of the architectural elements of a nagara, *temple, and in particular of the one at Bhubaneshwar in Orissa.*

Sanctuaries, Monasteries, and Temples.

The art of excavating and carving the living rock was pursued in India for over 1000 years. These centuries were marked by great and unusual works, carved deep into the heart of the mountains. It was a long period of synthesis in the plastic arts, because architecture, sculpture, and painting were all combined, in the hands of extraordinary artists, into a single work. Almost all the important religious monuments between the third or second century BC and the ninth or tenth century AD are caves and a total of some 1200 are known in the peninsula as a whole. The major ones are at Bhaya, Karli, Kanheri, Bedsa, Nasik, Udayagiri, Aurangabad, Bagh, and, above all, Ajanta, Ellora, Badami, and Elephanta. Many of these caves are in Maharashtra and in certain parts of central India. The architectural sculptures of Mahabalipuram in the south are not underground but in the open-air. They are ridges carved to form temples and subsequently they became the stylistic models for all Dravidian temple architecture.

Although temples and palaces cut into the rock first occurred in Egypt (the Tombs of the Kings, the Temples of Abu Simbel) and later at Petra and then in Persia, the cave art of India only really got under way at the time of the Maurya dynasty in the third century BC, just after Alexander the Great's expedition to Asia. The Chinese caves of the Six Dynasties and the Tang dynasty, as well as the colossal Buddha at Yungkang, clearly display Indian influence.

The first sculptors were the monks of the Buddhist and Jain sects, at the time of the appearance of sophism, the metaphysical schools, and the ascetic sects. They were men inspired by the philosophy of renunciation and 'retreat into the forest', in search of the fusion of Nature with the Whole, but also by the yearning to 'shelter in the forest to escape from the brutality of the cities' — at a time of profound crisis and difficulties. In the middle of the millennium, with the decline of Buddhism and the renaissance of Brahmanism, the prestige of the *sannyasi*, the

Hindu monk, in harmony with the ideals of religious education of the priestly caste, increased. 'The power of the brahmin derived from the ardour of his ascetic practices, and the desire for heroic spiritual exercise drove thousands of men and women into the forest at the time of the spiritual revolution' (Deleury).

Initially, the monks lived on their own but later the rock cave centres grew and their excavation involved whole teams of stone-cutters who were famous for their skill, supported by the patronage of rich merchants and rulers. Gradually the hermitages became places of pilgrimage for the laity, despite their isolation and the wild animals that infested the forests around them. For the Hindus in particular, the forests were places of momentary retirement where they could practise exercises in meditation and penitence with the monks, before returning to their lay existence and the activities of man.

The architecture of the caves is complex and although on the one hand it exhibits an extraordinary richness of formal imagery and is designed to meet the cult and liturgical rules, on the other it answers the practical requirements and the community life of the monks. In it one can clearly see the symbolic and stylistic characters of the art of various periods, the Gupta and post-Gupta period, the transition from Hinayana Buddhism, with its monastic rigour, to Mahayana Buddhism, which places more emphasis on ritual and the cult. However, with the subsequent involvement of Hindus the formal and iconographic variety is accentuated by the strong expressive requirements of the Brahmanic world in the ritual and representation of the celestial myths. It is with Brahmanism that Indian art in the artificial caves (the same is also true of 'built' architecture) reaches the peak of its formal and expressive possibilities and it does so in conjunction with bold spatial solutions of the architecture carved out of the rock, which are right at the structural limits of the technique.

The most constant Buddhist spatial forms, which became models and standard types that were to influence even Hindu architecture, are the *chaitya*, a broad basilican hall, and the *vihara*, a monastery with individual cells and chapterhouses. The ornamentation in Buddhist sanctuaries is more sober and static than in Brahmanical ones, where the sculpture and ornamental motifs often display exuberant and fantastic forms. The columns and capitals are adorned with ever more elaborate ornamental motifs. The rock art of the early period (Bedsa, Bhaja, and certain caves at Ajanta) continues to copy the forms used in wooden buildings — wood being a widely used building material at the time — or added the bare symbol of the *stupa*, the hemispherical or bell-shaped reliquary tumulus of early Buddhism, which was originally always positioned in the open. In Mahayana Buddhism the image of the Buddha appears. Previously he had never been represented other than by symbols but now he appears in various yogic postures lying down at the moment of death (*paranirvana*). The forms emphasize themselves and become more eloquent; in addition to the Buddha the figures of the *bodhisattva* start to appear, and sometimes statues of rulers and other patrons of the sanctuaries. At Ajanta (and also at Ellora and Badami, although the wall paintings have now almost completely disappeared) the monasteries were full of colour and great frescos, which represented the Buddhist community and illustrated the life of the great cities of the period. The peaceful iconography of Buddhism gave way, at Ellora and the temple of Kailash in particular, to the grandiose and irrepressible visions of the cult of Shiva and the Brahminic pantheon. It was during this so-called late period, from the sixth century onwards, that the great monumental complexes of Ajanta, Ellora, Badami, and Elephanta, which mark the full maturity of cave art, were created.

In these works India developed its most original contribution to the language and forms of sacred architecture and indeed there is perhaps nothing else in Indian art or indeed in the rest of Asia which achieves the same originality of vision and

The three-headed bust of Shiva Mahadeva, carved from the rock in the cave at Elephanta (from Dubois and Raymond, 1846).

formal capacity as these artificial caves. At the beginning of the second millennium cave art disappeared completely but the Hindu cults retained, and still do, the myth of the pregnant image of the cavern, intended to receive the emblem of the divinity. In 'built' architecture it was to be the *garbha-griha* (literally womb or uterus), the centre of the Hindu temple, on which the acts of devotion and ritual would converge. This in fact was a tiny, underground cell with no light and resembled a cave going deep into a mountain. Almost all the monastic centres were abandoned and some were forgotten for centuries and invaded by the jungle, becoming a lair for wild animals; they were only rediscovered, quite by chance, in the last century. In 1819 a group of British officials making a tour of the uninhabited central regions stumbled across an enormous complex of rock caves, which were called Ajanta after the name of a nearby village. The monastic centre of Ajanta comprises twenty-nine artificial caves, basilican halls, chapterhouses, and monks' cells, richly adorned with sculptures and elaborate decoration, particularly on the facades. However, the greatest discovery was an entire cycle of wall paintings, which, by itself, is the greatest masterpiece of Indian pictorial art. The paintings can be dated to between the first century BC and the seventh century AD and at that time covered almost all the walls of the monastery. Those that have survived are sufficient to give us a complete record of the painting of ancient India. The technique used is fresco, with the successive application of either secco or tempera colours and the subject matter comprises edifying scenes from the last life of the Buddha or from his earlier lives, taken from the *Jataka*, the ancient Buddhist tales. The art of Ajanta reveals the daily life of the refined society of the Gupta period, through stories which are simultaneously told in the form of friezes along the walls of the vihara. The figures are given relief not by chiaroscuro, which was unknown to Indian painters, but by modelling them, hollowing out the flat surface. The human figure predominates, with a few glimpses of the countryside and buildings. Men and women crowd the pictures in a great variety of postures, bringing life, movement, and grace to every scene. The frescos at Ajanta were not the work of one-off painters but of corporations of artisans and schools of painting. The importance of Ajanta is underlined by the very few paintings, either before or after this period, which have survived in India and which can offer an exhaustive picture of the history and evolution of Indian pictorial art.

Not far from Ajanta is the other great monumental example of cave architecture, Ellora, where there are thirty-four caves carved out between the sixth and tenth centuries AD and subdivided into three groups: the Buddhist group, the oldest one; the Brahmanical one; and the Jain one. Amidst these there is the most extraordinary piece of rock architecture in India, an immense monolithic temple dedicated to Shiva, and carved out of the living rock in a form which represents the sacred Kailash — hence it is called the temple of the Kailash, the paradise of Shiva. Proceeding from the top of the mountain to the bottom, thousands of stone cutters carved out the entire temple (200 feet long, 100 feet wide and 100 feet high); the result is a free-standing monolithic block of rock, of which the inner and outer surfaces, sculptures, and bas reliefs are treated as a single, total vision. Another major work and an example of the great capacity for artistic synthesis is the Great Cave of Elephanta, on an island in the bay of Bombay. Inside it, amongst the reliefs which depict the major manifestations of Shiva Mahadeva, is the gigantic, triple head of Shiva Mahesamurti, whose faces represent the three fundamental manifestations of the god as creator, preserver, and destroyer. According to Malraux, the Shiva of Elephanta is not only 'one of the most beautiful statues in India... but first of all the unique creation by which the Shiva of Elephanta is also the symbol of India'.

The sculpture-architecture of Mahabalipuram, a few hundred miles south of Madras, another example of fully mature rock carving, also dates from the seventh century, and is contemporary with the Kailash of Ellora. Besides the masterly relief of 'The Descent of the Ganga', a short distance away, there are five temples carved out of granite ridges, called *ratha* (processional carts), which are dedicated to the five Pandava brothers, heroes of the *Mahabharata*. The largest ratha, called Yudhishtira or Dharmaraja, displays marked affinities in its form and lay-out with the famous temple of Kailash at Ellora. Smaller in size, the Dharmaraja represents the most complete model of the formal, ritual, and cosmological principles which are at the root of Indian architecture and in particular its form is the result of the projection of the plan based on the *mandala*, the cosmic diagram.

In this survey of the development of Indian sacred architecture, rock cut architecture has deliberately been kept separate from 'built' architecture. This has focused attention on the extraordinary originality of the rock excavations, which have produced a human and artistic experience that is perhaps unique in the world. However, from the point of view of chronology, styles, and cultural cross-references, we must recall that this art is clearly interwoven with the history of built architecture, with which there is an intense cultural and formal exchange. Although the earliest examples of buildings that have survived are Buddhist, the full development of built temple architecture coincided with the period of the Brahmanical renaissance, about half-way through the first millennium. At this

The Shore Temple at Mahabalipuram (engraving by W. Daniell, 1834).

point two distinct architectural styles arose. The first of these is the 'style of the north', also called *nagara*, whose major centres are Bhubaneshwar and Khajuraho, although examples are found all over the north. The distinctive feature of the northern style is the *shikhar*, a prominent tower with a square base, curving up to a flat, round summit. At the base of the shikhar, on its vertical axis, is the cell which contains the emblem of the divinity (in Shaivite temples it is usually the *lingam*). Another particular feature of the nagara style is a rectangular hall preceding the sanctuary called the *jagmohan*. The second style is the 'style of the south' or *dravida*, whose development runs between the two poles of the monolithic ratha of Mahabalipuram of the Pallava in the seventh century AD and the tower sanctuary of Thanjavur of the Chola dynasty in the eleventh century before exhausting itself in the art of the Vijayanagar, the last dynasty to have left its mark throughout southern India, particularly in the temple-cities. The striking features of Dravidian architecture are the *vimana*, a central, pyramidal structure standing above the sanctuary of the divinity; the *mandapa*, a columned portico with a flat roof used to shelter pilgrims to the temple; and the *gopura*, the entrance towers standing along the circuits of walls of temple-cities. The latter are pyramidal and sometimes climb to dizzying heights.

Indian sculpture, which is so intimately connected with the evolution of the temple, is far from simply decorating the architecture. Its fundamental purpose is the illustration of doctrine and the depiction of myths and divinities. Bharbut, Sanchi, and Amaravati, and the later caves of Ajanta and Ellora, contain the most beautiful examples of bas-relief. Sculpture in the round appeared in India for the first time in the third century BC and in the north, at the beginning of the first millennium, the Hellenistic school of Gandhara emerged, developing an art that was partly Graeco-Roman in derivation but which was predominantly employed on Buddhist temples and images. The period of the Kushana dynasties is characterized by the Mathura school but the classic period in bas-relief and sculpture in the round was the flourishing Gupta and post-Gupta epoch, which produced the most beautiful figures of the Buddha in the whole of Asia. Further south, the classic period coincided with the Pallava and Chola dynasties. Under the Chola in particular the greatest expressive possibilities of bronze sculpture were reached in a series of extraordinary works depicting, amongst others, Shiva

Mural from the cave at Bagh, in Madhya Pradesh.

Nataraja in the full movement of his cosmic dance.
Sanchi, commissioned by the Buddhist Emperor Ashoka Maurya, was one of the major Buddhist monasteries and a sacred object of pilgrimage. Amidst the archaeological remains of the monastery, the *stupas* still stand intact on the hillsides. These reliquary tumuli were venerated symbols of the doctrine of the Englightened One and geometrical projections of the Buddhist cosmology. The beauty of the stupas (they date from the first century BC) is not only the result of the geometrical perfection of the hemispherical bell but also derives from the balustrades and portals which surround the walkway around the reliquary. The narrative bas-reliefs, carved on long stones with great decorative detail, illustrate episodes from the life of the Buddha (not yet represented as a human figure but with symbols: the *pipal* tree, the ceremonial umbrella, the stupa itself).
The basic prototypes of Hindu architecture in the medieval period are the temples of Pattadakal and Aihole (also Badami, although this is cut into the rock), the ancient capitals of the Chalukya kingdoms from the sixth to the eighth century AD. Taken as a whole the old capitals form a vast architectural anthology, offering a variety of styles and spatial solutions, models for the later nagara and Dravidian architecture. The most beautiful examples of Jain architecture are the Dilwara temples of Mount Abu in Rajasthan. Inside they exhibit highly elaborate marble work, based on overlapping mandalic-geometric figures which illustrate the projections of Jain cosmology and the magic *yantra* diagrams.
The name of Bhubaneshwar in Orissa is associated with some thirty temples, almost all Shaivite, the last remnants of the 7000 which stood there in the seventh century AD. They represent various stages in development, from the beginnings to mature classicism — from the seventh to the fourteenth century — of northern religious architecture. They were built in accordance with a rigorous architectural treatise, the *Shilpa-prakasha*. This architecture — without a facade and lacking in perspective — is inspired by symbolism and geometry, in which the dominant feature is the tall sikhar tower, which metaphorically represents a 'peak' or 'flame'.
The even more famous temples of Khajuraho, the sacred city of the Chandela dynasty, owe their fame principally to the erotic figures which adorn the outer walls of the temple. Built in the eleventh centuries the temples of Khajuraho, like those of Bhubaneshwar, are regarded as the masterpieces of northern medieval architecture. The names of the different parts of the nagara temple bear witness to its symbolic and metaphorical identity with the human body, the temple being the 'architectural repeat of the cosmic body of the Purusha'. The reliefs, projections of Tantric rites of esoteric sects, are based on the cult of the 'mystic' union of Shiva with his 'shakti'. Khajuraho, together with Konarak in Orissa, is one of the most extraordinary monuments of Tantric art; the *mithuna* (pairs of lovers) of the reliefs along the walls of the temples reflect the ancient cosmic concepts of the Tantra. Erotic figures were confined to esoteric cults, who thought of sexuality as the highest peak of existence and by ritualizing it took it as a means of self-realization and liberation. These cults practised a religion of 'ecstasy' in which sexual activity plays a central role and expresses an ideal model of perfect union with the divine. The isolated, giant temple of Konarak, built by the Ganga dynasty in the thirteenth century, is dedicated to Surya, a divinity which personifies the sun and was subsequently identified with Vishnu. Its form symbolizes the chariot of the sun, a typical Hindu concept of the cycles and cosmogony of the universe.
Southern architecture's masterpiece is the *vimana* (sanctuary-tower) of the temple of Brihadishwara at Thanjavur. Dating from the eleventh century, it is the pinnacle of the Chola's achievement in the art of building, although the dynasty was also responsible for all the great temples of the south. It is a daring pyramid

structure, rising thirteen storeys to a granite monolith weighing some eighty tons. The temples of the Hoyshala dynasty, the most beautiful and best preserved of which are the sanctuaries of Belur, Halebid, and Somnathpur, belong to the *ersara* form of the dravida style. They are famous for their highly refined sculptures running in continuous bands along the outer walls; but the temples are also distinctive in their form. Both in plan and elevation they are governed by an elaborate geometrical calculation of a star-shaped plan.

The final phase of southern architecture saw the completion of the great temple-cities. These are not homogenous pieces of architecture based on a single plan. Instead their building lasted centuries and the various dynasties which followed each other made differing stylistic and cultural contributions. Many art historians maintain that the southern art of the sixteenth and seventeenth centuries displays decadent character. The elaborate decoration of the gigantic tower and the profusion of sculpture inside lack the religious and aesthetic force which was such a feature of the plastic ornamentation of the temples of preceding periods. According to others this architecture does not deserve the harsh judgment of the historians; the grand scale, the cosmic feeling in the building of the 'city of god', as they maintain, comparable to the great structures of the Gothic cathedrals of Europe with their universe of symbols and myths, and is the product of centuries of culture and popular religion.

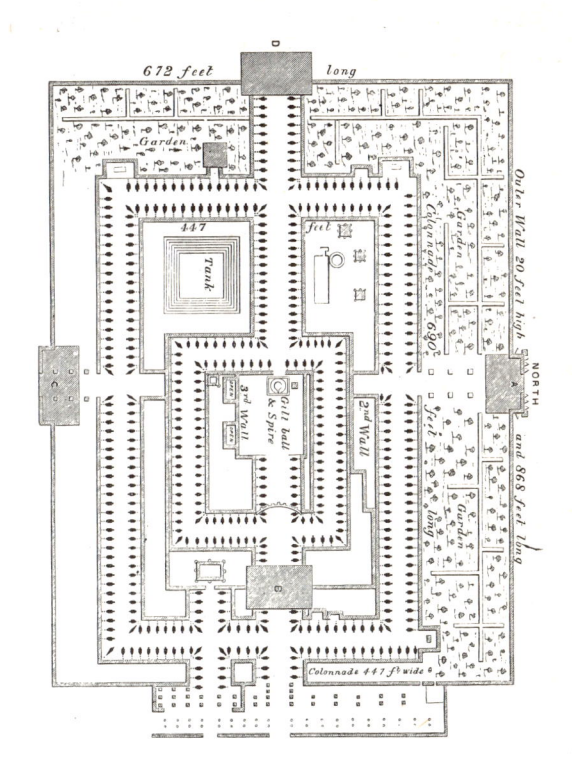

A drawing of the ground plan of the southern temple at Rameswaram (by J. Fergusson, 1876).

Indo-Islamic Architecture and Art

Of the various Islamic arts, architecture is clearly the most important. There are various reasons for this but most fundamental seems to be the prohibition in Muslim law of the depiction of figures or representational images, which has fettered the development of painting and sculpture whilst favouring the art of building. In the religious sphere, it is absolutely forbidden to depict the human figure and as a result mosques and other religious edifices turned to a refined decorative art marked by abstract and calligraphic geometrical patterns. All painting and drawing, portraits and miniatures are confined to the secular domain. This state of affairs holds true for India, although the Islam of India has not always been rigidly orthodox. Instead there have been ups and downs and all the great Mogul Emperors, with the exception of Aurangzeb, were regarded as deified beings and maintained legions of painters at court, for whom the emperor himself served as the highest model.

The aggressive cultural policy of Muslim society in India led to a radical change in literature, music, and especially in architecture, with the building of an enormous number of mosques, minarets, mausoleum, palaces, *madrasa* (theological schools), caravanserai, fortified citadels, and entire quarters of cities. Although Islamic architecture of the first period was still inspired by the styles of central Asia or by Persian or Turco-Afghan ones, during the Mogul epoch proper, and particularly under Akbar and Jahangir, the architecture incorporated Hindu stylistic elements and spatial arrangements, producing a new tradition which is referred to as 'Indo-Islamic'. What was absolutely new to India was that the invaders brought with them original forms and bold techniques, based on mathematical calculations and sophisticated geometrical concepts of space, which allowed spatial solutions never seen before in the peninsula. Such features include the dome resting on a drum, vaulting, and pointed arches, all of which created new spatial features both inside and outside buildings, leading to changes in the Indian townscape. Hemispherical or bulbous domes for mosques or tombs, wings with pointed arches and lattice-work screens, and tall minarets mushroomed after the turn of the millenium in Indian cities, particularly in the north. The greatest successes of Muslim

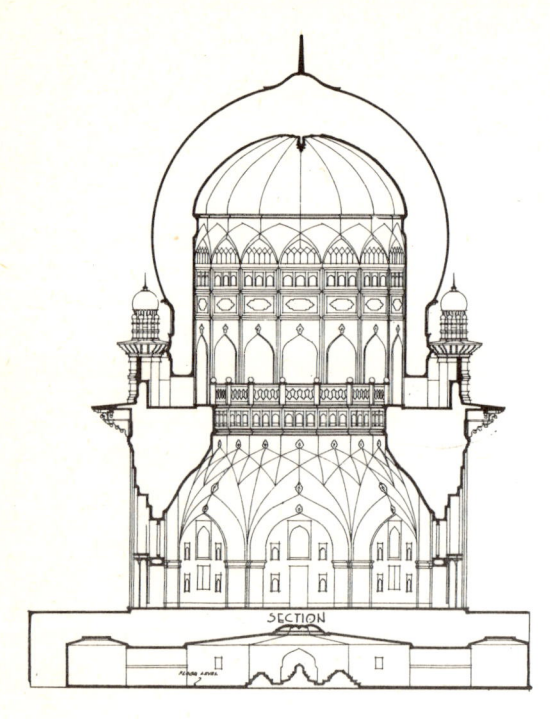

Section drawing of the Islamic mausoleum at Bijapur (by C. Batley, 1934).

architecture are almost always in an urban setting. Islam, which is essentially a town-based religion, found a genuine partner in urban architecture, often turning what was merely a collection of buildings into a true city. The palaces, mosques, porticoes, covered markets, and squares of cities such as Lucknow, Hyderabad, and Bhopal are examples of Muslim architectural mastery and of its important cultural contribution to India.

The oldest architectural complex in India, the Qutb Minar and the Quwwat-ul-Islam mosque, is at Delhi. The tall minaret, which is perhaps the most beautiful in India, was built during the reign of the first dynasty of the Sultanate of Delhi in the twelfth century. The red sandstone tower has a star-shaped plan and was intended, as a superb inscription tells us, 'to throw the shadow of God on the east and on the west'. At its base lies the vast mosque, which incorporates materials from Hindu and Jain temples destroyed by the Muslims. Even this early building shows clear signs of a blending of styles (Hindu workmen were employed) and the fusion of two different ways of conceiving architectural form. The architecture of the period of the Sultanate of Delhi and of its peripheral sultanates (Gulbarga, Jaunpur, Mandu) was inspired by Persian and Turkish styles. Its buildings are distinguished by their simple and austere forms and by the great sense of proportion between the various parts, especially under the Tughlaq dynasty.

Fatehpur Sikri, the royal city built near Agra by the Emperor Akbar in about 1570, is the first great architectural undertaking of the Mogul dynasty. Although abandoned after a few years when the court moved to Lahore, the city has remained virtually intact over the centuries. It is a vast collection of different styles and spatial forms, including a considerable Hindu contribution, and it is the greatest example of the architectural eclecticism of the period of Akbar. Built almost entirely of red sandstone, the city comprises a number of palaces several storeys high grouped around two great courts, with private apartments, areas for recreation, the extraordinary small audience chamber, the vast, open mosque which has at its centre the exquisite white marble pavilion forming the tomb of Salim Chisti, the Sufi saint who was the emperor's guru. Fatehpur Sikri, both in its plan and elevation, is an example of an organic spatial organization based on rigorous geometrical concepts, which bear witness to the high level of the architecture of the period.

Numerous mausoleums were built in India during the Islamic period. These included the tomb of Humayun in Delhi, whose Persian-style dome was later to be the model for another, more important tomb, the famous Taj Mahal at Agra, which is the greatest masterpiece of Muslim architecture in India and is known and admired around the world. It was built by the Emperor Shah Jahan in memory of his wife Mumtaz Mahal, who died young in childbirth. Work began in 1632 and according to a contemporary witness, the French merchant J.B. Tavernier, took twenty-two years of intense activity involving thousands of workers, including inlayers, marble carvers, engravers, and mosaic artists. It is not certain who was responsible for the design; the names of the Turkish architects Ustad Isa or Isa Mohammed Effendi and the Venetian architect Geronimo Veroneo are known, although the last of these would only have been involved in laying out the gardens. The Taj Mahal was built of white marble from Makrana in Rajasthan and, according to C. Tucci, stands 'in the evolutionary line of Mogul architecture and its features are such as to indicate that it is the fruit of a fusion between the taste and techniques of the Orient on the one side and those of the Christian West on the other'.

Shah Jahan was passionately fond of architecture and he often imposed his personal tastes on the style of buildings. He established an era of great structures which came to be called the 'kingdom of marble'. No sooner were the palaces and pavilions of the fort of Agra finished than the court moved to Delhi, where a new palace, the Qila or Red Fort, was built and a city which was to bear the name of Shajahanabad was planned. The palace is a citadel of gigantic proportions with fortified outer walls enclosing palaces, colonnaded pavilions, baths, fountains and gardens, and on all sides precious, inlaid marble decorated with arabesques. In the fort at Delhi there is a return to the orthodoxy of the Persian Safawidi styles. Garden design is an art that was particularly cultivated by the Mogul dynasty, beginning with Babar, the first emperor, and it displays a vast range of layouts and spatial forms, as in the gardens of Lahore, Srinagar, the fort at Agra, and the Taj Mahal. This art, which reaches its maturity in the fort at Delhi, harmoniously integrates the values of landscape with the functional rules which govern the layout of the entire complex. The Diwan-i-Khan, the private audience chamber, contains extremely beautiful marble inlays. In India inlay is called *manabhat-kari*, after the hard Indian stone which in Europe is called 'Florentine'. The art of marble inlay with precious or semi-precious stones was patronized by the Mogul Emperors and used in the great projects of the period, including the Taj Mahal and the palaces of the Agra and Delhi forts. One of the most refined examples is found in the small Itimaud-ud-Daula mausoleum in Agra. The Koranic texts on the outside of the Taj are inlaid in the *tughara* style of ornamental Arabic calligraphy.

Paradoxically, the true heirs of Indo-Islamic art are the Hindu Rajput races of Rajasthan, a land of feudal rulers who were once fierce opponents of the Islamic invaders. However, in the final period they became allies of the imperial dynasty through a series of marriages with Mogul princes. Beside a certain similarity in customs, the cultural and formal result of these alliances can be seen in the royal citadels of the ancient caravan cities of the deserts of Rajasthan. However, the Rajputs do retain numerous elements from their original culture from before the Muslim invasion, even though many stylistic and architectural features have been fused with contributions fron the new culture. The result is found in splendid, fortified royal palaces, with their typical cupolas and rich eclectic ornament, vaulted halls covered with mosaics of small, convex mirrors, lattice-work windows and screens. In the middle of the arid Thar desert stands what is perhaps the most beautiful of all the Rajput cities of Rajasthan, Jaisalmer. Still in perfect condition, the city forms a rich anthology of Rajput art and architecture, since work on it continued from its foundation in the thirteenth century up until the last century. Jaisalmer is a fully mature example of Rajput art and architecture, which reflects not only the particular climatic and environmental demands of the desert but also the complex formal and decorative projections of a refined culture. Some of the most elaborate buildings are the *haveli*, highly decorated palaces of the great merchant families.

Towards the end of the sixteenth century Indian painting found new life in the Mogul courts; and in particular the art of portraiture, which was introduced to India by Akbar. Jahangir, his successor, was even fonder of it than his father and his reign saw this art reach the height of its popularity. Under Akbar there was even a certain amount of influence from the art of Renaissance Europe, especially Italian, on Indian painters, who were influenced by the pictures and portraits which were presented in homage to the Emperor by travellers and Jesuit missionaries. The Emperor valued them greatly and ordered his painters to copy them. Mogul paintings, which are mainly miniatures on a full page, often reflect the taste and personality of the various sovereigns and the official life of the court, with great importance being attached to the figure of the Emperor, who was portrayed in his palace, in large hunting parties or in the midst of his troops drawn up for battle.

Although Mogul painting is aristocratic, academic, austere, and eclectic, Rajput

A Mogul prince in the middle of a group of palace women (from Dubois and Raymond, 1846).

The Taj Mahal at Agra (by W. Daniell, 1834).

painting, although it too is aristocratic, is also popular and lyrical. It reflects a more authentically Indian way of life and responds to Indian sensibilities in its colour values and in its exquisitely religious themes. The greatest source of inspiration for Rajput art, which was at its peak in the seventeenth and eighteenth centuries, is the poetic world of the god Krishna. The principal themes of Rajput painting are taken from poems which tell of the life and loves of Krishna; the *Bhagavata Purana* and the *Gitagovinda*. In the north various distinct traditions with their own characteristics developed, although they were inspired by shared cultural and aesthetic criteria. They included the Mewar, Bundi, Kotah, and Malwa schools. Later, *pahari* painting, 'of the mountains', became very important, particularly the Kangra and Basohli schools; its subject matter is almost always religious and it centres on the figure of the god Krishna.

Dance, Music, and Literature

In the past dance was essentially religious in function and all the great temples had a pavilion reserved for dancing within their sacred precinct. The *devadasi*, 'handmaidens of god', the dancers 'dedicated' to the temples danced and sang in the religious celebrations and in the processions. As a ritual function in the more important temples, the dancers were also involved in sacred prostitution. In the last century, as a result of a campaign by British and Indian moral reformers, the figure of the devadasi was officially abolished. The recent revival of dance that has occurred throughout India has produced various important innovations, although this revival is purely cultural and the religious and cult connections which dance had in antiquity have largely been lost. The Bharata Natyam, the 'classical' dance of India, is inspired by the 'treatise of dance, music, and the theatre', the *Natya Shastra*, composed by the 'wise Bharata', possibly at the beginning of the first millennium. The treatise deals with 108 basic figures (*karana*) and codifies the movements of the body, which may be upright or bent positions, the undulations of the body, the expressions of the face, and above all the vast range of gestures with the hand (*mudra*). Every movement is a 'sign', an expression, message, emotion, or formalized taste (*rasa*) and these signs linked together form an expressive language, whose subject matter is generally religious and connected with the narration of the myths. In the past there were also male dancers and epic and erotic characters were introduced, although the dance still maintained its religious character. In the modern versions the erotic elements, which were traditionally expressed in esoteric rites, have disappeared. Dance is taught from a very young age by masters of various schools and it requires total dedication. The period of apprenticeship is marked by the typical discipline of the discipline of the Yoga. The Bharata Natyam originated in the south in the ancient cultural centres of the Chola: Thanjavur, Madurai, and Chidambar. In the last of these there is a great temple dedicated to Shiva Nataraja, 'King of the Cosmic Dance', who is regarded as the divine model of the dance. The bas-reliefs of the temple illustrate in stone the figures which form the expressive vocabulary of Indian dance.

The other religious dance is the Kathakali, which originated in Kerala. It is a work which fuses dance, music, drama, and pantomime with a narrative thread. The traditional Kathakali, which is more than 1500 years old, is a form of theatrical performance which developed from the needs of the brahminical caste, the Nambudiri, to transmit the religious message of the great epics and the mythological tales of Hinduism to the people. At the celebration of the religious mysteries in the festivities in honour of the god Krishna of the temple of Guruvayur in Kerala, the Krishnanayapattam, an ancient form of the Kathakali, is still performed. Over the last few centuries a specific literature has grown up, an anthology of poems sung during the execution of the Kathakali, known as the 'Aatta katha'. The dancers are subjected to a severe discipline and it takes fifteen years of daily exercises under the guidance of a master to train a dancer. The costumes, the masks, and the make-up, which are governed by highly detailed rules, are very elaborate and require hours of preparation. The principal roles of the Kathakali are distinguished by their costumes and their facial masks, which express the moral character of the figures by means of their colour and other symbols. The female, as well as the male parts, are all taken by men. There is no specific set, everything is conveyed by the rich masks and by the vast range of gestures, symbols, and signs which govern the development of the theatrical action. Two singers recount and comment on the unfolding of the tale. Drums, cymbals, and a small harmonium govern the rhythm of the movements. The stage area of the Kathakali is filled with various mythical characters, virtuous divinities and gods, saints, devils and evil figures, mythical birds, and various animals. It is, in essence, a titanic confrontation between gods and demons, between wise men and wicked ones, the arena of the eternal conflict between the *sat* and the *asat*, the true and the false. The performances take place in the open air, generally within the temple precincts, and they last all night, from dusk to the break of dawn.

There are other forms of dance in India. The Kathak is mainly concerned with the various legends of the loves of Krishna. It is divided into the schools of Jaipur and Lucknow. The Kuchipudi, a local dance which originated in a village in Andhra Pradesh, celebrates the religious mysteries connected with the Krishnaite mythology. The Manipuri from the northwest of India, where there are Tibetan and Burmese populations, is danced by men and women with a choral accompaniment.

All Indian artistic expression, whatever the form, is dominated by the same spiritual principle, in that the artist believes his art is the way through which he will realize the divine. Music is another means for such realization, and the song in particular is a *yantra*, an ecstatic means and technique. The ancient theoreticians of the Sanskrit language studied the nature of sensations, the essential forerunners of perceptions, the invisible signs of the human soul. A thousand years before Christ, Indian music was already governed by precise rules and complete theories were developed on its function. Music is laid down as an activity and language controlled by means of a *rasa* or 'taste', which gives the performance its dominant character and determines the quality. The *Natya Shastra* conceives of music as one of the various forms of art but in the later texts, such as the *Sangita Ratnakara*, it receives individual treatment. Indian music may be defined as a diatonic and modal system and at the same time a mathematical process of changes on the basis of a continuous re-elaboration of the fundamental elements, although the most immediately apparent aspect is its purely melodic nature. Like all melodic systems, Indian music was born out of its relationship with the human voice, which in the past was the Vedic song, the most ancient musical form. Vocal music, therefore, represents the high point of Indian music and the singer enjoys a pre-eminent position among musicians. The Indian musical scale is divided into twenty-two microtonal fixed intervals called *shruti*. The notes are called *swara*, of which there are seven main ones, the rest being marginal. There is also a sol-fa system, used for notation both of composition and vocal improvization, which is represented as *sa-ri-ga-ma-pa-dha-ni*. Combinations of a minimum of five and a maximum of seven swara form the scale on which every composition is built. The swara may occupy different positions and may be sharp or flat and this offers the theoretical possibility of an infinite variety of 'scales' or 'models'. The modal scales or models are called *raga*, a term which has been in use since the medieval period and which is derived from *ranj* meaning colour. As with chromatic values, it expresses the range of emotions evoked by each scale. Tradition lays down that each raga has its particular hour, day, and season, which correspond to particular states of mind or sensations. There are six basic ragas, from which all the others, classed either as male or female, are derived. The origins of Indian music go back to the Vedic period and the original forms have been preserved up to the present day and handed down by generations of great families and guilds of musicians. Two major schools developed, the *Hindustani* or northern school and the *Karnatic* or southern one. Although they share a common origin, they differ in stylistic features, musical forms, and the use of different musical instruments. The northern school has been influenced by the Islamic musical tradition, particularly in the Mogul period. In the northis the ancient vocal '*dhrupad*' tradition of songs in which the voice, like a musical instrument, covers a vast tonal range. The southern school produces longer compositions, with more elaborate musical forms.

There are numerous Indian musical instruments, perhaps even more than in Western music, even though Indian orchestral groups are composed of relatively few players. The most widespread string instruments are the sitar, the *sarod*, and the *sarangi*; whilst in the south the *vina*, similar to the sitar, is used. In the north, the most widespread percussion instrument is the *tabla*, a double drum, which is not simply used for accompaniment but as a means of expression in its own right. The commonest wind instruments include the bamboo flute, the *shahnai*, and a kind of oboe, whose southern version is the nagasvaram.

The rural and tribal world of India offers a rich variety of musical traditions, often connected with sacred representations and community dances. The figure of the strolling musician or singer is still common, moving from village to village and singing the mythological stories of the epics or the religious hymns of the mystic saints. Classical or cultured music is certainly distinct from the music of the popular tradition but the real difference between the two is in the quality of the performance rather than in the nature of the music itself.

Just as in other aspects of its culture, Indian language and literature displays an extraordinary variety. The census of India lists 844 languages and dialects spoken in the various parts of the country but there are in fact many more. If one groups the languages by the size of the ethnic groups one ends up with about 130. Of these, about a score are literary languages and are spoken by about 85 percent of the population of some 700 million. These enjoy the status of national languages, recognized officially by the constitution. Politically, the borders of each state of the federal union are drawn on the basis of the range of the major linguistic groups. There are also some thirteen different alphabets, including the Latin one, and numerous languages or dialects still lack a written form, whilst others are still in the process of developing one.

In general terms, the subcontinent may be divided into two major language groups, with a further two less important ones. Indo-Aryan languages cover the whole of northern and part of central India; Dravidian languages cover the south; Tibeto-Burmese languages occur along the northern borders with China and Burma; and Munda or 'Austro-Asiatic' languages are spoken by tribal minorities, particularly in central India.

Sanskrit is the classical and sacred language of India. It is closely related to the ancient 'avenstan' Persian, Latin, classical Greek, and the ancient Celtic languages. Virtually all the modern European and Indian languages derived from Sanskrit display more or less profound links, as was recognized by Sir William Jones in 1784. Sanskrit is not only the language spoken by the Indians of antiquity; it is also widely used today for literary works, as well as scientific studies and treatises.

Sanskrit traditionally begins with the *Vedas*, which were composed in an archaic Sanskrit defined as 'Vedic' that subsequently developed into classical Sanskrit with a rigorous grammatical structure. The tradition of the oral transmission of the *Vedas* during the early period of the formation of the language has permeated the character and style of this literature. The *Upanishads*, the epics of the *Mahabharata* and the *Ramayana*, the *Purana* and the *Tantra* were all composed in Sanskrit. Besides the philosophical and religious literature, all kinds of literary and scientific works flourished in Sanskrit, from lyric poetry to the theatre, from legend to novels, from treatises on the various sciences to those on the arts, from music to dance and architecture. The golden Gupta period saw the composition of the works of the grammarian Panini, of Patanjali, who codified the techniques of Yoga; the political work of Kautilya, the 'Indian Machiavelli'; Vatsyayana, who wrote the *Karma Sutra*; and Kalidasa, the master of the lyrical epic. The *Panchatantra* or 'Five Books' are the archetype of all Indo-European fables. From later periods, there are the poet and dramatist Harsha and the philosphers Shankaja and Ramanuja, who all wrote in Sanskrit, the Jayadeva lyric and mystical poets, Chaitanya and many others.

Sanskrit literature has continued unbroken for 3000 years, giving it the longest history of all the world's literature. During the first millennium of our era the 'language of the gods' retreated and became restricted to the intellectual and academic elite, whilst 'medieval Indian' languages, spurious and popular dialects, established themselves and, in a sense, opposed the hegemony of Sanskrit. Many Buddhist scriptures were composed in Pali, and Pakrit dialects spread through the north of the peninsula. These were later to give rise to the modern Indo-Aryan languages such as Hindi, Bengali, Marathi, Gujarati, Punjabi, Oriya, Assamese, Kashmiri, Maithili, and Urdu.

With its innumerable dialects, Hindi forms the largest group of languages spoken in northern India, comprising just under half the population. Hindi is spoken by a varied array of peoples with differing cultural and religious traditions and as a result of its widespread use it has ambitions to become the national language of India. As a language and literature, Hindi began to establish itself around AD 1000 but it was not until the twelfth century that it began to assume a dominant position. Under the Moguls Hindustani, a language with different roots, began to spread through northern India. Two variants of it were spoken. The first is an

71. Sculpture of a dvarapala, *or guardian of the temple, at the beginning of the portico of the 'thousand columns', inside the great temple of Madurai dedicated to the goddess Minakshi. In the background there is a great bronze chola which represents Shiva Nataraja, the 'God of the Dance'. Shiva is regarded as the husband of the goddess Minakshi and the festival of their marriage is celebrated every year. Madurai was an important centre for the Dravidian world and for Tamil culture and literature.*

On the following pages:

72. Great relief inside cave II in the rock cave complex of Ajanta.

Islamic one with an Indian grammar but a largely Persian and Arab vocabulary and a Persian alphabet. This is Urdu or the language of the 'orda' (military camp or bazaar), and was spoken by Muslim Indians, although not by all of them. The other form of old Hindustani was literary Hindi, which had a largely Sanskrit vocabulary and a Sanskrit alphabet known as *devanagari*. It was widespread throughout northern India for about 100 years, although the traditional regional dialects continued. The complex evolution of Hindi has not prevented the formation of a literary tradition of the highest level. Devotional religious poetry and the hymns of the mystical lyric poets have always been of great importance in Hindi, particularly in the fifteenth and sixteenth centuries: examples being the philosophical and religious works of Ramananda and the lyrics of Kabir and the poetess Mirabai. Subsequently Hindi literature diversified into prose, novels, essays, drama, literary criticism, and journalism.

The Dravidian languages form a massive and entirely separate block which extends over almost the whole of the Deccan. The oldest and richest literature culture amongst them is the Tamil. In the first century AD, when almost all the other modern Indian languages were still in the process of formation, Tamil had already achieved a high degree of maturity and was able to bar the expansion of Sanskrit. It was in fact the only language of the south, although it was influenced by the court language of the north, to remain virtually intact in its form and syntax for about two millennia. Tamil also gave rise to the other Dravidian languages of the south, such as Telegu, Malayalam, and Canarese. The languages have been more profoundly influenced by Sanskrit.

The first important Tamil literary works are lyric poems, followed by linguistic studies which laid down the grammar of Tamil in a definitive form. The most widely known classical text is the *Kural* or *Tirrukural*, based on a didactic ethical work composed in verse and attributed to Valluvar, who appears to have lived in the fifth century AD. The sacred *Kural* is regarded as the greatest masterpiece of Tamil literature and is admired for the perfection of its form, its conciseness, and the liveliness of its portrayals. The outstanding works of the oldest phase of Tamil literature are the verse pieces by the poets who together form the legendary figure of Sangam, and the epic romances inspired by Buddhism and Jainism. The literature of hymns is represented by a collection of hymns dedicated to Shiva by various poet saints of the bhakta tradition (sixth and seventh centuries BC) and by the Alvar, mystical Vaishnavite singers. The Tamil masterpiece, the *Ramayana* of Kamban, dates from the twelfth century, during the height of the Chola. In the course of its long period of development Tamil literature has been enriched with important works and treatises in the sciences, arts, linguistic, and other fields.

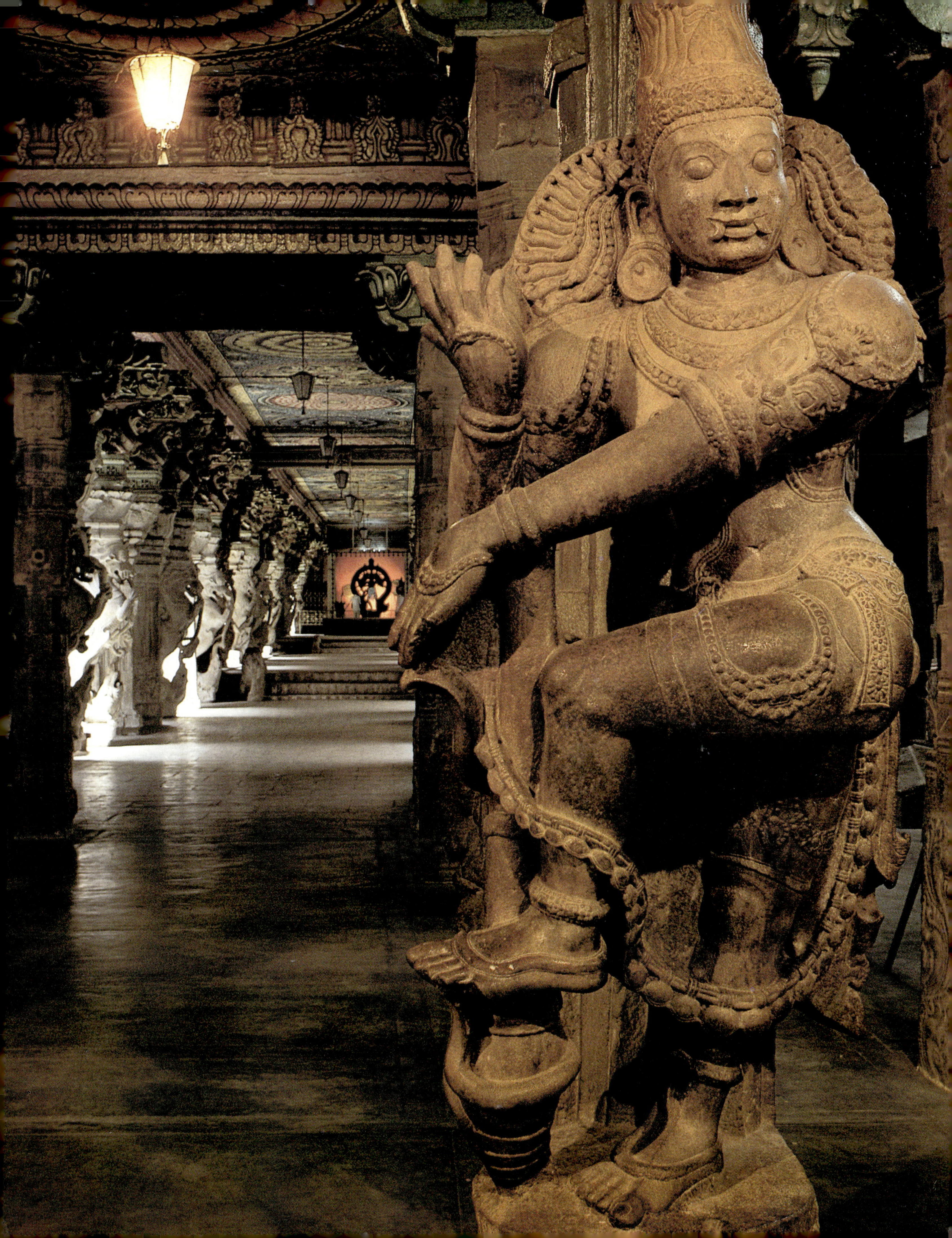

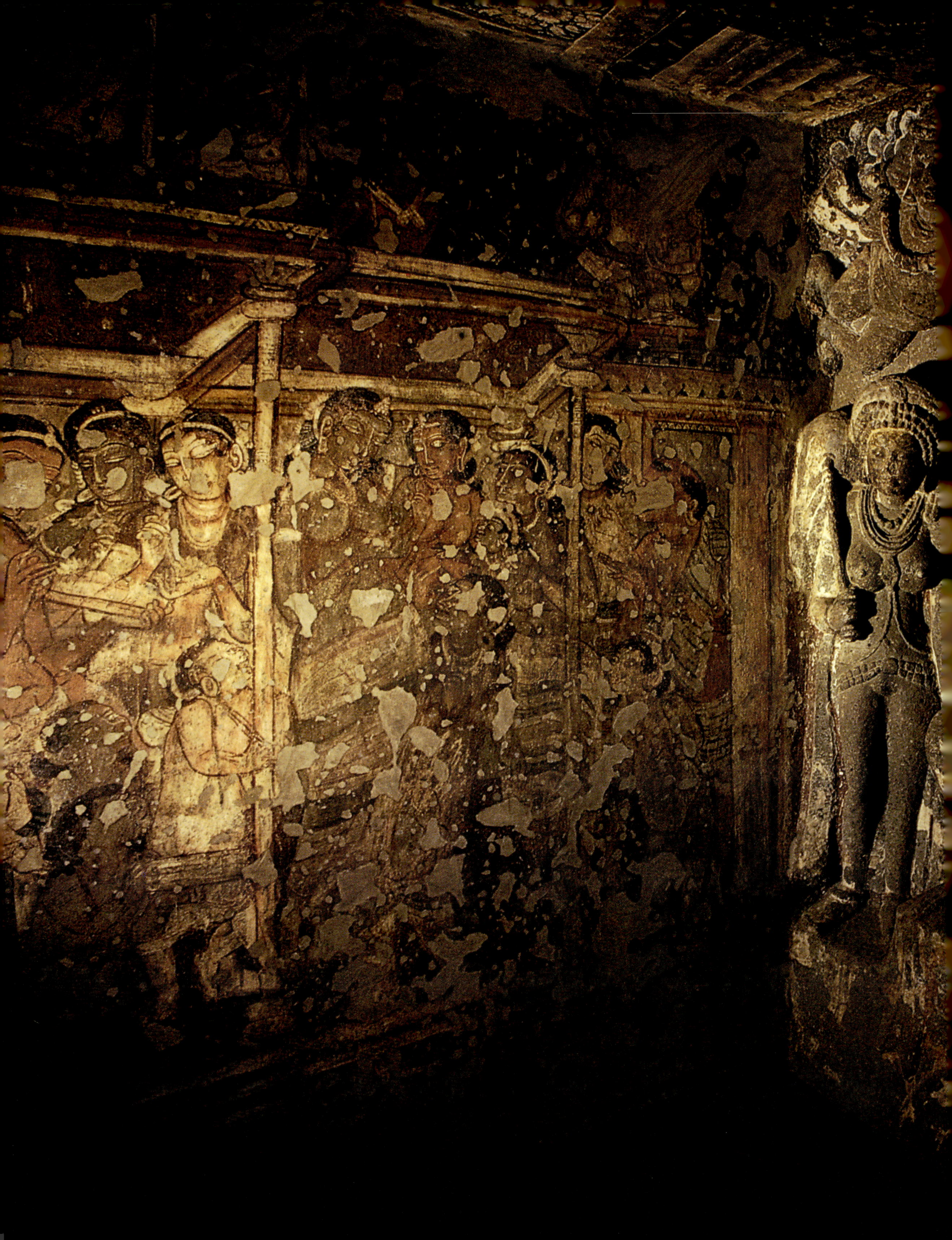

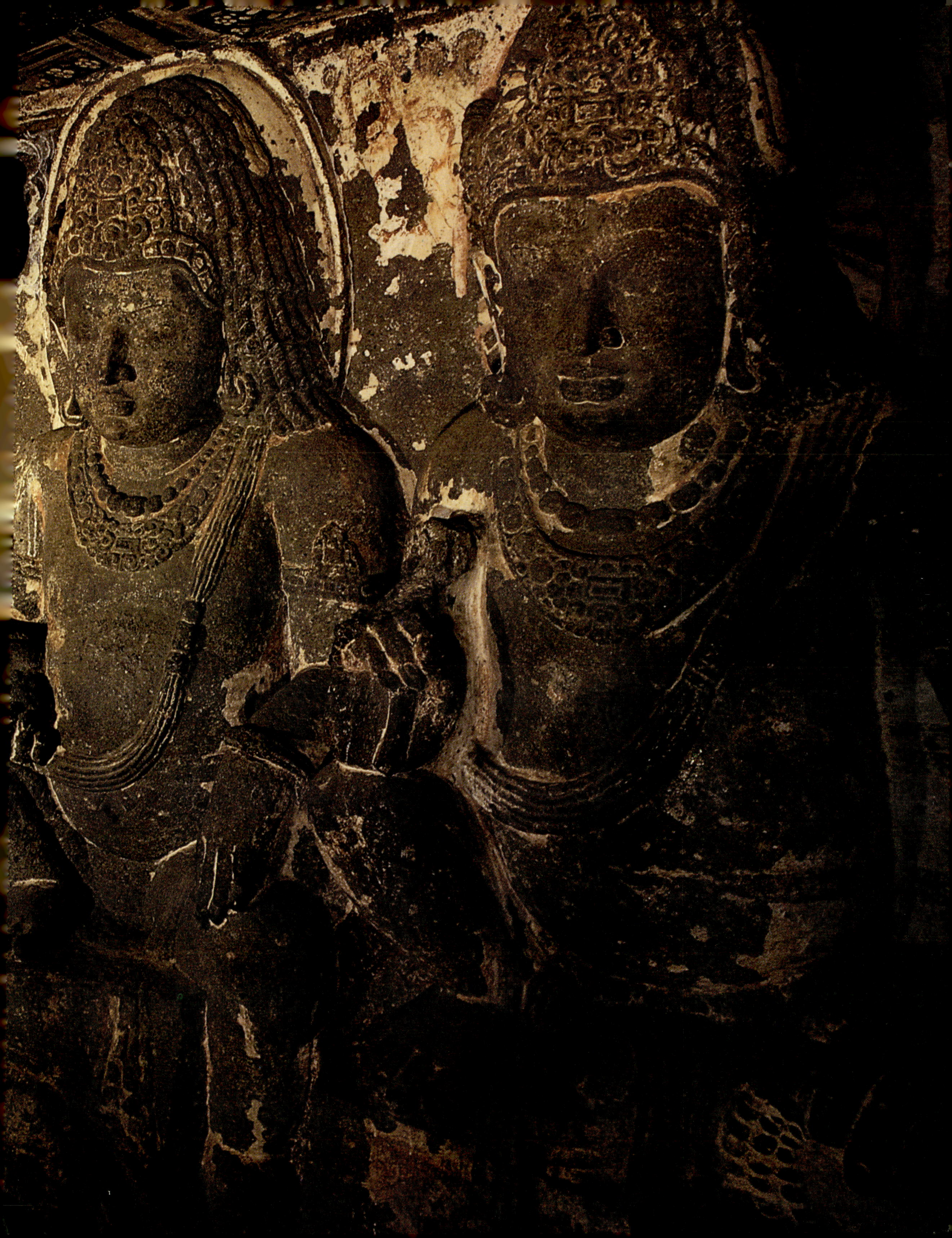

73

73. Buddha shown reclining at the moment of total extinction (paranirvana), in cave XXVI at Ajanta. The twenty-nine caves of Ajanta constitute one of the largest Buddhist monastic centres in Asia and they were occupied throughout the whole of the first millennium AD. Besides the beautiful sculptures of the Buddha and the bodhisattva (Buddhist saints), Ajanta is renowned for its well preserved wall paintings, which date from the first century BC to the seventh century AD.

74. The face of a sculpture of the Buddha cut into the monolithic stupa at cave II, Ellora. Not far from Ajanta, Ellora, is the other great centre of rock architecture, with temples and monasteries for monks and ascetics cut into the rock. It consists of separate groups of buildings belonging to three different religions, Buddhism, Hinduism, and Jainism.

On the following pages:

75. Wall painting in cave II at Ajanta with countless Buddhas representing the earlier lives of the Enlightened One.

76. The small temple of the lingam, the phallic symbol of the god Shiva, at the centre of the cave at Elephanta, with enormous statues of dvarapala at the sides.

77. The ruins of the great Buddhist university of Nalanda. Founded by a Gupta sovereign in the fifth century AD, Nalanda was for centuries a famous centre for the study of Mahayana Buddhism. It was destroyed in the twelfth century by the Muslim invaders.

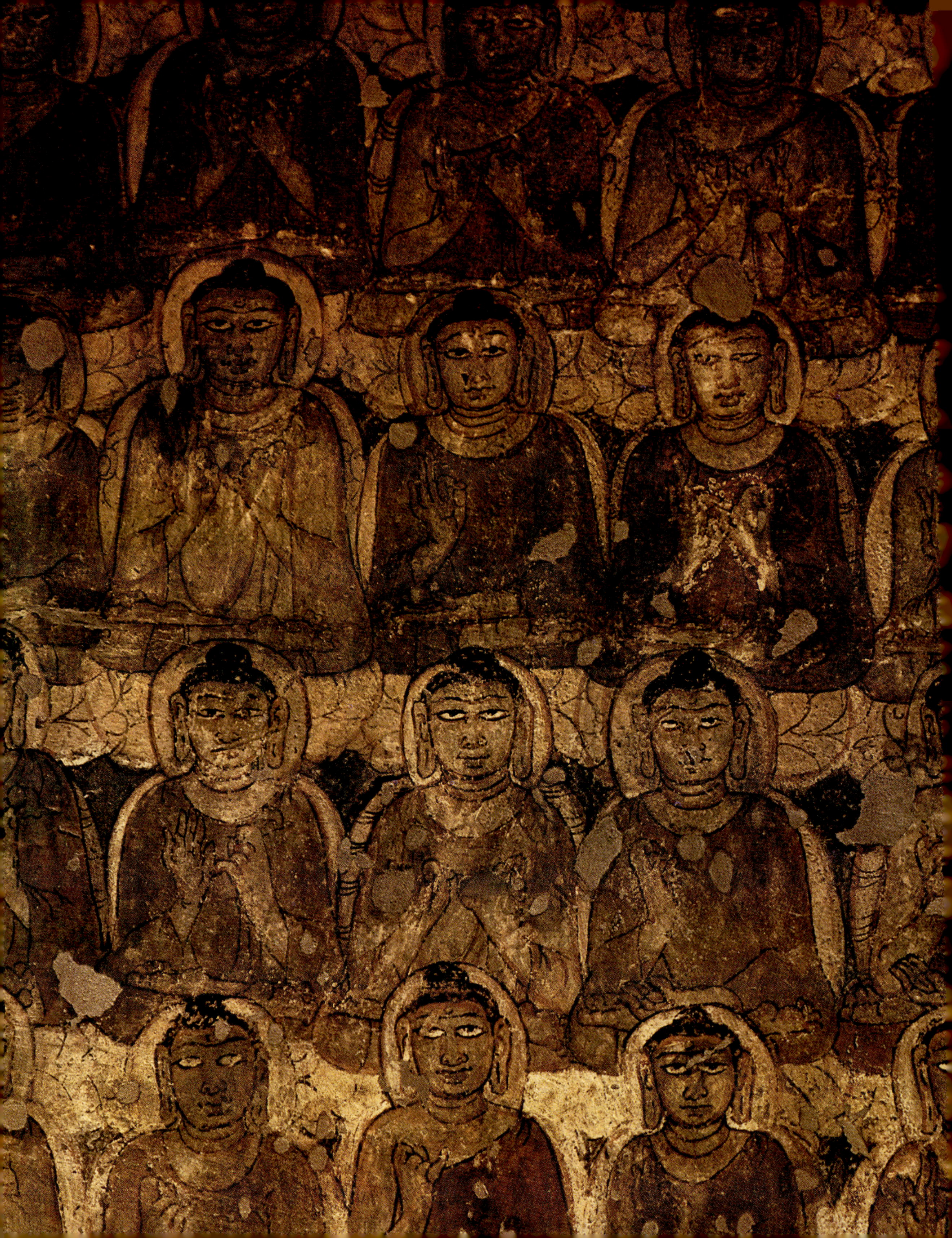

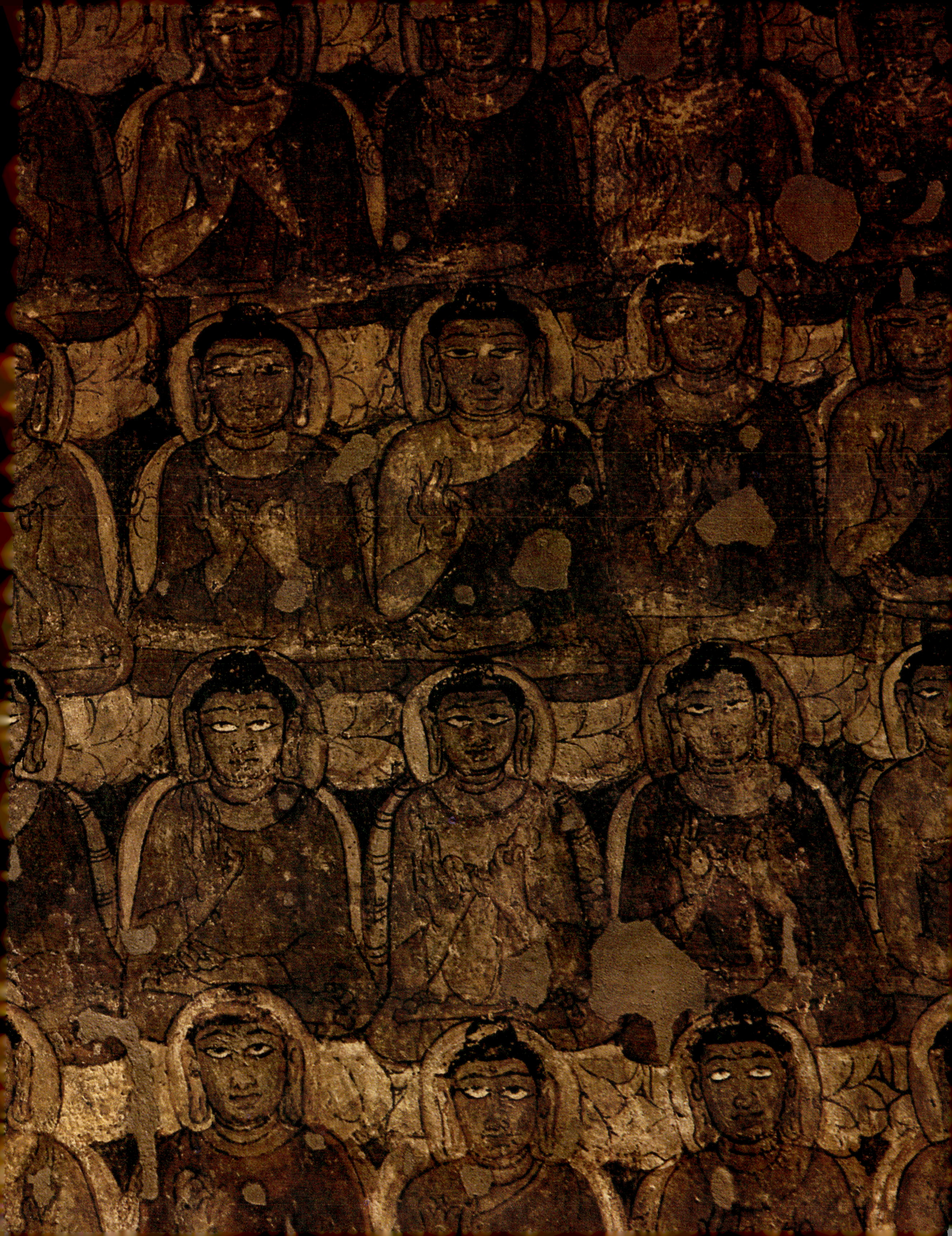

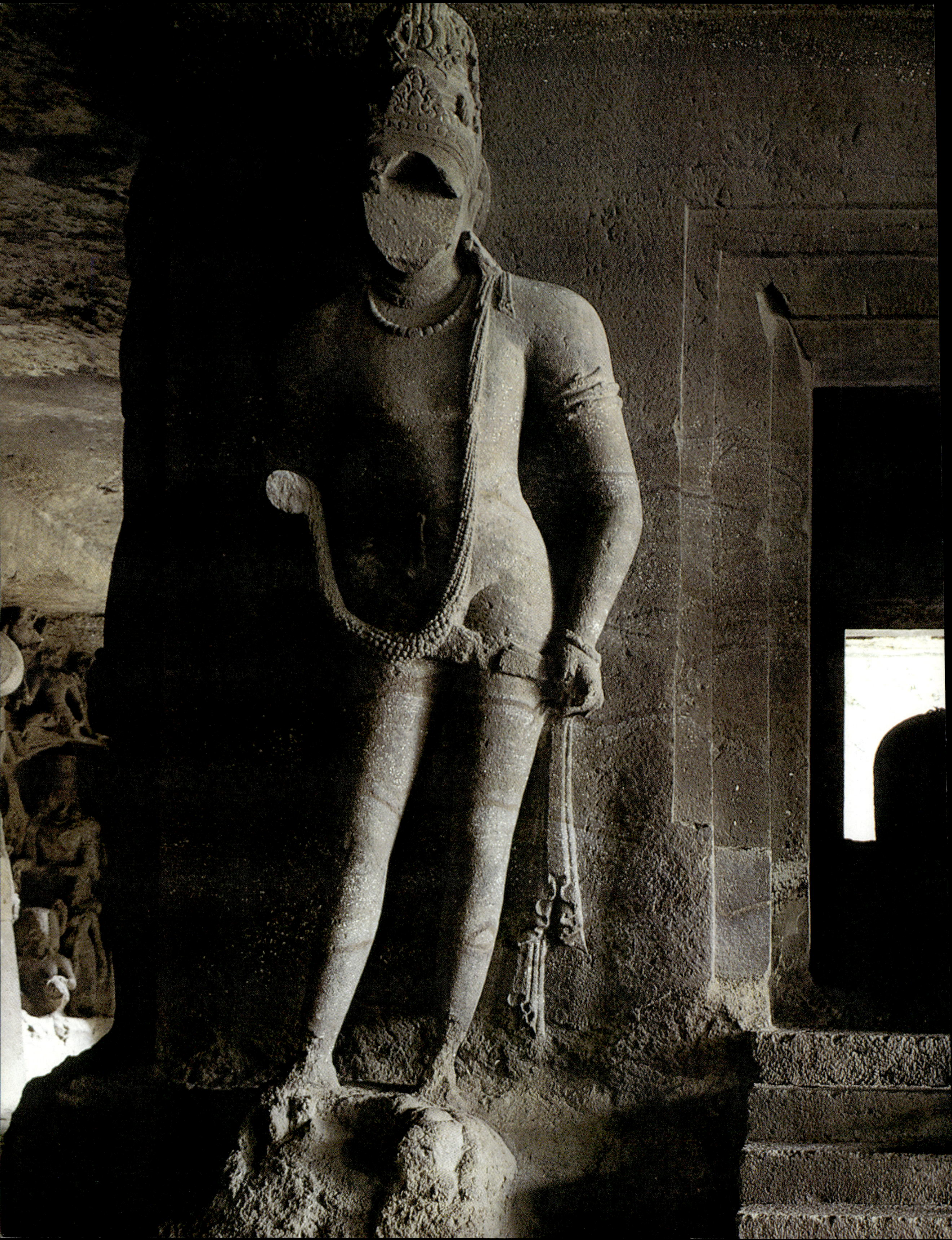

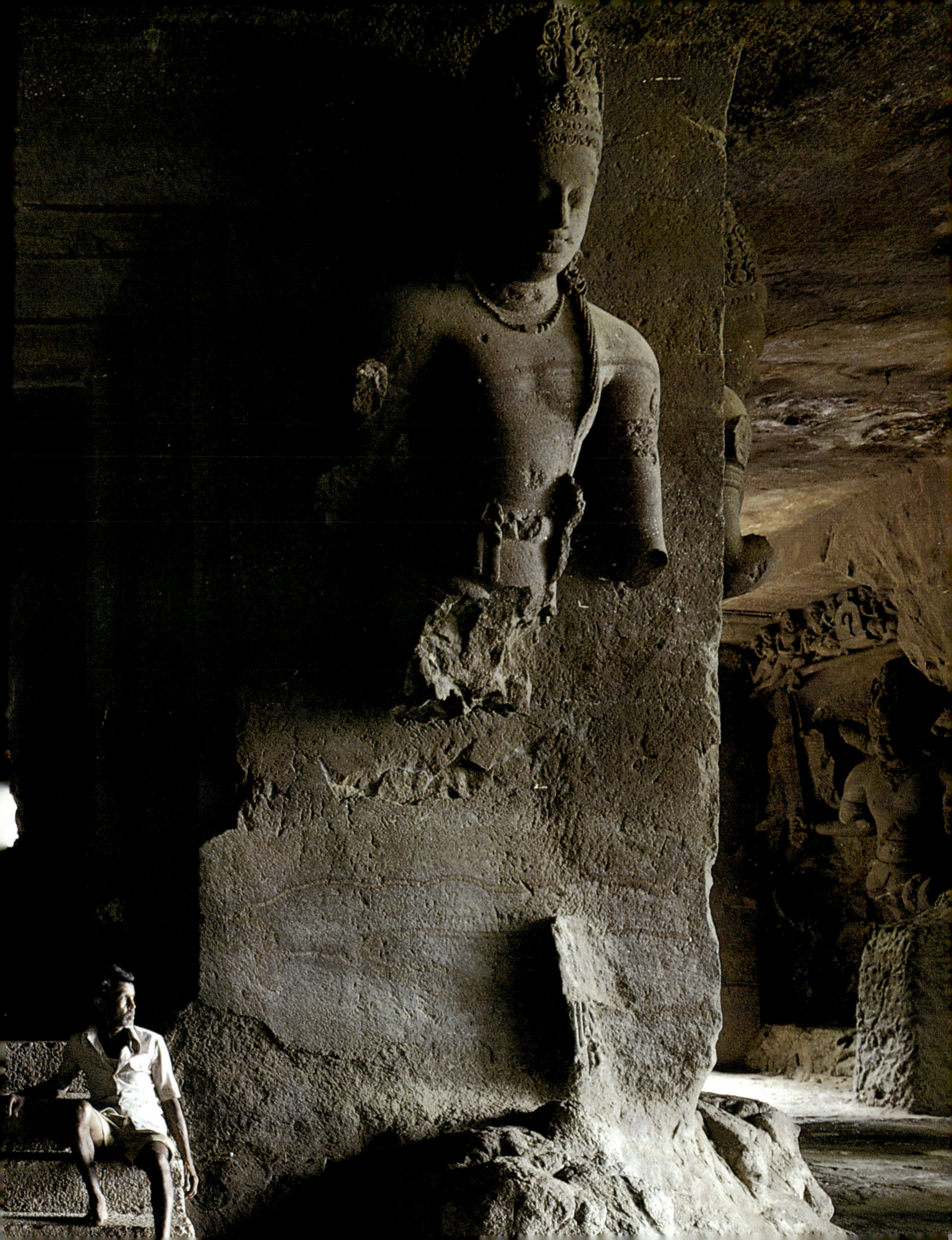

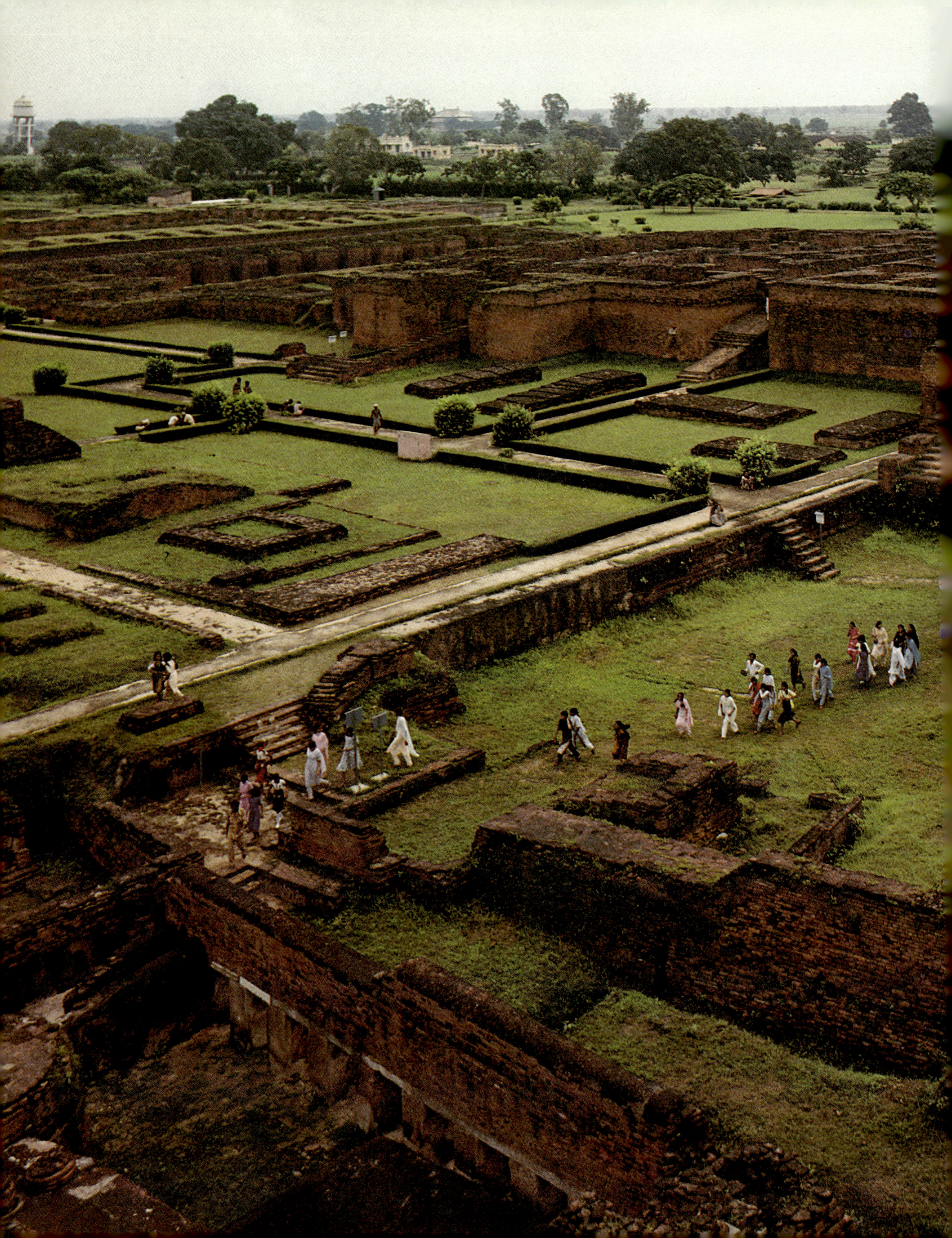

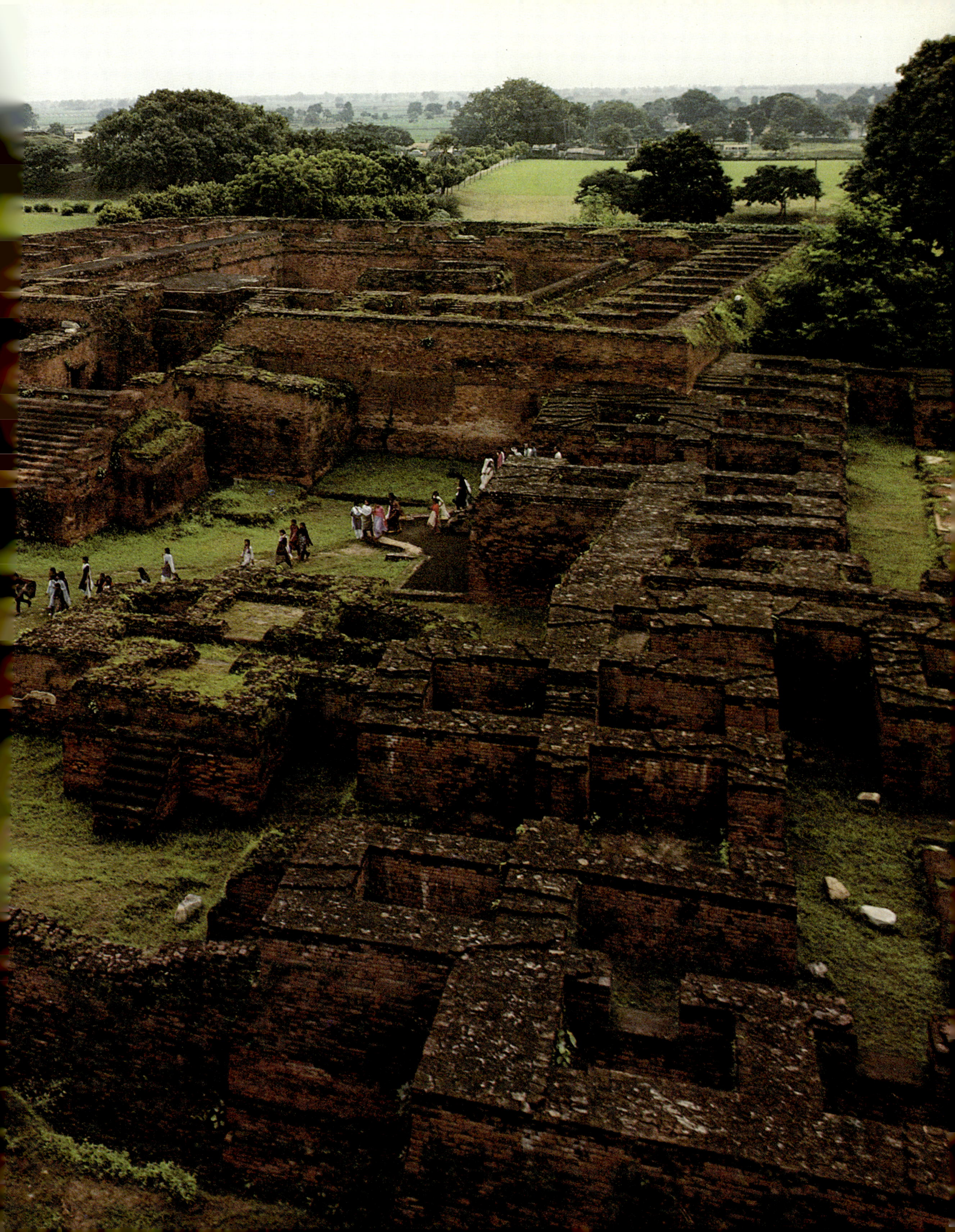

78

78. The colossal temple of Konarak in Orissa was never completed and, standing a short distance from the sea, in the last century it was covered by sand. At the end of the nineteenth century, the central tower, the shikhar, which was still standing at that time, collapsed completely despite restoration by the British government. The first European navigators named the temple the Black Pagoda, to distinguish it from the temple of Puri, which was called the White Pagoda: they provide two important landmarks for voyages along the coasts.

79. One of the countless images of amorous couples which adorn the outsides of the temple of Konarak.

80. Relief from one of the temples of Mahakut in northern Karnataka.

81. The deep stone steps of the pool in the temple of Mathura, dedicated to the sun god Surya. Since antiquity, all Hindu temples have had sacred pools for the purificatory ablutions which are essential before entering the temple and taking part in the rituals.

82. View of part of the largest temple in Bhubaneshwar; dedicated to Shiva and called Lingaraja, it was built in the eleventh century.
Bhubaneshwar is now the capital of the state of Orissa but in the past it was a city of temples; indeed in the seventh century AD there were perhaps as many as 7000 of them. Today there are the remains of about 500 and thirty of these are still intact. As a group they show the various stages in the development of the northern nagara *style of temple architecture. One of* the distinctive features of this style is the central tower, the shikhar, *with a pointed, circular crown.*

83. Peasants resting in the temple area of Khajuraho. Situated south of the Ganges plain, this was the capital of the Chandella dynasty, which, between 950 and 1050 AD, built about 100 temples here, almost all being dedicated to Shiva. There are also some Jain temples. The remaining sanctuaries, which are now only architectural monuments, are, like those of Bhubaneshwar, examples of the northern nagara *architectural style. The temple of Lakshmana is regarded as the architectural masterpiece of Khajuraho. These temples are widely known for erotic images which adorn their outer walls and which comprise one of the major expressions of Tantric art.*

84. A group of local tourists crowding into the entrance of a temple in Khajuraho.

84

85

85. One of the three sanctuaries of the temple of Somnathpur, in the south of Karnataka; it was built by the southern dynasty of the Hoyshala in the thirteenth century and dedicated to Vishnu-Krishna.
86. Detail of the relief frieze which runs along the outer walls of the temple of Halebid in Karnataka, a never-ending gallery of black stone images of the Brahminical pantheon, episodes from the sacred epics, mythical and grotesque animals, dancers, and musicians. The sculptors of what is known as the medieval period displayed an exceptional mastery in the working of steatite, the material used in the building of the Hoyshala temples.

On the following pages:
87. View of the ruins of the ancient Islamic city of Golconda, in Andhra Pradesh.
88. The exquisite white marble mausoleum of Salim Chisti, the spiritual master of the Mogul Emperor Akbar, situated at the centre of the royal city of Fatehpur Sikri, which the emperor built in the sixteenth century.

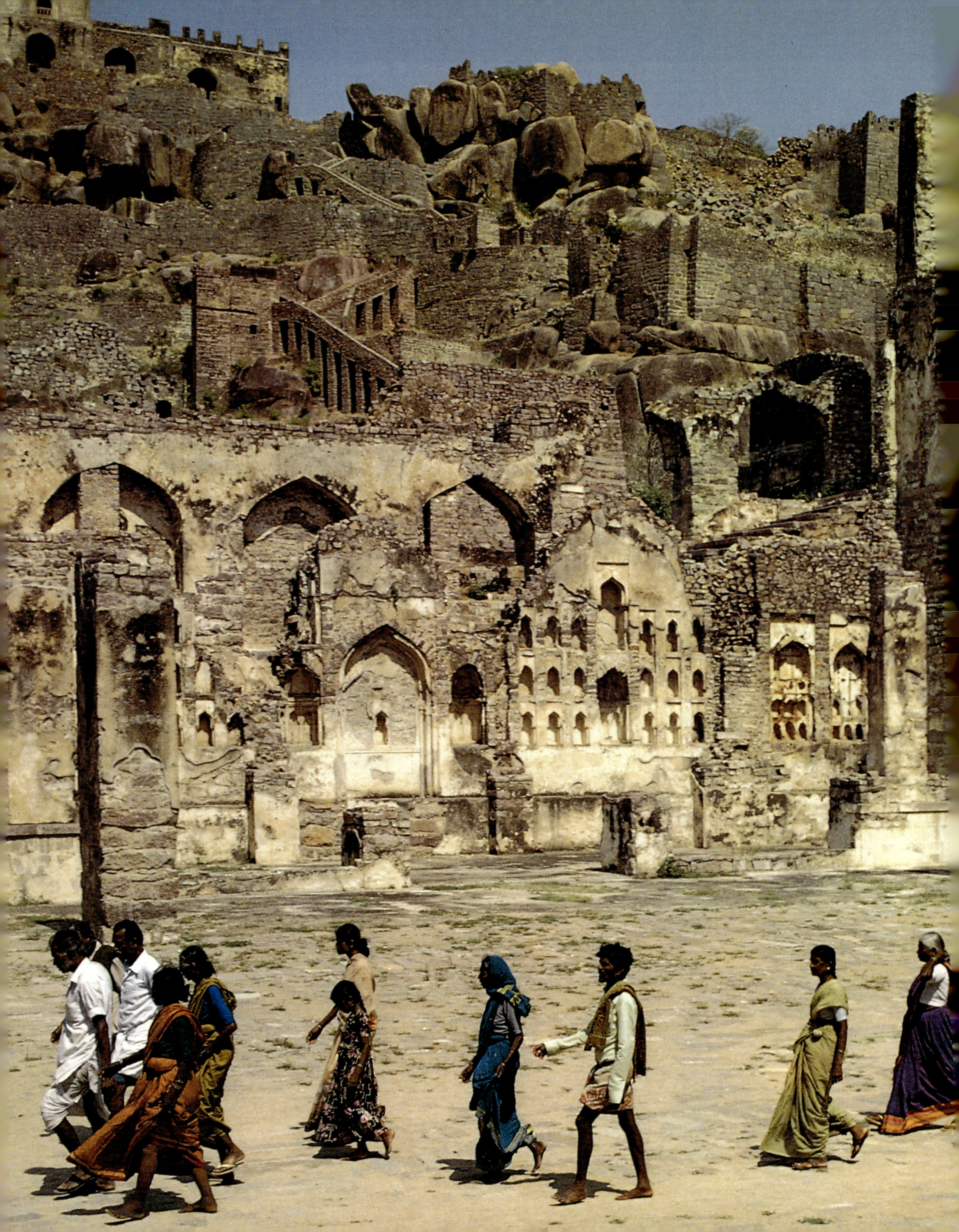

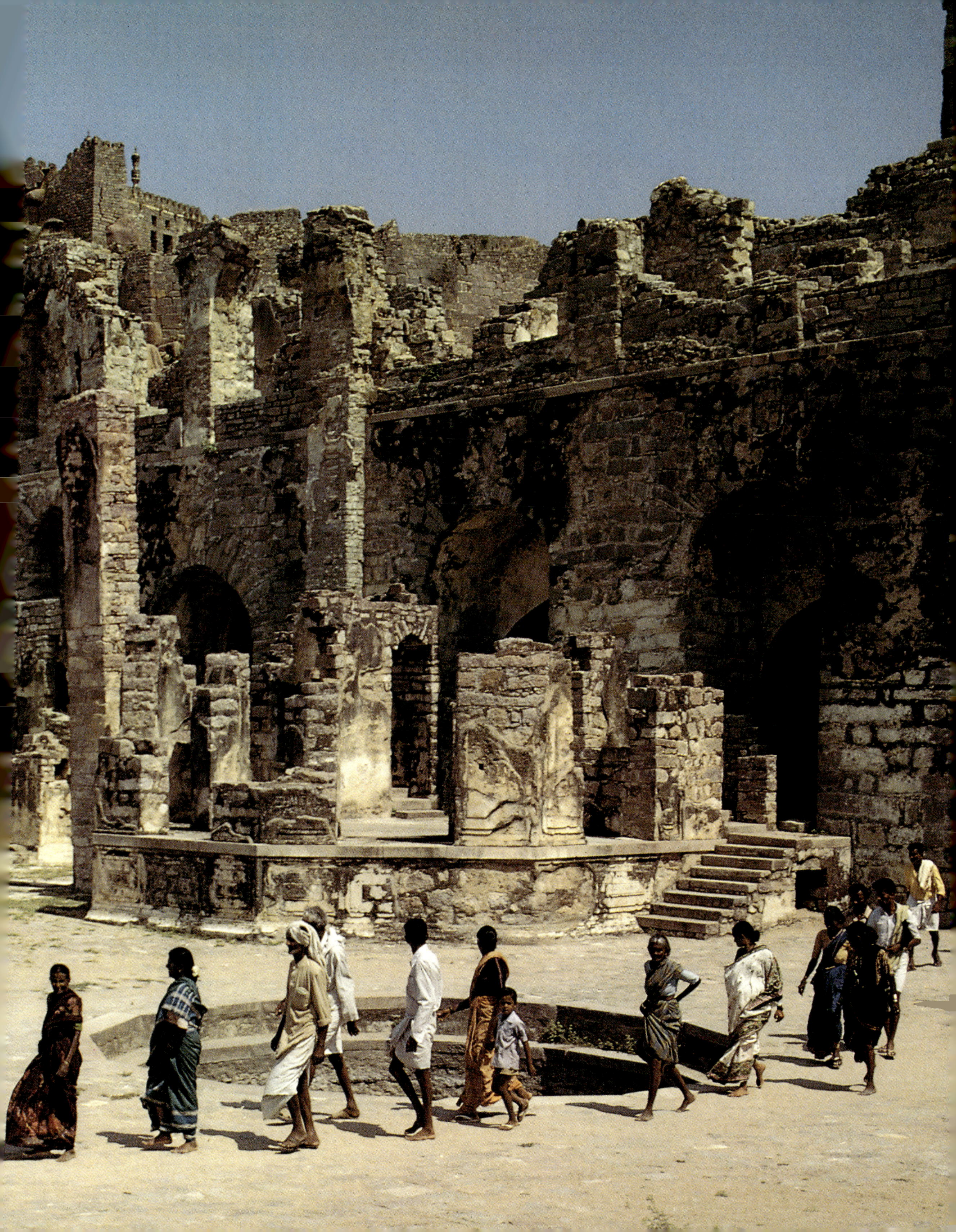

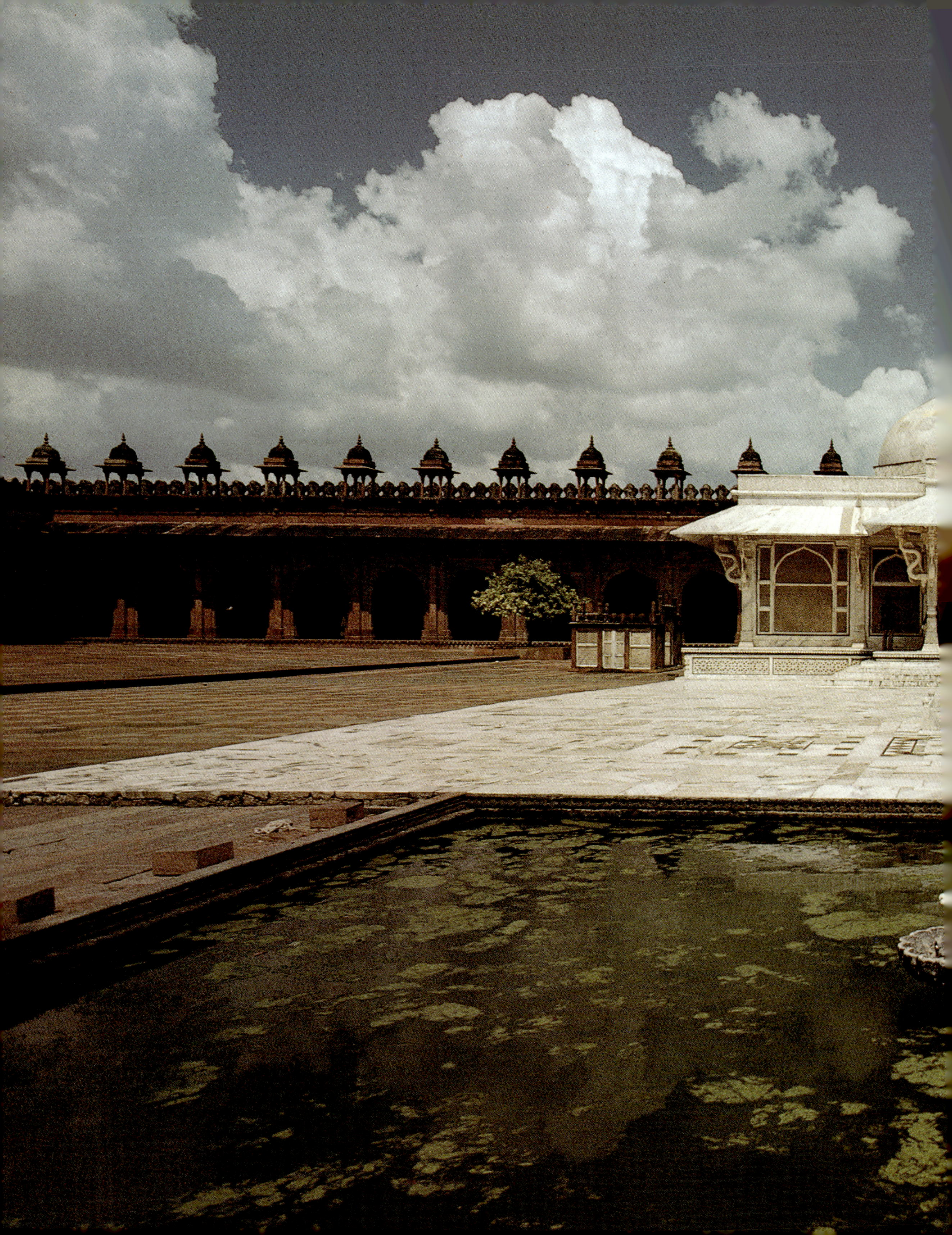

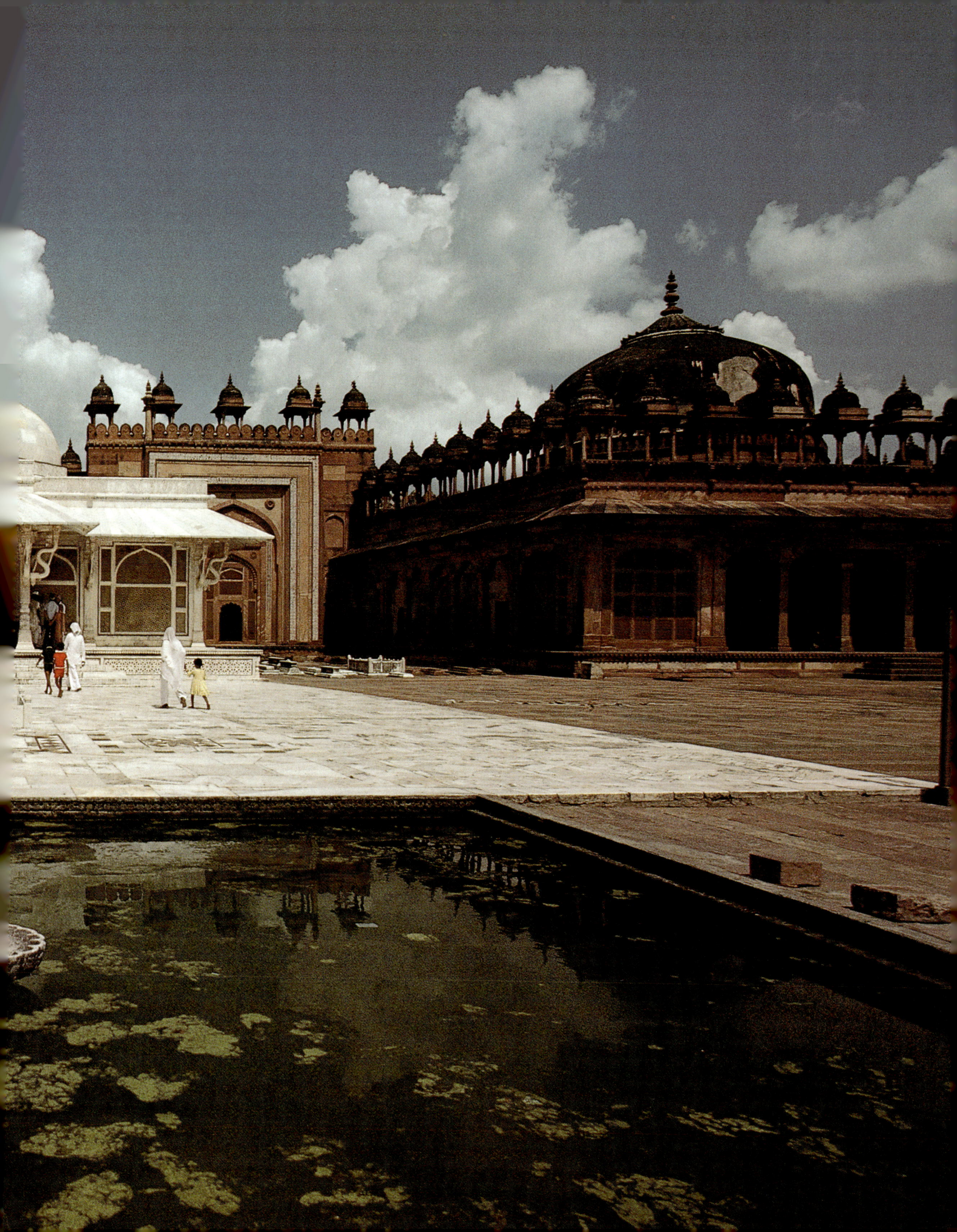

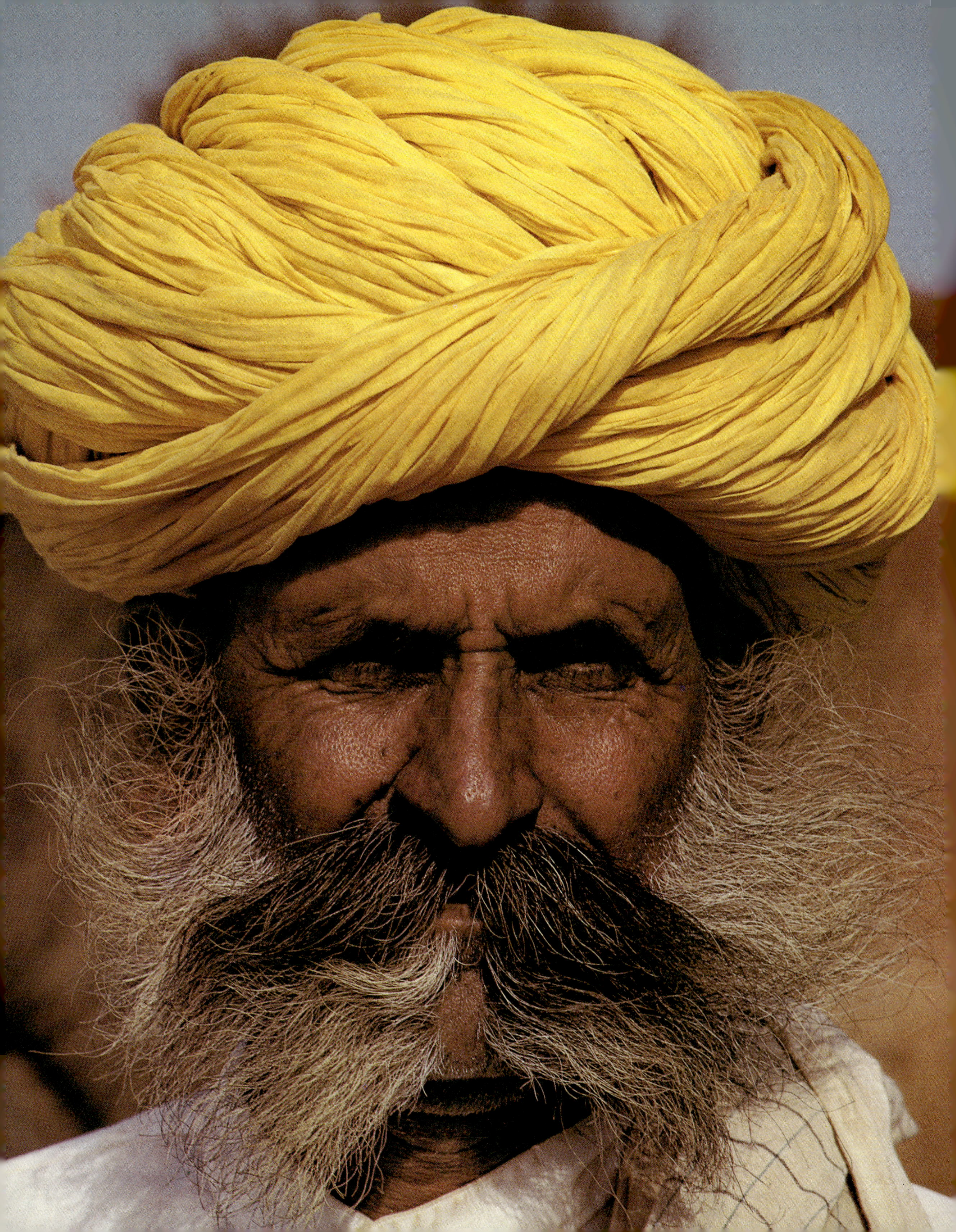

'In reality, Indian society is anarchy. It is a curious mixture of extreme social discipline and anarchy of thought. You can do what you like and think what you like, in philosophy or any other field... but you must respect the rules of caste. Once the rules of caste are broken, everything is anarchy: unless you put something else in its place...'.

Jawaharlal Nehru, from T. Mende's *Conversations with Nehru*

Society and Caste

The ancient Indian scriptures mention caste and in the *Rig Veda* (X, 90, 10-14) there is a definition of the castes, although the passage is controversial and interpreted in various ways. The *Ramayana* speaks of it explicitly and so does the *Bhagavad Gita*. For the *Manava Dharma-Shastra* of Manu (perhaps first century BC) it becomes the only possible order for Brahmanical society and it adds theological justifications to its *raison d'être* and several sanctions for transgressors. In the Constitution which independent India adopted in 1949, the caste system although it was fully discussed was not abolished, but no legal validity was conferred on it. What is unequivocally condemned is 'untouchability'. Today, castes are still a concrete reality, the backbone of a social organization so specific to India that it is difficult to find analogies in other parts of the world — a system that perpetuates itself despite the enormous changes that have taken place over the last few centuries and the stresses imposed by the modern world. Indian society is open to the outside world, part of its economy is now international in character, and relations with other countries are now both frequent and extensive; urbanization and industrialization have partly broken down the old ties between castes and their work and, finally, new social ideas, inspired by the concepts of progress and equality, form part of the culture of the new generations. All this might suggest that the caste system was on its last legs and that its total eclipse was imminent. However, this is far from being the case and it still forms the key to relations between individuals and groups. To a large extent this is due to the continuance of the old economy of the country, which is still largely based on farming, and to the fact that the majority of people live in villages. However, the inhabitants of cities, although they have altered their customs and habits, still in fact respect the fundamental rules of the system such as, for example, only marrying members of their own caste. Furthermore, the sense of identity of the caste groups has been strengthened. The religious belief is still accepted everywhere that membership of a caste, even the lowest one, is not the result of chance or a blind or perverse mechanism but rather depends on the laws of causality of the individual karma. Membership of a particular caste or the lack of one is determined by personal conduct and by deeds performed in innumerable previous lives. For Hindus, this is an unavoidable inheritance and it is shared not only by believers but by everybody, even Indians who have rejected the caste system. If anything has changed in the system, it may be seen, for example, in the formation of new alliances, in the consolidation of caste groups, which, in a new economy that is becoming increasingly capitalist and entrepreneurial, tend to become united pressure groups — lobbies or party organizations — locked in perpetual antagonism but also ready to make alliances for common objectives or purposes. The harijans, for example, the discriminated against 'children of god', have used the ballot box and also their numerical predominance to obtain political advantages or special benefits at work or when studying in certain areas, at the expense of groups who in the past were at the top of the caste pyramid. The system survives through its capacity for continual transformation. New dominant castes arise and new hierarchies; nevertheless, in the villages one can still get an idea of its original structure.

The term 'caste' (from the Latin word '*castus*', pure) was first used by Portuguese

89. *An old man wearing the traditional Rajasthani turban. The population of Rajasthan, a partly desert region, is predominatly made up of small peasant farmers who own their own land. Most belong to the Rajput races, which are descended from the ancient warrior caste, the* kshatrya, *especially the noble families and the dynasties of the various feudal kingdoms. The Rajputs, who are Hindus, are divided into thirty-six clans, almost all from Rajasthan, but for historical reasons – mainly as a result of the Islamic invasions – they are now scattered throughout northern India.*

missionaries in the sixteenth century. The term stuck and it is still difficult to avoid using it, even though it is not sufficient to explain the realities of the system. The more correct terms are *varna* and *jati*. The first, a Sanskrit word literally meaning colour but also 'covering' or 'appearance', is used for caste in the classification of the four subdivisions of brahminical society in the Vedic epoch: brahmins, warriors, merchants, and servants. The second term, also Sanskrit, means birth, origin, kind and refers to the groups which share specific common characters by birth. They are in fact the sub-castes and their numbers ar unlimited. Outside the varna are the great mass of the so-called *a-varna* (non-varna), groups of lower rank and the 'untouchables', now called the *harijan* ('people of god'), as defined by Mahatma Gandhi.

The division of the social body into four varna has never reflected the true state of affairs in India; rather it is a scale of religious and ethical values. The divisions were built into a pyramidal hierarchy, governed by hereditary rules which placed the brahmins at the top and the a-varna or harijans at the base, with the intermediate castes in between. It is the religious concept of purity which governs the hierarchy of the castes, high and low. A certain ritual status corresponds to the degree of purity of each caste or sub-caste and this is associated with a certain position in the caste hierarchy. Beside various factors connected with customs or behaviour (for example, non-vegetarianism increases the level of impurity), the degree of purity is governed first of all by the profession or trade the caste exercises. Some occupations are extremely pure, brahmins in the priesthood being one, whereas others are completely the opposite and are regarded as sources of impurity. These are in general trades which come into contact with things or materials which are subject to organic decay or anything connected with death or putrefaction, such as the sweepers who remove refuse or the tanners of leather who treat the skins of dead animals, and so on. This leads to the other cardinal factor of the caste system, the 'principle of contamination', which in social terms is the risk of a group or individual falling in the hierarchy of the caste system. A higher and hence purer caste may feel itself contaminated by contact with a lower caste and so over the centuries the system has developed a body of rules governing conduct, the so-called 'rules of avoidance', to prevent this problem. The rules of avoidance are regarded as essential for the preservation of the ritual purity of the caste and they entail the acceptance or non-acceptance of certain contacts and, in unavoidable instances such as at work, the ritualizing of them or the performance of purification rites. The case of the village sweepers, who remove the refuse, is most informative. The higher castes regard their work as absolutely essential and acknowledge their right to share in the benefits of the harvest or, in modern terms, the just reward for their services, but they avoid any social or physical contact with them. The obsession with the idea of purity and impurity is found at all levels, so that a barber, who belongs to an artisan caste that is very low in the hierarchy, will not cut the hair or beard of a harijan for fear of being contaminated. Naturally, the rules of avoidance are much more strictly observed by the higher castes and much less so amongst the untouchables. In many parts of the country, and not only in the towns, the rules of avoidance have become much diluted or in some cases have even completely disappeared. However, what has remained and which testifies to the permanence of the caste divisions is the fact that in the villages, with very few exceptions, there are no marriages which link families belonging to different castes.

Over the centuries caste society has gradually become more complex and there are now several thousand basic caste groups. Each main caste group has an even larger number of sub-castes, the *jati*, which are essentially geographical divisions of the caste group. The brahmins for example — a group present throughout India — are subdivided into about 2000 independent sub-castes or jati.

Maratha leaders giving food to a group of brahmins (from a print by T. Baxter, 1818).

Theoretically the main caste group is characterized by its members having the same profession, whilst the sub-castes are an infinite number of subdivisions of it and are associated with an area or village. In other words, the jati is a sub-group which belongs through its profession to a larger group (which may occur throughout India), but whose specific members are tied to a precise geographical locality. Consequently, the jati have developed distinct characters and traditions, their own codes of behaviour and rituals such as marriages, funerals, and religious festivals, as well as different habits and customs in clothing, food, mode of speaking, and relations with other groups. Frequently, groups belonging to different jati of the same caste display virtually no similarities. In any given situation, the jati claim the highest caste and ritual position which the other groups will acknowledge.

The jati are subdivided in their turn, particularly in the higher castes, into a number of *gotra*, a kind of clan or extended family. The members of a gotra are descended from a common ancestor and as a result of this they have an overriding obligation to marry out of their group, the rule being to marry within ones jati but outside one's gotra.

The cohesion of the jati, continually strengthened by the rigid rule of marriage within it, is based on the productive role which it performs within the structured organism that is the village, which often extends to the neighbouring villages. Although there is no longer an absolute correspondence between jati and profession, almost all the major jati have exercised the same profession for generations, giving the group a high level of specialization and a certain stability in its relationshps with other castes. In carrying out its profession, each jati becomes mutually dependent upon other jati; thus farming castes require the services of artisan castes (blacksmiths, carpenters, potters, barbers, tanners, and so on) and the latter, in exchange for their services, may receive the produce of the former, and so on.

This web, which in some ways seems harmonious and logical, is today being transformed drastically through changes which in the end will break down the insuperable barriers of the caste system. The introduction of monetary exchange rather than barter, the creation of a huge array of new trades (what caste does a mechanic or a tractor-driver belong to?) have markedly affected the relations between castes and also the social and caste rituals (the *jajmani* system, for example) whose function is to ritualize these relationships so as to neutralize the

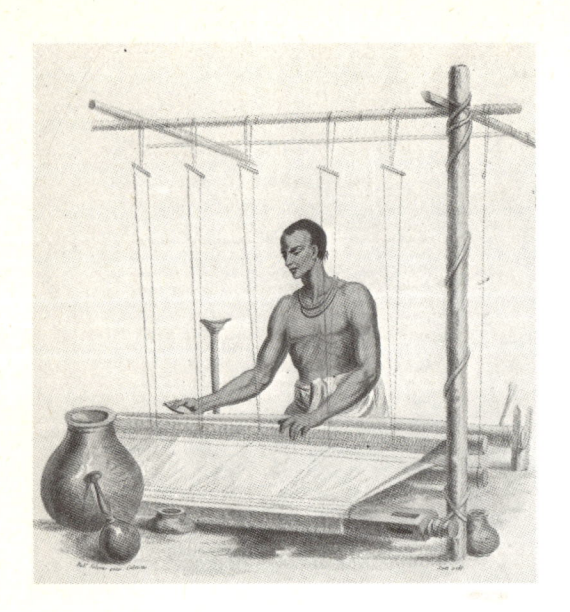

A weaver at work (by Solvyns, early nineteenth century).

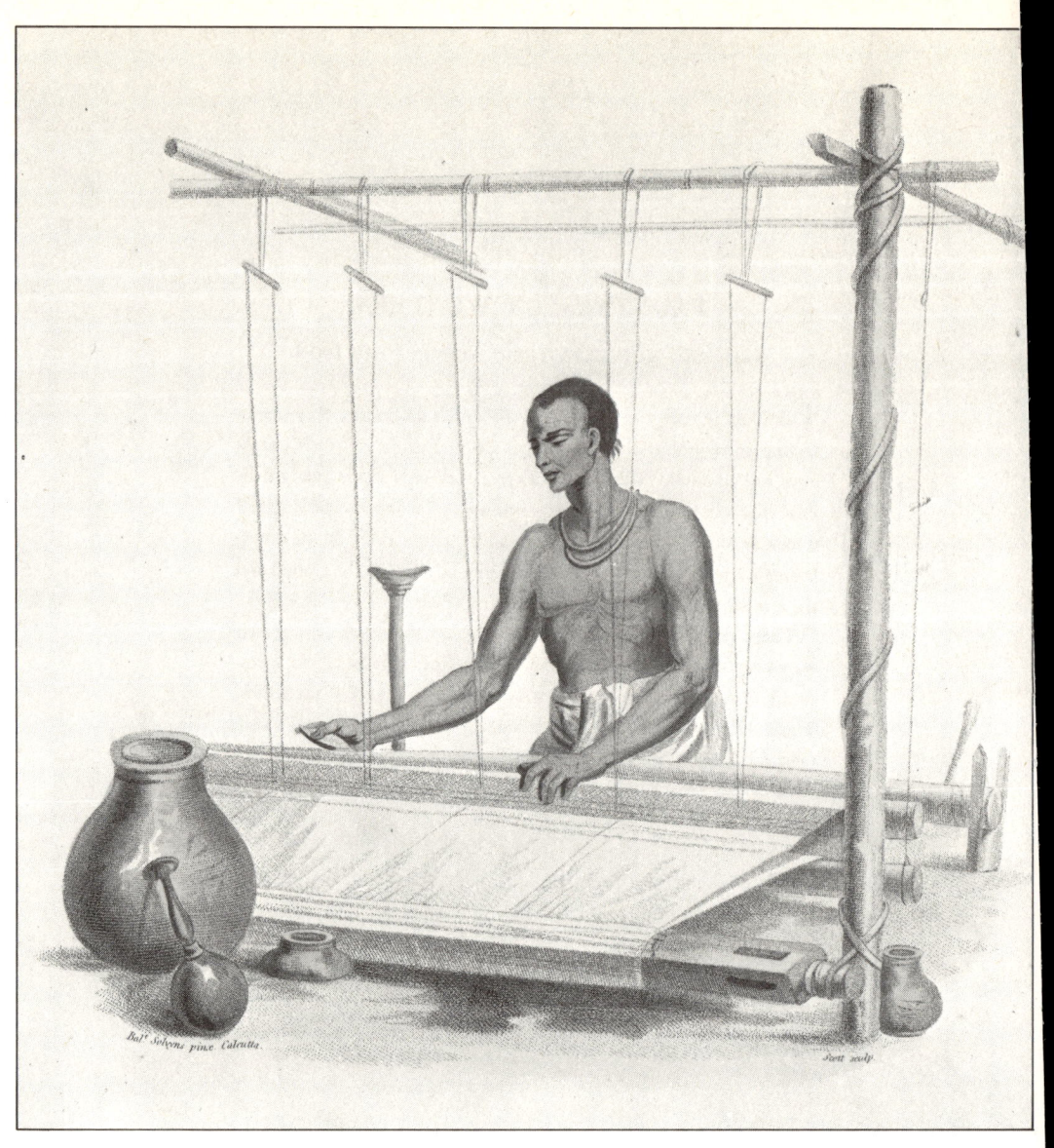

problems of contamination.

The most mobile in this respect are the former untouchables, who according to an approximate calculation, form between 10 and 15 percent of the population of India. They are found in almost every village and are usually employed in some form of service. Although untouchability has been legally abolished, the harijans are still widely discriminated against.

They are the poorest members of society, they are barred from entering temples of the Sanskrit rite and their homes are segregated in special quarters of the village. It is they who swell the ranks of the new city-dwellers and when they remain in the country they are engaged as seasonal labourers and so are subject to the ups and downs of the uncertain agrarian economy.

The caste system is, however, less rigid than it might seem. Changes are occurring amongst the lowest castes, a gradual movement up to higher ritual ranks, and the same is also true of certain groups of harijans or recently detribalized families. What is occurring is what the Indian sociologist Srinivas calls a process of 'Sanskritization'. This entails the abandonment by the lower castes of habits and customs which the caste system regards as extremely impure and contaminated; and the adoption of the rules of high castes and their style of life. Such changes may include the rejection of a non-vegetarian diet (the eating of meat by orthodox brahmins produces impurity) or the adoption of Brahminical rites and divinities in place of lower or tribal ones. It is a kind of social and caste climbing which often leads to the change of an improved position in the caste hierarchy, with all the resultant benefits in mutual relationships and, therefore, economic ones too.

The Indian Village

The history of India is identified with and blends into its spectacular rural nature. It is the history of a predominantly agricultural economy, which, in its turn, has stamped distinctive features on the civilization. Although, as will be seen later, an urban culture existed, it is the village which has been the constant and unvarying socio-economic element in a philosophy and way of life. The reality of the village, which is to be found in every part of the subcontinent, has remained largely intact and it is hard to think that its future will be radically different.

It is in the villages that the castes are still fully expressed in the well-defined system of rights and duties which characterize them. Despite some progress in the mechanization of farming and the application of certain agrarian reforms, the relationship with the land is still largely the same as it was a century ago and the farming techniques and the methods of cultivation have not changed much.

It is estimated that within the present borders of India there are 560,000 villages and that just under 80 percent of the population is supported by farming. In the near future changes are forecast, with a sharp drop in the numbers employed in agriculture and a simultaneous growth in urban life, but at present this process is still slow and gradual.

The widespread dominance of rural life gives the country a uniformity. With some exceptions, the methods of cultivation, the agricultural techniques, and the relationship with the land are not very different from one region to another. However, the social composition of villages displays considerable variety. There are multi-caste villages, comprising several distinct castes or jati, single-caste villages, and some villages consisting of just one large, extended family. There are villages made up solely of harijans (untouchables) and tribal villages. Religion also plays a role, because there may be exclusively Hindu or Muslim villages, as well as integrated ones. Climate, surroundings, and relief may all influence the kind of settlement. Almost all the villages of the Ganges plain and of the low plateau of the Deccan display similar physical characteristics. However there are marked differences in the settlements in the desert regions of Thar or the mountain belt of the Himalayas, and in coastal villages or ones situated on inland mountain ridges, or the high plateaux of the Ghati. Obviously the farming techniques and the types of crops also vary. The commonest type of village has a central nucleus but in Kerala the villages are more linear, being strung out along the banks of rivers and canals or along roads. Villages vary in prosperity from region to region. Some have benefited from agrarian reforms or the building of reservoirs or dykes for irrigation, whereas other regions are still threatened by flood, drought, and famine as a result of the variability of the monsoon rains. In the north the Punjab, with its extensive water courses and its modern farming equipment, has become the most fertile region in India, the national granary, whereas certain parts of central India, such as Bihar and Andhra Pradesh, are historically 'depressed'. The relationship between land and ownership and the scarcity of available land are crucial problems throughout India. Since British rule the country has been subject to a number of reforms and following independence a series of five-year plans have been applied, whose main aims have been the transformation of the system of land ownership and the partition of the great estates. The suppression of agrarian feudal systems (zamindari, malguzari) and the application of other ones (raiyatwari) have resulted in the appearance of large numbers of small cultivators and share-croppers. The attempts by the government of an independent India to break up the large estates has failed because as a result of the caste system and

A silver-worker in the Kutch (by P. Brown, 1902).

the inefficiency of the laws much of the land is held by a small number of families. The rest is divided into large numbers of plots of land, whose owners today form the great mass of small cultivators in India. In the present market economy the holdings of these small cultivators are hard pressed to survive in an economy dominated by the great agricultural concerns which have superior means of production at their disposal. The phenomenon of urban growth in India is also created by the imbalance in land ownership, because many families have been forced to sell their land and to become agricultural labourers or seasonal workers — it is then but a short step to move to the city in the hope of better work opportunities. The caste system forms the basic social structure of the village, with the family forming the smallest unit and the caste group the largest one. A typical multicaste village generally comprises 'farming castes', who form the largest group and have worked the land for generations. The majority own land, which they work and from which they obtain the means of subsistence. The village also contains 'artisan classes', who perform the various trades and professions connected with farming and, depending on the village's size, it will have one or more families of smiths, carpenters, barbers, potters, and so on. Finally, there the 'service castes', who perform the menial, unspecialized tasks. These are generally groups of harijans or proscribed castes who are employed as launderers or sweepers, etc.

In the past, virtually all the artisan and service castes were paid with a share of the harvest, the exchange being governed by a code of behaviour known as *jajmani* (from the Sanskrit *yajamana* 'he who performs the sacrifice'). This system can also be viewed as the patronage of one caste by another or simply as a socio-caste contract, which governs the transactions and exchanges of goods and services between different caste groups. This web of mutual obligations, which because of the peculiarity of the caste system took on the character of a ritualized relationship, has almost entirely vanished as a result of the increasing tendency to pay for services with money rather than in kind, and also because of the complexity of modern means of production, the rise of new, specialized occupations and, finally, because of the modern village's reliance on services from outside which would once have been provided from within the village.

Normally, the village is divided into similar quarters called *mohalla, basti, cheri*) composed of families of the same caste and the same profession. In an average-sized village there may be a large number of quarters. The typical subdivisions are between the sub-castes or jati of cultivators, between the craftsmen and merchants and, above all, the quarter for the lower castes and harijans, who are kept at some distance.

The various quarters for the castes have communal wells, where the women gather at certain hours in order to collect water. Almost all villages have a square or *chok* at their centre. It is here that the market is periodically held and the various village institutions are located in its vicinity. These include the *panchayat*, a form of council made of representatives elected by the various groups and sub-castes, although in the past it was hereditary and was made up of the elders and prominent members of the dominant castes. Rural temples are almost always for a particular caste and are situated in their respective quarters, with enough space in front of them for the gatherings to celebrate the various festivals. On the banks of the rivers or lakes, a short distance from the houses, most villages have traditional stone structures, or steps down the bank, where the groups employed in the washing of clothes carry out their tasks.

The typical rural house is built with techniques and methods that have remained unchanged for centuries. Villages are mostly composed of 'poor' houses, built of stone or clay and surfaced with animal dung. Dung, which is commonly used as a domestic fuel, is a natural and cheap cement. When it has dried after application or after being touched up from time to time, it forms a perfect plaster, which withstands the heaviest of downpours. In northern India houses built with poor materials are known as *kachcha*, whereas houses built with brick and cement are called *pakka*. Although the pakka is greatly coveted, and in general such houses are at the centre the village and belong to the richer families, the kachcha matches the economic resources of the average peasant, who, with the guidance of a *mistri* or master builder, can build it himself. There is an ancient skill in the building and rebuilding of the house. Its periodic repair also has a purification value, connected with the thaumaturgical value of cow dung.

The most widespread type of house in the Indian countryside is a large structure that can shelter a joint family. It consists of a series rooms on a single storey grouped around an open courtyard, which forms the heart of the dwelling. This central court often has a well and, on one side, a stable. Surrounded by verandahs, it forms the focal point of the whole family's life and, except for during the monsoon period, everybody sleeps in it, in the open. The plan and distribution of areas in the country house are not the same everywhere but vary with climate (mountain or coastal), regional or caste traditions, and the economic status of the family. The houses of poorer families often have just a single room, which also serves as a shelter for the animals. If there is no central court there is often a verandah by the entrance, and this becomes the communal area of all the members of the family, although it is often only used by the head of the family for meeting friends and acquaintances.

Family and Festival in Village Life

The basic family of just parents and children is the exception in India, particularly in the countryside. The traditional Indian family is patriarchal, an extended core of at least ten and possibly twenty, fifty, or even a hundred members. This is known as a joint family, because it includes under the same roof and as part of a single economic unit all the brothers of a family with their respective wives and children. At its head is the father of the brothers or the eldest of the brothers, whoever is the oldest man in the house. The home of such a joint family may house three or four generations and therefore it is built to provide the facilities and space that such a large group requires. The head of the family has complete authority and enjoys the absolute respect of the whole family in any decision he takes concerning the administration of the common goods and the conduct of members of the family.

In the world of the peasant there is no alternative to the joint family and an individual cannot exist either socially or economically on his own without belonging to a family group. In its turn the family belongs to a larger social group, the caste. Each member of the family, besides sharing in the economic benefits, obtains protection and a sense of identity from his clan. In order for even a small holding of land to function properly, rigidly laid down rights, duties, and, above all, roles have to be established on the basis of an accepted hierarchy of authority. Men must attend to their duties in the fields or in the workshops; the women must work in the house and raise the children.

It is always the head of the family who decides when it is time for the children to marry and who selects their husband or wife. Given that one must marry within one's caste or *jati*, the choice of partner follows rational and practical principles, such as the economic status of their family, as well as such factors as astral combinations and the horoscopes of the prospective parties. Occasionally there is what is termed a 'marriage of love' — although even this is within the caste — which results from a meeting between a man and woman, which has either been concealed from or is outside the control of the families. The couple who are to be married may never have seen each other before the wedding but in general the young people place their trust entirely in their parents and the wisdom of their choice. In effect, an Indian marriage is an alliance between families which, besides consolidating the bonds of caste, tends to assure the economic security of the couple to be married and the continuity of the clan. Consequently it involves all the members of the family, not just the couple in question, and matrimony with few exceptions is regarded as a duty incumbent upon everybody. It is regarded as *shankar*, that is 'propitious', because it gives physical form to the natural cycle of life and perpetuates the family lineage. Despite its legal prohibition (Sarda Act, forbidding marriage before fifteen and subsequently eighteen years of age), many rural communities still practice child marriages, involving children of about ten years of age. However, such marriages are less absolute than those of adolescents; they are rather a mutual obligation on the part of the two families, followed by a betrothal ceremony with a brief symbolic ritual. At the appointed time the proper wedding ceremony is celebrated but this, although final, is merely formal, since the children immediately return to their respective families until the time when, after puberty, they will live together. Another of the major problems of marriage is the dowry, which is termed more precisely in India as the 'price of the husband' or the 'price of the wife' (the latter still being known by the ancient term of *arsha*). In general the predominant system is the dowry which the bride brings with her. In recent years, as a result of the government's Dowry Prohibition Act, 1961, an anti-dowry movement has developed whose objective is to free families from the heavy obligation of paying dowries; but its effect in the villages has been very limited. It is not uncommon for families to become saddled with debt for life in order to obtain good marriages for their daughters. Many communities or caste groups are changing the dowry system of their own accord, ritualizing it with a simple ceremony in which the family of the husband is offered a single rupee, a symbol which seals the contract. Elsewhere, in village as well as cities, more modern values, such as the educational level, health, and physical appearance of the young people, are becoming more important.

There are countless types of marriage in India, depending upon whether the parties are Muslim or Hindu, the traditions of their caste, the differences between north and south, and numerous other factors. In modern India it is the Sanskritic marriage which is tending to prevail. This is monogamous and indissoluble and is observed by the higher castes in particular. In the lower ones there are many variants and the practice of divorce is accepted. The modern Hindu code of marriage allows various forms of contract (the Muslim one allows a man up to four wives) and divorce. However, as is usual in the countryside, the law is only partly respected, because caste traditions and interests are still very important. For example, in central India, certain castes of Hindu farmers have a form of polygamy that allows them to take a second wife, usually a younger one who can work in the fields. In return for such a wife, the husband-cum-employer will pay the girl's family a large sum.

If the variety of marriages in India is infinite, so are the wedding ceremonies, which reflect ethnic and caste traditions and also economic conditions. The most widespread rite is the brahmanical one, which provides for a series of ceremonies, such as the celebration of the betrothal before the sacred fire, almost always held in the open beneath multi-coloured tents; the ritual offering to the fire, the *homa*; the clasping of hands by the couple, *panigraha*; and the seven symbolic steps around the flame, *satpadi*. The ceremonies may last for several days in front of a crowd of relatives and friends and the religious rite may last from evening until dawn. It is the woman who enters the house of her husband, never the opposite. The separation of the young girl from her family is never easy and sometimes causes great suffering. She will enter a family of people she doesn't know, the brothers of her husband with their wives and children, and frequently the not-too-kindly mother-in-law, who has absolute power over domestic arrangements and the behaviour of the women of the family. The severity of mothers-in-law is proverbial throughout India. With the exception of virtually all of the south, the tradition of *purdah* (a Persian term meaning curtain) persists, particularly in the villages. This is the custom which segregates women in particular areas of the house and which also governs their behaviour, determining their reserved and modest attitude towards men, even the men of their own household. The higher the caste, the more rigid is the system of purdah, although in many communities today it is losing its force. Purdah curbs the freedom of women in accordance with the Indian view that women are more vulnerable when exposed and, even more significantly, it continues the ancient Indian tradition, exacerbated by the long Muslim presence in India, that a woman is owned by her husband and is absolutely dependent upon him. In the north in particular, the laws of the ancient Indian legislator Manu have not entirely disappeared, indeed in many cases they are followed and venerated as divine laws. They have affected the customs of India for thousands of years and even today they confirm a state of inferiority and total submission for women. Despite modern legislation, some customs have not entirely disappeared in many parts of India. The archaic and absurd practice of *suttee*, the self-sacrifice of the widow on the pyre of her dead husband, still rears its head every so often, and, despite its widespread condemnation, there has even been something of a revival in certain parts of the north.

The other important aspect of the woman's lot is widowhood. Remarriage is unlikely, even if the woman is young. Instead she is isolated and in certain ways segregated, having very little to do with her family and village. Amongst the lower castes or harijans the remarriage of a widow is not so uncommon and in some cases it is even encouraged.

It is unbecoming for a man to remain at home but it is even more so for a woman to go outside, except amongst communities of cultivators or harijan labourers, where even the women labour in fields. The traditional role of women is performed within the walls of her home, where she keeps it in order, prepares food, and cares for the children, in conjunction with the other women of the house. If she is of high caste — although not necessarily rich — she will be helped by a swarm of servants, in general the children of castes employed in services. Women guard the morals of the house and a feature of women's behaviour is the rigid observace of the rituals which call for penitences and fasts during the various religious festivities.

A woman acquires greater authority and power when she becomes a mother, particularly when she has a son. With a son the Indian family is complete; other sons and daughters may be born later but the essential need has already been satisfied. The importance of male offspring in patriarchal families is well known, not only for practical reasons connected with subsistence, but also for religious reasons; the birth of a son completes the chain that connects the past to the present and, above all, it absolves the parent's moral obligations to their ancestors. Consequently there is still a certain amount of hostility towards the birth of girls and in the past, and still occasionally today, female infanticide was practised.

In general, peasant families tend to have large numbers of children and each couple within the joint family may have between five and ten children. Despite the government Family Planning programme and laws allowing abortion and the free distribution of contraceptives, the cult of fertility and the large family survives. The situation is changing gradually but conditions in the countryside are still much as they were and the security that a large family brings a peasant is still a

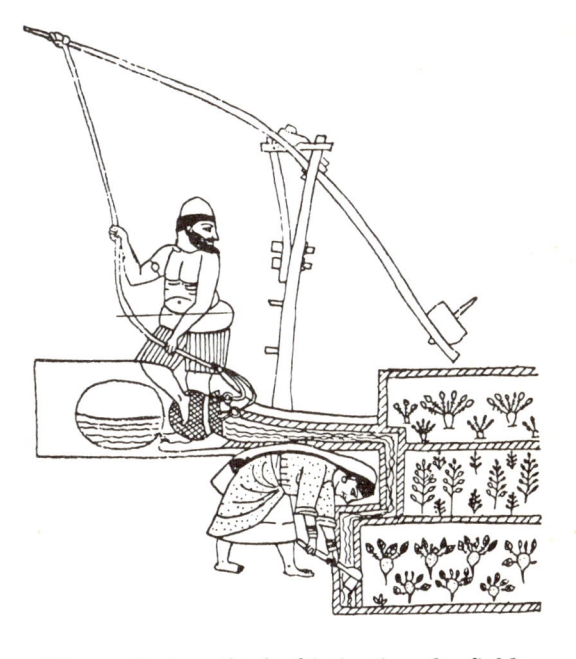

The ancient method of irrigating the fields, still widely used in India today (by D.D. Kosambi).

powerful force.

The Indian family is authoritarian and rigid in its upbringing. The children are educated with severity and discipline is the order of the day both in the house and outside it, at school or at work. Junior schools in Indian villages only teach half the children of school age; the others, despite the fact that school is compulsory up to fourteen years of age, are sent to work in the fields or in workshops. These are the children of the countryside's poorest communities, the lowest farming castes and the harijans, not to mention the children in tribal villages.

The smallest unit of the Indian village is the joint family; a more extensive one, composed of several families, is the caste group. As was seen in the previous chapter, most villages are multi-caste, and each caste is associated with a particular trade or occupation. The interdependence of the various professions enables the village to function as an organic and productive system. All the castes, the 'farming castes' or those providing services, depend on each other and work closely together for the common good of food production. The unifying principle is farming the land, in which everybody, with their own particular trade, co-operates. Although the caste system divides, the interrelationship between the castes allows the village to function and co-operate as a collective unit. However, the village is not merely a productive unit, although this is of fundamental importance; it is also a social one, an organic community where the divisions between castes can be suspended or overcome. It is above all in the cult of the tutelary divinities of the village, the *gramdevata*, or in certain festivals associated with seasonal events that the entire community of the village displays a certain unity of purpose. Almost all the castes of the village, especially the dominant high ones, have exclusive temples and cults, reserved for the members of that particular caste, but in many cases the rules separating the castes may be suspended. This is so with the rural festival of Hola, which is celebrated throughout India. It is a kind of saturnalia in which every form of liberty is allowed, even the most provocative — men and women throwing coloured water at each other, men singing obscene songs or jokes, etc. In the southern regions of Tamil Nadu and Karnataka the Pongal Sankrant is celebrated, a typical rural festival dedicated to the harvest. Cows and bullocks are fed large amounts of special food, and there are painted and led in procession to the sound of music and the beat of drums. In some villages the bullocks are allowed to run through the streets, whilst the local youths attempt to halt them by seizing their horns. In the north a popular rural festival is that in honour of Krishna, the herdsman god (Gobardhan), and the celebrations are in honour of cows and livestock in general.

The Hindu liturgical year is densely packed with festivals, some of which are national while others are local, possibly being celebrated in just a single village. The celebrations may last several days and they consist of games, athletic displays, illuminations, collective puja, and sometimes processions through the streets. They are also occasions for markets, with the buying and selling of various products, utensils, and items produced by local craftsmen, as well as religious symbols and images.

The most popular of the Indian festivals, which are celebrated throughout the country, are Diwali, or the 'festival of the lights', at the beginning of the Hindu new year (October-November) and in honour of Lakshmi, goddess of prosperity. The whole house is refurbished and painted in order to welcome the spirit of the goddess; in Dassehra (September-October) or Durga Mataji Puja, an extremely popular festival in Bengal in particular, Durga, the warrior goddess, represents the triumph of good over evil. Other popular festivals are the anniversaries of the births of Krishna Janmashtami and Rama, Ram Navami; Shiva has the 'great night of Shiva', Mahashivaratri.

In the local cults and in the popular Hinduism of the countryside, all the major divinities of the Hindu pantheon are regarded as protectors of the house or of the crops in the fields. Special prayers and rituals are addressed to Indra, an ancient Vedic divinity, ruler of the natural elements, in order to avert drought. The hierarchy of the universe of the gods changes according to local traditions which result from the crystalization of Hinduism within the devotional framework of the *bhakta*, inspired by the sacred epics and by the ancient mythological tales, the *Purana*. Here, the devout Hindu, the *grihasta*, removed from ascetic practices and monastic discipline and daily immersed in the hard labour of the countryside, finds comfort in a world of tutelary divinities for his family and fields to whom he dedicates his *puja*, or act of veneration. It is in this sphere that Ganesh, the elephant-headed god, enjoys his great popularity throughout India, even amongst the more urbanized populations. An easy-going and benevolent god, he is regarded as the 'protector of harvests' and as he 'who removes obstacles' and who has the power to bring fortune to any project. The athletic monkey god, Hanuman, venerated only by men, is another pan-Indian divinity. He is the symbol of absolute faithfulness to the divine couple Rama and Sita, who in their turn are the ideal model for the life and behaviour of a married couple. Their images are found in every house and also in shops, either printed or painted on the walls. Household altars also have depictions of the joyful god Krishna, who is popular and well-loved. Depictions of his deeds as a child are particularly popular.

In addition to the Brahmanical divinities there are the cults of the tutelary gods or deities of the village, the *gramdevata*. These often share the position and popularity of the great Brahmanical divinities and are sometimes considered as their particular manifestations, although the gramdevata are very often indigenous and independent and at the centre of cults which veer between local myth and tribal animism. They are in general rather ambivalent divinities, the bringers of well-being but also of unlucky influences and calamities. Usually they are female, sometimes being regarded as wives of Shiva, as is the case with Shitla Devi or Shitla Mata, who still has a strong cult in central India and in Bengal. In the south, the goddess is called Mariyamman by the Tamils. Shitla or Mariyamman is the goddess of smallpox or cholera and she could inflict the disease or threaten the entire village with an epidemic; equally, if suitably propitiated, she could drive the disease away. The children of the village are adorned with amulets bearing effigies of the goddess in order to protect them from disease. The crude image of Shitla Devi, painted vermilion and venerated by the women of the village, is placed on simple altars outside the boundaries of the village, often in the shade of a *kikar* tree, the Arab acacia. After a wedding ceremony, it is traditional for the couple to visit the altar and a brief puja is held.

These regional divinities do not always represent opposing powers and forces; there are sometimes divine pairs, who manifest themselves in a complementary but antagonistic fashion; Panchika-Hariti for example, comprising the god Panchika, the dispenser of riches, and the evil goddess Hariti. Hariti, however, in one of the frequent metamorphoses of Indian cultural forms, has now become the protectress of children. Aiyannar and Karuppu, who are very popular in Tamil Nadu, display elements specific to Dravidian Hinduism; they not only represent the relationship between high and low castes but also the synthesis of the Aryan, Sanskrit cosmology of the north with the belief of the Tamil world. Aiyannar is one of the commonest and most popular of southern divinities. He guards the fields and protects the harvests and his is the commonest image of a divinity to be found in the fields, in the forn of terracotta statues painted in bright colours, with his band of attendants on horseback (the god Karuppu, his squire, representing the lower castes). The horses are commonly a votive offering made by the villagers to help the god protect their crops during his watches. Like all ancient peasant cultures, the world of the Indian countryside is pervaded by beliefs and superstitions and

A drawing showing the rite of sati *(suttee) in which widows sacrifice themselves on the funeral pyre of their dead husband (by Nicolo Manucci, seventeenth century).*

exists in a magico-religious universe populated by occult forces that dominate the environment and domestic life. This culture weighs heavily on the lives of groups and families, demanding a vast array of auspicious practices and formulas of exorcism in almost any activity or undertaking. In order to withstand baleful or evil spirits the Indian peasant relies on an infinite number of exorcisms, charms, incantations, amulets, talismans, *mantra* (oral magic formulas), or *yantra* (magic diagrams). The village contains astrologers, palmists, exorcists, and formulators of mantras (*mantrvadin* or *mantrin*), who read the omens and perform exorcisms to avoid the evil consequences of a curse or to ward off a bad omen. Often it the local *pandit* or village priest, a man who knows the ancient texts and the movements of the stars and who can read horoscopes, who performs these functions. Such men are continually consulted, both over marriages and births but also over whether or not to undertake a journey or a piece of business. The reading must be careful and precise and every detail scrupulously defined, even the correct moment, because some exorcisms only work at dawn and others after dark. The movements of the stars constitute an open book in the sky which can be scrutinized for signs auguring a fortunate or unlucky future. Comets, shooting stars, and eclipses, though rare, are crucial omens. According to mythology, it is a great demon of the skies, Rahu, the devourer of the sun and the moon, who causes eclipses.

The science of prediction and the techniques of exorcism have ancient origins; the first mention of the evil eye appearing in one of the *Vedas*, the *Atharva Veda*. According to some it is a science, codified in the ancient treatise, the *Shakuna-Shastra*, which was handed down in a form of initiation by the god Shiva to his son Karttikeya, during the terrible battle with Taraka.

Before beginning a task, undertaking a journey, or abstaining from sexual contacts, the days which coincide with the full moon or the very end of the moon's waning are determined. During the full moon one should sleep under cover, in a place sheltered from the cold, silver light of the moon. Drawings and graffiti, known as *kolam* amongst the Tamils and *rangoli* in central and northern India, are periodically made on the pavement in front of the door of the house by its womenfolk in order to bring good fortune on the house and family. Besides frightening birds, scarecrows are normally intended to ward off the evil eye or misfortune cast by anyone. People in the village who can cast the evil eye or who practise witchcraft are feared in the village. Everyday behaviour is a source of good or bad omens and there is even a science of sneezing, which, depending upon the circumstances, can bring good or bad luck. The sight of a cow, a horse, an elephant, or two or more brahmins is universally considered lucky whereas it is thought unlucky to catch sight of a crow on one's left, a kite to one's right, a snake, a widow, and so on. A cat crossing the road you are on is an omen of death. If a crow caws during the night it is a sure sign of a death in the neighbourhood and if a crow enters the house it augurs ill for its prosperity. It is also considered unlucky if a stranger praises a house; one should not say that a house is beautiful or pleasant, nor praise the food or even make the usual compliments about the children of the house. When one enters the house of a practising Hindu, it is best to be silent or to speak as little as possible, otherwise the praise offered will attract influences.

There are deep beliefs that 'negative forces' can possess a place or a house, poisoning ponds, trees, and fields. These include the feared 'wandering spirits' of the dead (*preta*) who, if not suitably propitiated, may return to their old earthly residences, bringing baleful influences; and the *bhuta*, evil spirits, demons, or souls of those who have died a violent death or because the prescribed funeral rites have not been celebrated. The bhuta are feared because they can poison wells, make fields barren, and sicken children and livestock. They infest forests and ruined houses. Other feared spirits include the *rakshasa*, nocturnal demons, and the *pishacha*, carnivorous demonic beings, sometimes associated with the bhuta and which have the power to enter people. They dwell near burial places and may assume any form or even make themselves invisible. Offering and oblations (*bhutabali* or *bali*) are prescribed to placate or propitiate them. One of the eight branches of ancient Indian medicine, the science of spirits or demonology (*bhutavidya*) treats illnesses caused by demonic possession and deals with formulas for exorcisms. There are many *bhagavati* temples (one is near Ernakulam, in Kerala), where people bring the mentally ill or hysterical, who are cured with mantras and special pujas. For exorcisms connected with the evil eye specialized exorcists are engaged. They are found everywhere in India and they

A public religious ceremony which serves as a ritual for the devout and as a test for the ascetic (from a nineteenth-century print).

may be Hindus, Muslims, or belong to other religious groups.

Belief in witchcraft is widespread amongst the aboriginal tribes but it also persists in many groups or lower castes who are of tribal stock and who in the course of many generations have become completely Hinduized.

The world of magic and the occult in India is vast, pouring forth from the deep spirit of the peasant and tribal soul of Indian culture, although in some areas it is now contracting and declining. The Hinduism of the high theological and intellectual concepts has always tolerated, and almost always absorbed, in its characteristic fashion, the occult practise and esoteric rites of the aboriginal and pre-brahmanic communities. The enormous process of brahmanization has swallowed these cultures and conferred on them a cloak of orthodoxy. The peasant world is based, moreover, on a view of the cosmogonies, the forces which govern the universe, that is coherent with the sacred scriptures and with the profounder Hindu doctrines. One might view the situation as a symbiotic relationship between the high, intellectual Hinduism of the brahmin castes and the popular Hinduism of the lower castes and even the groups that have still to be Hinduized.

There is in India a particular cult of power — of the way of acquiring the energy which acts on inert matter. It is pervaded by arcane and subtle forces and it is behind every phenomenon or existential manifestation. Nevertheless, these forces are often believed to be unfavourable to man, unless placated by exorcism or ritual sacrifice. The most spiritual and elevated way of controlling these forces is the asceticism of the yogi or the brahmin, with its deep meditation and concentration. However, the bulk of ordinary men resort to magic and the occult arts, exorcistic practices and the reading of omens. Occultism is like a defence against the suffering imposed by nature and the particular hardship of the environmental conditions of India. Characteristically, Indians believe that the spirits, both favourable and unfavourable to man, have one origin, just as 'good' and 'evil', projections of the desires of man and therefore of the *maya* ('play of illusion'), have the same identical nature. The philosopher saint Shankara, who laid down the lines of Shaivite monism, stated that 'compared to the condition of the undifferentiated spirit, even the gods are demons and the worlds to which they belong are demonic'.

Sanskrit formulas for exorcising the evil eye and other malevolent spirits, and also for curing various diseases (by P. Thomas, 1966).

The India of the Tribes

It is difficult to draw a clear boundary between the populations of the villages and the tribal world, that great mosaic of the aborigenal peoples of India who are also called the *avidasi*. Gradually the ancient avidasi are coming to adopt ways of life which are not very different from those of normal Indian villages as a result of contacts with the Hindus, Hinduization, and now, their dependence upon a rural economy, which has transformed them from hunter gatheres and forest-dwellers into agricultural labourers. On the other hand, the rural Hindu world, in particular the lower castes and the detribalized groups, retain traditions, cults, and rites which are not greatly different from those of the tribal world. The avidasi are losing the isolation in which they have lived since pre-Aryan times and their integration, inevitable though often unfair, will result in the complete loss of their distinctive characteristics. The latest censuses suggest that 'tribal peoples' total about 40 million and are divided into more than 400 major tribes having from several thousand members or even a few hundred to ones with three or four million. They are found all over the subcontinent although they are concentrated in certain regions such as the Northeast, Assam, and the adjacent areas. The main tribes include the Khasi, a large group divided into twenty-five petty states, each with a recognized leader; the Naga warriors, ex-head-hunters who used the heads in magic rites and who have settled in a recently formed state (Nagaland). Another area where there are tribal concentrations is the central belt, in the states of Madhya Pradesh, Orissa, and Bihar and the Bastar and Chota Nagpur regions in particular. In the west there is the large Bhil group and to the east the Santhal and Gond tribes, each numbering four million and belonging to the Dravidian and Munda language groups, as well as the Oraon, Muria, Khond, and others. In southern India (which includes Andhra Pradesh) there are large numbers of small tribal groups located along the western Ghati, on the Nilgri, Badaga, Kota, Toda mountains and there are also the Kanikkar and Kadar. With the exception of the Toda, they are regarded as of Veddid stock (like the larger tribe in Sri Lanka), the so-called proto-australoids. There are also nomadic or semi-nomadic tribes, including the Banjara from the deserts of Rajasthan, and the Kalbelia. They move from village to village as snake charmers, fortune-tellers, minstrels, and sellers of amulets and medicinal roots, or, like the Gadoliya Lohar, they may sell the peasants rudimentary tools that they have made. They are matriarchal and the nomad group is always led by a woman. Other nomads live by stealing livestock and consequently are generally not welcome in the villages.

Almost all the tribal groups base their subsistence economy on gathering the produce of the forest: roots, tubers, fruits. Some hunt with the bow, others fish, and others are herdsmen. Certain customs survive but the deforestation of the areas where they live, amongst other factors, is forcing the hunters and gatherers to turn in part to agriculture, as labourers in the fields and plantations. The majority of them live in villages that are not very different from normal Indian villages, whilst others shelter in huts on the edges of the forests. Their employment as seasonal labourers leads to the building of temporary tribal camps outside the villages. In the south the Irular hunters and gatherers are now employed by government agencies engaged in forest exploitation or in land improvement. Tribal populations are employed in all parts of India by organizations undertaking public works projects such as the building of dams and roads. It is impossible to provide a complete picture of the customs and social relationships of so many different communities, but in general marriage is almost always within the group and monogamous, although some communities do practise polygamy and polyandry. There are innumerable rules concerning sexual customs, often based upon the religious concept of purity. An unusual social institution amongst the Muria of central India is the *gothul* or collective dormitory where all the young men and women of the village live together for a period as a test of communal life, after which they may marry, even though their spouse, as with Hindus, will be chosen by their parents. The collective propitiation dance is an ancient tribal tradition and is performed at certain festivals and also at marriages. There is a considerable amount of craft-based industry, ranging from the production of fabrics to silver and argentan necklaces and from wooden or metal sculptures to idols made of plant fibre and wall drawings. Often these represent their divinities and the various symbols of their cult. Many tribal divinites are transformed Hindu ones, as in certain incarnations of Shiva, Durga (Bhairavi), and Ganesh. The Kannadiga from the south perform a 'dance of the spirits' or the ritual of 'walking on hot coals', which is also a Hindu custom. The Khond of Orissa once ritually sacrified human beings, but this practice has now been superseded by the sacrificie of buffaloes. The Santhal, a proscribed caste who live to the east of the central zone, have women who are regarded as witches and their tutelary deities are witchlike divinities or spirits known as *bonga*. They formulate special mantras to cast the evil eye on certain people or to exorcise curses that have been uttered by others. Santhal witches, who are called *ojha* or *sakha*, enter a trance during particular black magic rituals or formulas and merge

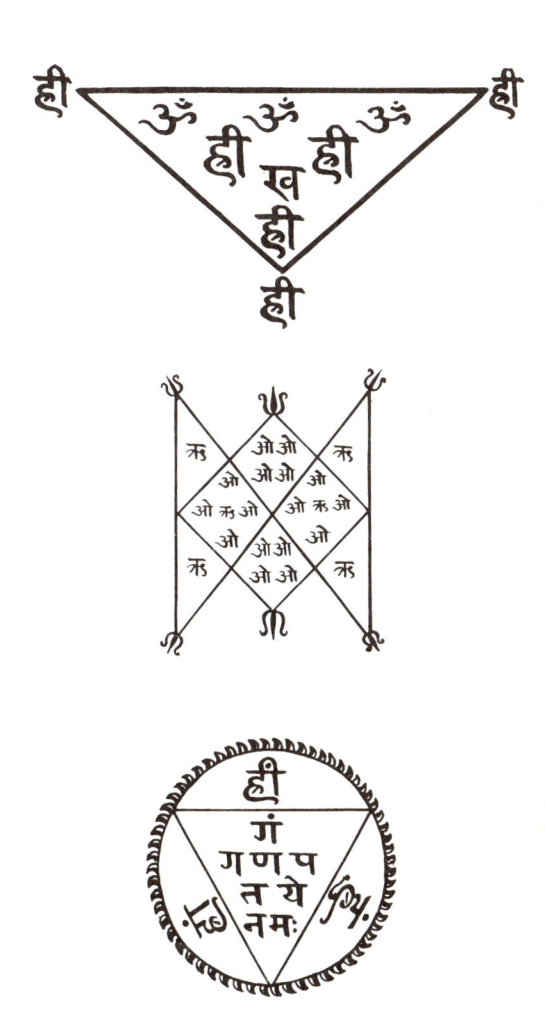

90. A woman cooking on the verandah of her house in Orissa.
On the following pages:
91. A large camel market, held in February, at Nagaur in Rajasthan.
92. A caravan of nomads on camels in the great, arid plain of the Kutch. They carry all their domestic implements and their tents as they move and most tend flocks of sheep or goats and breed camels.

with the evil spirit in order to propitiate it.

It is worth describing the specific characters of two tribes in more detail; one is amongst the largest of the northern tribes and the other is one of the smallest tribes to be found in the southern part of India.

After centuries of contact with Hindu communities, the Bhil, with more than four million members, have absorbed certain brahmanic beliefs and cults, such as the figure of Shiva, who they call Mahadeo. They venerate a 'magic' drum and they believe in a supreme divinity called 'Bhagwan'. They believe themselves to be the true descendants of the Rajput races of Rajasthan and in the past they had the right to place a ritual mark made from blood, the *raj-tilak*, on the forehead of a new Rajput sovereign upon his accession to the throne. The Bhil were mainly semi-nomadic hunters and forest gatherers and some of them still use the bow to hunt game. However, the majority are now involved in agriculture, though it is unusual for them to own land; instead they are usually labourers or herdsmen.

They and their families camp around Hindu villages and everybody, including the women, is very active. Recurrent famines have reduced the Bhil to absolute destitution and bloody fights often break out amongst them.

The pastures of the Nilgiri hills ('blue hills'), between Kerala and Karnataka, are occupied by the Toda, who live in scattered villages, usually consisting of six or seven huts. It is essentially a pastoral tribe whose features are possibly unique in the whole of India. Today they may number as few as 1200 but the exceptional interest that they excite is due to their being of pure 'Europid' type, with their pale skin, Dravidian language, animist religion, and practice of polyandry. Some farm but the Toda principally live by rearing buffaloes, which they consider as an emblem and source of fertility. The buffaloes are divided into domestic and sacred ones. The milk of sacred buffaloes, which are only milked by the priests, is kept in conical huts. Men and women dress in the same garment, which resembles the Roman toga. The houses are most distinctive, with ogival pitched roofs, a very old kind of structure, which can be seen in Indian sculpture that is centuries old. Every Toda woman can marry several times and has marital rights over a number of 'friends', which are officially recognized; at the same time she can be the wife of the brothers and cousins of her husband. Each of these has wives and 'friends', and these are changed every few years for others. It is not a proper matriarchy, but the women are a form of common property. The question of paternity is resolved by naming a father in a special ceremony during the seventh month of pregnancy and the children in this way belong to the community.

The Toda have a system of justice which is exercised by a council of five elders, the *naim*, to which a member of the Badaga tribe belongs. This is an example of ritual co-operation between different tribes. The naim, which presides at great ceremonial functions, settles disputes and imposes fines (always levied in heads of buffalo) for the small number of minor crimes committed. Death comes easily to the Toda, for with them it is merely a move from one part of the Nilgiri to another, which is called Amrov or Amnor, the underground world, where the deceased will continue in the same way as they did when alive. All a man's property will therefore be cremated with him and some buffaloes will be sacrificed by the priests. The Toda do not appear to have been part of the invasions of Aryan pastoral tribes, but seem to be a relic of an early Indo-European descent into the peninsula. This population has adapted to local conditions and, although it has remained distinct, it has absorbed the customs and habits of the Dravidian people as well as their language.

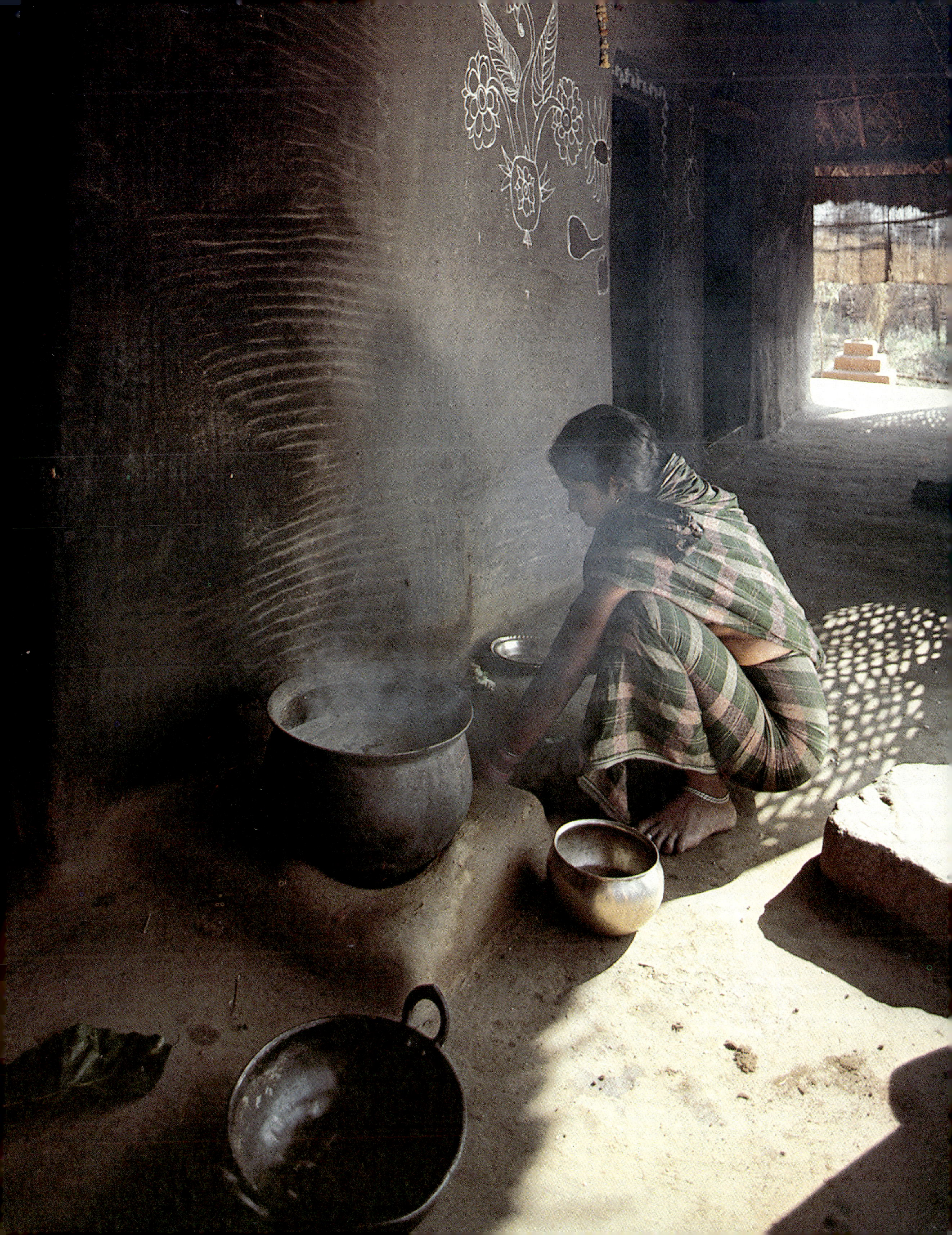

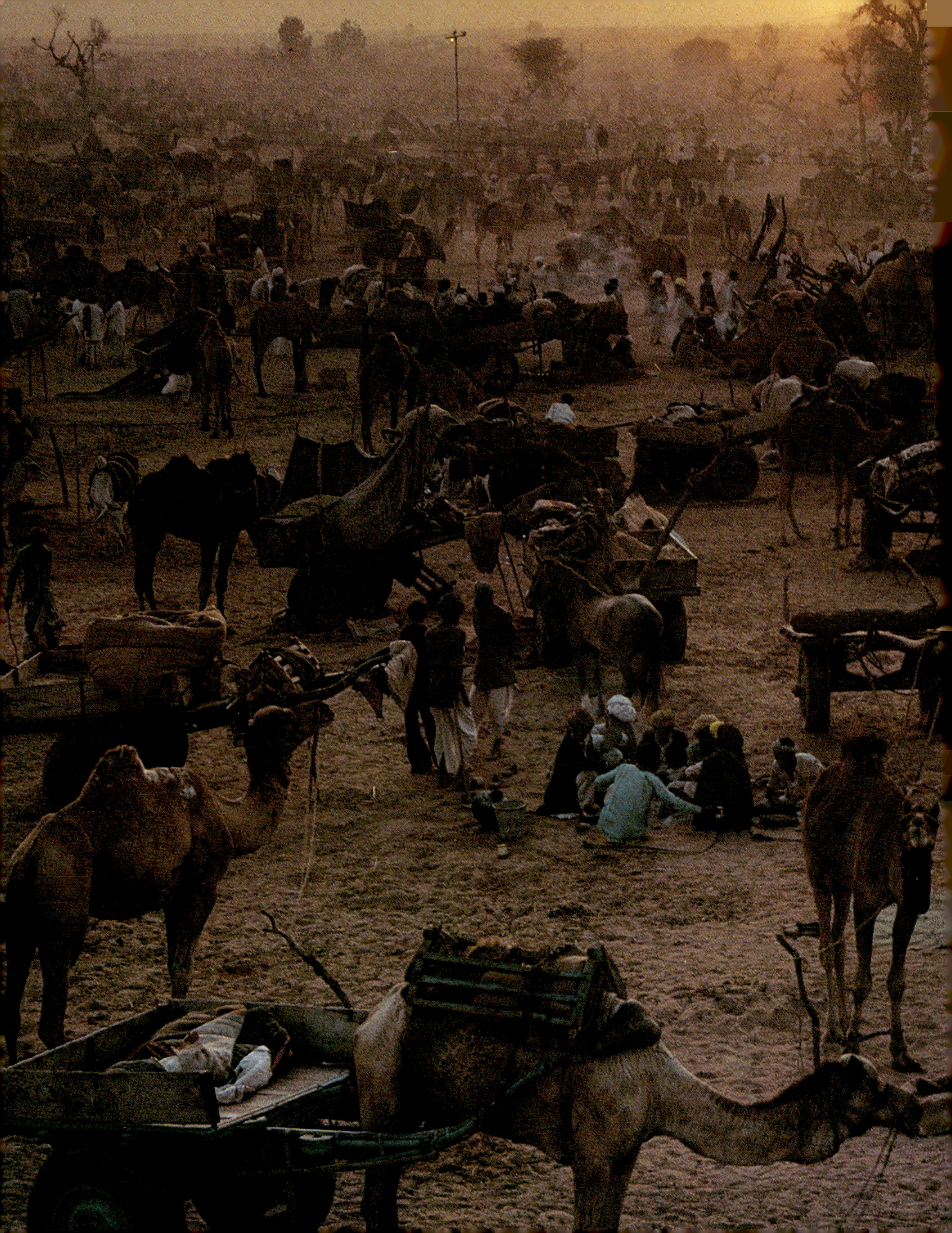

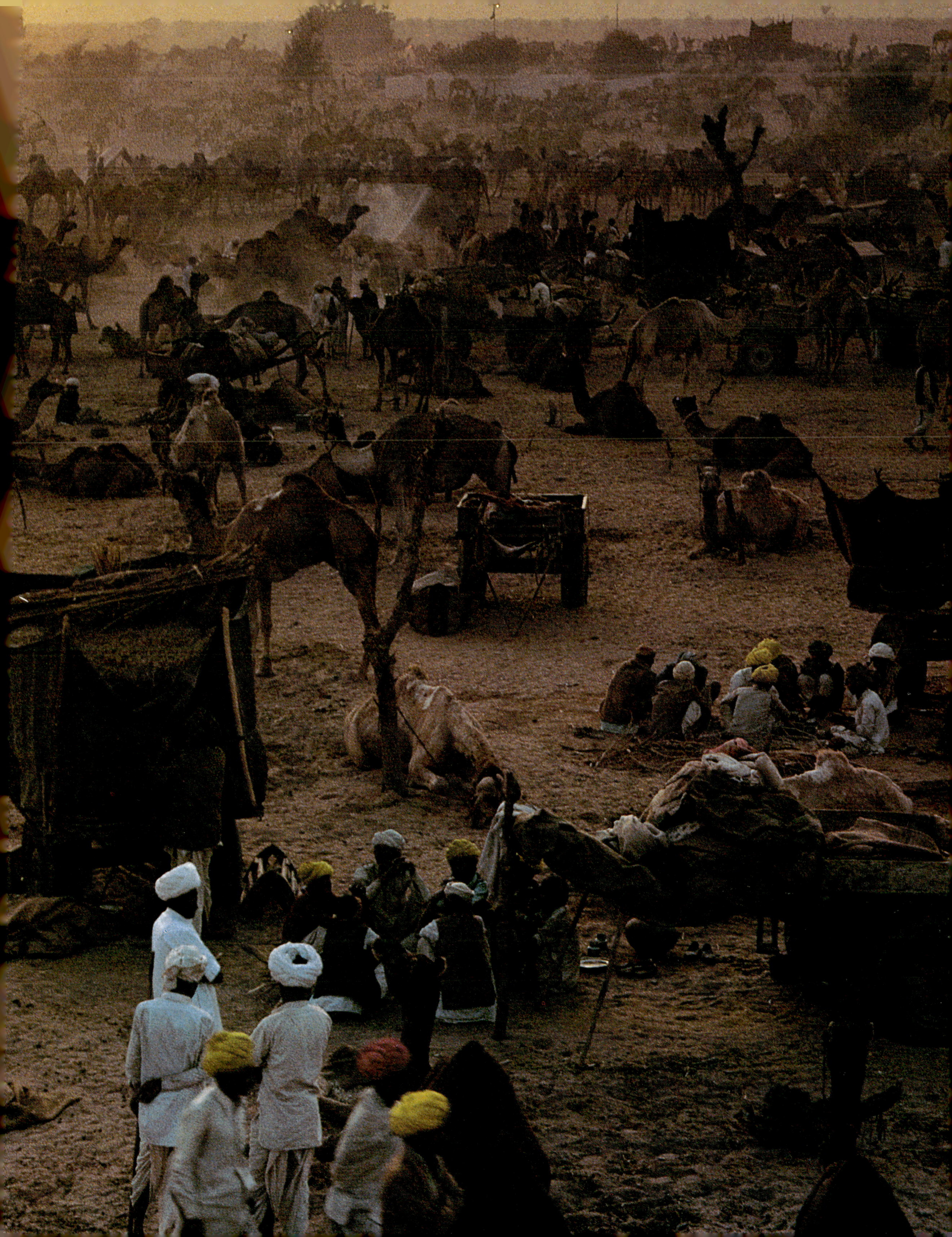

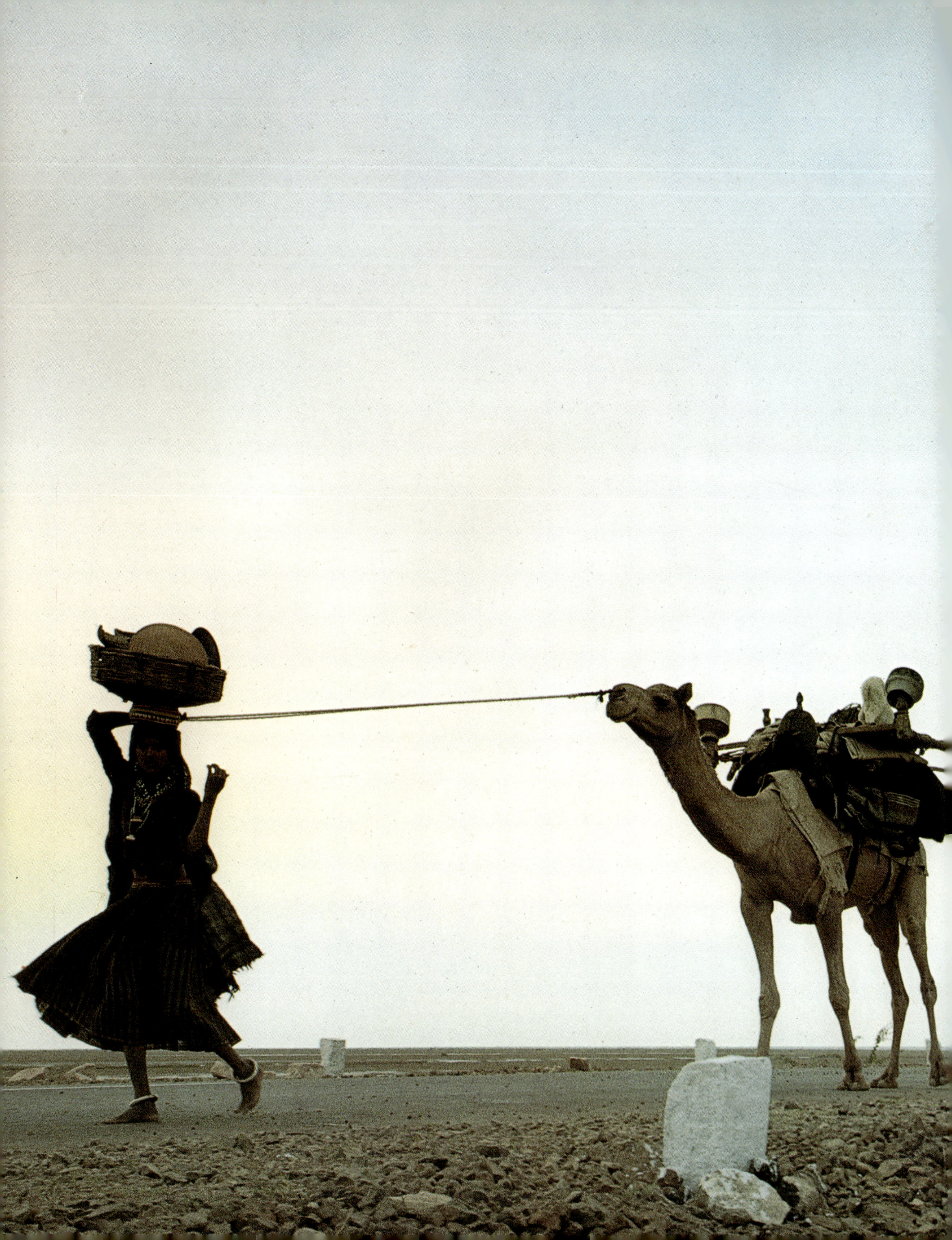

93. *A beautiful house, the home of a Muslim in the Kutch. All the furnishings are raised off the ground to avoid being damaged by the floods which occur in this region during the monsoon season. This house is in the village of Dordo about sixty miles south of Brij, the capital of the Kutch. The region is known as Bunni, a name it has earned from a type of grass that is widespread in the region and which provides good grazing for the livestock.*

94. A Kutch peasant repairing the walls of his house. The main materials are mud and cow dung, which is a good binding material and which, when dry, gives a smooth and impermeable surface.

On the following pages:
95. In the courtyard of a small village temple some pilgrims rest in the dharamshala, a space set aside as a shelter for pilgrims which is to be found in every Indian temple. The village is Kathiawar, in Gujarat, and the festival of Tarnetar is being celebrated. The statue on the left painted red represents Hanuman or Maroti, the athletic monkey god, who is almost as popular as Ganesh. In mythology and in the sacred epic of the Ramayana he appears as the faithful servant of the god Rama.

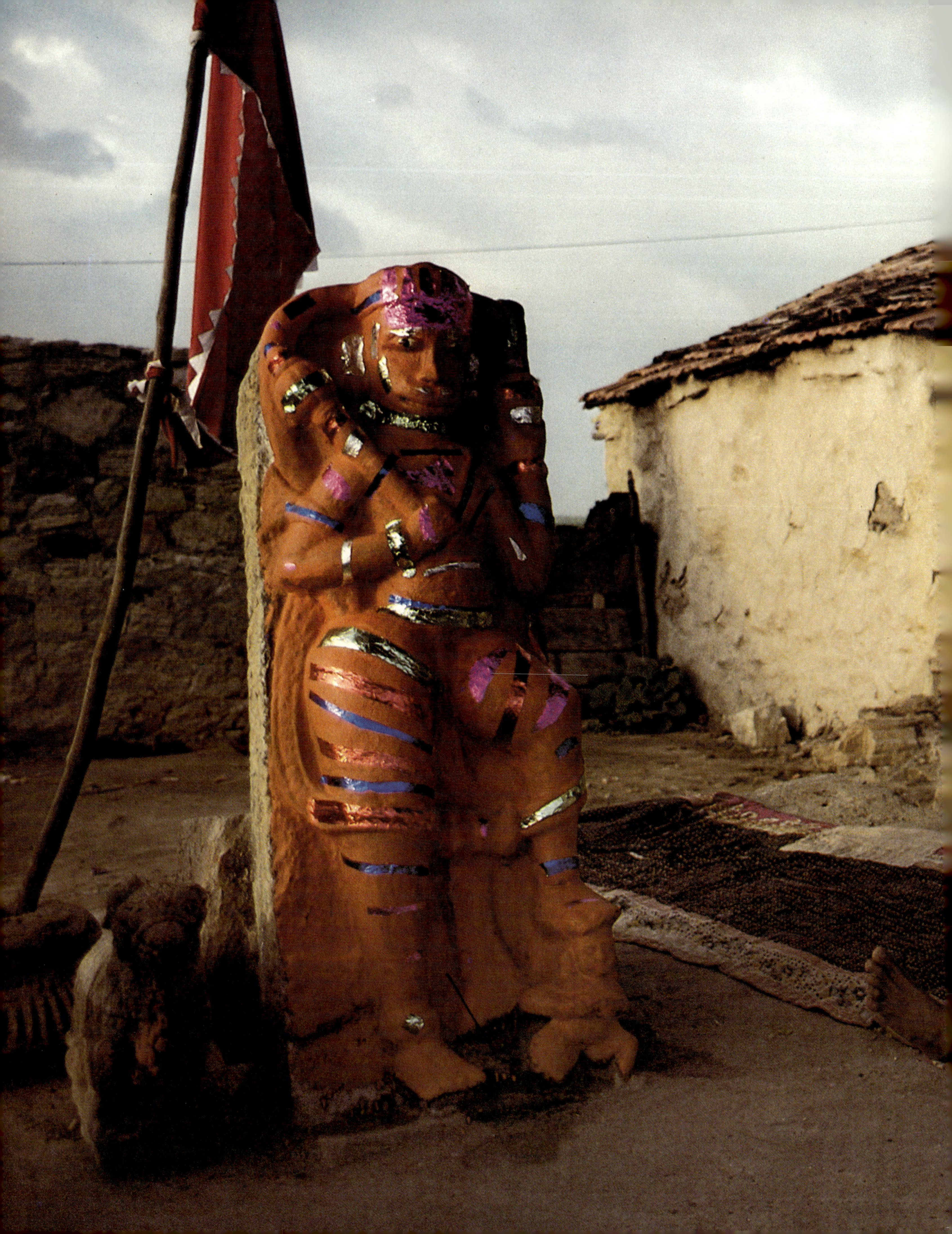

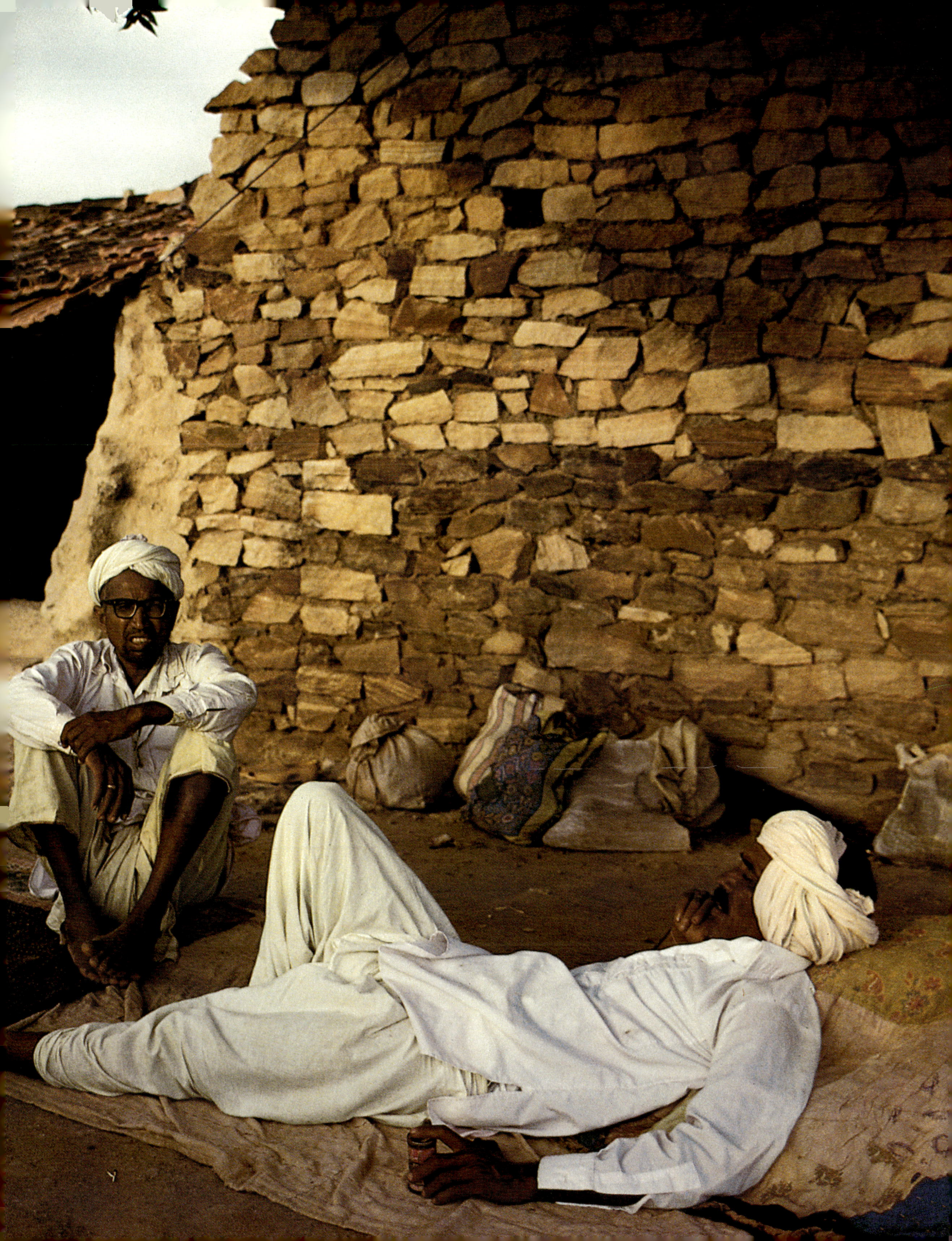

96

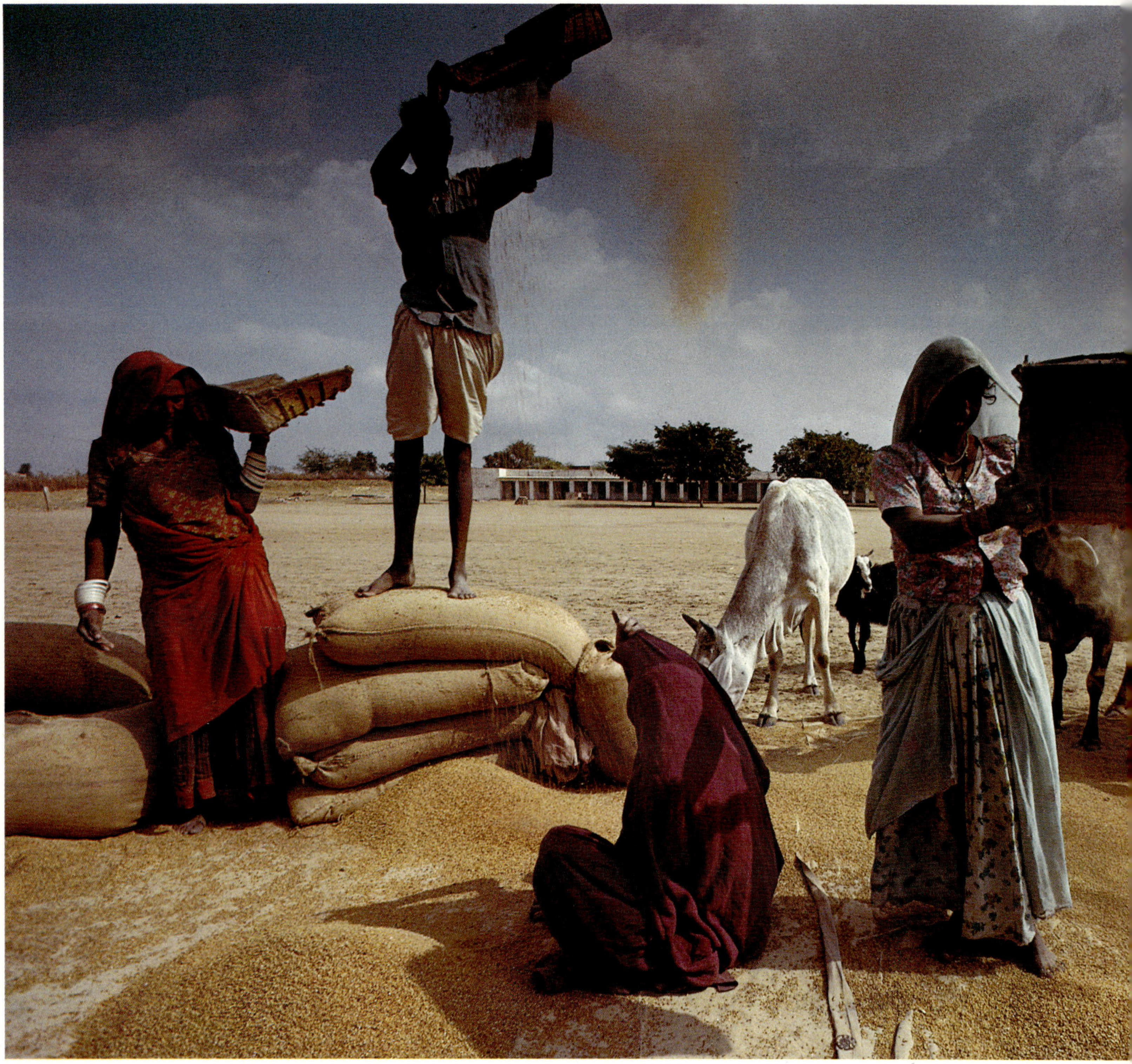

96. Winnowing grain in Rajasthan; this traditional method is still common throughout India. Farming techniques are fairly primitive and threshing is done by one or two oxen walking in a circle and turning a heavy cylindrical millstone with a rod attached to a central axle. Winnowing is generally done by women and children, as is the washing of the grain in the river in order to remove the earth and lumps of mud. Almost everywhere the rainy season kharif is the richest harvest. The most important harvests are in July, November, and March-April.

97. The entrance of a mud house at Kannoy near Jaisalmer, with the walls painted with religious decorations and signs and lucky charms.

98. The local bus, which covers vast stretches of desert from one village to the next, finally arrives in the city of Jaisalmer.

99. In the space in front of a 'hotel' in Pushkar, at a café offering tea and other beverages, a group of Rajasthani peasants rest and chat. The women are huddled together to one side and crouch on the ground. Pushkhar is one of the holy cities of Rajasthan and the object of pilgrimage but it also has a market and fair.
On the following pages:
100. Nomads, camped in the open, with their traditional decorated carts and merchandise. They are probably Gadoliya Lohar, nomadic smiths who make crude utensils on the spot which they sell to peasants in the villages. These tribes display a form of matriarchy and the women actually make the utensils.

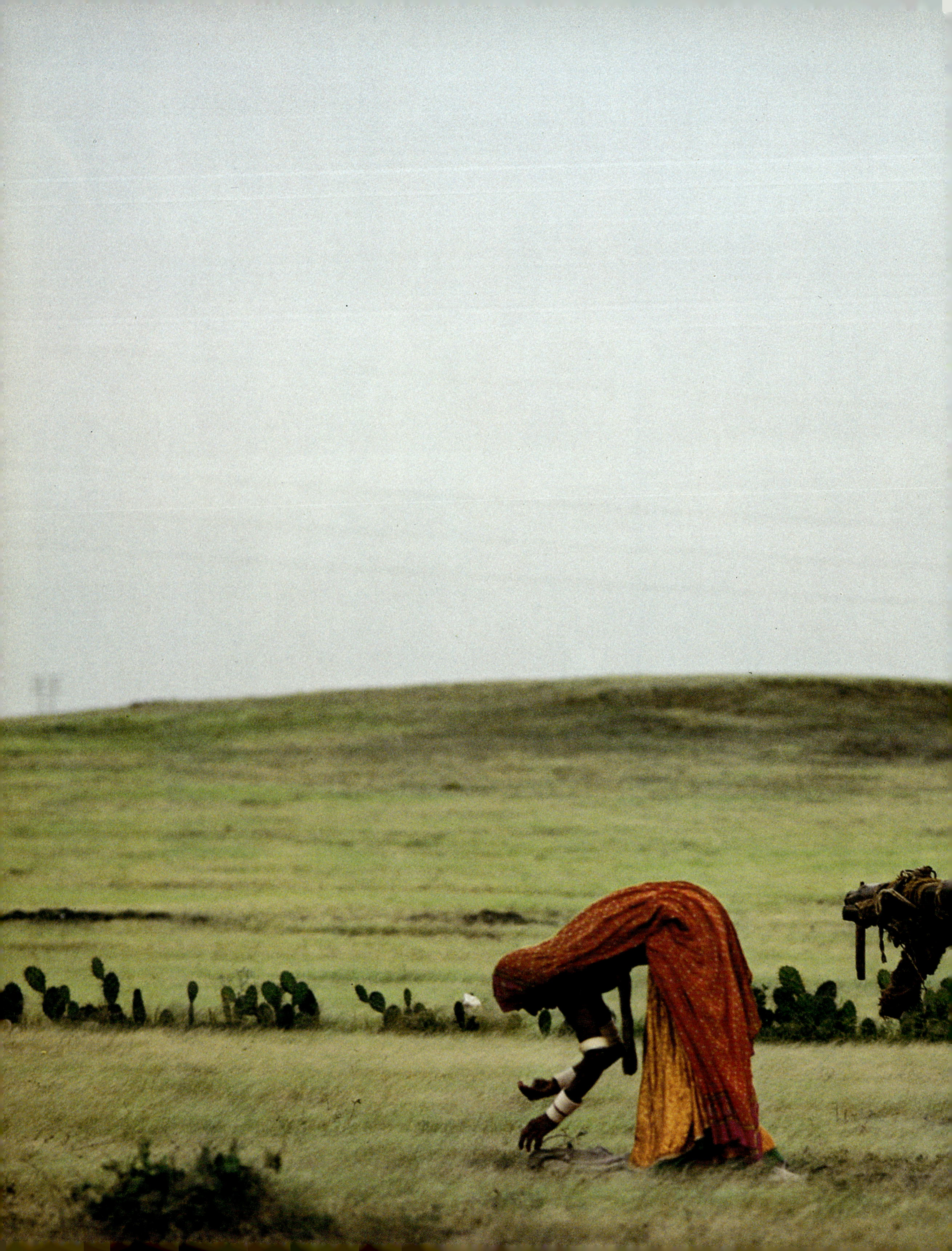

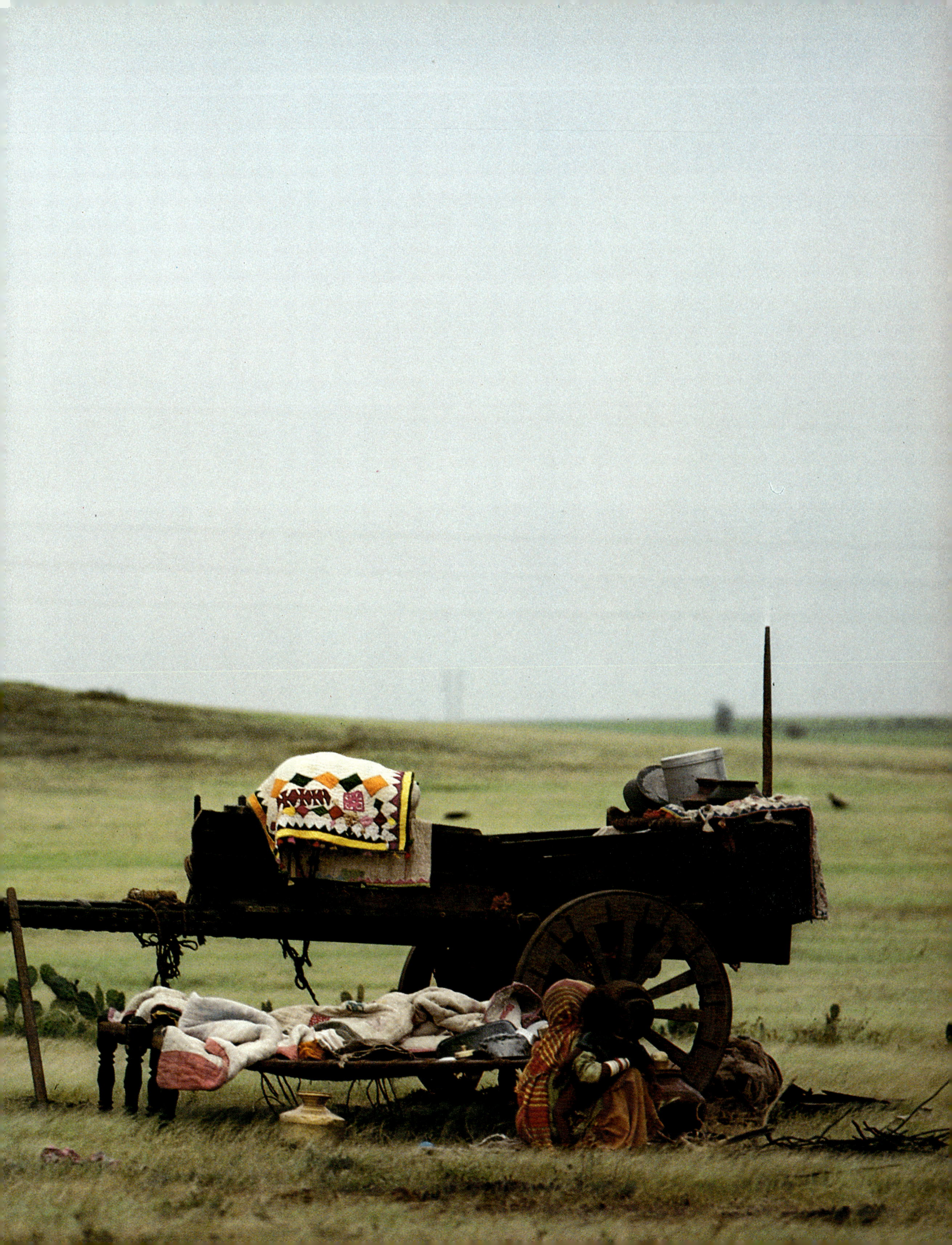

101

101, 102, 103. *The middle of the monsoon with torrential rain and rivers in full spate, in the countryside of central India. Indians, particularly in the country, are not bothered by the rain, indeed they are overjoyed by the atavistic feeling of gratitude to the sky and the knowledge that the water brings new life to the fields.*

102

103

201

104

104. Peasants in the middle of the fields rest during a heavy downpour of the monsoon.
105. On the road to Udaipur. The subcontinent is today criss-crossed by a dense network of roads and few regions remain isolated. However, the traffic is not segregated and there are no motorways reserved for motor vehicles. Instead, whole families and groups can be seen walking along the roads, along with herds, bullock carts, bicycles, cars, and large, overladen lorries all jumbled together in a disordered chaos which surprises the foreign visitor but which is moving faster than it might appear.

106

106. Terracotta statues of the god Ayannar and his squire; this rural divinity is regarded as the tutelary divinity of the fields and harvests in Tamil Nadu.
107. Young women, after their ablutions in the holy basin, prepare to enter the temple to do homage to the divinity of Dwarka, Krishna, on the anniversary of his birth.

On the following pages:
108. Earthenware vases at Ramdeora in Rajasthan. The vases are made by a caste of vase-makers, the kumhar.
109. A street in Udaipur, an important town in southern Rajasthan.
110. An entire Bhil clan rests on the steps of a lake at Mandu in Madhya Pradesh.

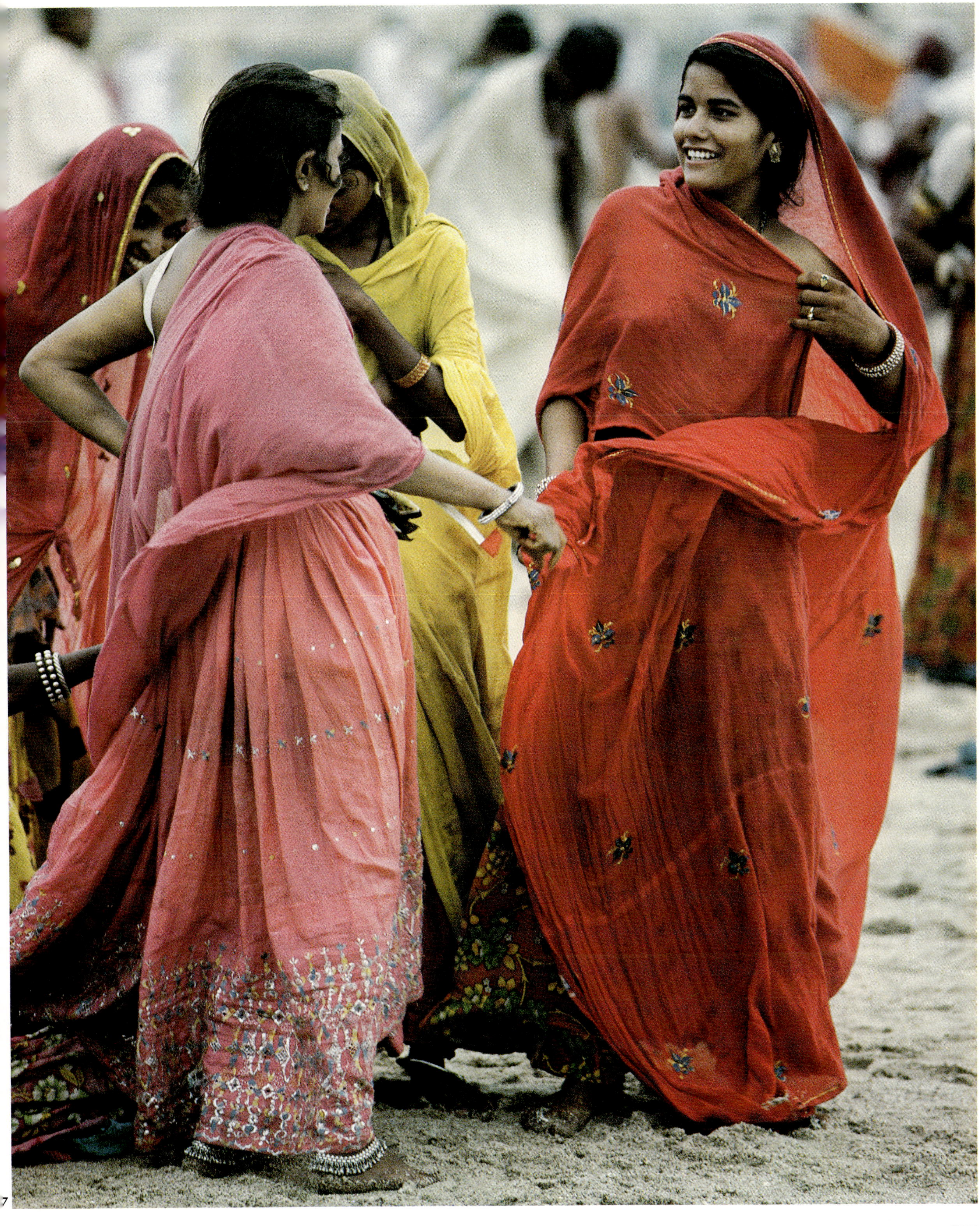

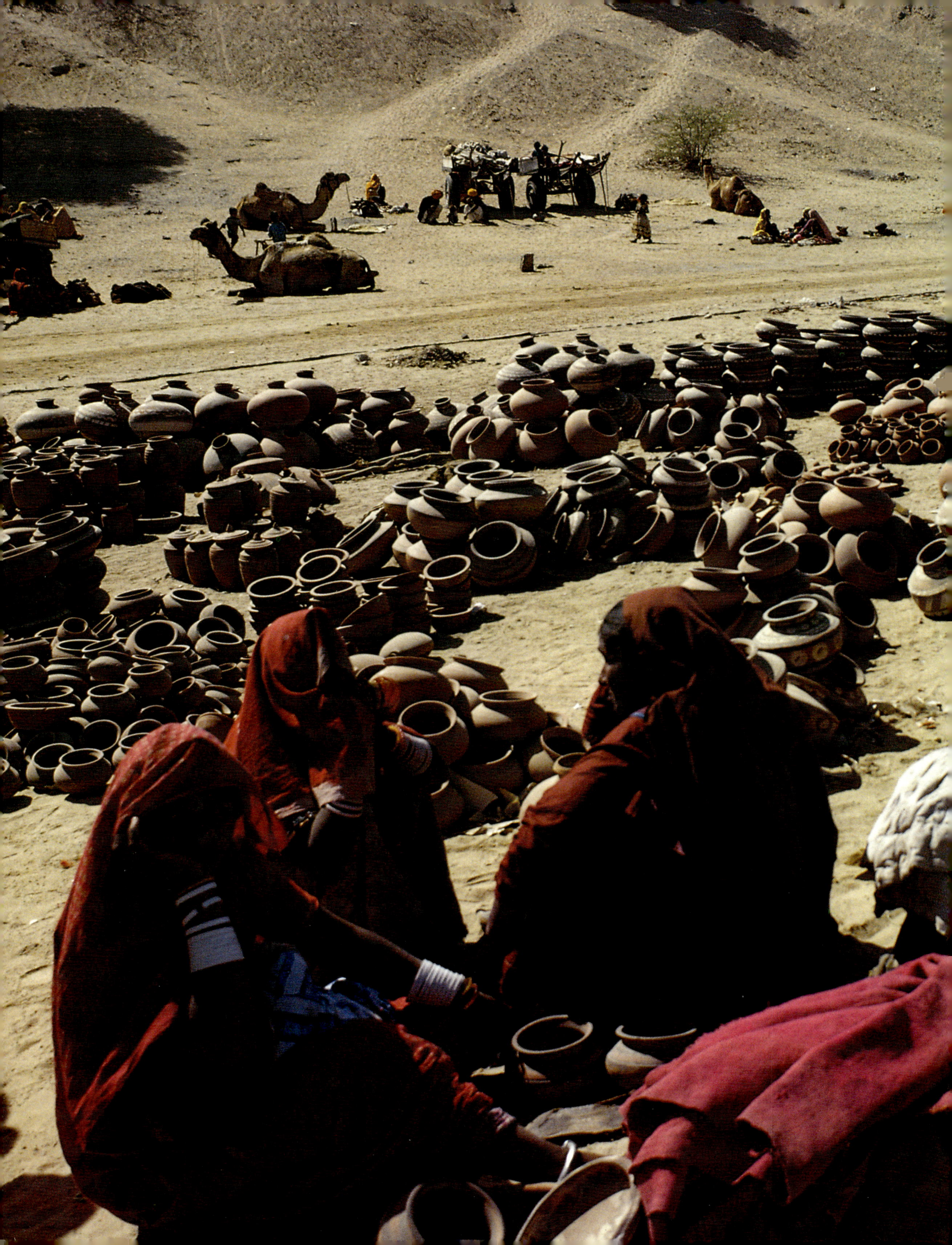

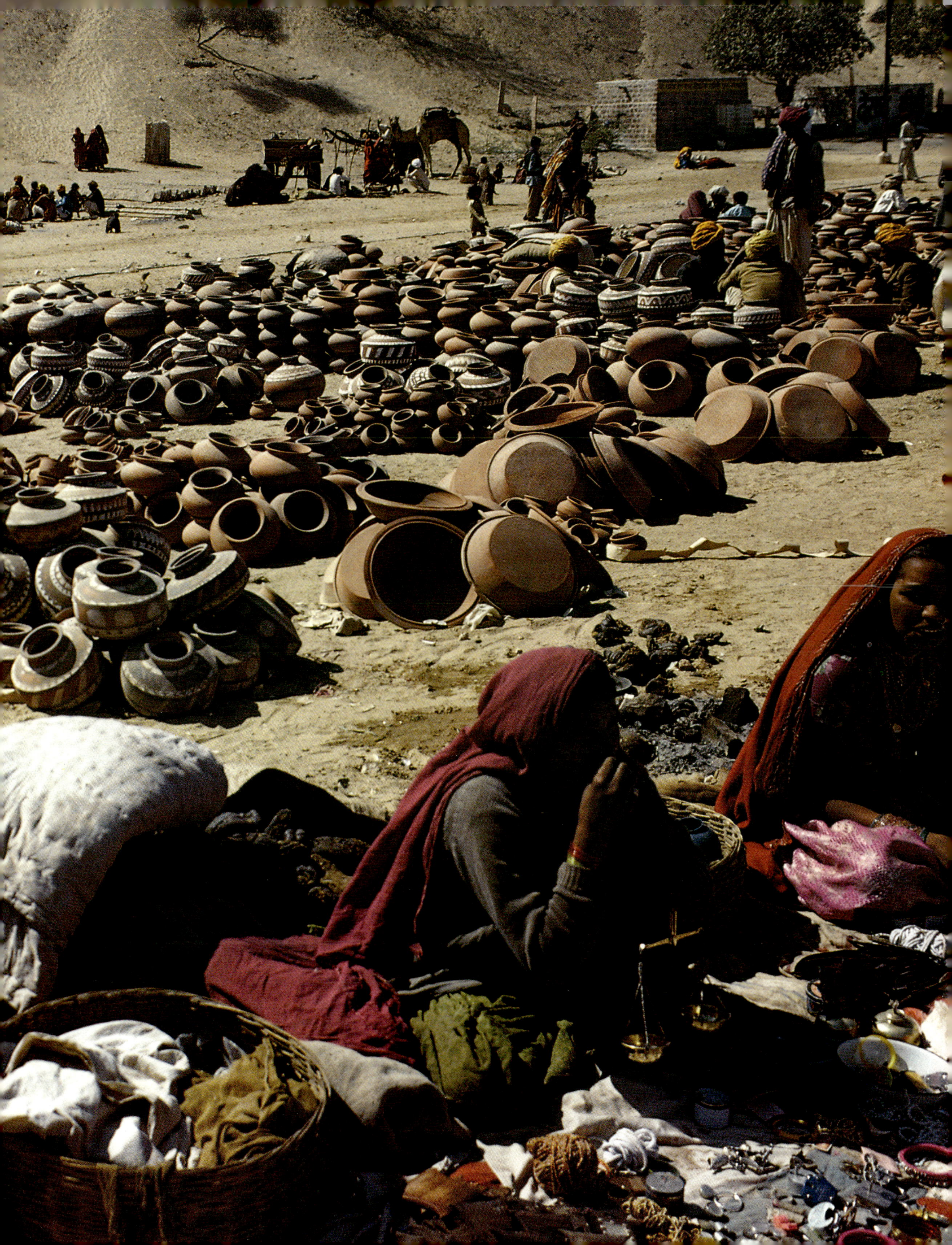

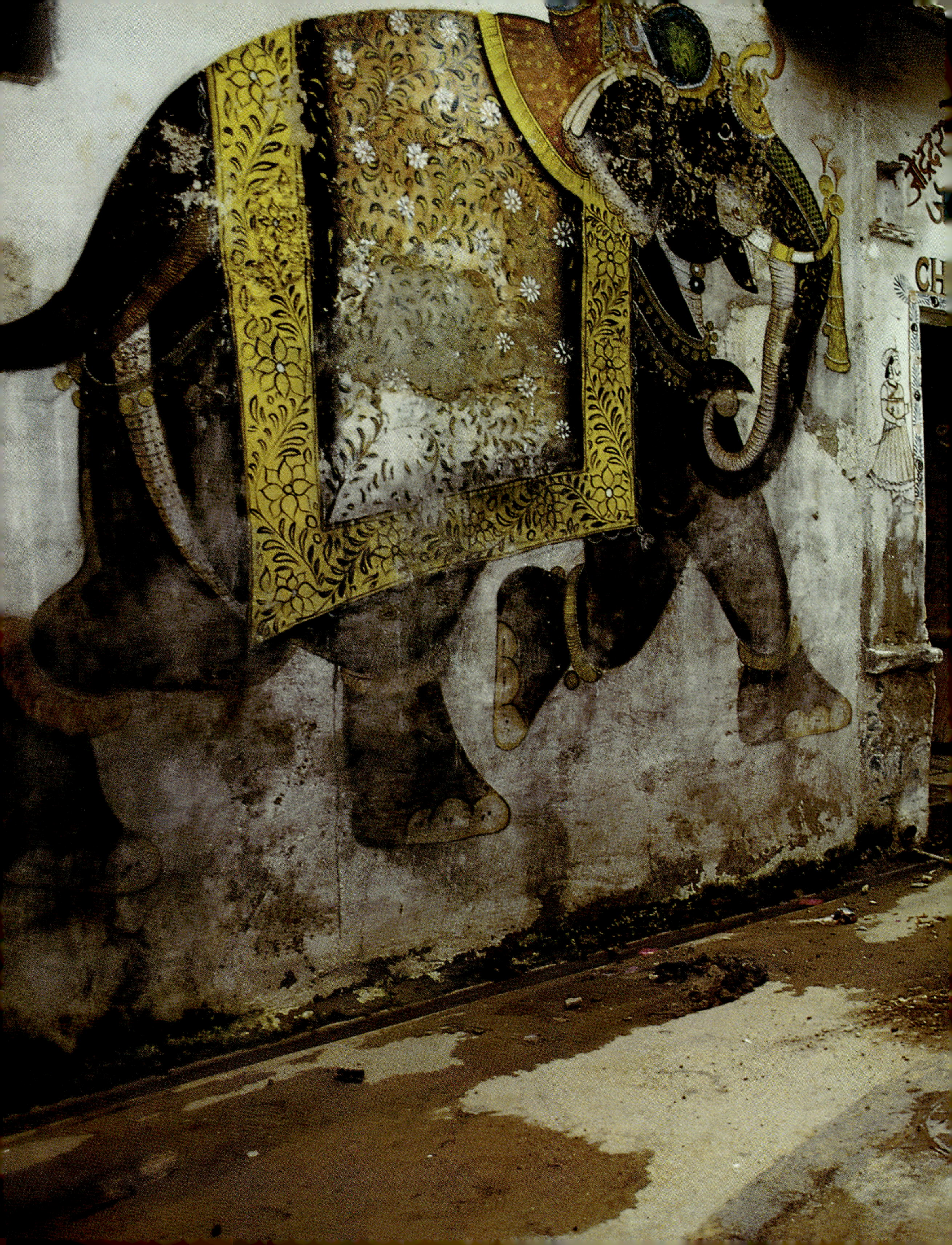

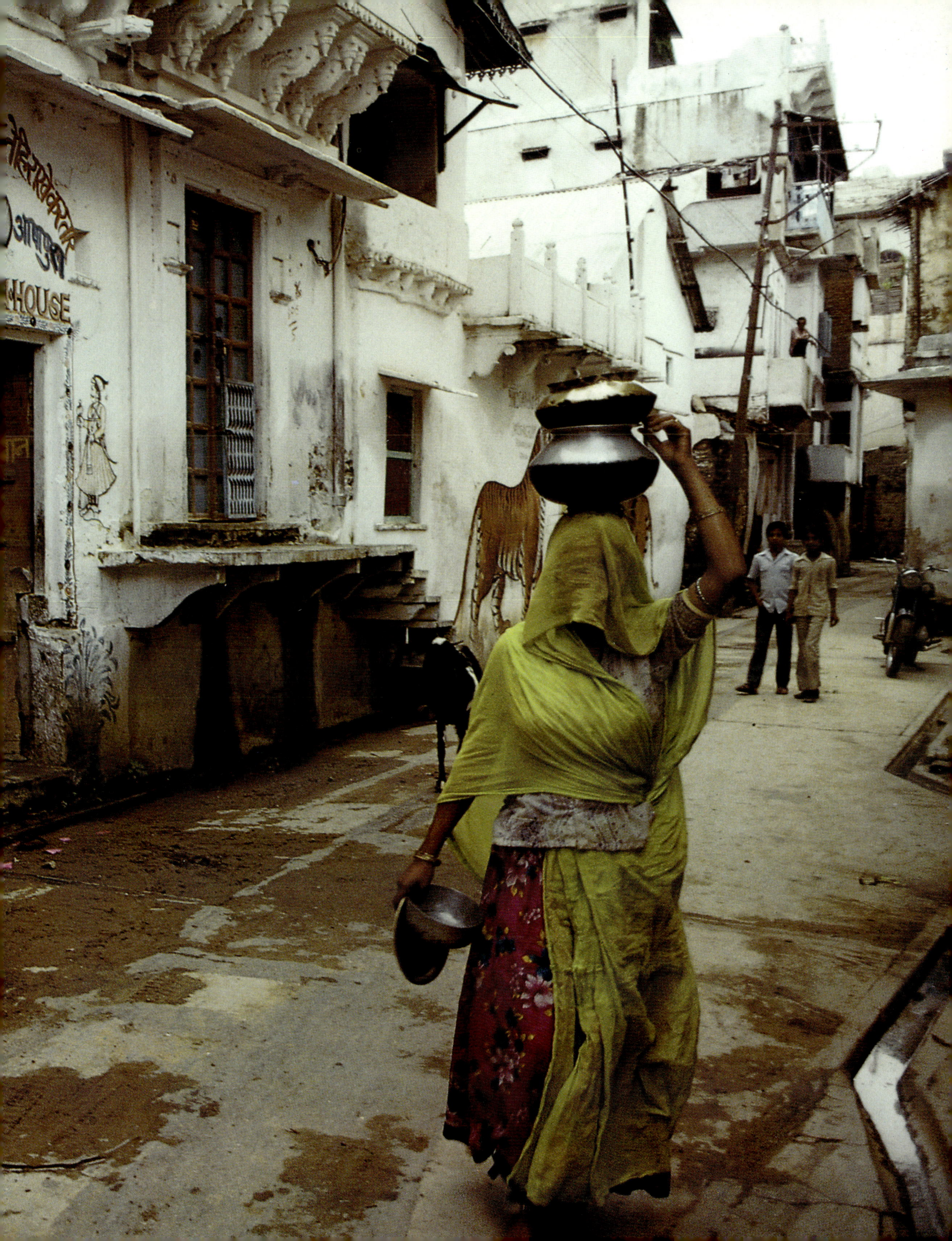
HOUSE

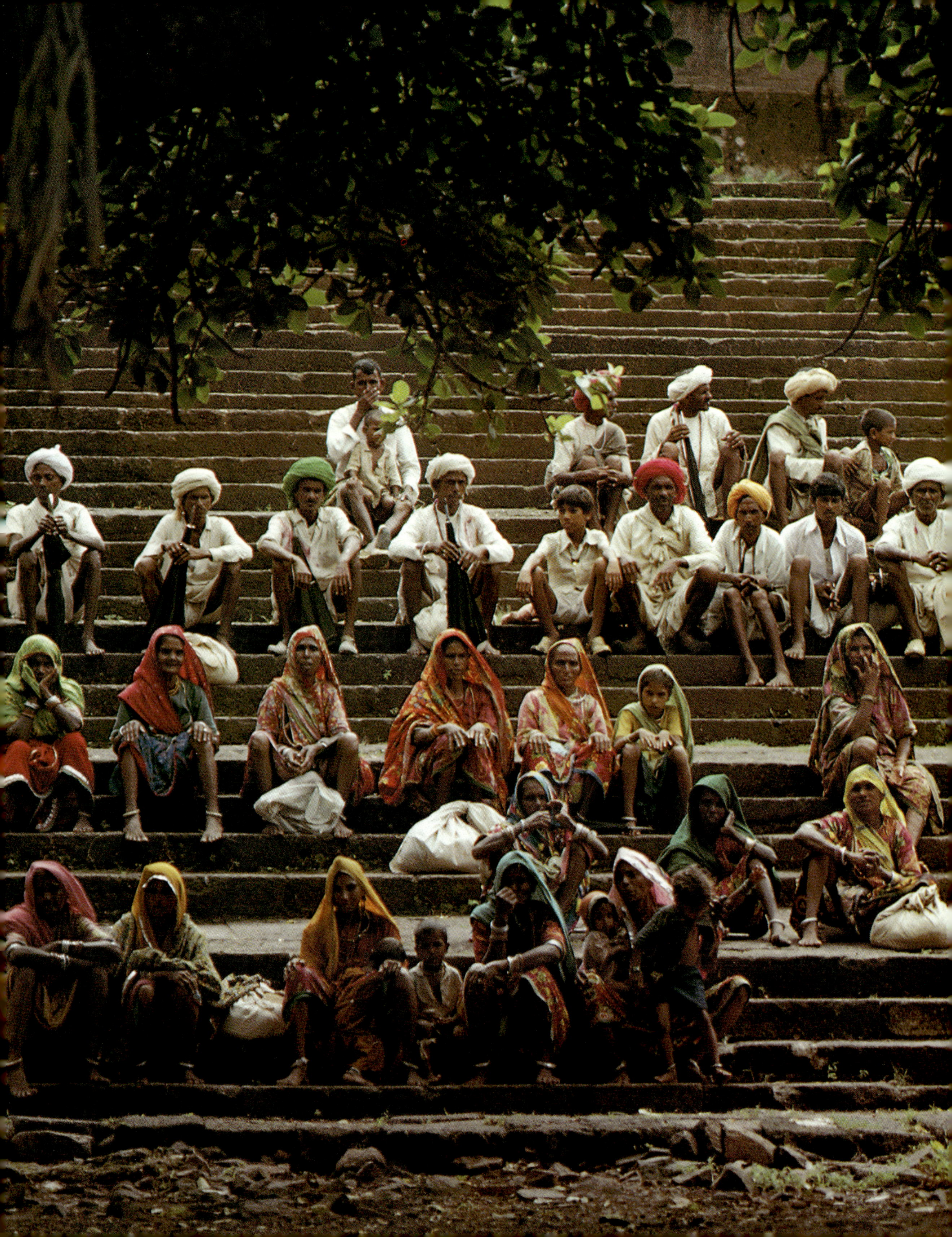

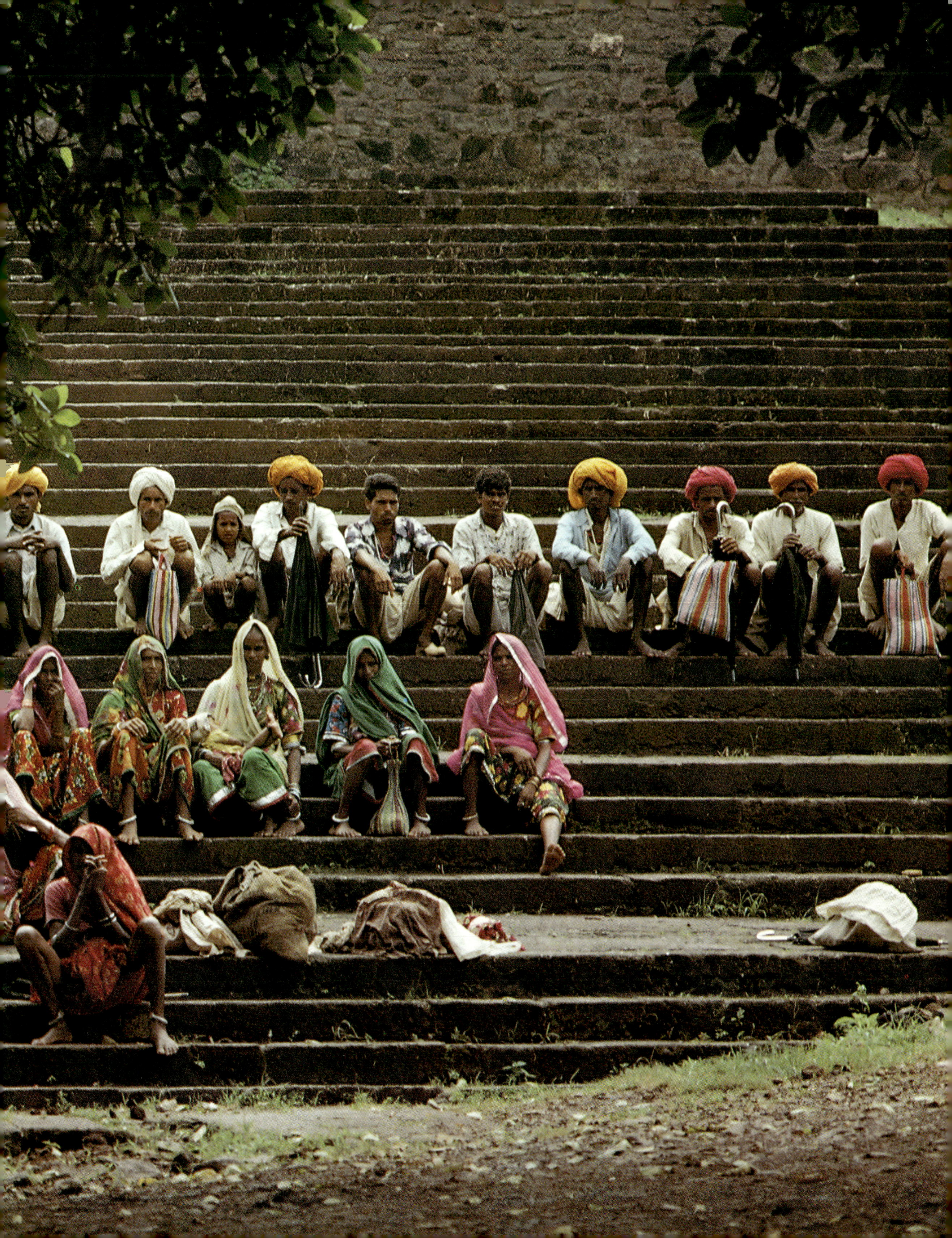

111

111. On the beautiful beaches of the Bay of Bengal, level with Konarak in Orissa, fishermen assess the morning's catch.
112. Fish market at Diu, the small island off Gujarat, a former Portuguese colony.
On the following pages:
113. Harvest time in Orissa, north of Bhubaneshwar.

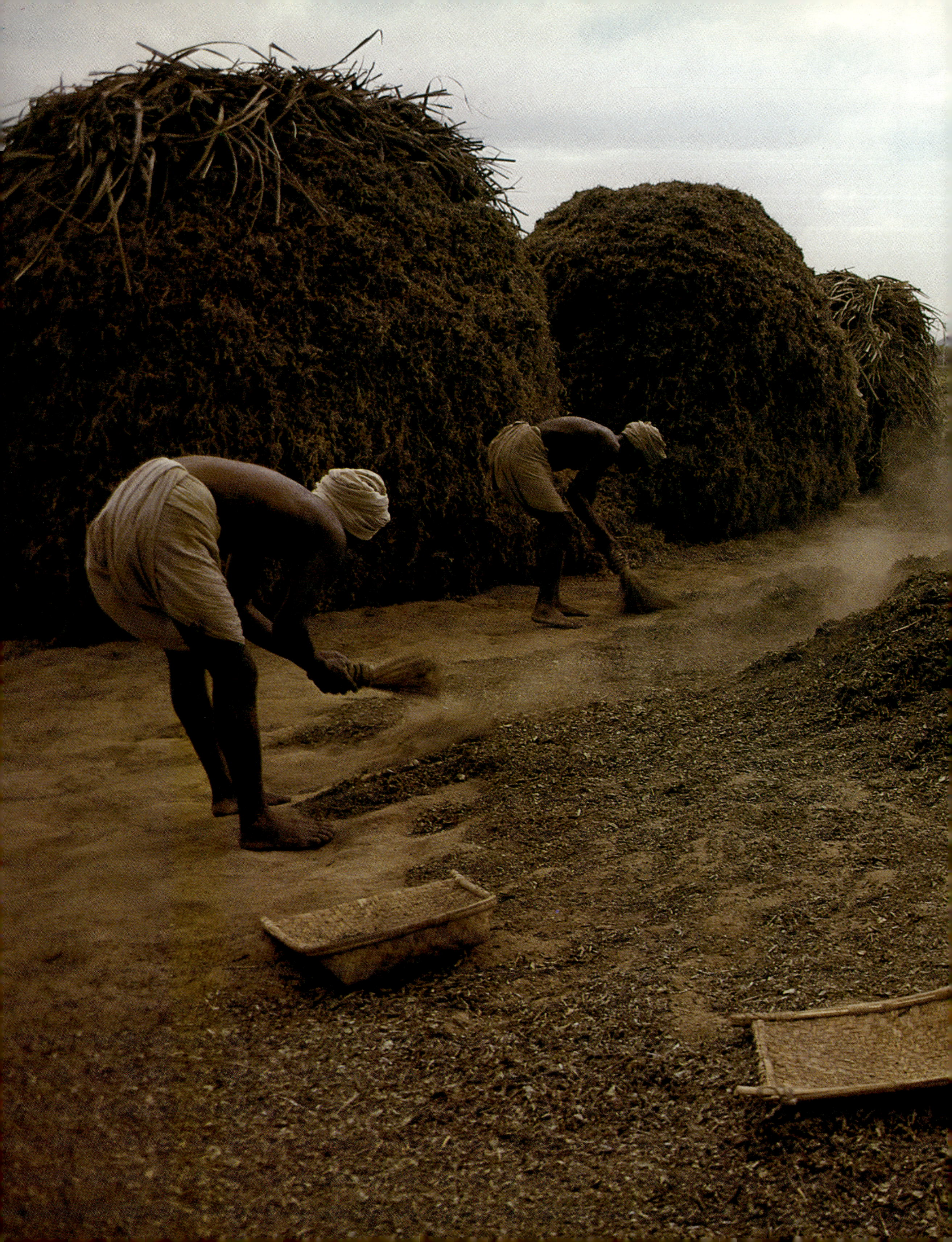

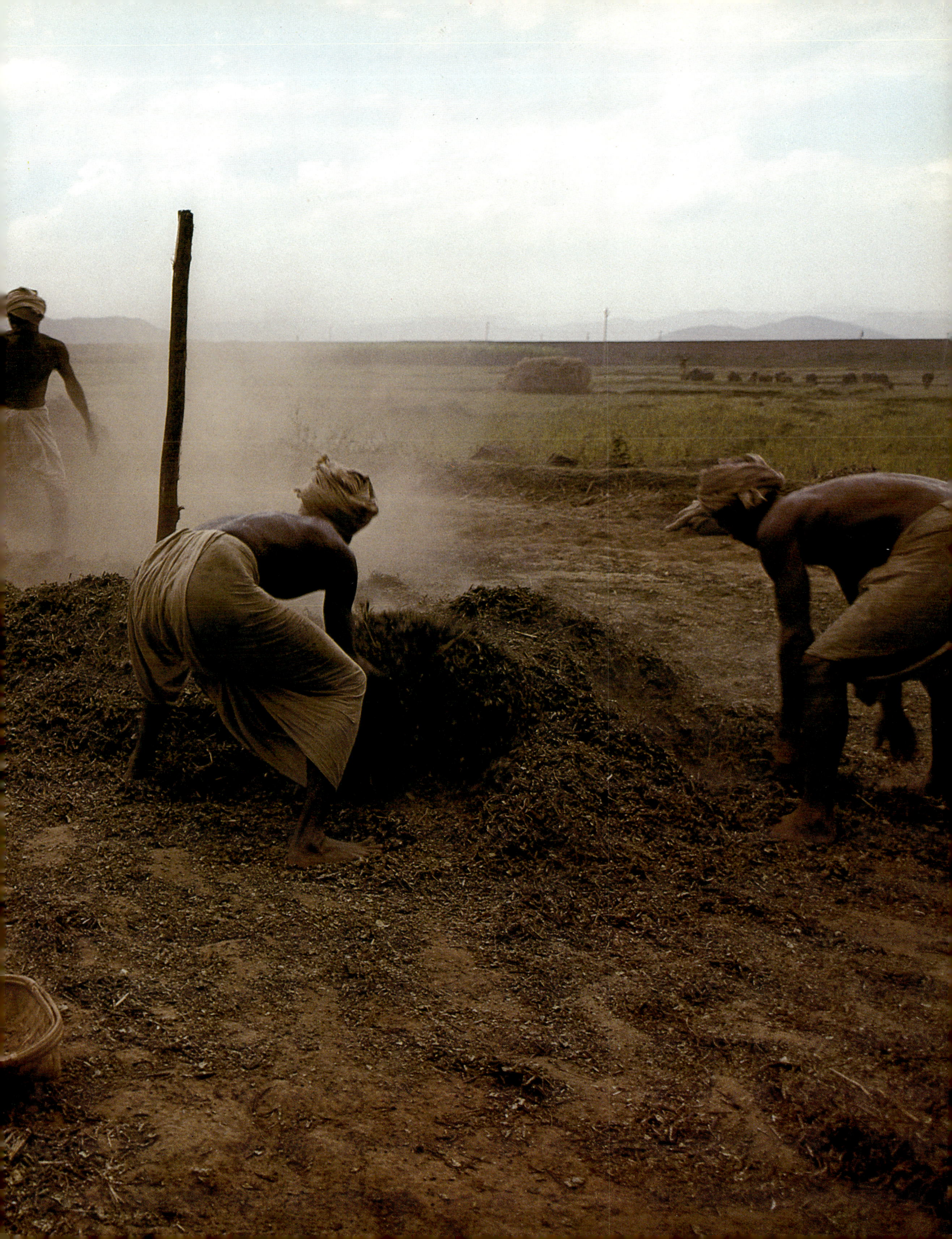

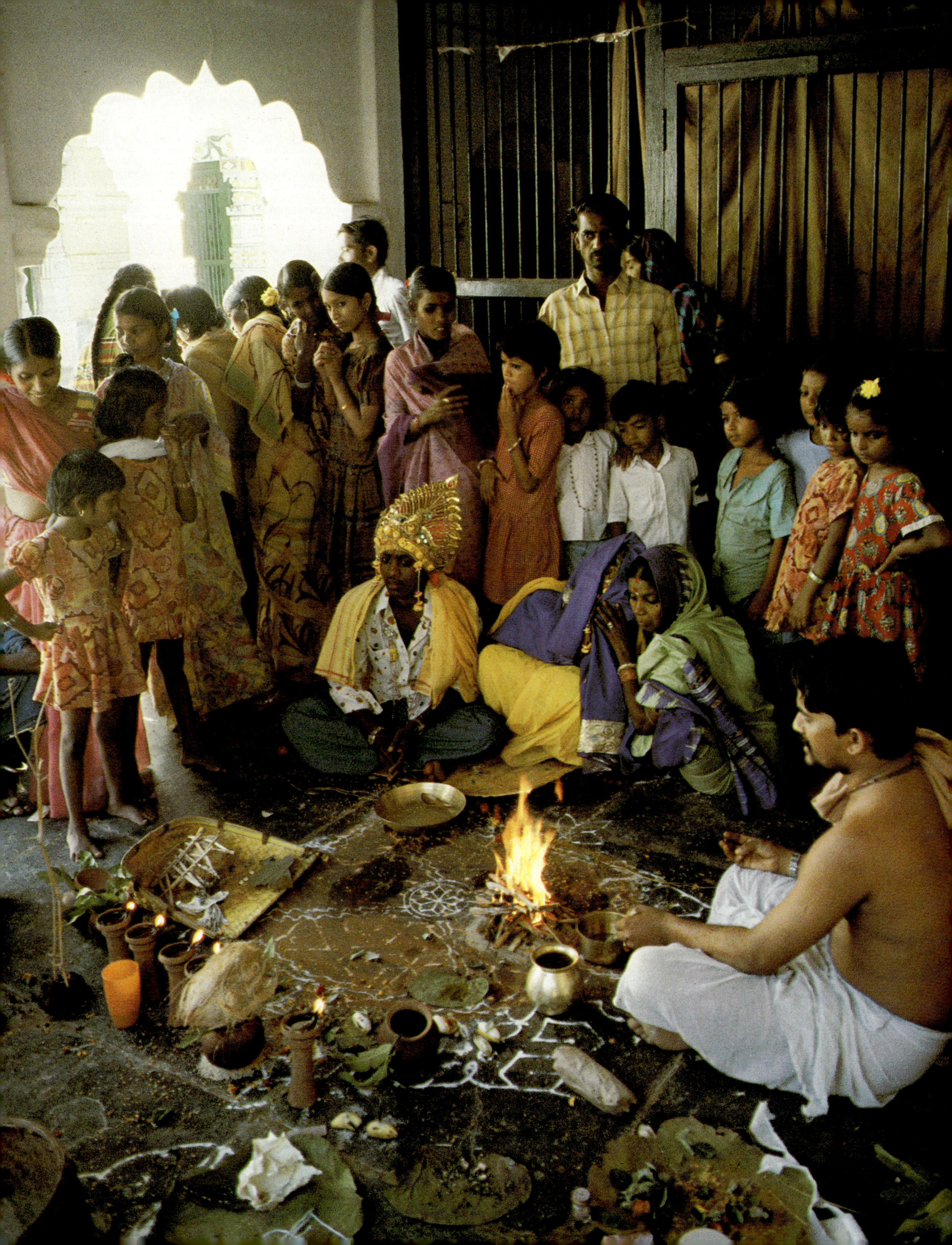

114. *A marriage being celebrated in the precinct of the temple of Gopalpur in Orissa, dedicated to the god Krishna. In India, the rites, ceremonies, and festivities associated with a wedding last two days and sometimes a whole week, and involve relatives, acquaintances, and members of the caste to which the couple belong. The types of wedding and ceremonies vary markedly from region to region and even from village to village.*

115. *Rishikesh, in the north, is the holy centre of the sannyasi and the ascetics and religious schools; it is also frequented by westerners on a spiritual quest. The owner of a small restaurant invented this original advertisement.*

116

116. At work in the fields, at Hampi in upper Karnataka. The colossal statue is of Narasimha, the lion man, a classical incarnation of Vishnu. This area is the site of the great city of Vijayanagar, the last Hindu empire of the south and it is littered with the partially ruined remains of buildings, temples, statues, and other important archaeological finds.
117. A Tamil peasant ploughing.
118. A Tamil peasant carrying an enormous earthenware vase.
On the following pages:

119. Banjara nomad women in picturesque dresses. The gypsies now found around the world appear to have originated from India, and from the Banjara peoples in particular.

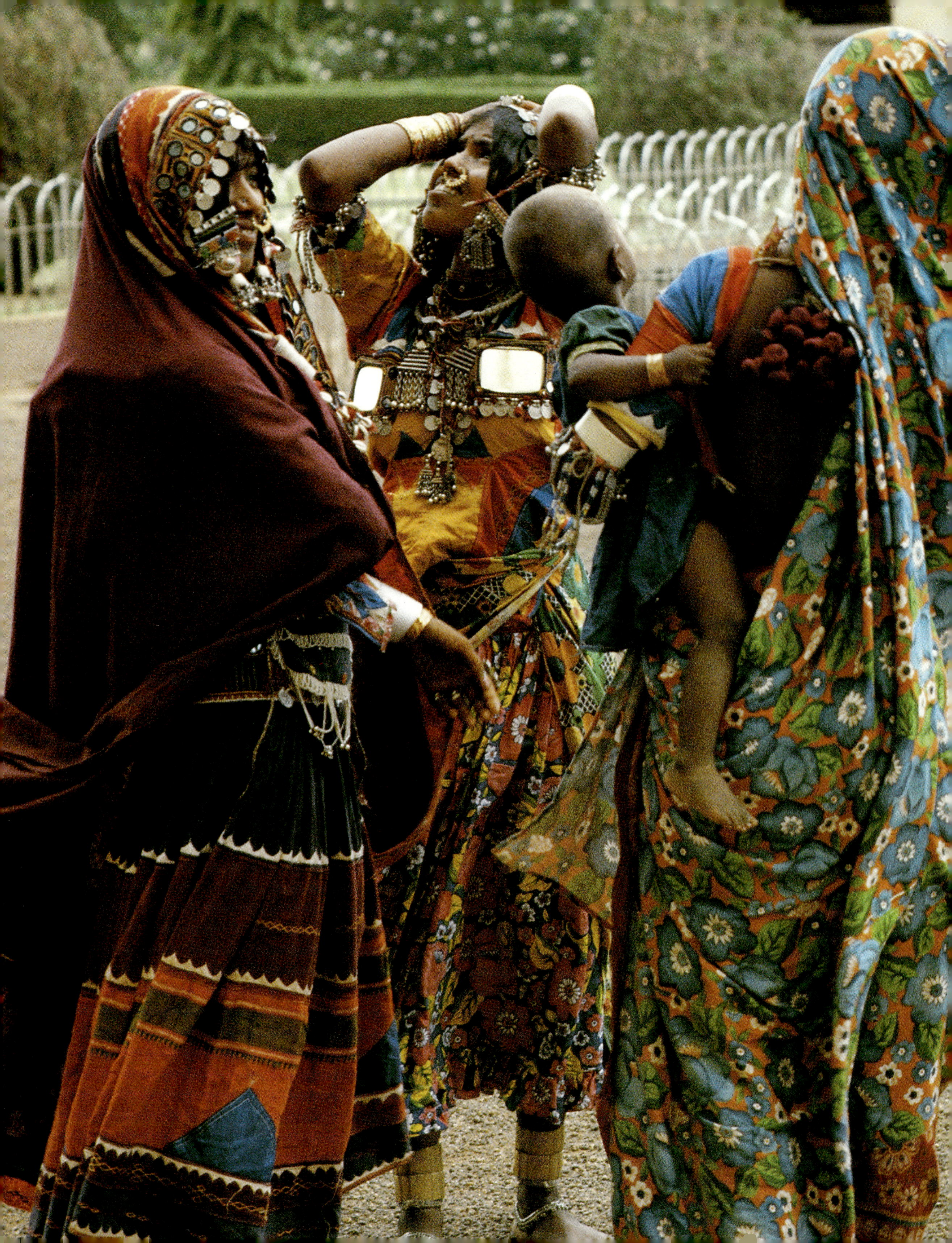

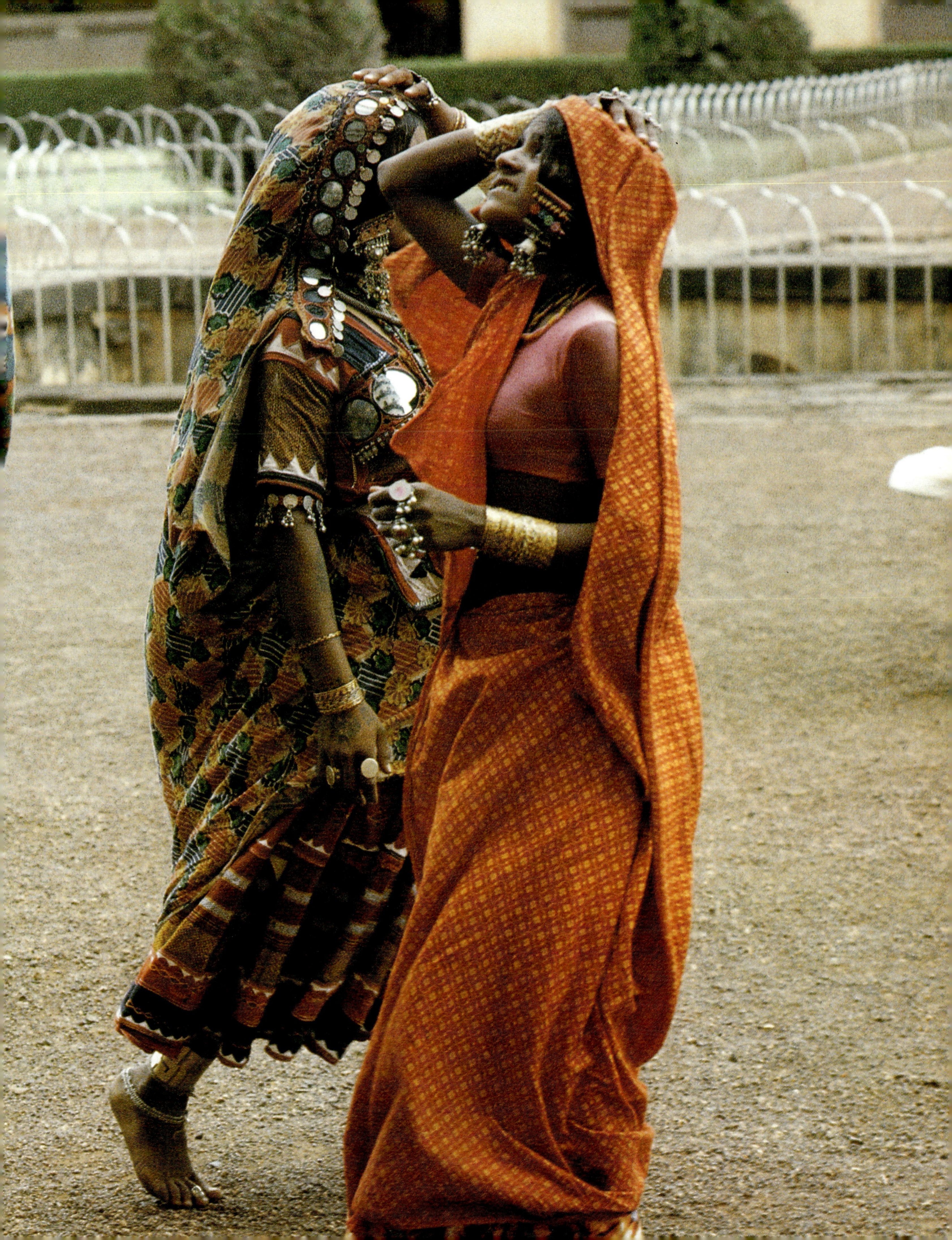

120, 121. Often called 'hotels', these places of refreshment are very common throughout India; they serve coffee or tea, as well as local dishes. This one is in the deep south, near the city of Trivandrum. The religious and racial composition of the peoples of Kerala is very varied; half are Hindus, a fifth Christian and there are three million Muslims. A feature of this tongue of land along the coast of the Arabian Sea is the fragmentation of land ownership into small plots and villages. Following independence, Kerala was the first state in India to vote in a government controlled by the Communist Party, which continued in power until very recently.

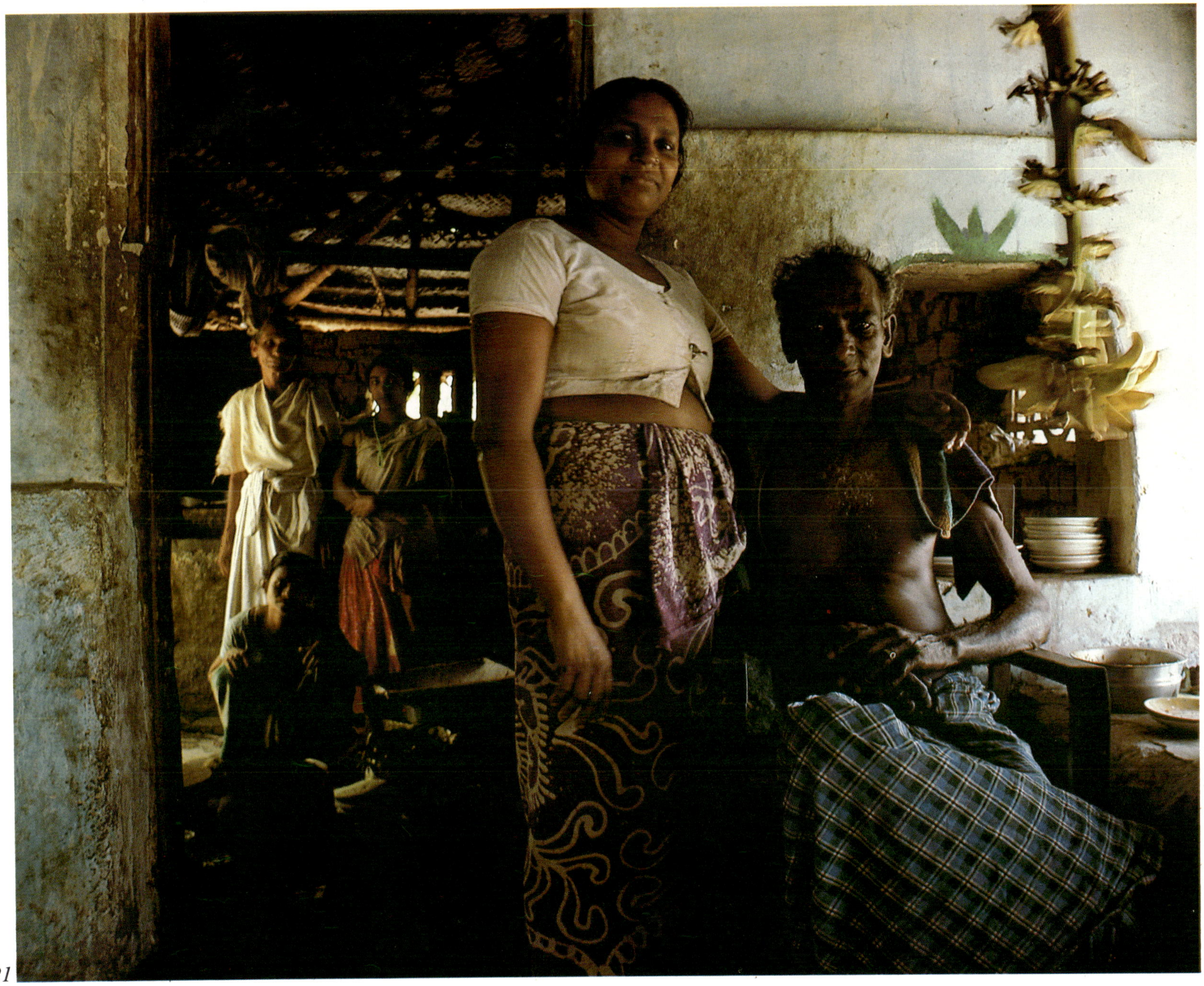

21

122. A shikhara, *a typical Kashmiri river boat, with a family of Kashmiri peasants.*
123. *The kitchen of the lamaist monastery of Rizong Gompa in Ladakh.*

123

On the following pages:
124. Life on board one of the typical river boats of Kashmir.
125. Peasants harvesting rice in southern Rajasthan, near Udaipur.
126. A snake charmer in the open-air studio of a local photographer, beside the Palace of the Winds, Hawa Mahal, in the centre of the city of Jaipur. There are still many such snake charmers in India and some communities have cults of snakes, particularly cobras. They are regarded as sacred and a symbol of fertility, often being depicted beside the great divinities and even the Buddha. In Maharashtra and in Gujarat a festival dedicated to the cult of the snake, the Nag-panchami, is celebrated every year.

225

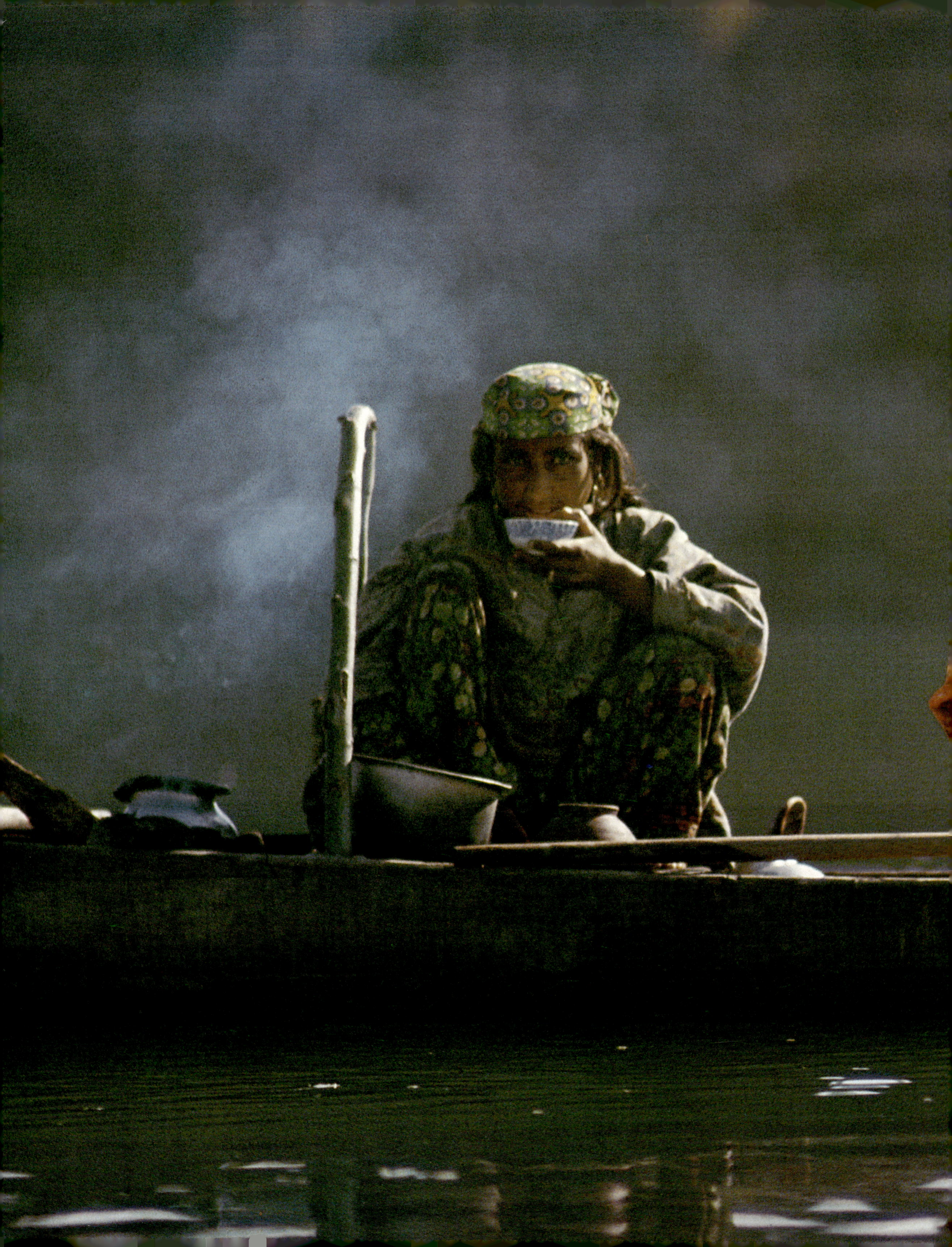

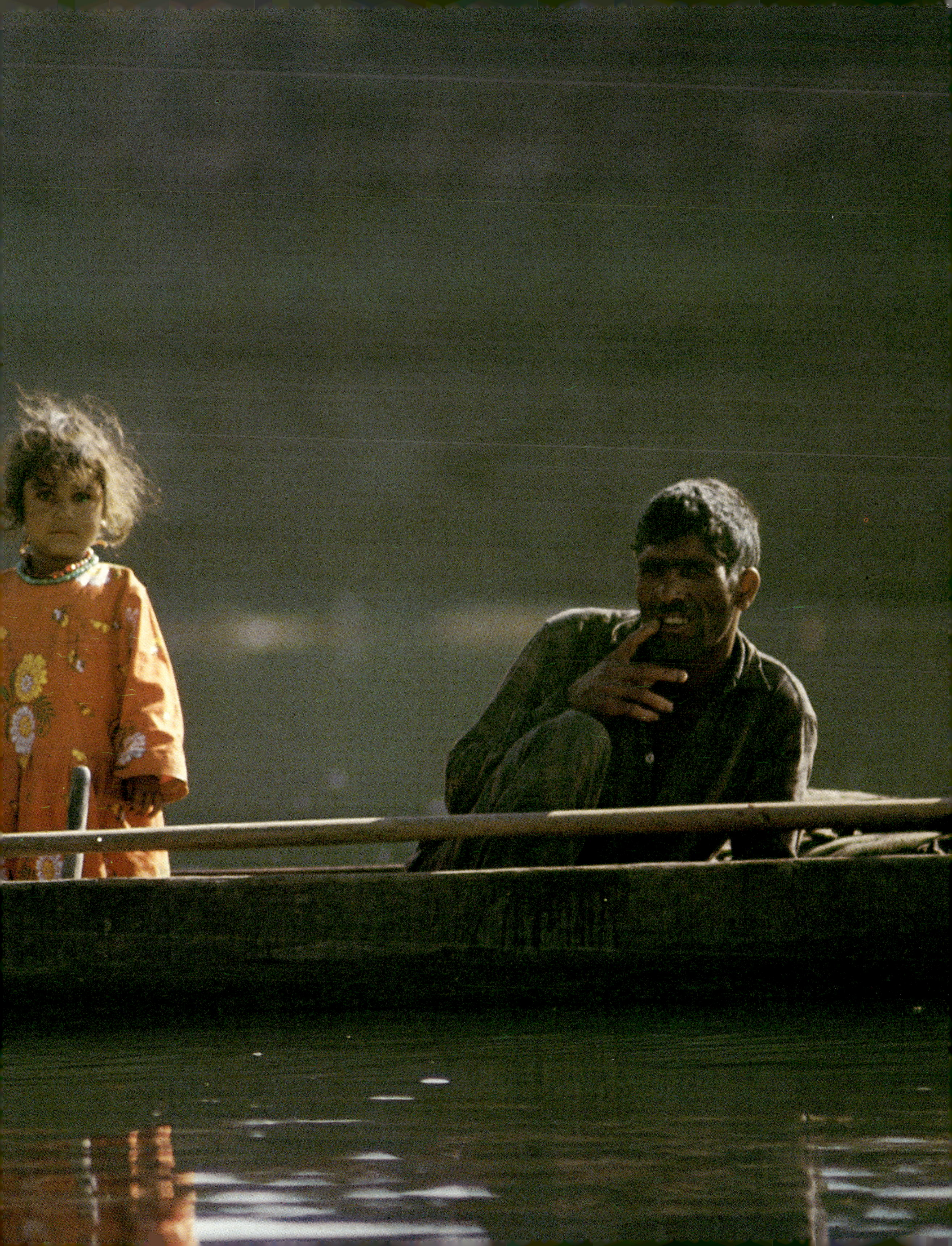

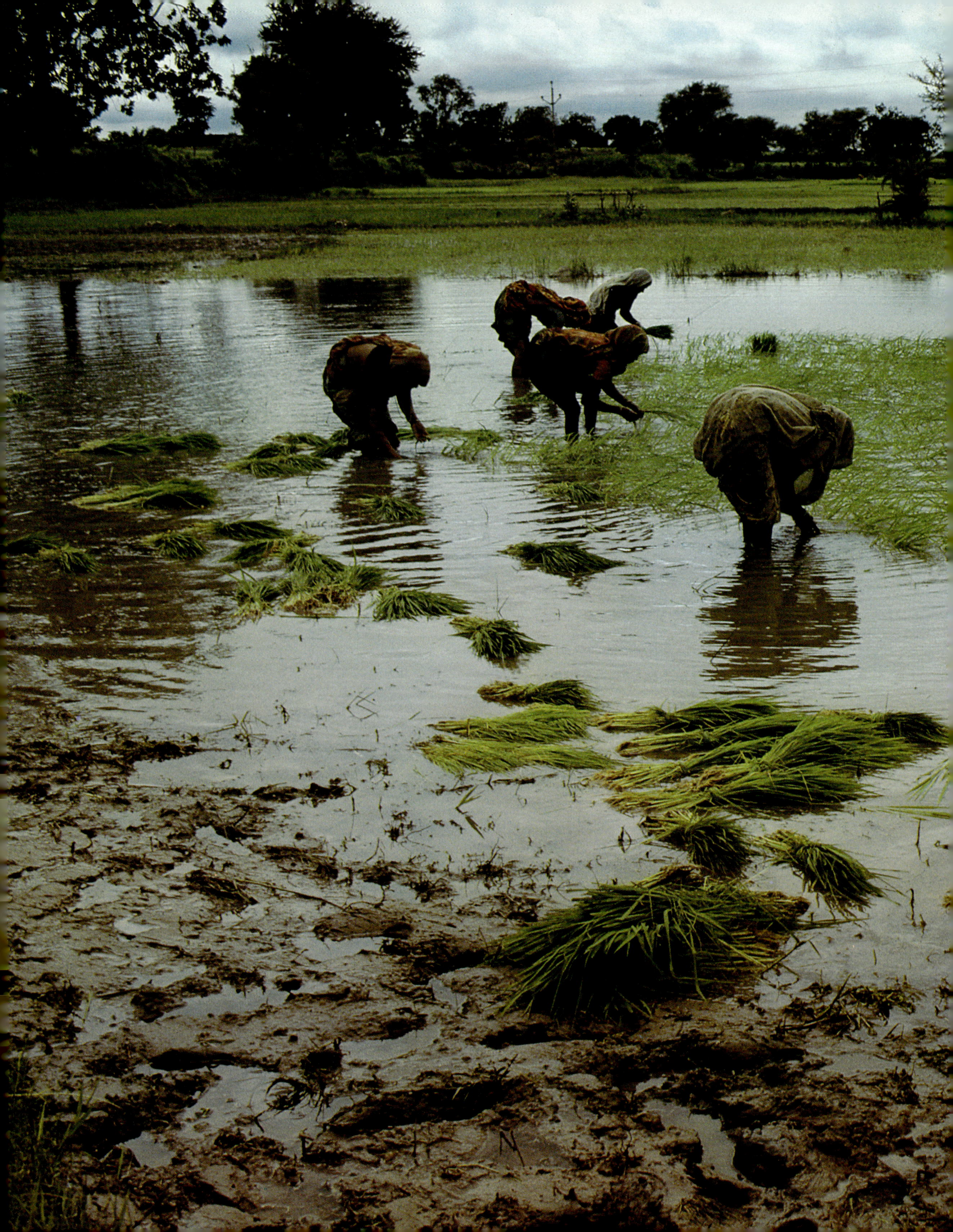

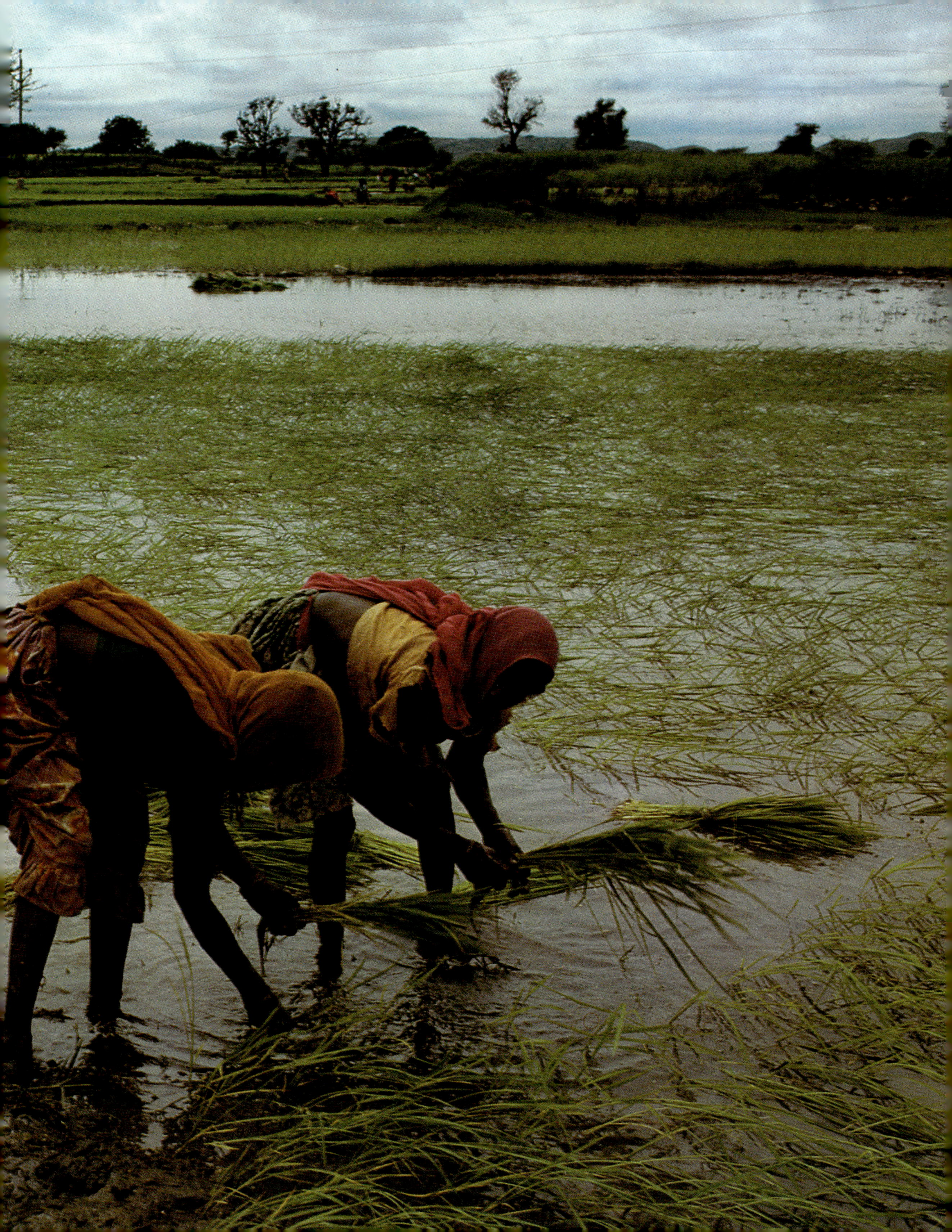

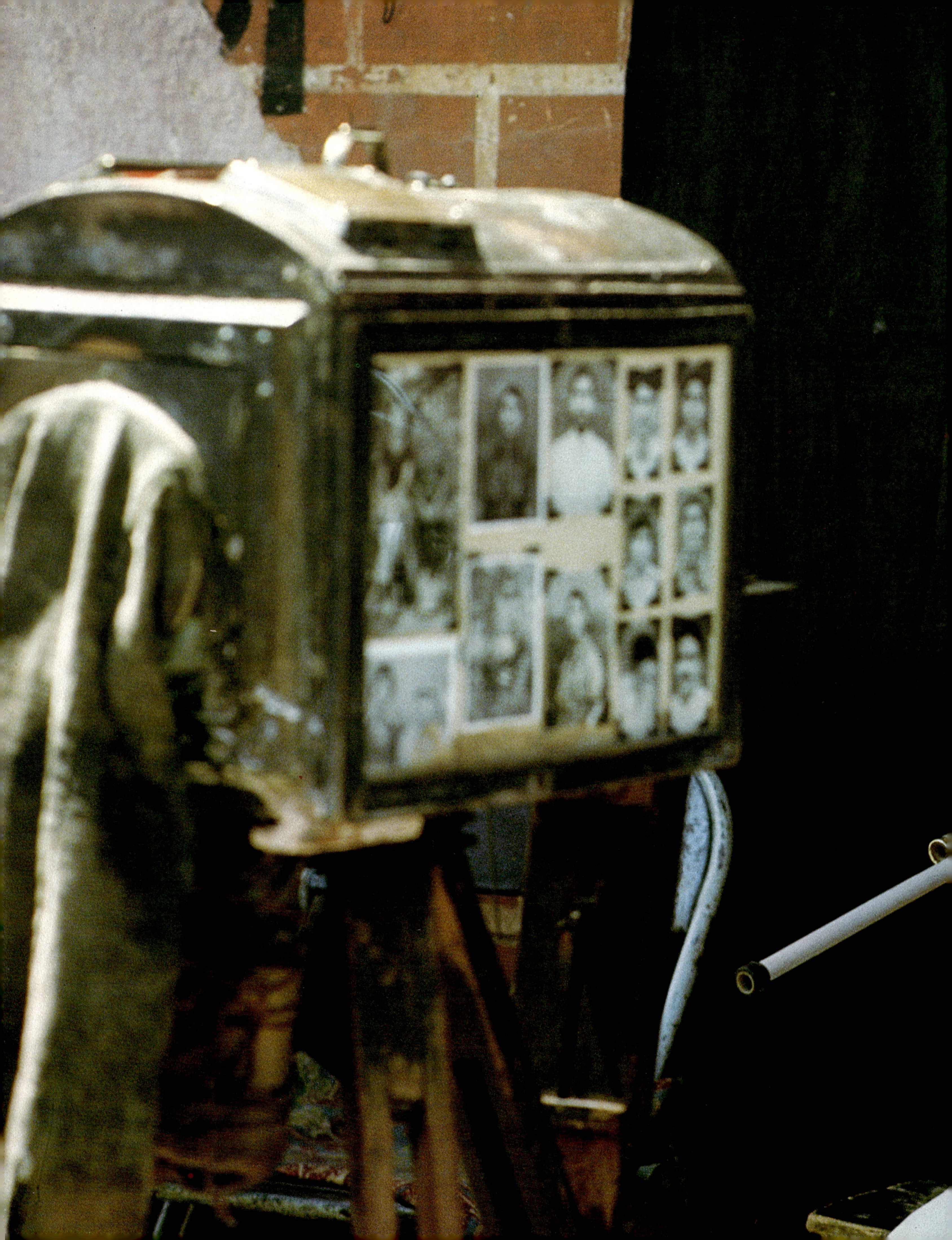

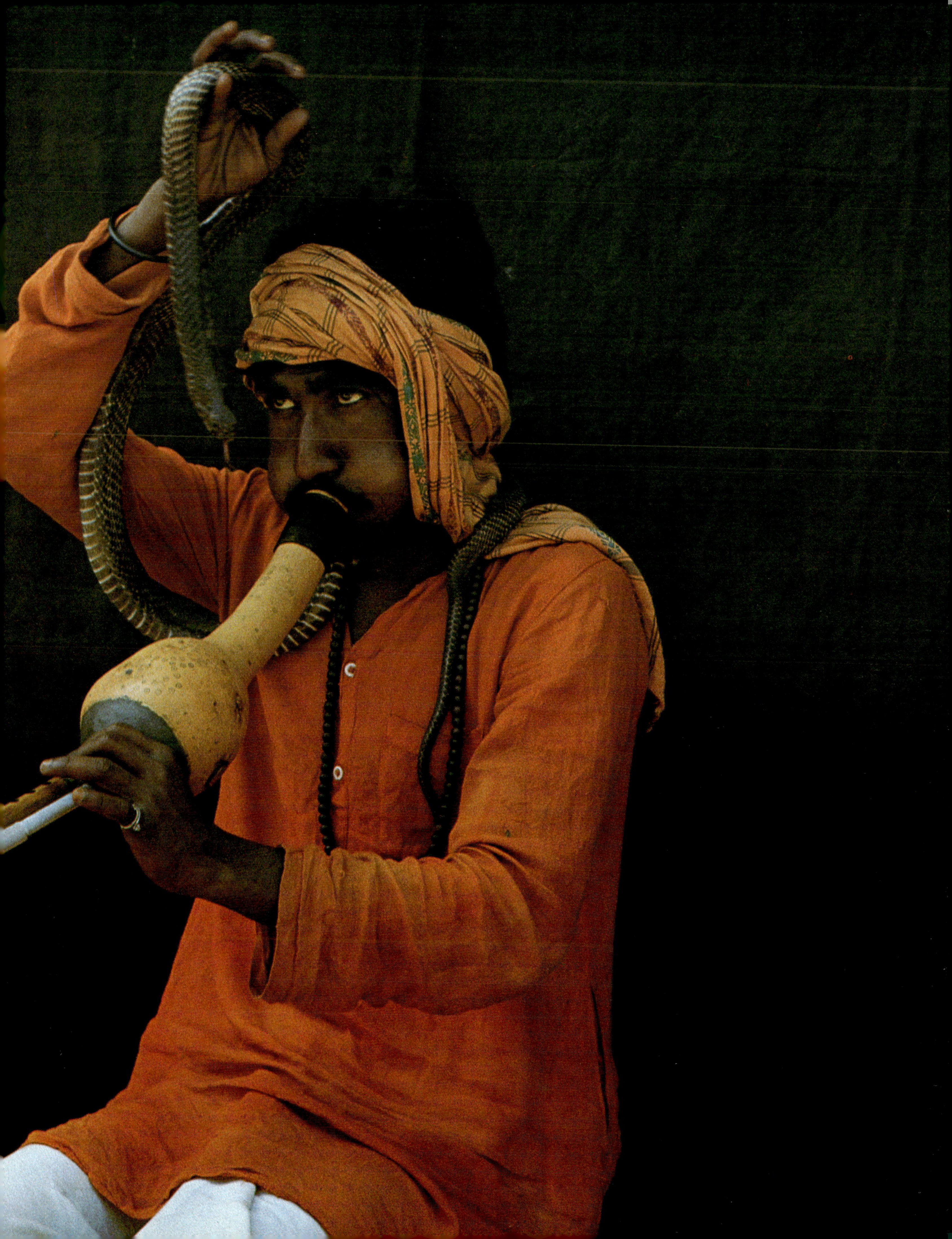

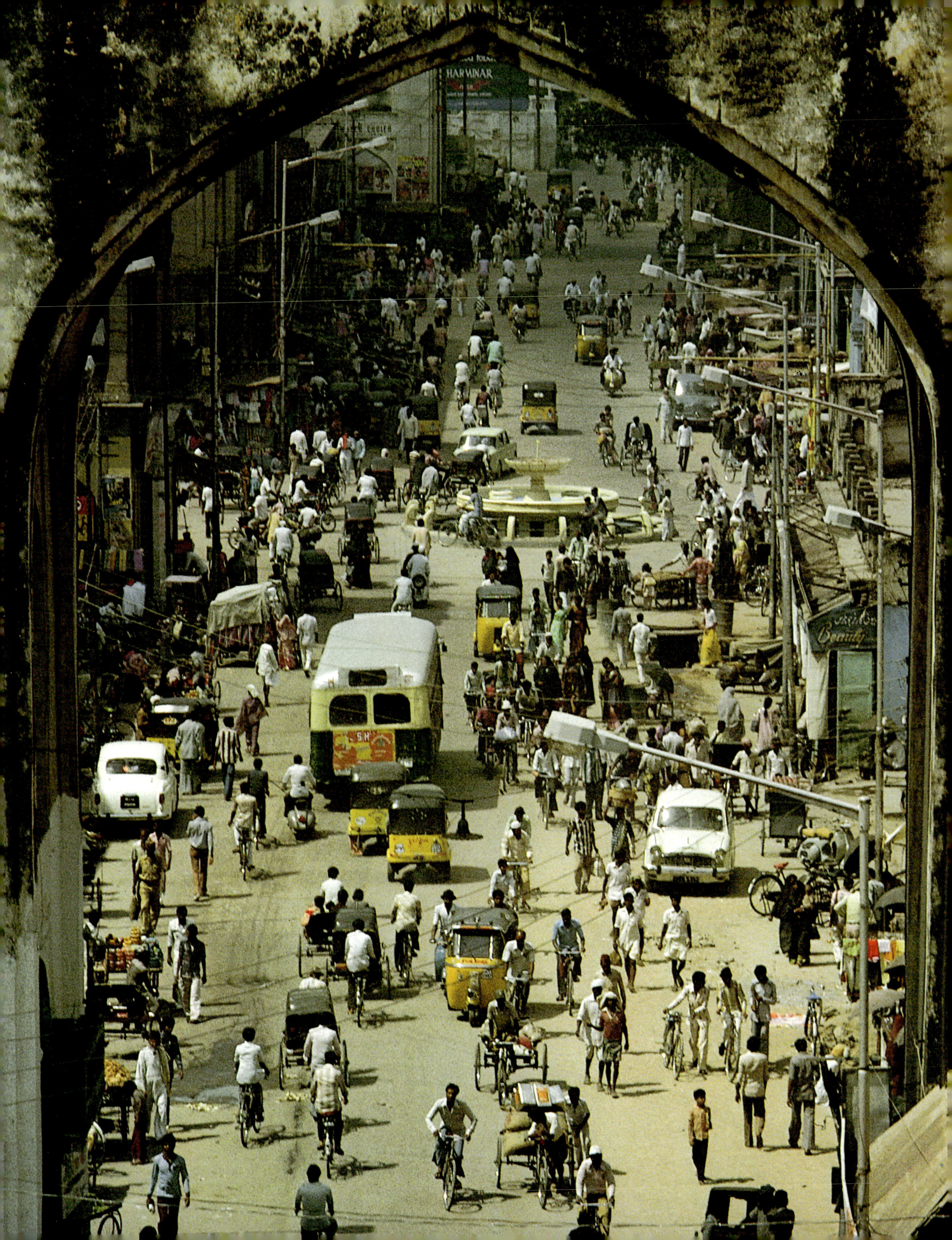
HARMINAR

'The famous Kamasutra *has as its protagonist the urbane and cultivated* nagaraka — *the man-about-town* — *and the entire setting of this treatise on the art of love is urban. The most mature phase of Urdu literature has as its setting the cities of Agra and Delhi. A saying from this time states that the tail of the crow pointing towards the city was superior to its head pointing towards the village'.*

Romila Thapar

The New Urban Condition

The theory was long held — and was widely accepted by historians, particularly during the Empire — that the basic element of Indian civilization was the village and that a city culture had never existed on the subcontinent. It is true that the country's economy has been, and for that matter still is, predominantly agrarian and its culture a peasant one. But it is equally true and verifiable that over the millennia of India's history there have been innumerable settlements whose size and organization have been such as to rank them as cities. Some were trading cities, some state capitals, some were on caravan routes, others were ports. There were garrison cities and great religious and pilgrimage centres. The tradition of pilgrimages, the collective liturgies of the great Hindu assemblies, led to the birth of religious centres, holy cities, in which the presence of crowds of pilgrims invariably stimulated production and the great commercial markets. Benares is one such example, as is Kanchipuram in the south.

The cultural legacy of brahmanical India includes complex theories of cities laid down in ancient treatises on architecture or town planning. The *Mansara*, for example, a sort of Indian Vitruvius compiled in the sixth century AD, offers models and types for the foundation of new cities for commercial, administrative, or religious purposes. Methods of town planning are laid down, involving the arrangement of quarters according to the division of caste and trade, the open spaces, and the public institutions of the town. Technical problems are also dealt with: sanitary arrangements, drainage, the distribution of wells and water reservoirs, green spaces, and defensive works. Plans were based on astrological and geomantic studies into the hierarchy of cosmic forces which governed the orientation of the roads according to the cardinal points, but they were also governed by the demands of ritual, such as the need for a processional way for the circumambulation of the temple, situated at the centre of the built-up area (Maduraine is an example of this, as are other temple cities).

Recent archaeological excavations have revealed the high level of the civilization in the two capitals of the proto-Indian Indus civilization (2000 BC), Harappa and Mohenjo-daro. The migration of the nomadic Aryan herdsmen in around 1000 BC towards the upper Ganges valley and the transformation of their communities into a farming society led to the development of various urban commercial centres, associated with river or land routes. Environmental and climatic factors were of some importance in determining the distribution of cities but so too were historical events, with the political fragmentation of the region into numerous small kingdoms, each with its own capital. In the third century BC a trans-continental network of trading and caravan cities developed extending beyond the traditional boundaries of India to China and the lands of central Asia. At the same time Buddhist and Jain religious centres grew up with the support of both rulers who had been converted and guilds of merchants. The repeated incursions of the Huns into India held back the development of the city for a whole millennium and led to an extensive process of de-urbanization.

With the coming of Islam to India a new period began in the development of the city and the organization of the territory, processes which would reach their climax with the rise of the Mogul dynasty in the sixteenth century. Almost all the regions of India were to be systematically planned, with the building of a dense

127. *A street seen from the top of the most important Islamic monument, the Char Minar, in the capital of Andhra Pradesh, Hyderabad. The city was a great cultural centre and the seat of the Muslim Asafia dynasty, which ruled in the eighteenth century with the title of Nizam. The Nizam was regarded as the richest ruler in the world and was highly regarded by the British government.*

network of roads, hydrographic projects, and the foundation or enlargement of cities intended to become the capitals of vassal sultanates. Agra, Lahore, and Delhi, which were to succeed each other as capitals of the Mogul Empire, had great palaces and fortifications built to accommodate the court and the army. They expanded enormously as their populations rose sharply, as a result of the way the Mogul emperors stimulated trade and manufacture. This stimulus was to bring new life to the guilds of craftsmen, *shreni*, and the professional, city-dwelling castes, on whom the city depended in order to function. At the end of the sixteenth century Agra and Lahore were described by European travellers as being much bigger and more populous than London or Cairo.

During this same period, coastal cities like Surat, Bombay, Goa, Tranquebar, Pondicherry, Madras, Calcutta gradually grew from simple villages into the factories of the various European companies and some of them would grow to such an extent that by the end of the nineteenth century they would be amongst the largest cities of Asia.

Jaipur, perhaps one of the most beautiful and well thought out of Indian cities, is the product of the meeting of Mogul culture with the ideas of the ancient Hindu writers. The creator of the new Jaipur at the beginning of the eighteenth century was Jai Singh II, who was from an ancient Rajput dynasty and a scientist, astronomer, and founder of five astronomical observatories, which he had built in various Indian cities. Jaipur is planned on enlightened principles, with a regular grid and a hierarchy of streets. It incorporates the ideas of the ancient Hindu texts for plans based on cosmological and astronomical criteria but the architecture of the city displays the influence of Mogul styles.

The growth of the colonial cities, Madras, Bombay, and Calcutta and so on, based on exporting and on maritime trade, continued throughout the nineteenth century, first with the territorial expansion of the East India Company and, towards the end of the century, with the final establishment of the British under the aegis of the Crown. The overriding objective of colonial policy was to alter the economic systems of the colonies to serve British interests. In the mid-nineteenth century there was no part of the Indian economy or aspect of its production, whether in the country or in the great manufacturing centres, which had not undergone a profound transformation. The strategy of the colonial government included a policy of urban development and control of the territory from the towns. The age-old rural economy, and much of the land, was transformed into monoculture for export by means of a system of taxation and capital investment, whilst, at the same time, the major urban centres of the country were expanded and new ones founded. The communications network in particular was extended and strengthened, the key element of this being the completion of the railway system.

The collapse of the economy and of manufacturing produced a phenomenon that had no precedents: the mass exodus from the countryside to the industrialized cities, a movement that was aggravated from time to time by such natural disasters as flood and drought. The cities and new industrial zones acted as a magnet to the masses fleeing the ruined countryside. The nineteenth century was the period of the terrible famines, which began in its early years and killed millions of Indians as they recurred throughout the century, reaching their most disastrous at its close.

In such circumstance it was essential for the colonizers to consolidate the role of the city as a model of their cultural hegemony in the country and as an organizational and administrative centre. This was the birth of the modern Indian city and Calcutta, Bombay, and Madras have grown into major cities with industrial zones around them. In the great cities and in the capital cities of the principalities and seats of local government the buildings that housed the new

Plan of the city of Jaipur as it was in the eighteenth century (from C. Batley, 1934).

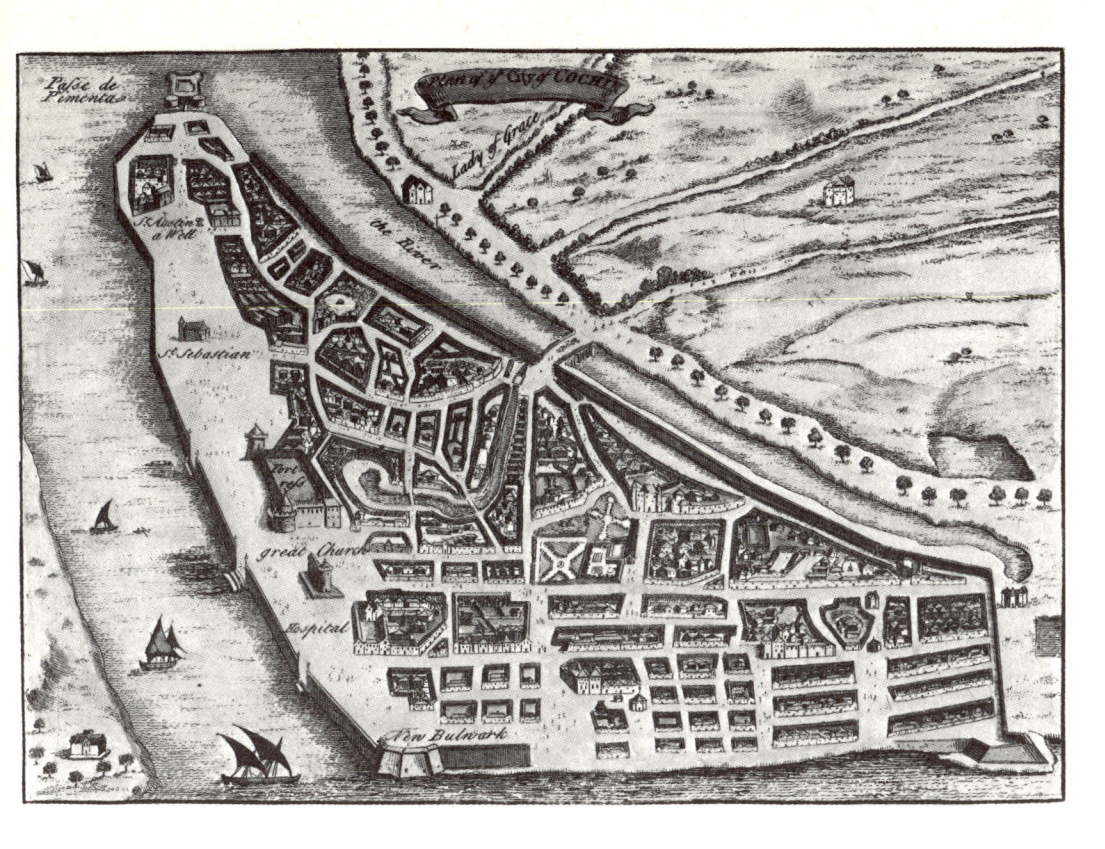

Detailed plan of Cochin, the city of lagoons on the Malabar coast (from an eighteenth-century engraving).

insititutions were often built in a markedly European style.

The urbanization of India is unstoppable and it is violently transforming the countryside as all India's energy and resources are diverted from the rural areas and concentrated on the urban centres. Although 80 percent of the present population of India live in villages, it is forecast that by the end of the century only half will. Demographic models suggest that in the year 2000 the population of the metropolitan area of Bombay will number 16 million and that in addition its boundaries will have pushed out and swallowed up all the adjacent towns and villages to form an enormous conurbation of some 40,000,000 people.

Mass migration to the cities shows not the slightest sign of falling. Bombay, Calcutta, Delhi, Kanpur, and, to a lesser extent, Madras and Bangalore are surrounded by tumbledown suburbs of huts without any facilities or water. They are home to millions of people — in Bombay's case to almost half the city's population — and in addition there are the hundreds of thousands who live on the pavements, on the railway embankments, and under bridges.

It is typical of such suburbs that, despite all the squalor of the city and with none of the advantages of the country, they are arranged in the same ways as the caste quarters of the original villages. They often form organized conglomerations with proper caste solidarity and a rhythm of life, festivals, cults, services, and even a bazaar that are not very different from the village.

The towns and federal governments have made attempts to halt the growth of these slums by offering loans and by the building of subsidized homes — the Pakka Housing Scheme for example — but the phenomenon is so vast that such attempts do not even scratch the surface of the problem. There then arise such paradoxical situations as the fact that the slum dwellers, although they live in houses without any facilities at all, often possess modern luxury products such as televisions and fridges, which are uncommon in India. In general the highest authority recognized in these suburbs is a sort of feudal protector (who in Bombay, for example, is popularly known as the *dada*) and who is regarded as a sort of 'tutelary deity' of the shanty town. In fact he is a racketeer who, in return for a tax, protects his 'subjects' from attacks and theft and guarantees them the right to remain in the slum.

A street in Agra (from an engraving in The Mutiny *by Havelock, 1858).*

However, leaving aside the miserable conditions in which the bulk of the inhabitants of the cities live, what has really changed in the style of life and in the traditions of Indian families so recently urbanized? Industrialization and urbanization are fairly new phenomena and, as in other countries, India is living through a period of transition and transformation, with all the contradictions that are the corollary of such phases. City life inevitably creates new customs and ways of life and an extensive range of new occupations and trades, but it also tends to break down the economic basis of the caste system, eating away at the old bond between caste and occupation. A class structure is developing on top of the caste system, with white-collar workers and those involved in trade and finance forming the basis of a bourgeoisie whose values and solidarity differ in a number of specific ways from those of the ancient caste guilds. Nevertheless the caste system and the compactness of the jati are far from disappearing in the urban environment. The bond resulting from marriage within the caste means that the group perpetuates itself even though some of its members live in cities whilst the remainder have stayed behind in their home villages. This extensive network of caste and blood ties has an economic effect, because the group, by means of its traditional bonds of solidarity and collaboration, can extend its sphere of activity to the market place of the town. This is what has happened with the *banya* caste of merchants, who are found in both cities and villages and who have built up a more extensive and profitable business network by making use of their existing caste co-operation. However, this is not always the case. The past dominance of the brahmins is now almost extinct and it has completely disappeared in the cities, because the kinds of occupation that the brahmin jati performed almost never meet the new demands of life in the cities; indeed the brahmins have never been an occupational caste, performing distinct but interrelated roles. They must adapt to new trades to be carried out by individuals or which at any rate are completely different from the brahmin's ancient occupation. This, together with the irreversible secularization of urban society, is why the brahmins have lost their traditional dominant position in the move to the cities.

However, not everything changes. Certain atavistic habits and traditions have not even been scratched as a result of the compactness of the groups and in many cases they are becoming more firmly established as cults or specific religious practices of certain castes. They are still powerful symbols of community identity

Neo-classical buildings in Calcutta (from Havelock, 1858).

and their preservation answers the deep need to distinguish oneself from the process of undifferentiated levelling so typical of the urban environment. Almost all the recently urbanized groups resist the assault launched by the customs and life styles imposed by towns. Although certain outward features or aspects of behaviour, for example eating habits and modes of dress, are modified, the more essential values, such as the hierarchical nature of the family and of marriage, are clung to. Inter-caste marriages, in the sense of a union between different castes, still only form 5 percent of the total, the remainder conforming to the rule of marriage within the caste to a spouse chosen by their parents. Even the use of the new media, such as marriage advertisements in the major dailies — which are a rather unorthodox, but rapidly increasing, means of seeking partners — emphasize how little the urban condition has affected the behaviour of groups. Very few of the advertisements state that a difference in caste would not be an obstacle to a good marriage (caste no bar); the majority however stress the caste of the advertiser, implicitly requesting that potential partners should come from the same jati (community). However, these new forms of communication do subtly display the alternative ideas and customs of the new city classes, with their gradual transformation of mentality and morals.

The Great Cities

Purana Delhi, New Delhi; two cities, one capital. The first built over 300 years ago by the Mogul emperor Shah Jahan; the second planned and erected only fifty years ago by another empire, the British Raj, which moved its capital to Delhi in 1911. The decision was taken, despite the clear disadvantages of a transfer from Calcutta, because of the prestige attached to Delhi, which, historically, had always played a dominant role in India. According to tradition, seven cities have stood on the site, each the capital of an empire. Delhi has always been the target aimed at by other peoples and invaders; the idea that 'whoever is master of Delhi is master of India' being a view shared by all. Its geographical position has allowed it to dominate the routes from the valley of the Indus and the Punjab to the west and the plain of the Ganges to the east. Its history goes back 3000 years and over the last 700 it has been the capital of kingdoms associated with the coming of

Islam to India. The most recent, the fortified city of Shahjahanabad, which was built in the eighteenth century, is still packed with inhabitants, even though it has now lost its ancient splendour. The Mogul Empire gave way to the British, who did not consider themselves legally master of India until the Union Jack fluttered above the towers of the Red Fort.

The transfer of the capital was announced by Edward VII on his first visit to India; as was the plan to build a completely new city to house the Viceroy and the administration. However, it took a further twenty years before New Delhi was officially inaugurated in 1931. The new city was laid out on a plain dotted with the ruins of earlier settlements, lying some four or five miles from Shahjahanabad, the old walled city. The focal point of the new city was a manificent avenue, flanked by rows of trees and canals, running eastwards for some two miles from the Viceroy's residence and the government offices. Its course is divided into great hexagons intersected by broad diagonal streets. To the north there is the great, circular Connaught Place, with its neoclassical buildings and porticoes. It is from here that the main streets radiate out to the centre of government and other parts of the city, such as Old Delhi. Connaught Place is still the commercial heart of the city and today it is packed with commercial and administrative buildings of every type and style.

New Delhi was designed by the English architect Sir Edwin Lutyens, a convinced proponent of classical European styles, with specific reference to imperial Roman and classical Greek architecture. He took the then widespread view that only the classical style could meet the requirements for majesty and dignity of an imperial capital. Lutyens also designed the Viceroy's palace, now the residence of the President of the Republic of India; and here he blended certain Indian, particularly Mogul, elements with the European styles.

The metropolitan area of New Delhi, which was designed for a population of 65,000 now has one of over 3,000,000 and its chaotic development has exploded the imperial Delhi of Lutyens. The city has expanded in every direction and everywhere there are public and private buildings in the hybrid 'international style', which is unsuited to the Indian climate. The British, who were concerned to build a city that was a symbol of their empire, totally neglected the functional and social aspects which are vital to a city, particularly if it is a capital. From its inception no thought was given to the housing of the lower classes or even the relative locations of places of work and residence. As a result New Delhi has become an immense, sprawling city, ill-adapted to meet the everyday needs of its inhabitants. On the other hand, its founders could not have foreseen what India would achieve within a few years. Just sixteen years after the inauguration of the new capital, the Indian people finally gained self-government and independence after a long and hard struggle. Delhi remained the capital of the new republic, which faced an uncertain future but one full of hope and significance.

Like the other major cities of India, although possibly on a smaller scale, the capital has its city of slums, which lies to the north and has a population of over a million, the product of the flight from the countryside and the political instability at the time of partition in 1947. This part of the city does not immediately impinge on the visitor because Delhi the capital has adopted a firm, hard line in containing the growth of the slums and keeping them separate, as they would detract from its role and prestige as the capital of modern India. Consequently, in addition to Old and New Delhi, which are so different from one another, there is a third, equally different city which gives Delhi a diversity not found elsewhere in the world.

Although New Delhi, the city of the ministries, government, embassies, and the vast army of bureaucrats and employees, does not have a cultural life to match its importance, there is still the glorious Old Delhi, the city which for centuries

Plan view of New Delhi, made by the British architect Sir Edwin Lutyens.

View of Old Delhi from a palace in the city (from Havelock, 1858).

dominated Indian culture and history. Though overcrowded, Old Delhi is still the most interesting part of the capital, because it still retains some of its original features. Chandni Chowk, the great commercial artery which leads to the Red Fort, and the roads running to the city's gates are today clogged with heavy traffic. However the tortuous and labyrinthine streets within the various quarters often surprise those walking along them. The *mohalla* are quarters for social, ethnic, and caste groups who are almost always involved in a particular craft or industry. There are the ancient guilds of smiths, silver workers, jewellers, weavers, tanners, and dyers, who live and work within these quarters, which are often surrounded by walls. The houses have beautiful decorated doorways and the passageways offer views of oases of peace and intimacy, along the lines of an Islamic kasbah. The colour and life of the old city stem from the numerous bazaars, large and small, the spices and perfumes, from the markets for glass bangles to the riot of colours of the bazaar for fabrics, which are hung out in front of the shops. Just as any other Indian market, there are numerous small kiosks selling *pan* and *bidi*. The first of these, consisting of green betel leaf, aromatic spices, a pinch of lime and areca nut, is eaten after meals as a digestive; the other is an Indian cigarette of dried leaves and tobacco.

Delhi, as we have seen, is an ancient city and it was only in the last few years prior to independence that the British began to make their mark. Calcutta, on the other hand, more any other Indian city, owes its very existence to the British, who established themselves there very soon after their arrival in India. Its history begins with the founding in 1690 of a small agency of the East India Company at a site in Bengal surrounded by tiger-infested forests and near three small Hindu villages. One of these, Kalikata — which was regarded as sacred because of the legend that the goddess Kali had lived there — gave its name to the future city. The rapid growth of Calcutta during the last century was due to the fact that the British made it the geopolitical centre of their mastery of India and it was in fact the capital of British India until 1911. It was the port established on the river Hooghly, a few miles from the coast of Bengal, which was to be crucial to the success of the city. Just like Bombay in the same period, Calcutta was adorned with buildings in a variety of styles, with a marked preference for neoclassical European ones, which were suited to its role as capital.

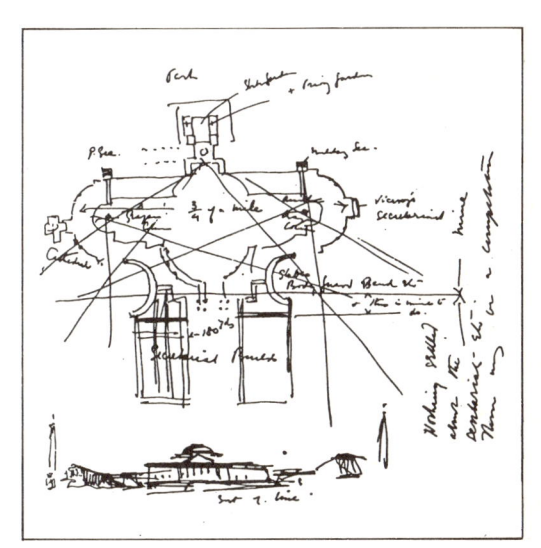

A sketch by Sir Edwin Lutyens for the Viceroy's Palace, now called the Rashtrapati Bhavan, the residence of the President of India (R.I.B.A.).

Chitpur Road, the ancient pilgrimage route which linked Murshidabad, the old capital of Bengal, with the venerated temple of the goddess Kali at Kalighat, formed the original axis for the development of modern Calcutta. It was to become the major commercial street of the native town. The movement of Fort William further south and the creation of the *maidan*, an immense open park typical of many Indian cities of British origin, flanked by Chowringhee Road, the main street of Calcutta, have together opened up an otherwise tightly packed city. The city as it now stands cannot leave the visitor indifferent: 'fascinating' and 'monstrous' are the adjectives which recur through all the vast assortment of descriptions of Calcutta offered by its famous and not so famous visitors since the beginning of the last century, even during the height of the British Raj. Although Calcutta may be the great commercial, industrial, and administrative centre of northern India, it has the unwanted fame of being the distressing symbol of all the urban problems of our time: large-scale and chronic unemployment, vast areas of slums, and a degradation of the surroundings that has no like in any of the other great cities of the world. Even in the grander areas an uncontrollable mass of the poor live and sleep on pavements. Over the last twenty years, this situation has been made even worse by an influx of refugees from Bangladesh, whose border is not far from Calcutta. It is estimated that some ten million refugees have settled in Calcutta and its hinterland.

'Buildings. Crowd. Rags. Filth. Laughter. Lethargy. Movement. It is a naked city, without a mask. Overpopulation, unemployment, hunger, disease, appear here in all their crudity in a jumble of great vitality and chronic exhaustion, but an exhaustion from which a new vitality arises...' (Merton).

It is precisely from this vitality that another of the fascinating aspects of Calcutta emerges. From the cultural and political point of view it is the liveliest and most active centre in the whole of India. Rightly or wrongly, it is universally acknowledged as the most intellectual city in the country, with hundreds of literary and political magazines, intense cultural activity and enterprises, shows, concert, and the theatre. The cinema, both Indian and international, has an enormous following of enthusiasts and the population of artists, painters, actors, musicians, and actors exceeds that of the rest of India put together. The films produced in Calcutta are highly refined, although it does not match Madras and Bombay in terms of quantity, and its major producers and writers have established schools. In clubs, film libraries, and even in the shabbier cafés it is not unusual to hear well-informed talk of the major western directors and also of the literature and arts of distant parts of the world. Politics is another of Calcutta's passions, and the extreme politicization of its students is a characteristic feature (the university of Calcutta has 200,000 students). West Bengal has elected a number of Communist coalition governments and the history of this region has been that of an endless sequence of bitter and sometimes bloody conflicts between the various political groups.

Bombay too is colonial in origin. Once a small village, it owes its enormous growth to the arrival of the Portuguese in the sixteenth century and the subsequent growth of Dutch and British trading posts. At that time the township was virtually non-existent and the group of islands, which formed the base on which the city grew, was covered by wild vegetation with marshes and swamps, pestilential places where, as the colonists said, 'two monsoons equalled the life of one man'. The Koli fishermen, the tribe who originally inhabited the islands (named the 'Heptanesia' or seven islands by Tolomeo), called the area *Mumba-Ai*, after their tutelary goddess Mumba (Mumba Amba, Great Mother), wife of the god Shiva; this was subsequently corrupted to the present name of Bombay. Bombay passed to the British Crown in 1674 and it became the headquarters of the East India Company, which led to the rapid development of the port and the

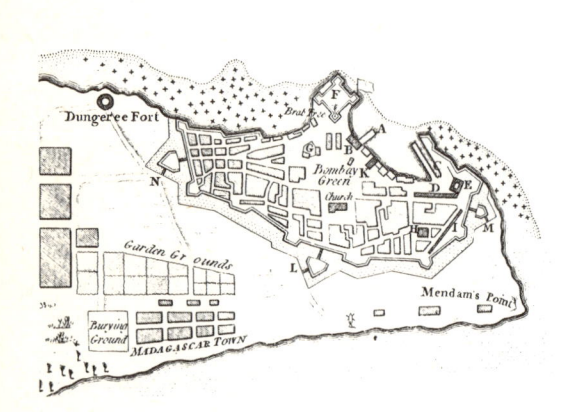

A plan of the fortress and city of Bombay at the end of the seventeenth century (by W. Nicholson).

settlement. The opening of the Suez Canal in 1869, which encouraged the transport of goods to Europe by shortening the distance, and the building of the subcontinent's railway network with Bombay as its largest terminus, turned the city into a great manufacturing centre and the major cotton and textile market. At that time Bombay's population grew rapidly and it became the nerve centre of a vast area as well as a major financial and entrepreneurial market. In competition with Calcutta, Bombay proudly assumed the motto of 'Urbs prima in Indis'. Around the end of the last century it was laid out anew, with the building of the majority of its public and commercial buildings in the City and a new street plan. The superb array of Victorian-Gothic styles has given Bombay its distinctive appearance, which is known around the world.

At the beginning of this century, during the Edwardian era, it was already regarded as an 'international city', and it still retains the title. Today, the Bombay-Poona district is perhaps the largest industrial and commercial conurbation in Asia. The importance of Bombay, the 'Port of India', lies principally in its role as a port and in the massive movement of goods. Industry employs almost half the working population and the chemical, mechanical, and engineering industries are the most important in the country. It also has the greatest concentration of companies and firms in India, as well as banks, shipping, insurance, and financial companies.

Bombay grew from three million inhabitants in 1951 to more than eight in 1981. Such uncontrolled growth has affected almost the whole city, leading to a severe degradation of the environment and almost intolerable living conditions. Everywhere, rich quarters and the most sordid of slums, known locally as *zopadpatti*, clusters of tumble-down huts and high-rise blocks of flats, exist side by side. Bombay rivals Calcutta as the most socially committed of Indian cities, being the centre of the unions and the scene of the bitterest conflicts in the labour world.

The variety of groups and ethnic/caste minorities to be found in Bombay makes it one of the most extraordinary examples of city life in Asia. To the north of the business centre is what in the days before independence was known as the native town. This was, and to a large extent still is, the area where communities from all over India settled. In certain quarters the population is a mixture of different races, castes, and beliefs whereas others have a homogenous character and a shared style of life. The dwellings are clustered around the places where the crafts and industries are pursued, the sites of the workshops, and the stores of the merchants. A vernacular style of architecture is often apparent. Multi-storey timber houses are still built, many in the Gujarati style, and these are intermingled with Hindu temples, mosques, churches, and *gurudwara* (Sikh temples). The markets and bazaars are often organized by the trade guilds and run by groups of Hindus of the same caste or by Muslim professional groups as in any other Indian city.

It is the multitude of languages that are spoken which makes Bombay's status as a great metropolitan centre clera. The languages which are spoken allow one to establish the sizes of the various different communities. English is the language of business and official culture. About half Bombay's population speaks *Marathi*, the language of the state of Maharashtra, of which Bombay is the capital; this is followed by *Gujarati, Hindi, Sindhi, Urdu*, the languages of the Deccan and Tamil ones. A fifth of the population is Muslim, both Sunni and Shiite, with merchant communities from Bohra, Khoja and Memon. The Christians can often be identified by their Portuguese surnames and belong to minorities of southern origin. The small group of Jews, the Beni-Israel, speaks Marathi, whilst the Jain, who are associated with trade and the liberal professions, speak Gujarati. The Parsi community has been of great importance in the city's history. Of ancient,

This sequence of five stages in a typical 'squatting' operation shows a merchant making steady progress — not too drastic or noticeable — to avoid attracting attention.

Persian origin and Zoroastrian in belief, it is perhaps the most eminent ethnic group in Bombay, occupying top positions in the liberal professions, in finance, and in industry. They are known for their modern spirit of initiative and for their philanthropic works. One characteristic of Parsi customs, which aroused the curiosity of European travellers in the past, is the funeral rite, which involves the exposure of the bodies on the *dakhma*, also known as the 'towers of silence', in order for them to be devoured by carrion-eating birds. The object of this is to avoid the contamination of the four elements considered sacred by Zoroastrians: water, earth, fire, and air.

The city has always been a magnet to the other parts of India since the days of the 'great boom', as the late nineteenth century was called. In the hymn to Bombay, Rudyard Kipling has it say '... a thousand factories roar in me, whilst I gather the races of all the lands'. This influx gives no sign of abating. However, the city still retains a specific character — something which other Asian cities do not have to such an extent — a character that is more than just the contrast between wealth and poverty and lies rather in the bizarre amalgam of east and west. Despite the immigration of millions of Indians from all parts of the country, Bombay has never become an 'Indian' city, nor is it a western one. Perhaps its unchanging hybrid nature is due to the growth of two different but interdependent factors. Every modern establishment has spawned areas of slums in its vicinity, inhabited by people who in the main have never been fully urbanized. An acute observer at the beginning of the century highlighted a feature of Bombay which is still true today: '... although the immigrants to Leeds or London have, within a generation, virtually forgotten their rural origins and formed a new urban proletariat, the same has not happened in Bombay... the workers think constantly of the village of their birth and when times are hard in Bombay they return there' (Tindall).

Plan drawing of sector 22, part of the architectural plan for building Chandigarth, capital city of the Punjab, prepared by Le Corbusier (from Architectural Design, *1974).*

Modern Architecture

Not only the great cities of India but also the small and average towns are today crowded with modern buildings; tall skyscrapers, huge, heavy public buildings, post offices, universities. And in the suburban areas endless rows of concrete bungalows, of over-decorated villas and 'rational' housing blocks, spring up like mush rooms. All this goes under the definition of the great boom of 'modern architecture' in India, brought about by the constitution of the new nation.
In India, too, the modern movement in architecture has gone through the different phases of evolution which came about in Europe, from its origins in the eighteen hundreds to the avant-garde happenings in the twentieth century. The birth of modern architecture in India and of a movement which breaks with antique traditions dates back to the experience of European stylistic eclecticism at the end of the nineteen-hundreds. It is India in the full bloom of her British period, the moment of the formation of the great urban centres marked by the tragic phenomena of urbanism. But it is also the moment of the policy of embellishment and architectural decoration of the towns and capital cities of the various principalities.
Almost all the urban institutions are built in styles taken from the vast anthology of European revivals, Victorian and Edwardian, with a sprinkling of elements recovered from Indian, particularly Hindu-Islamic, decoration: neogothic university colleges, town halls in Anglo-Hindu-Islamic style, railway stations in Venetian-Gothic, buildings in art nouveau, and palaces in art déco. The Victorian city of Bombay and the Imperial Delhi of Lutyens are the finest examples. It is the triumph of the Beaux-Arts schools, of hybrid architecture, but also the

opening up of India to the modern internationalism of the arts and the beginning of the formation of a proper Indian school with 'modernist' tendencies. Of course, much of that period was the product of the imposition of the policy of westernization operated by the British Raj, of the predominance of one culture over another, favoured by the representative ambitions of a particular Indian middle-class (amongst which the dominating communities of the Parsi, Marwari, and Bohra stand out), and by the formation of an academy at university level. But what clearly emerges is the great Indian capacity to absorb and to adapt to integration which demonstrated that despite her long history of foreign domination she possesses a culture resistant to unification, to the imposition of a homogeneous formal world, but open to new contributions from outside, in a continuous process of assimilation and reinvention.

The rationalist architectural movement created an entire school in India even when in the nineteen-fifties the Punjab government commissioned the great rationalist architect, Le Courbusier, to build its capital, Chandigarh. After independence, grandiose urban programmes and the construction of 'new towns' inspired by the English models were planned. Over the years the accumulation of the different historical and cultural experiences has brought out the need for a 'national way' which would take into account not only the recovery of tradition in order to consolidate a real cultural autonomy but also, above all, the real practical and social needs of the population such as the enormous demand for popular housing and the renewal of urban centres.

Advertisements appearing in a Bombay newspaper announcing the films showing at the various cinemas in the town.

The Indian Cinema Industry

The most striking social phenomenon of modern India is the success of the cinema amongst the masses. In terms of quantity India ranks first amongst the world's film producers and with an audience of 75 million every week it also has the largest viewing public. Other figures confirm this primacy: between 700 and 800 films are produced annually, almost all in Hindi and Tamil and then in part dubbed in about fifteen Indian languages. Indian cinema magazines are published in thirteen languages and exceed in number the rest of the world's press in this sector. Bombay, Madras, and Calcutta are the major centres of film production; Bombay, where the Indian film industry was born, is the main centre for films in Hindi, Calcutta is devoted to Bengali films, and Madras is the home of the most flourishing industry in the south. Originating in the nineteen-forties, Tamil cinema has turned itself into a popular propaganda tool and means of self-determination for southern culture, a form of Tamil 'nationalism', opposing the cultural, linguistic, and political pressures of the north. It is not by chance that the various Chief Ministers who have succeeded each other in the state of Tamil Nadu have been either screen writers or actors idolized by the public, beginning with M. Karunanidhi up to the present minister, M. Ramachandran, who, as an actor, had over 20,000 clubs dedicated to his name all over the south. Recently, Rama Rao, an extremely popular actor in mythological films, has enjoyed political success as Chief Minister of the state of Andhra Pradesh.

At the moment, television, which is confined to the major cities, steals few viewers from the cinema. Abroad, Indian films are only distributed in certain Middle Eastern countries, South East Asia, and parts of Eastern Europe. Virtually no Indian films reach the West, although some are shown in immigrant communities in Britain. The differences in culture, taste, and the peculiar film language mean that the majority of Indian films would not be well received by the western viewer. Hindi or Tamil films generally last three or four hours and are a blend of melodramma, romantic comedy, and a story with a sentimental

128. One of the rooms of the guest house next to the Jain temple of Kanch Mandir also known as the temple of Hukamchand at Indore.

background. Dance, music, and song are of prime importance in any dramatization. The sets are sumptuous and in a sense reflect the life styles of the actors and the luxurious surroundings in which they live. Comic films enjoy great success and many Hindi films reserve a place for comic roles, readopting the old tradition of the Indian theatre. The so-called mythological films depict popular stories or religious legends, exploiting the devotional attitudes of the Indian masses. The nineteen-seventies saw the success of films with violent scenes, set in the great cities and showing the contradictions of urban life, but in a fantastic, never realistic, way. Although the sexual element is essential for the film's success, there are strict limits on the depiction of erotic scenes. For some obscure reason it was not permissible to show a kiss until a few years ago but caressing was. Now kissing too is allowed. Over the last few years slightly risqué films, known as 'massala-movies', have tentatively begun to make their appearance.

India is one of the few countries where the star system still operates and the popularity of the actors is the basis of a film's success, rather than the quality of the subject or the skill of the director. The most popular actors receive huge sums, which are in a completely different league from those of internationally renowned actors.

India does not just produce films with box-office appeal. Films of a high artistic level are made but these are generally regional and remain restricted to selected cinemas in cities or film libraries.

The urban landscape is now dominated by the vast cinema hoardings and this is just as true of small, out-of-the-way towns in the interior as it is of the great cities. They cover the old and new facades of buildings or they are hung from specially built structures and in the most unlikely places. Almost all are hand-painted on the spot by skilled painters and they often attain the expressive and technical level of a true art. This is a popular art, with idealized figures, strong colours, erotic attraction, not explicit but slightly suggestive, the faces of the heroes and heroines, the dramatic gestures and the expressions charged with emotion. Often they reflect the ideals, in terms of appearance and status, of the common Indian spectator and it surprising to find formal and symbolic affinities with the present-day, popular iconography of the divinities in the millions of highly coloured prints which are on sale everywhere and are hung on the walls of houses and shops. This extraordinary urban stage setting is unique of its kind and has no parallels anywhere else in the world.

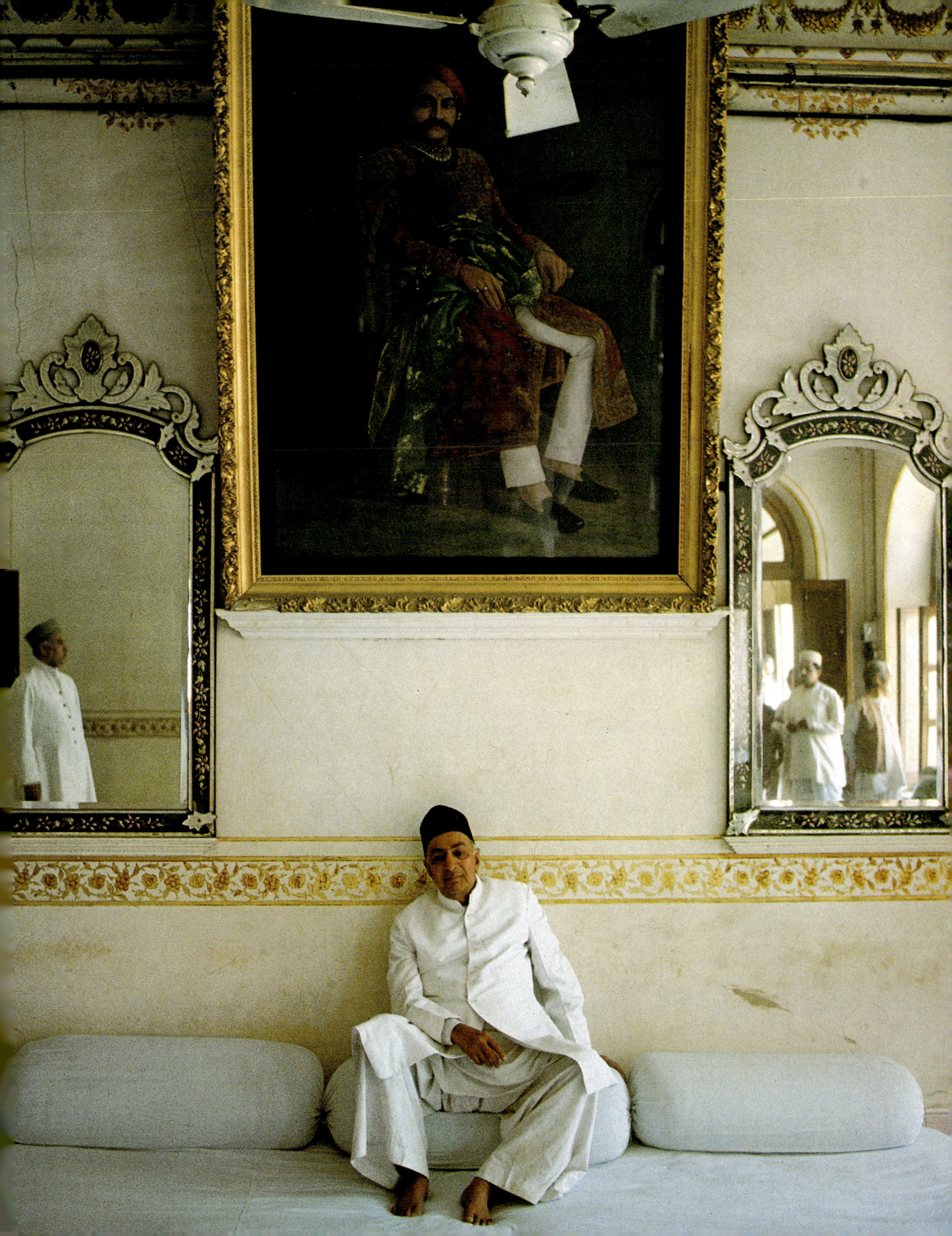

129 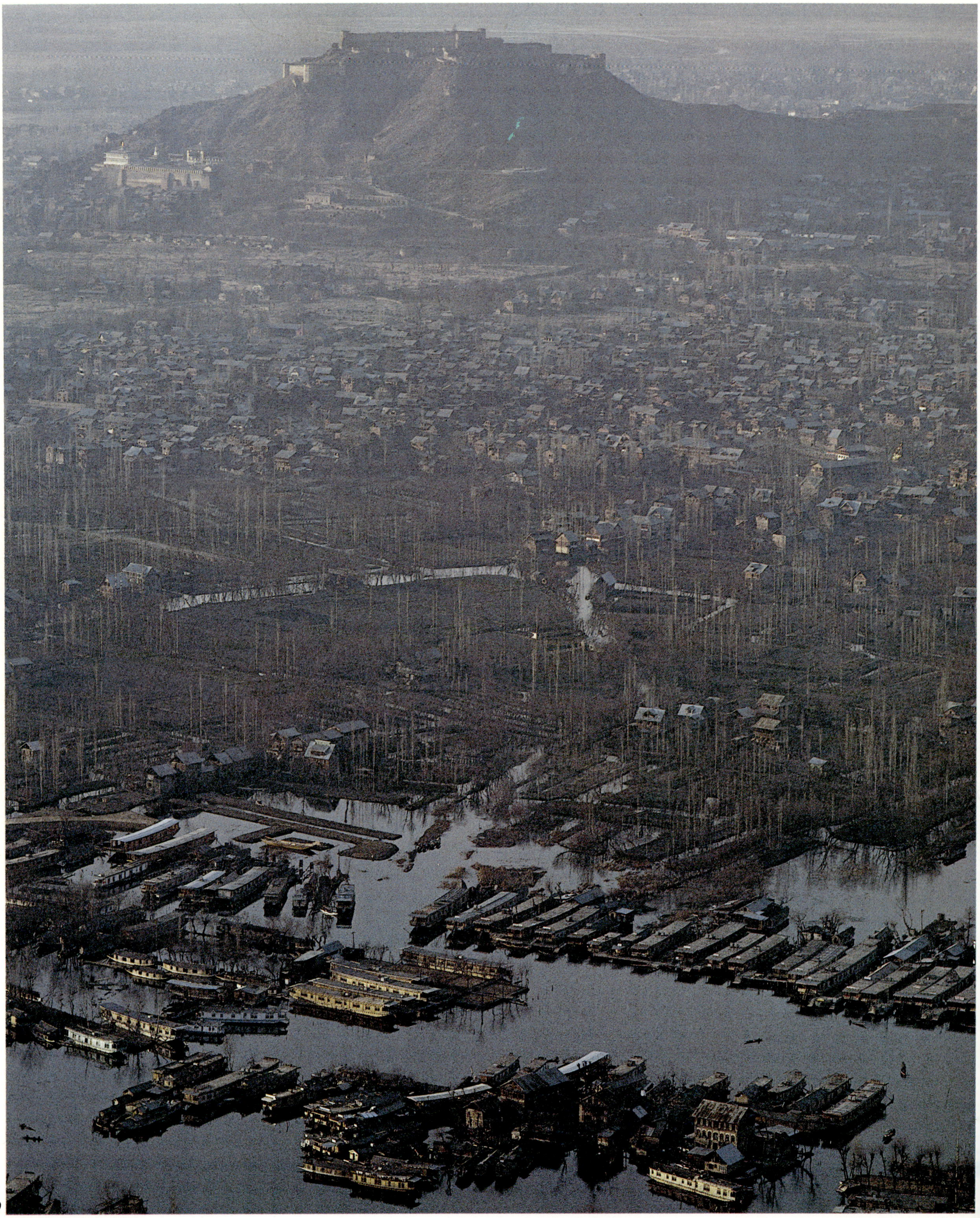

129. A view of Srinagar, the capital of Kashmir, with the densely packed houseboats moored along the banks of Lake Dal. The boats are proper houses and today most are rented out to tourists. On the slopes of the hill there is a dargah, the tomb of a Muslim saint, and on the summit there is a fort. Srinagar is in a temperate valley, with mountain lakes, rivers and canals, and lush vegetation. The floating gardens along the river and lake are famous, as are the geometrically laid out ones of the Moguls. The best known of the latter is Shalimar, which occupies several terraces with pools and cascades. About half the population is Muslim, the remainder belong to various Hindu castes.
130. Winter on Lake Dal at Srinagar.

131. View of the city of Ajmer in Rajasthan. It is a holy city for Shiite Muslims and a centre of pilgrimage, with one of the most venerated Muslim mausoleums, the dargah of Khwaja Moinuddin Chisti, the founder in the twelfth century of a Sufi community.

132. Dominating the city is the rocky spur on which the fortified palace of the ruling Rajput princes of Jodhpur stands. The fort, which was defended by a series of fortified approaches and by a high wall, was considered impregnable. In the sixteenth century the Mogul Emperor Akbar found it so difficult to subjugate the Rajputs of Jodhpur that he made peace by marrying a Rajput princess to a Mogul prince. Jodhpur is on the edge of the Thar desert and, despite the plethora of modern buildings, it still retains some areas and remains which recall its past as a caravan city. From the top of the rock one can see the blue-painted houses of the brahmins.

133. *A quarter of Old Delhi, known locally as* mohalla, *near the Jama Masjid, the great mosque of the Muslim Congregation. The old quarters are occupied by one caste or community, which often practises a single trade.*

134. A rikshaw *in the rain. These bicycles have a small cab for passengers and are still common in the cities, although they are gradually being replaced by motor vehicles.*
135. Sellers of live poultry near the mosque.
136. Cooked chicken on sale. There are numerous shops like this.
On the following pages:

137. Daytime traffic along Chandni Chowk, the ancient artery which runs from the Red Fort to the mosque of Fatehpuri. It is the centre of life and a market but it has completely lost its old charm, and the beautiful decoration of its palaces, which is such a feature of old descriptions, has also disappeared. The traffic is very heavy and the buildings are almost totally hidden behind hoardings, most of which are advertising films.

ROOP
SAREE
KENDRA
(AIR CONDITIONED)
KATRA CHOBAN
CH. CHOWK. DELHI
Jyaram's
SHIRTINGS
CITY
LODGE
CHAINS

Indian Bank
SONEX
TWO-IN-ONE
TAPE RECORDER
AMPLIFIERS
Seeta Studio
COLOR
LAB.
ROOP
SAREE
KENDRA
(AIR CONDITIONED)
KATRA CHOBAN
CH. CHOWK. DELHI
ROOP
SAREE
KENDRA
(AIR CONDITIONED)
KATRA CHOBAN
CH. CHOWK. DELHI
Esquire
VIDEO CASSETTES
COUNTER
श्री गौरी शङ्कर मन्दिर
SHREE GAURI SHANKER MANDIR

138. New Delhi, a great parade by the armed forces and by people wearing the local costumes of the various regions during the annual celebration of Republic Day on 26 January.
139. Soldiers mounted on camels, Rajasthan border guards, being reviewed in New Delhi with government buildings in the background.
140. Some inhabitants of the Himalayan region of Ladakh, 'Little Tibet', prepare for the parade wearing their regional costume.
On the following pages:
141. The shunting area and sidings in the railway station of Old Delhi.

139

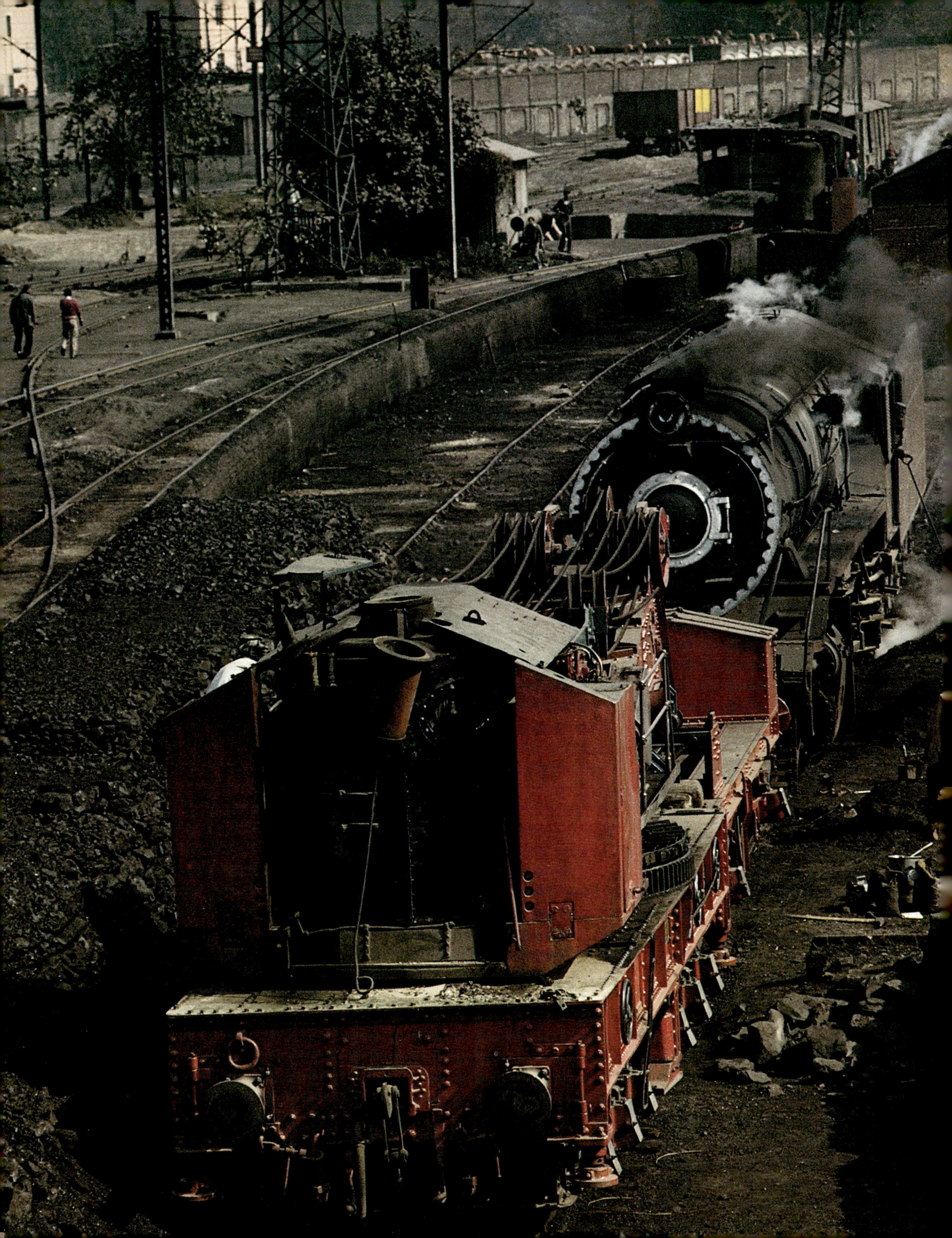

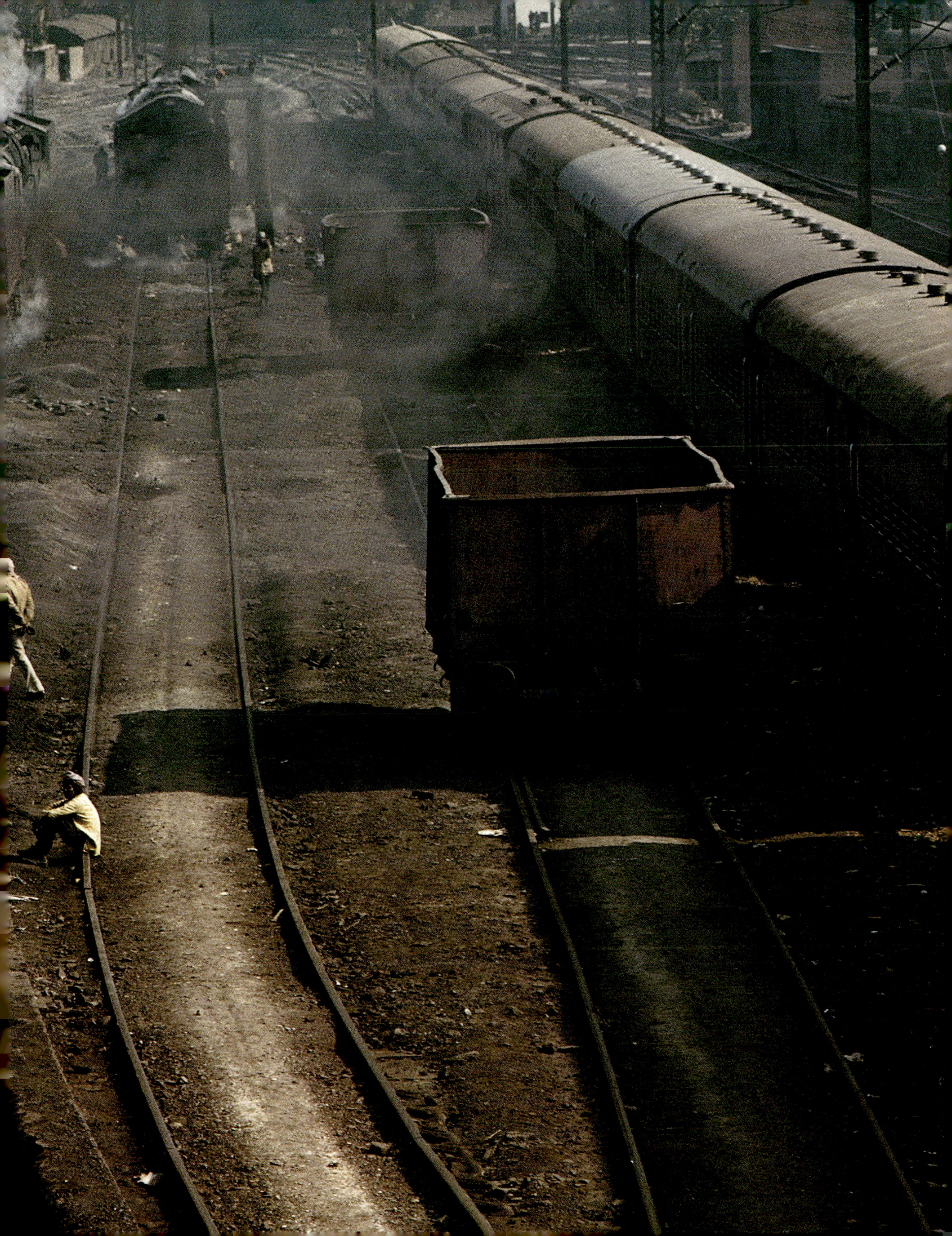

142

142. The temple of Dakshineshwar, near Calcutta, a Shaivite sanctuary dedicated to Kali and built in the nineteenth century. Sri Ramakrishna, the mystic saint of modern India, was a priest here. He was one of the major figures in the renewal of contemporary Hinduism. Throughout his life he was imbued with a desire for total immersion and realization in God, but in the female form and he had numerous visions of Kali, the Great Mother. His disciples, under the leadership of Swami Vivekanda, organized themselves into an order, the Ramakrishna Mission, which has centres scattered around the world.

143. View of part of Calcutta, with the outline of the famous Howrah iron bridge, which connects the two parts of the city, and which is used every day by hundreds of thousands of the city's inhabitants.

144. A gigantic poster advertising a famous magician covers the front of a Calcutta house.

145. A street of craftsmen near Kalighat and the temple of Kali, Calcutta, with a beautiful display of terracotta and papier-mâché statues along the pavement. These statues are made for the festivals dedicated to Shiva, Mahashivaratri. The busiest period for the makers of statues is during Durga Puja, which is much celebrated in Bengal and Calcutta. The images of Durga, the warrior goddess who killed the demon Asura, are very popular, but so too is Kali, the 'Black', who is depicted in her terrifying incarnation whilst trampling on Shiva. The temple of Kali is the centre of the spectacular and intense devotional life of Calcutta. Even today, animals are sacrificed daily to the goddess in order to placate her anger. Nearby, at Kalighat, the funeral pyres of Calcutta are permanently alight.

261

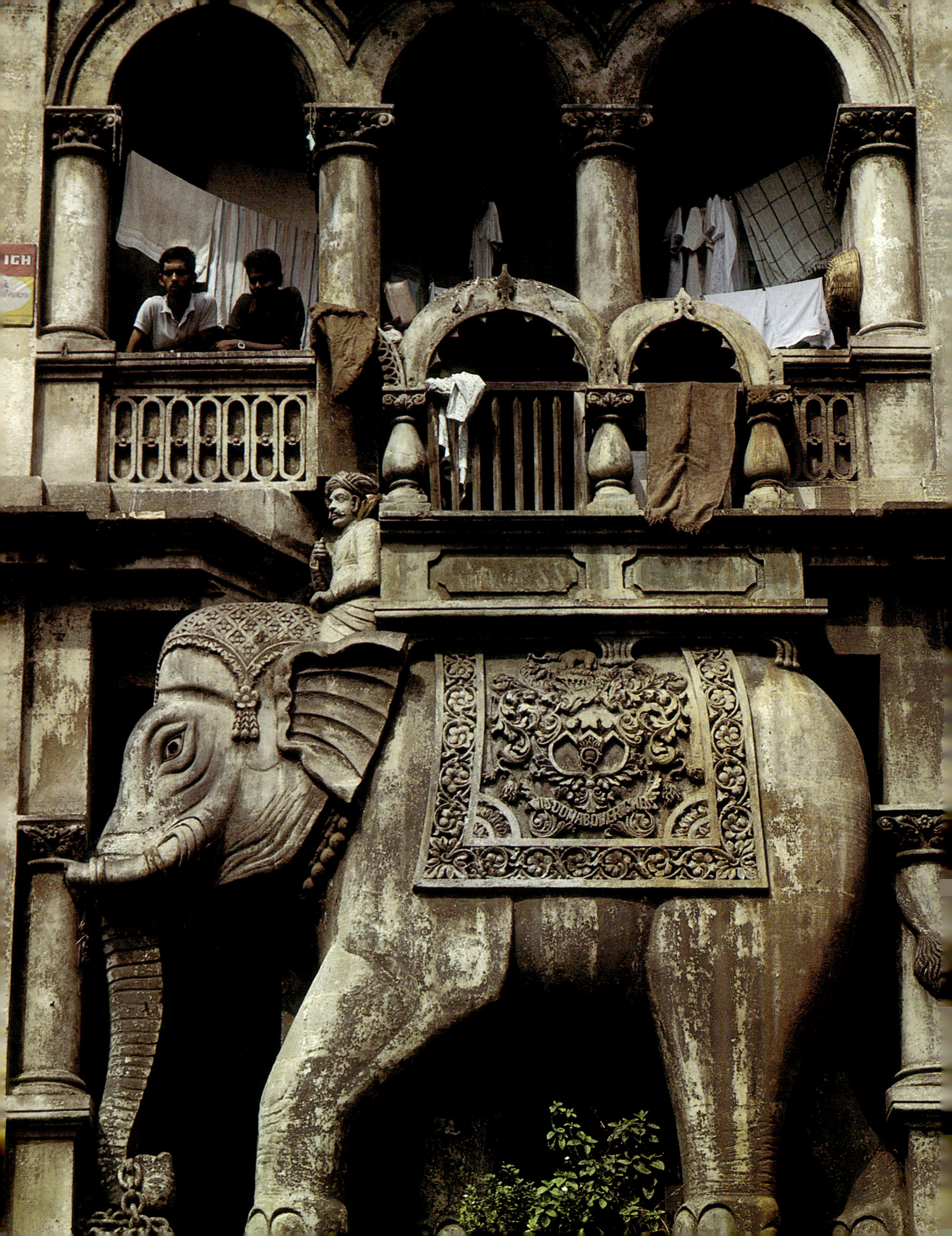

147

146. A large carving on the façade of a house in an old quarter of Bombay.
147. Victoria Station, Bombay, built in the high Victorian age in 1888 in an electic style — anglized Italian Gothic predominating but with certain Indo-Islamic decorative elements. During the rush hour the station is the centre of swirling vortex of people made up mainly of those who live in the suburbs and travel to the city to work. Bombay is the main terminus of one of the largest railway systems in the world, most of which was built under the British.

On the following pages:
148. Waiting for the open-air reception given in honour of the Prime Minister at Jamshedpur. Some sixty miles from Calcutta, Jamshedpur is an industrial city founded by Jamshedji Tata, one of the famous family of Bombay industrialists, which, at the beginning of the century, built up the first steel works in India.
149. Light fabrics for turbans exposed to the sun in a gurudwara, a Sikh temple, at Patna in Bihar.
150. Bombay's most popular beach, Chowpatty Beach, a favourite place for relaxation on Sundays and the site of large gatherings during festivals.

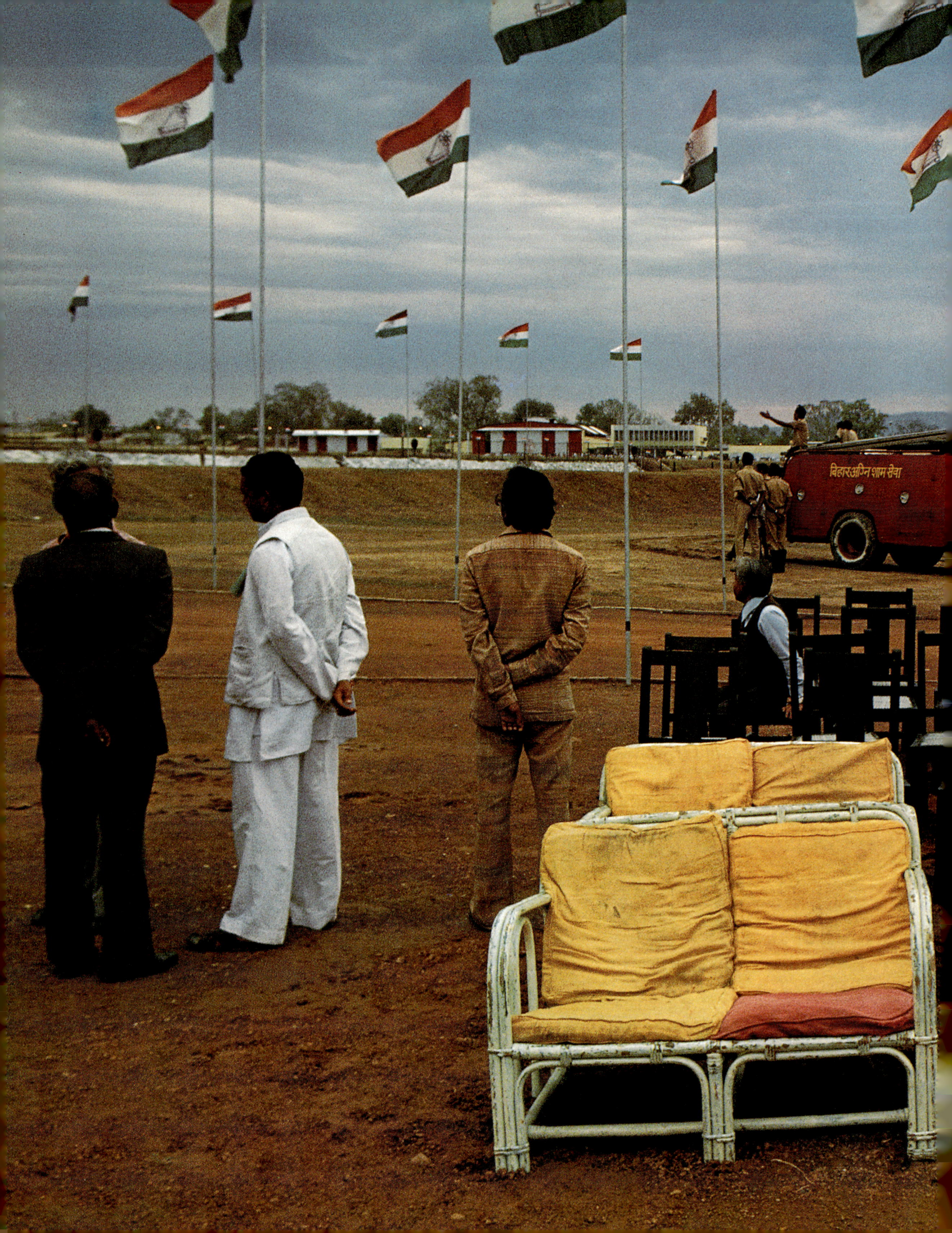
बिहार अग्नि शाम सेवा

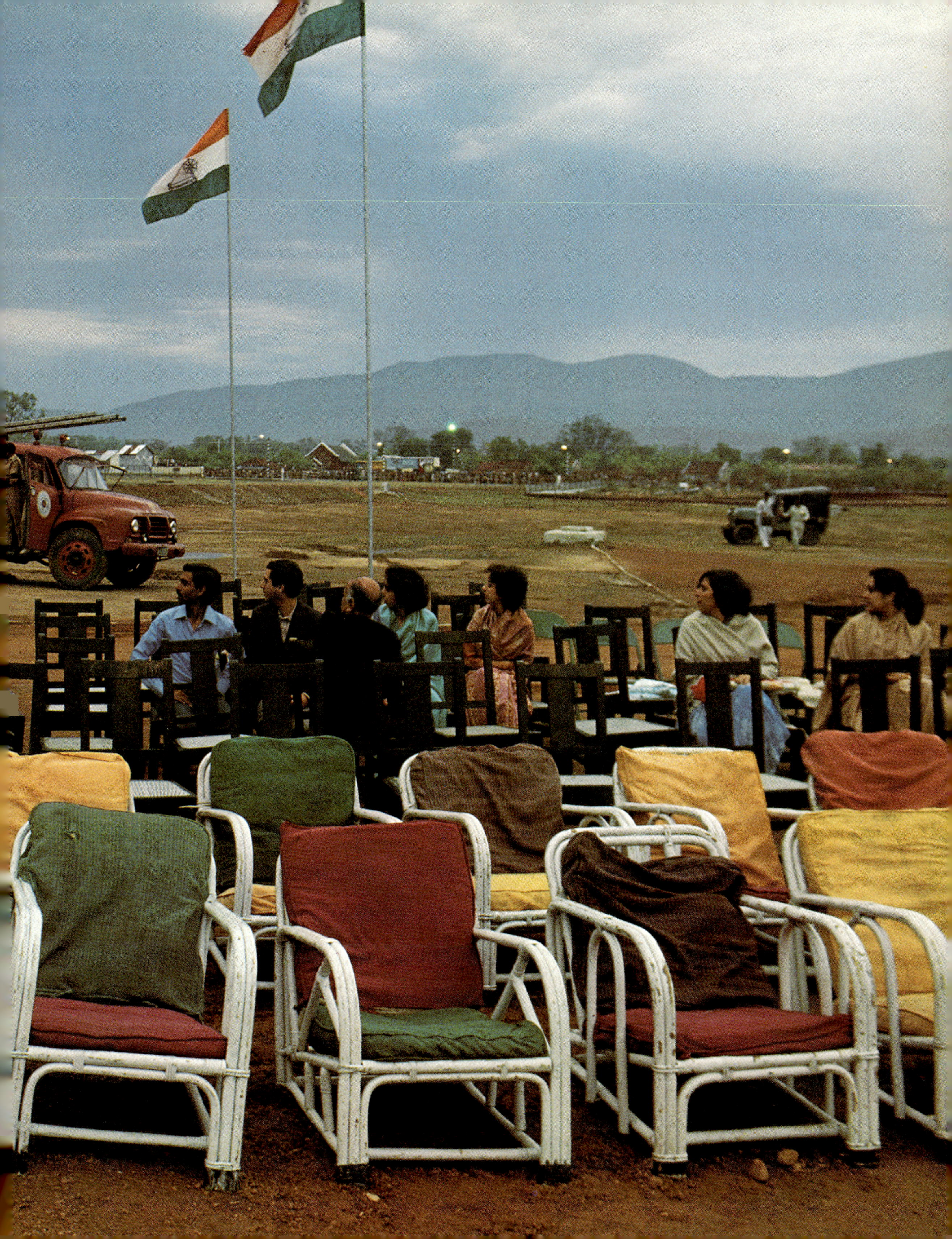

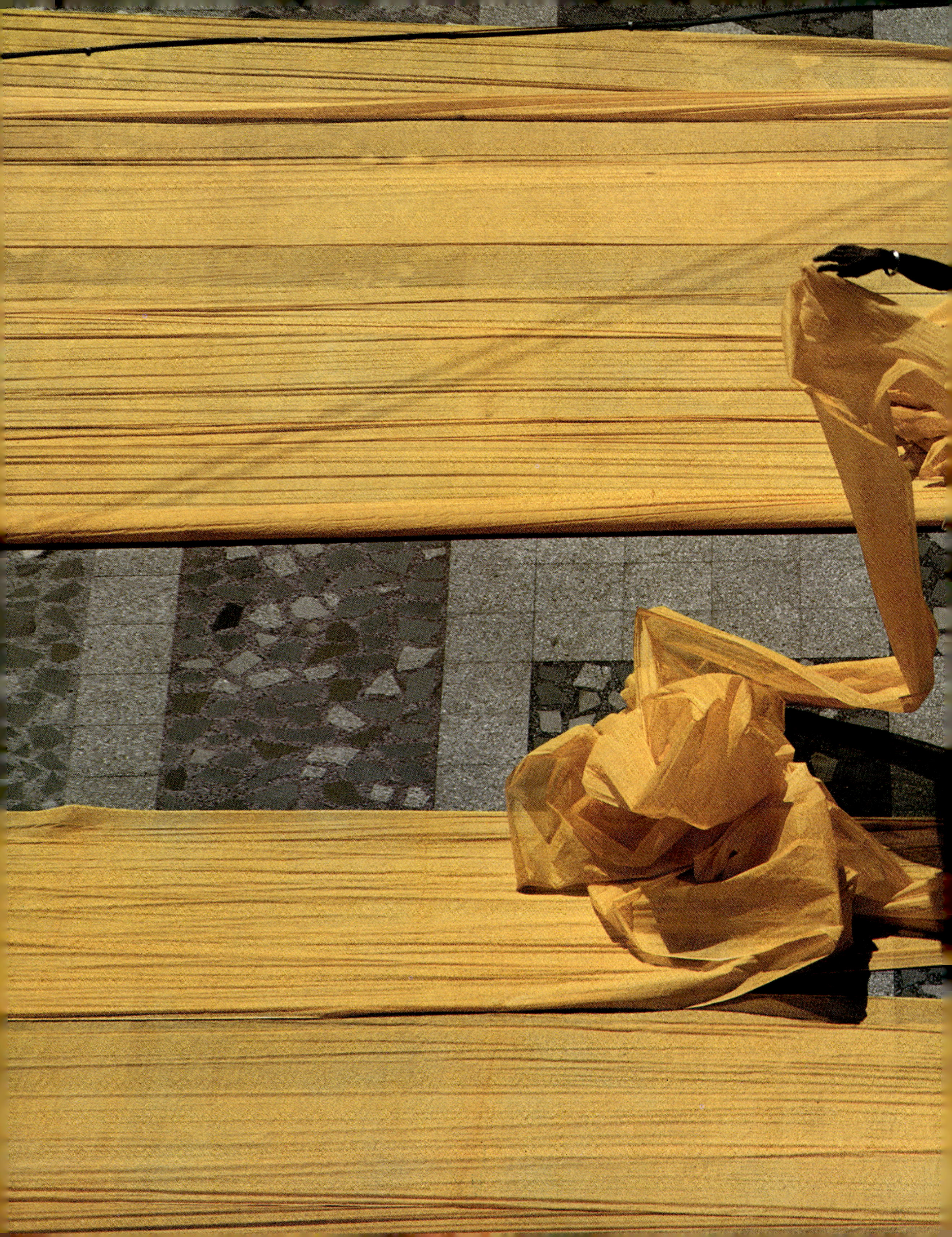

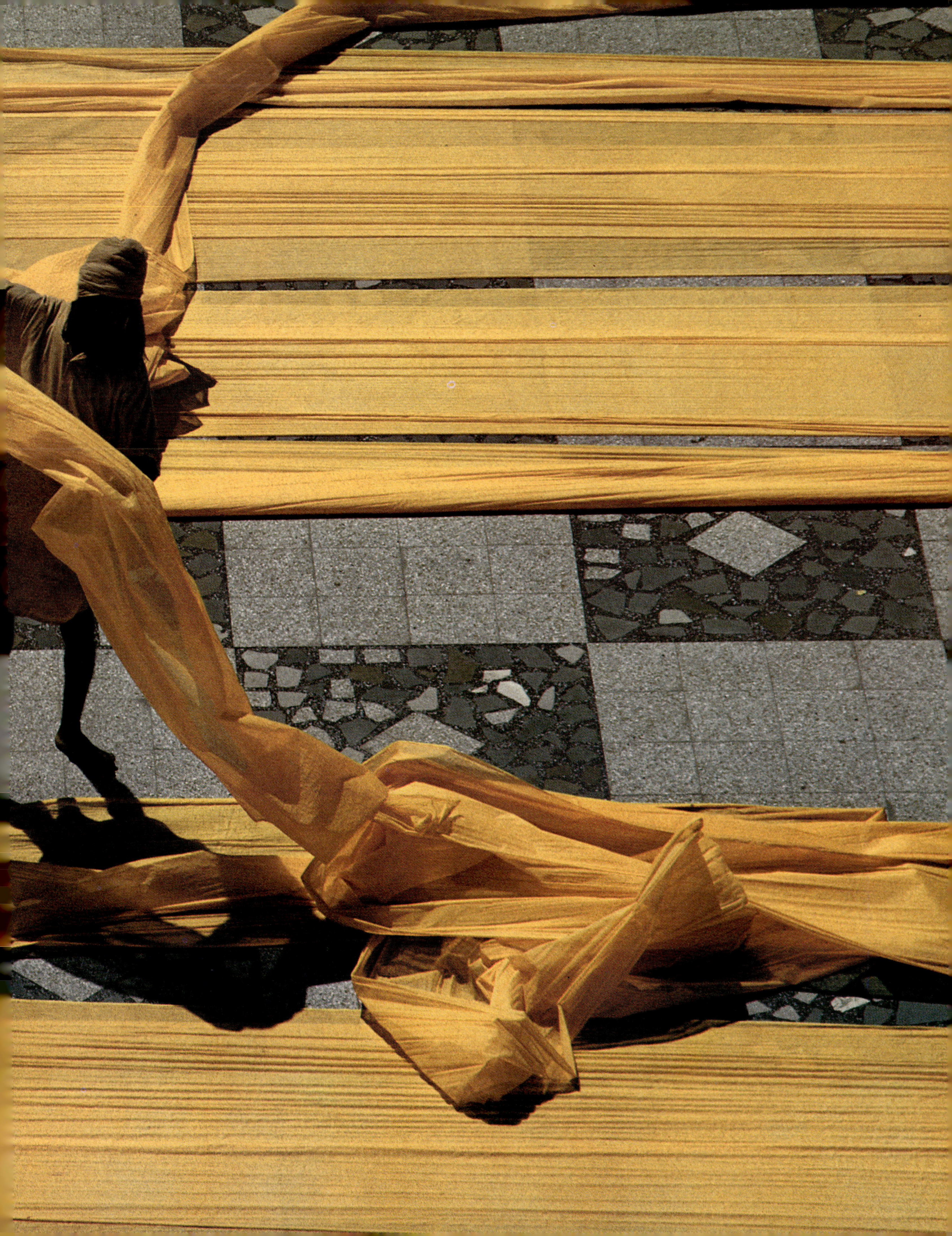

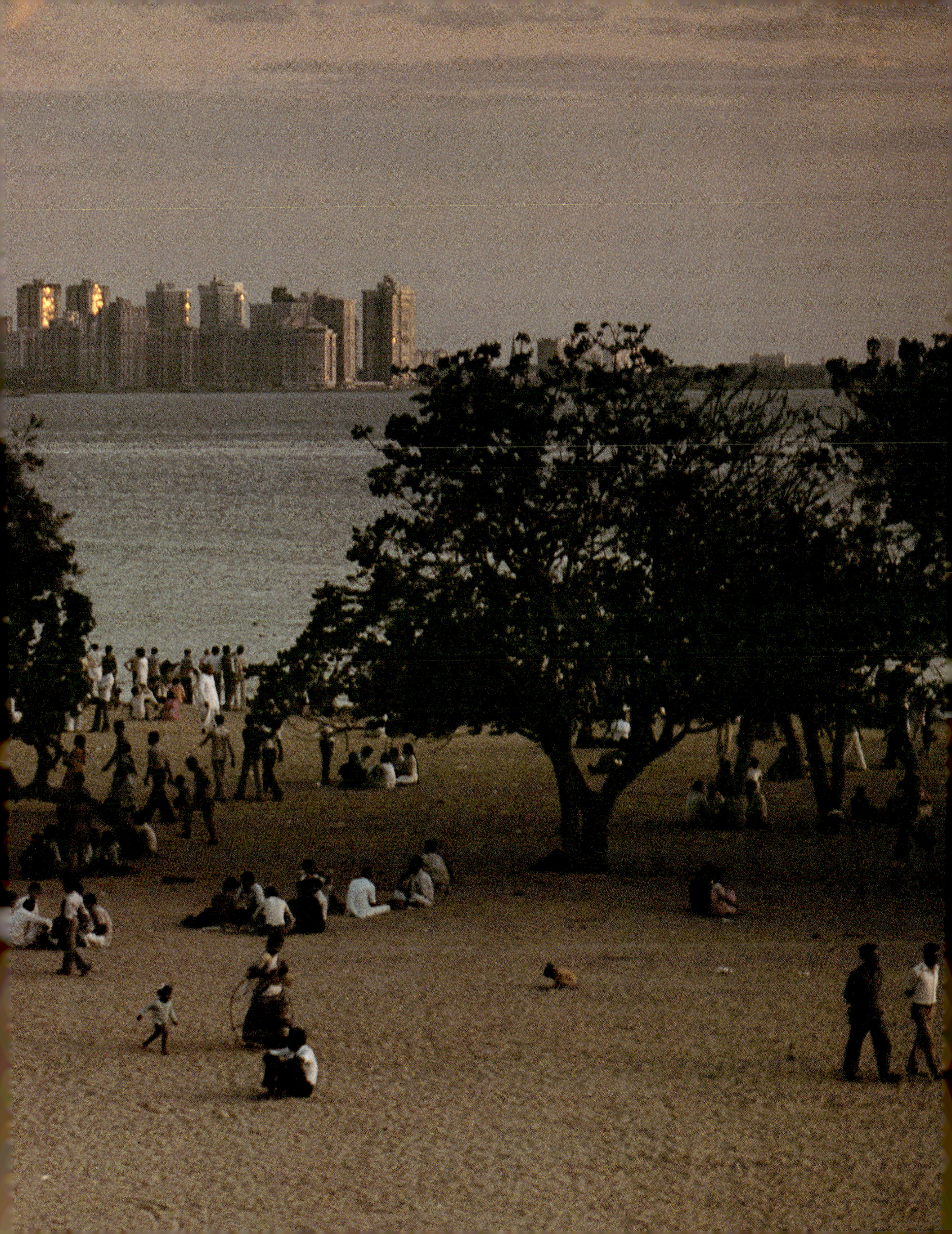

151. Young girls waiting in the red light district of Bombay. The bars on the windows of the houses have earned the area the nickname of the 'Cages'. It is also known as Falkland Road, from the best known and most frequented street, or Kamatipura, the city of love. Brothels are not illegal.
152. Soldiers on Chowpatty Beach, Bombay.

153. A sunday acrobat in the middle of the crowd on Chowpatty Beach. Because the population of Bombay is made up of groups and people who have come from all over India, the city has a vast variety of professions and trades, which are to be seen in the streets; it is a market place of hawkers and sellers, which offers an infinite array of wares and services.
On the following pages:
154. A typical, tiny hut by the roadside belonging to a mochi, *a semi-itinerant cobbler.*
155. The immense public wash-house of Bombay, known as the dobhi ghat.

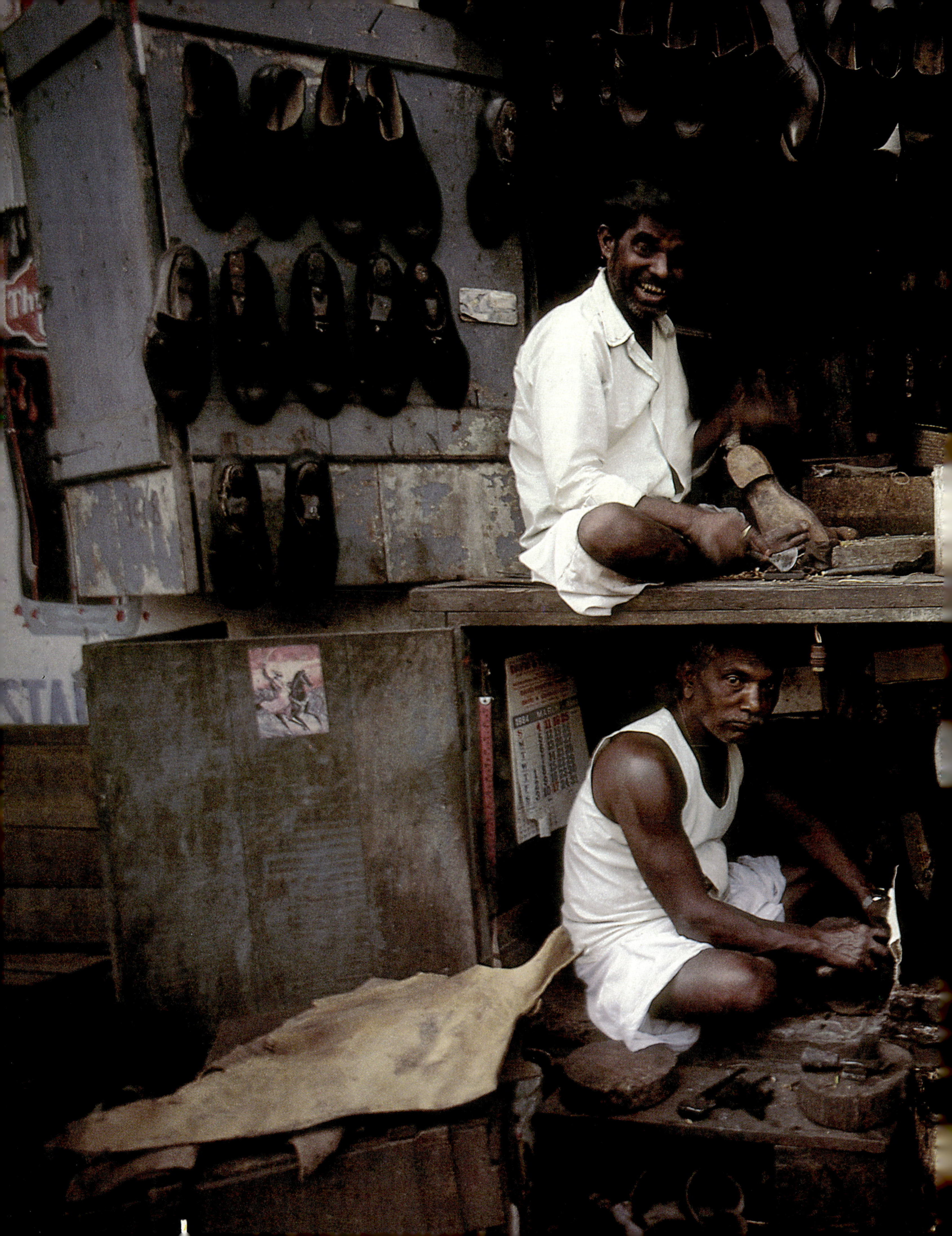

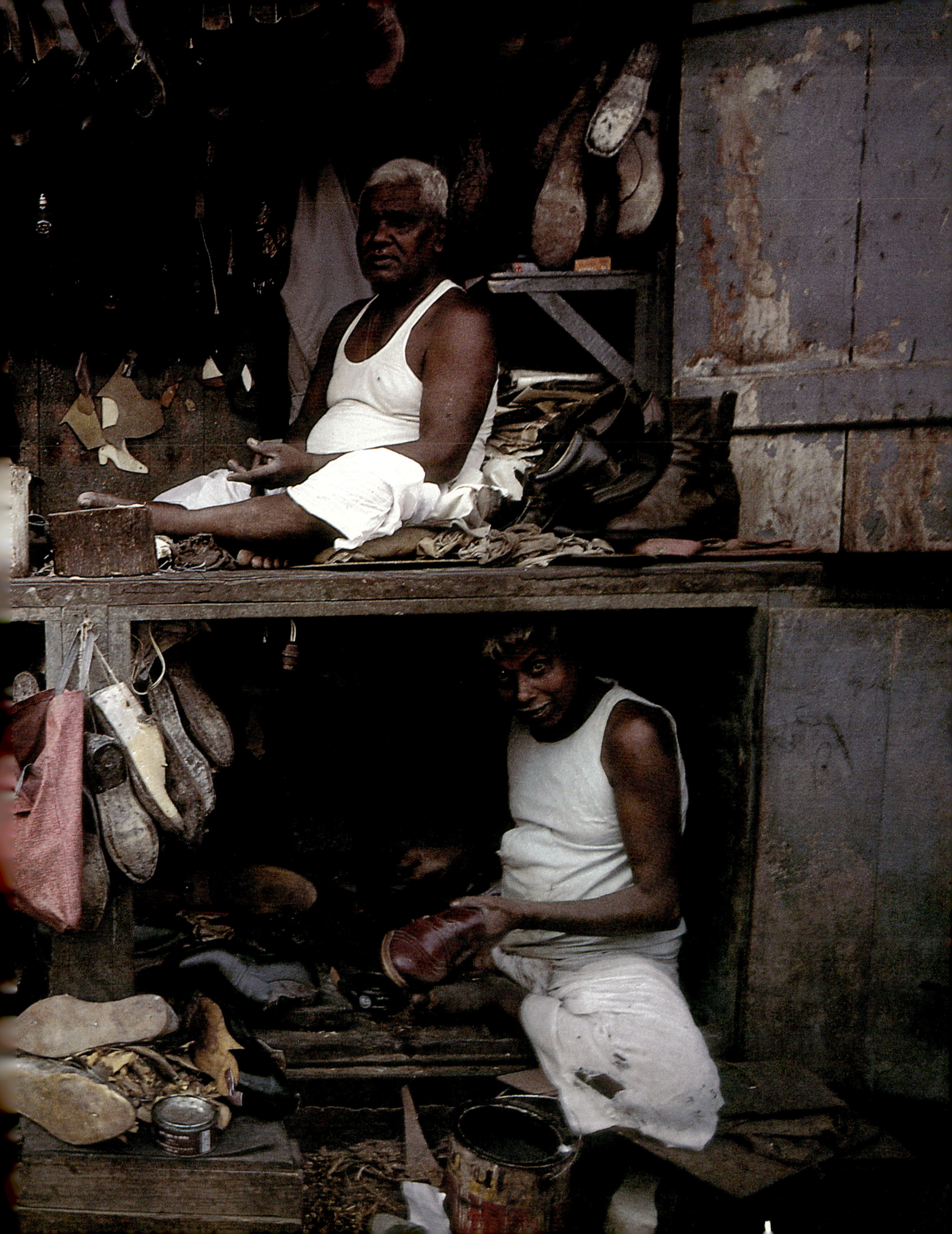

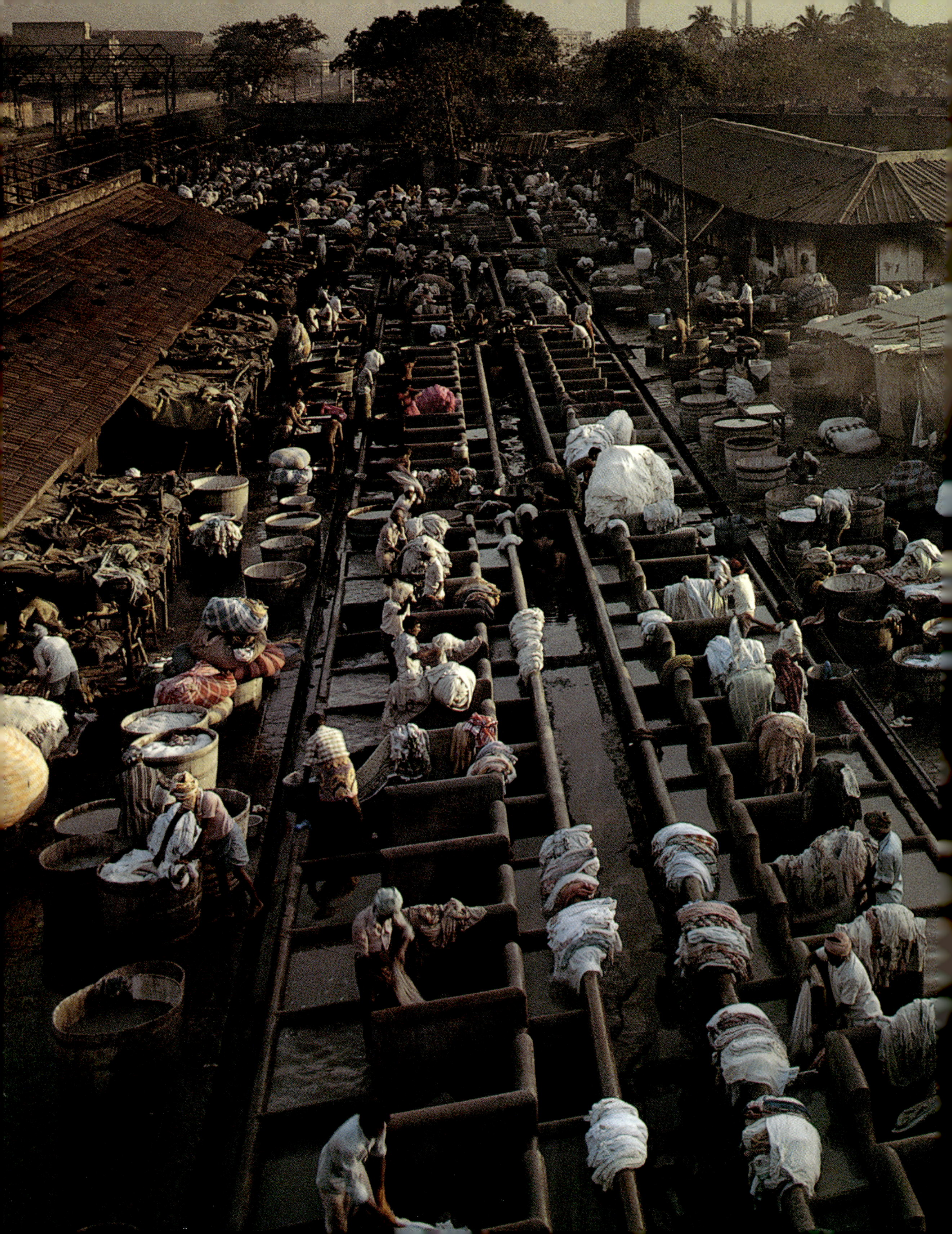

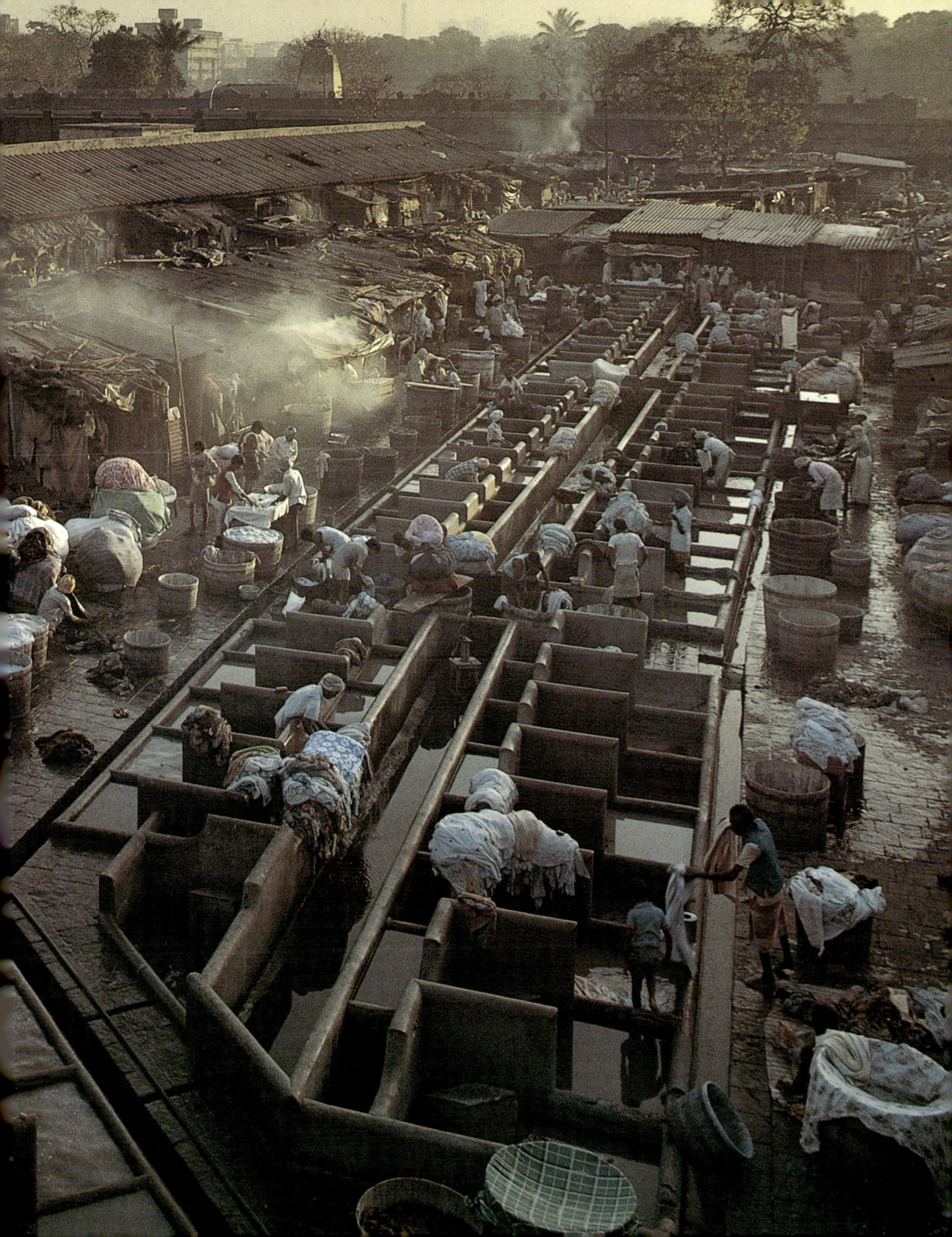

156

156. Muslims at prayers, facing towards Mecca, at noon on Friday in the middle of Bombay. Even in the great cities the religious processions and celebrations of the various denominations are performed in public, in the streets, and may even last several days. Wedding ceremonies too are often performed in the open air, under multi-coloured tents.

157. A vast cinema poster in a Bangalore street. The cinema is very popular in India, and so are the songs associated with the films. India produces more films than any other country.

158. *A game of polo, with the hills of Jaipur in the background. Polo is an ancient Asian game played by the northern population of Beluchistan and in Kashmir and Ladakh. The British adopted it and made it more widespread, although it was confined to the upper classes and the soldiers of the colony. Today it is widely played by rich and aristocratic Indians, and the last Maharaja of Jaipur was one of the world's best players.*

159. A silk mill at Ramanagram, near Bangalore, a large modern city in the south, and the site of the largest Indian silk market.

160. A gathering of Parsees in Bombay, during the holy day of the Avan. Parsees are Zoroastrians and are concentrated in Bombay, where they are mainly to be found in the liberal professions, in commerce, and in finance. They are famous for their philanthropy and for the numerous charitable institutions endowed for the city by rich Parsees.

161

162

161. *In the heart of the city of Bombay a small mosque which has been reduced to a traffic island. A fifth of the city's population is Muslim and is divided into two main groups, the Sunni and Shiites. The large Muslim communities of Bombay, the Bohra, Hhoja, and Memon, are largely engaged in trade.*
162. *The Anglo-Indian style house of a great Bohra merchant at Sidhpur in Gujarat.*

163

163. The vast crowd at the highly popular festival of Ganesh Chaturthi, on Chowpatty Beach in Bombay. It is perhaps most popular in Bombay, although it is celebrated throughout India. It lasts for about ten days in August and September and there are numeous collective rituals and ceremonies. On the last day hundreds of painted clay statues of Ganesh, the elephant-headed god and son of Shiva, are carried in procession and immersed, to the sound of music and with dancing, in the rivers, pools, and sea. The largest procession in Bombay ends on the popular Chowpatty Beach. Ganesh is one of India's most popular gods and he is regarded as the 'Great Guide' or 'He who removes obstacles' for any kind of venture or undertaking. His image is everywhere, on the doors of houses, in factories, in offices; in the countryside he is venerated as the tutelary divinity of harvests and fertility. At all ceremonies, apart from funeral rites, and at the conclusion of an agreement or a piece of business, Ganesh is the first, and sometimes the only, god to be invoked.

164. A craftsman of Ahmedabad works a clay statue made for the festival of Ganesh Chaturthi.

On the following pages:

165. A gigantic statue of Ganesh is carried along by the crowd in the narrow streets of Old Bombay. This particular idol is called the 'Sovereign of Gargaon' — a working-class district of Bombay — by the faithful.

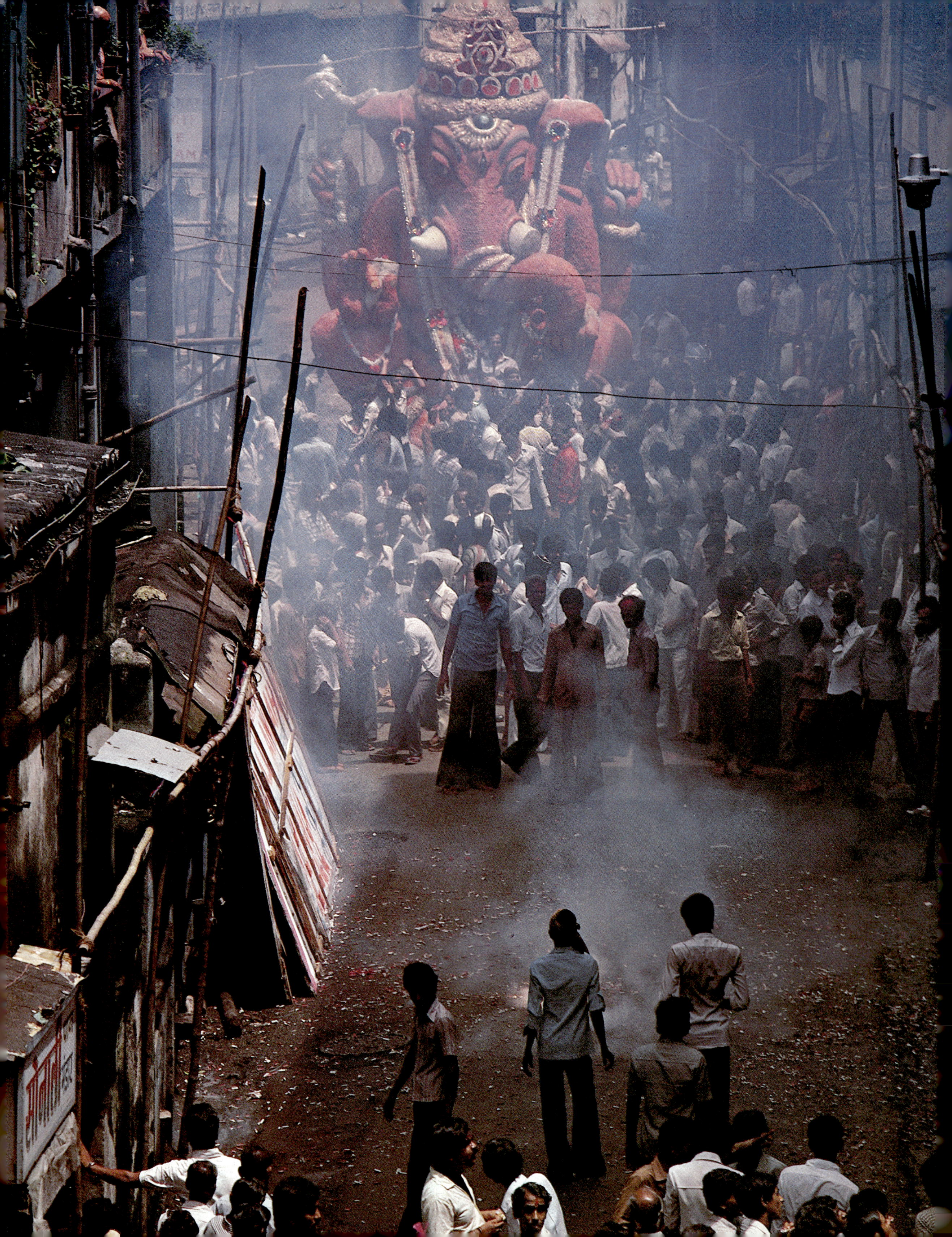

Chronology

3000-1900 BC Indus civilization and the Harappa Culture: principal cities: Harappa, Mohenjo-Daro, Chanhu-Daro, Lothal.

1900-1200 BC The descent of the Aryan peoples into the Ganges plain and the affirmation of the Vedic civilization; the composing of the *Rig-Veda*, the oldest of the four holy Veda scriptures.

1200-600 BC The expansion of the Aryan civilization over the Dravidian and aborigine areas; the formation of the caste system.

600 BC The Magadha Kingdom reigns in North-East India.

563 BC The birth of Siddharta Gautamo, known to the world as Buddha.

Fourth century BC - fourth century AD The great Hindu holy poems, the *Ramayana* and the *Mahabharata*, are composed; central to the latter is the *Bhagavad Gita*, the 'Lord's Song', which has become the most revered of the Hindu scriptures.

326 The army of Alexander the Great penetrates the Indus valley.

268-231 The empire of Ashoka of the Maurya dynasty is extended to nearly all India; the Emperor is converted to Buddhism, and unifies the Indian peoples with the Buddhist doctrine.

80 Sciti or Shaka take possession of the north-western territories; the founding of a Scita kingdom in the Gujarat region.

First century AD The period of the Kushan dynasty.

320-415 The sovereignty of the Gupta dynasty inaugurates a golden age of Hindu civilization, both through economic prosperity and through the impulse given to the arts and Sanskrit literature; with Chadragupta II the Gupta civilization reaches its highest point.

450 The invasion of the White Huns into north India.

606-647 The reign of Harsha in north India; the Pallava dynasty gains power in the south.

650-1000 The so-called Indian Middle Ages; political and territorial dissolution, rivalry and fighting between the various feudal states.

760 The birth of Shankaracharya, the greatest Hindu philospher; the beginning of a Hindu renaissance.

888-1280 Chola sovereignty in the south; expansion and conquest by sea of various territories of south-east Asia.

997-1526 Islamic invasions into the Punjab and the north, and battles with the Rajput clan, the only ones to oppose the invaders; the sultanate of Delhi and the Mussulman dynasties of Khilji and Tuglaq.

1366-1653 The south Hindu empire of Vijayanagar.

1498 The Portuguese navigator Vasco da Gama reaches Calicut on the Malabar coast; the beginning of the period of European penetration into India.

1526-1707 The great Mogul Empire, beginning with Baber, the head of the dynasty.

1556-1605 The reign of Akbar, the greatest of the Mogul emperors; territorial reorganization and religious peace between Muslim and Hindu.

1612 The opening of the first English agency at Surat.

1658-1707 The reign of the last great Mogul emperor, Aurangzeb; the Maratha opposition, led by Shivaji, undermines the unity of the empire; the successive conquest by part of the Maratha confederation of the greater part of India.

1757-1857 At Plassey the British East India Company wins the battle against the Sultan of Bengala; having also eliminated her French rivals, the British company proceeds in its territorial conquest of India; consolidation of the British possessions and application of British law and administrative reform, and acquisition of the means of production in colonial interest; enforced annexation of numerous Indian kingdoms; the collapse of the agrarian economy and of the native manufacturing industry; in the nineteenth century the period of the great famines begins.

1857-1858 The Indian Mutiny, the mutiny of the Sipahi or sepoys, the native troops of the Company; the revolt affects the whole of north India; it takes eighteen months to quell the uprising; the East Indian Company is abolished and the British Crown assumes the direct sovereignty of India.

1876 Queen Victoria is proclaimed Empress of India and reigns through her representative, the Viceroy; about 600 Indian principalities are recognized and are given sovereignty over their territories following an act of submission to the British Crown.

1855 The National Indian Congress is founded: it is the first step towards the formation of an Indian nationalist conscience and political unity.

1899-1905 Dictatorial ruling policy of the British government which radicalizes the position of the Indian nationalists led by Bal Gangadhar Tilak.

1906 Founding of the National Muslim League.

1914-1919 The great contribution of India to the British war effort during the First World War, which does not, as was hoped, lead to greater national autonomy, however; a state of permanent agitation following the massacre of an unarmed crowd at Amritsar by British troops.

1921 Mahatma Gandhi takes up leadership of the Congress and inaugurates a new method of resistance based on 'non-violence' and 'non-collaboration'; the Congress successively launches the civil disobedience movement and the boycotting of British goods, thus involving the rural masses; the colonial government reacts by imprisoning thousands of nationalists.

1933 Muhammed Ali Jinnah, the head of the Muslim League, proposes the setting up of an independent state which would be wholly Muslim to be called Pakistan; in the meantime differences grow between Hindu and Muslim.

1939-45 When the Second World War breaks out, Congress refuses to support Great Britain, but after Japan enters the war, India becomes a fighting base against the Rome-Berlin-Tokyo alliance.

1946-47 The end of the world conflict, India in a growing state of unrest; fighting and reprisals between the Hindu and Muslim populations increase. Britain decides it is best to retire from the country and recognize India's independence but imposes the separation of the territory into two distinct and independent states: India and Pakistan; the tragic exodus of Hindus and Muslims leads to the massacre of hundreds of thousands of people.

1948 Mahatma Gandhi is assassinated by a member of the extremist Hindu fringe. Jawaharlal Nehru assumes the leadership of the country and begins the application of a series of five-year plans for the development of an autonomous national economy.

1950 Proclamation of the Indian Republic and its constitution.

1962-64 Frontier skirmishes with China and Indian defeat, which sets in motion a rapid militarization programme; on Nehru's death, Lal Bahadur Shastri becomes Prime Minister.

1965 Indo-Pakistan War.

1966 Indira Gandhi, Pandit Nehru's daughter, becomes head of the government.

1971-72 Fresh conflicts with Pakistan and the creation of the independent nation of Bangladesh.

1975 Opposition to Indira Gandhi's government is followed by a constitutional crisis and the proclamation of a state of emergency.

1978 Indira Gandhi's party is defeated at the elections; a coalition government based on the Janata Party is formed.

1980 With the new elections the Janata Party falls and Indira Gandhi is re-elected.

1983-84 Agitation all over the country and secessionist movements in various regions, such as the Punjab and Assam; the Prime Minister, Indira Gandhi, is assassinated and her son, Rajiv Gandhi, is named in her place; a general election confirms the new Prime Minister's mandate.

Glossary

Ahimsa non-violence; doctrinally, non-interference in the karma of others.
Amrit the drink of immortality, the food of the gods.
Asana name of particular positions according to the schools of yoga.
Ashram hermitage, religious community; the name of the four stages of life.
Atman soul, principle of life, the self, according to brahmanical metaphysics.
Avatar divine descent or incarnation.
Banyan (*Ficus bengalensis*) a widespread Indian tree, whose branches often dip down and take root.
Bazaar market or market place, street with shops.
Bhakti devotion to god, love, adoration; bhakta is the devotee full of divine love.
Bhikku, bhikshu mendicant Buddhist monk.
Bodhi illumination, awakening according to Buddhist doctrine.
Bodhisattva Buddhist saint, not yet a Buddha.
Brahmacharya first stage of life, celibacy, vow of chastity.
Brahman the absolute, impersonal god, according to the metaphysics of the *Upanishads*.
Brahmin, brahman member of the highest caste in the caste hierarchy.
British Raj the period of British domination in India, as well as the domination itself.
Chaitya chapel, reliquary, altar, Buddhist temple.
Chattri literally 'umbrella'; small stone or brick pavilion.
Dargah memorial chapel, place of burial of a Muslim saint.
Darshan view of god or saint, philosophical-theological system.
Deva god, male divinity.
Devadasi sacred dancer.
Devata divinity; *gramdevata*, tutelary divinity of the village.
Devi goddess.
Dharma supreme duty, the law of the universe.
Dhoti male garment.
Dvija 'twice born', condition of the first three castes; title given at the caste initiation ceremony.
Fakir devout Muslim who has taken a vow of poverty; wrongly used for Hindu ascetics.
Garbhagriha literally womb, uterus, receptacle; cell of the divinity, holy of holies.
Ghat steps along the banks of rivers or the shores of lakes; mountain pass; range of hills.
Gopura entrance towers to southern temples.
Grihasta head of the house and father of the family; stage of life.
Guru spiritual master.
Harijan literally 'people of god'; name given to the untouchables by Mahatma Gandhi, now widely used.
Hartal strike or lock-out.
Jati literally, birth, origin; caste community, sub-caste.
Jiva soul, vital spirit, in Jain philosophy.
Karman literally, 'action'; result of actions in the cycle of rebirths.
Kharif monsoon harvest.
Kshatriya member of the second caste, the warriors or nobles.
Kuli porter.
Lingam, Lingan literally 'sign or symbol'; phallic organ; emblem of Shiva.
Lok Sabha one of the chambers of the Indian parliament.
Lungi male garment worn in southern India.
Madrasa Muslim theological school.
Mahal house or palace.
Maharaja literally 'great king', the usual title of Indian sovereigns.
Maharani consort of a maharaja.
Maidan open space in a town.
Manasara medieval treatise on architecture.
Mandala literally 'circle'; magic sign or diagram, cosmogram.
Mandapa columned, hypostyle hall or portico.
Mandir Hindu temple, cult site.
Mantra sacrificial formula, prayer or song of praise.
Marg path or way.
Masjid mosque.
Maya principle of illusion, unreality.
Mela festival, market; Kumbh Mela, literally 'festival of the vessel'; great religious assembly in various holy cities.
Mithuna pair of lovers.
Moksha salvation or liberation.
Morcha protest march or meeting connected with a strike.

Nawab Muslim title.
Nirvana nothing, annihilation, liberation in Buddhist metaphysics.
Om mystical syllable, origin of the universe.
Panchayat village council.
Panda officiating priest.
Pandit brahmin who knows Sanskrit and the ancient texts.
Pariah untouchable.
Patel village leader.
Pradakshina ritual circumambulation of a cult object.
Prashad literally, divine grace; food or flowers offered to the divinity and redistributed to the faithful.
Puja veneration, adoration; cult act before the divinity.
Purdah literally 'curtain'; term for the area reserved for women within the house; also, reserved female behaviour.
Pyjama Indian garment.
Qila fort.
Raga melodic unit, melodic base of Indian music.
Raj literally 'realm'; also government.
Raja Hindu king or prince.
Rani queen or princess, the wife of a raja.
Rasa literally 'taste'; emotion; emotive-aesthetic factor in the philosophy of Indian art.
Rath processional cart.
Rupee, Rupiya the basic unit of Indian currency.
Sadhu Hindu ascetic, saint.
Samsara transmigration, cycle of existences.
Sannyasa renunciation of the world; sannyasi, monk or ascetic.
Sari garment worn by Indian women.
Sepoy Indian soldier employed by the East India Company.
Shakti divine energy, power, often personified in the female principle.
Shanti peace.
Shastra scientific or religious treatise.
Shikhar central tower in northern temples.
Shilpin artist-craftsman.
Shruti literally 'revelation', name for the Vedic and Brahmanic doctrinal literature.
Shudra member of the lowest caste, peasant or servant.
Smriti literally, tradition, memory; the literature of the epics, the mythological tales and the *Tantra*.
Sthapati priest-architect.
Stupa reliquary, tumulus, or monument holding a relic.
Suttee the sacrifice of the widow on the pyre of her dead husband.
Swami member of monastic order.
Swaraj independence, self-government.
Tapas literally, 'warmth'; extreme asceticism.
Tilak, tiki, tika religious mark placed in the centre of the forehead
Tirtha ford or sacred place.
Tirthankara Jain saint.
Vaishya member of the third caste, merchants.
Varna literally, 'colour'; Sanskrit term meaning 'caste'.
Vastu literally 'to enclose'; term for architecture.
Vihara Buddhist monastery, chapterhouse.
Vimana pyramidal tower at the centre of a temple.
Yantra instrument, ritual diagram, magic figure.
Yoga literally 'yoke'; discipline of concentration and ecstatic technique.
Yogi practitioner of yoga, ascetic.
Yoni uterus, womb, emblem of the goddess in Shaivism.
Yuga age of the world.

Photographic credits
Numbers refer to the illustrations

Antonio Martinelli - Roberto Meazza: 14, 16, 17, 18, 61, 62, 64, 65, 76, 81, 92, 93, 94, 95, 100, 105, 107, 112, 126, 128, 131, 146, 147, 148, 152, 158, 159, 160, 161, 162, 163, 164, 165.

Antonio Martinelli: 1, 3, 5, 7, 8, 11, 15, 22, 24, 25, 26, 27, 28, 29, 31, 32, 33, 36, 37, 38, 39, 42, 44, 45, 46, 47, 48, 49, 50, 51, 52, 53, 55, 56, 58, 59, 60, 63, 67, 68, 71, 77, 82, 85, 87, 88, 89, 91, 96, 97, 98, 106, 108, 115, 117, 118, 120, 121, 122, 123, 127, 129, 130, 132, 133, 135, 136, 137, 138, 139, 140, 141, 149, 151, 155, 156, 157.

Roberto Meazza: 2, 4, 6, 9, 10, 12, 13, 19, 20, 21, 23, 30, 34, 35, 40, 41, 43, 54, 57, 66, 69, 70, 72, 73, 74, 75, 78, 79, 80, 83, 84, 86, 90, 99, 101, 102, 103, 104, 109, 110, 111, 113, 114, 116, 119, 124, 125, 134, 142, 143, 144, 145, 150, 153, 154.

Acknowledgements

The photographers wish to express their thanks to all those whose valuable assistance helped in the preparation of this book::
Mr. R. Anand; Mrs. Hira Chandran; Dott. Umberto Comellato; Mr. Noshir Desai; Arch. B.V. Doshi; H.H. Jamsaheb; Mr. J. Jeanghir; Kashmir Tourism Mr. Mohiuddin Shah; Mr. Gangouli; Indian Airlines PRO Mr. O.P. Garg; Rajastan Tourism Mr. S.L. Sankhla; Mr. Ravi Pasricha; Mr. A.K.A. Samad; Mr. Satish Sharma; Mrs. Parviz & Rusi Surti; TATA Ltd. Mr J.R.D. Tata, Miss. K. Divecha.